ANCIENT RECORDS OF EGYPT

HISTORICAL DOCUMENTS

FROM THE EARLIEST TIMES TO THE PERSIAN CONQUEST, COLLECTED
EDITED AND TRANSLATED WITH COMMENTARY

BY

JAMES HENRY BREASTED, PH.D.

PROFESSOR OF EGYPTOLOGY AND ORIENTAL HISTORY
IN THE UNIVERSITY OF CHICAGO

VOLUME V
INDICES

ISBN: 978-1-63923-646-6

Printed: January 2023

Published and Distributed By:
Lushena Books
607 Country Club Drive, Unit E
Bensenville, IL 60106
www.lushenabks.com

ISBN: 978-1-63923-646-6

ANCIENT RECORDS OF EGYPT

PREFACE TO VOLUME V

These indices are the work of my friend and former pupil, Dr. O. A. Toffteen. I would take occasion to express to him here my thanks and appreciation for the labor and care which he has expended upon them. While the author has constantly supervised the compilation, yet the work has been that of Dr. Toffteen, and he is fully responsible for it. It should be said in justice to him, as well as perhaps to the author also, that the latter's return to the Orient for another season left the compiler only a little over two months in which to complete his heavy task. He was obliged to work more hours a day and with more speed than was his desire, but I am sure that the usefulness of his work, and the persistent industry with which he has compiled his lists, will deserve lenient judgment, should any occasional errors in numbers be found. I hope also that the necessity for the separate publication of such exhaustive indices in a volume by themselves will be evident to any who may have expected to find them included in Volume IV. Aside from the fact that it would have rendered that volume (already far the largest of the set) much too bulky, it was thought highly desirable to give such a cyclopædia of the subject separate existence as a volume, rather than to absorb it in Volume IV, where it would be constantly lost to use, whenever anyone might be using Volume IV for some other purpose. Likewise if bound up with Volume IV, the employment of the indices by a reader would also have involved the needless use of Volume IV with them. The compilation of the index has disclosed an occasional inconsistency in rendering, and in a few cases also in the orthography of proper names, in view of which the author would only recall the long period of time and the numerous modifications involved in the slow progress of such a work as this.

In view of some remarks in one of the first reviews which have appeared, it should be stated that it was necessary to close the manuscript of these Records to any additions on October 1, 1904. Any works or texts which appeared after that date could not be included. An advance proof kindly sent me by Eduard Meyer enabled me to employ his invaluable *Chronologie* in revising the chronology in Volume I; and wherever possible I endeavored to insert in the proof important facts appearing in new books and current journals. But I could take up no new texts. The omission of Abydos texts, mentioned by Foucart (*Journal des Savants*, June, 1906, p. 336), was intentional, as no translatable document of importance is in Abydos, Volume I, the only volume out when my manuscript was handed in. Among these the inscription of "Nakhiti," which Foucart says I have overlooked, is in our own Haskell Museum, where it was received not long after its discovery. I was therefore not very likely to overlook it.

As I have stated in the general preface, circumstances beyond my control obliged me to read the proofs of these volumes, as well as those of my *History of Egypt*, between April and September, 1905, a period in which fell also the preparations for the expedition to Egypt under the auspices of the Oriental Exploration Fund, University of Chicago. There are therefore doubtless more typographical errors and corrigenda than I could wish. I have already noticed the following:

Vol. I, §§ 178–80. Please read in the following order: 180, 178, 179. The unpublished and also almost unreadable base-inscription should be mentioned here (see Maspero, *Les Origines*, p. 364, note 8).

Vol. I, § 182. The verb after "Ptah" is doubtless part of the name, so that the *ny* is dative and not the *n*-form. We should then render, "Ptahyutnai (*Ptḥ-ywt-ny*), who made this for him, etc."

Vol. I, § 185. For "field judge who," read "field judge, Kemethnenet (*Kmṯnnt*), who."

Vol. I, § 199. After "Upper," insert "Oleander."

Vol. I, § 538. For "count of Siut," read "official of Siut."

Vol. I, § 685. For "Nebkure," read "Nubkure."

Vol. I, before § 707, at top of p. 313. Insert as a title, "REIGN OF AMENEMHET III."

Vol. I, pp. 314, 316, 318, 320, 322, 324, 326, in running-title at the top of the page for "SESOSTRIS III," read "AMENEMHET III."

Vol. II, § 657. For "by the hair the Kode-folk," read "among the Curly-Haired," as in Vol. II, § 71.

Vol. II, p. 305, note a. For "has," read "have."

Vol. II, § 854. For "Ibbet," read "Ibhet."

Vol. III, § 309. For "*Ḳ ꜣ-r ꜣ-ḳy-kšꜣ*" read "*K ꜣ-r ꜣ-ḳy-šꜣ*."

Vol. III, § 498. For "*Ḥ ꜣ*," read "*Ḥ ꜣ m*." This change is due to a collation of the original at Abu Simbel.

Vol. IV, § 240. For "*s ꜣ mw*," read "*s ꜥ mw*."

Vol. IV, § 455. For "*ꜣ-ry-m*," read "*ꜣ-r-ry-m*."

Vol. IV, § 493. For "*Nfr-k ꜥ-R ꜥ*," read "*Nfr-k ꜣ-R ꜥ*".

Vol. IV, § 815. For "Zeamamefonekh," read "Zeamonefonekh."

Vol. IV, § 853. For "*ḥtm*," read "*ḫtm*."

Vol. IV, § 874. For "*Ḫnt-Ḫty*," read "*Ḫnt-Ḫty*."

Vol. IV, § 918. For "*N ꜣ-ꜥꜣ-t ꜣ ys-nht. t*," read "*N ꜣ-ꜥꜣ-t ꜣ ys-nḫt.t*."

Vol. IV, § 921. For "*B ꜣ-k ꜣ-R ꜣ*," read "*B ꜣ-k ꜣ-R ꜥ*."

Vol. IV, § 1028. For "*wḥm*," read "*whm*."

I would also note that the inscription recording a campaign in Syria, supposed to belong to Thutmose II (Vol. II, § 125), has been shown by Sethe's examination of the original probably to belong to Thutmose I. Hence Naville was right in attributing the monument to the last-mentioned king (*Deir-el-Bahari*, Vol. III, p. 17). This makes the reign of Thutmose II still more ephemeral and unimportant.

James Henry Breasted.

Haskell Oriental Museum,
University of Chicago,
September 1, 1906.

LIST OF INDICES AND HINTS FOR USE

			PAGE
INDEX	I.	DIVINE NAMES	3
INDEX	II.	TEMPLES	13
INDEX	III.	KINGS OF EGYPT	23
INDEX	IV.	PERSONS	35
INDEX	V.	TITLES, OFFICES, AND RANKS	51
INDEX	VI.	GEOGRAPHICAL	71
INDEX	VII.	MISCELLANEOUS	105
INDEX	VIII.	EGYPTIAN	173
INDEX	IX.	HEBREW	197
INDEX	X.	ARABIC	199
INDEX	XI.	LEPSIUS' DENKMÄLER AND TEXT	201

The temples (Index II) will be found supplementary to the geography in Index VI. Inscriptions, however, are not placed under temples. The inscriptions of all sites will be found in the geographical index (VI). In compiling the list of temples it was found difficult to distinguish between the different temples in a given city, when such temples have perished, as, for example, at Memphis and Heliopolis. The differentiations made are probably not always correct. The index of Pharaohs includes also such *queens* as actually ruled; otherwise the queens will be found in Index IV. The documents, monuments, wars, etc., of the Pharaohs will be found under the numbered name, not under the throne-name. Thus, look for Thutmose III under Thutmose III, not under Menkheperre; the references to the latter name will be found appended to those of the former.

The historical development of terms should not be forgotten in using these lists. "Count," "mayor," and "prince" are all renderings of the same Egyptian term at different periods. In the same way, different connection often demands a different rendering of the same title; thus, "chief," "overseer," "master," and "governor" may be rendered from the same Egyptian title. Such a series is also "lord," "nomarch," and "ruler."

INDICES

INDEX I

DIVINE NAMES

A

ALL-LORD, I 478; II 53, 314, 343, 812, 815; III 265, 281, 613; IV 47, 66, 356, 382; great house of, IV 8; city of, II 316; throne of, see Index VII; eye of, II 316, 815; applied to Re-Atum, IV 249.

AMON, II 98, 101, 120, 149, 153, 154 ter, 157, 162, 163, 165, 192, 193, 194, 195, 199, 205, 208, 209, 211, 216, 228, 244, 275, 283, 285, 294, 302, 310, 311, 314, 315, 328, 329, 332, 339, 374, 377, 383, 389, 402, 430, 431, 439, 451, 452, 455, 457, 549, 556, 557, 558, 559, 596, 608, 617, 620, 627, 628, 646, 784, 790, 791, 805, 827, 835, 836, 838, 856; III 27, 28, 34, 43, 71, 72, 82, 111, 134, 138, 155, 164, 165, 172, 177, 179, 195, 198, 204, 210, 224, 237, 261, 371, 386, 452, 455, 471, 498, 535, 560 n. b, 566, 575, 580, 615, 622, 623, 626, 642; IV 7, 13, 17, 40, 47, 50, 51, 54, 55, 71, 72, 78, 80, 82, 88, 92, 96, 103, 110, 122, 123, 125, 126, 127, 411, 412, 468, 497, 586, 591, 634, 661, 663, 688, 700, 702, 704, 705, 724, 743, 822, 836, 851, 855, 856, 868, 887, 888, 893, 925, 926, 943, 945, 958C, 958D, J, 988H; lord of eternity, IV 124; lord of heaven, IV 943, 945; king of gods, II 412, 891; III 30, 72; IV 483, 498, 945; lord of gods, II 253, 351, 645, 881; III 215, 515, 625, 626; ruler of gods, IV 943; lord of Karnak, II 149, 150, 377, 378, 423; presider over Karnak, II 200, 203, 253, 271, 282, 315, 402, 568, 569; lord of Thebes, II 44, 45, 87, 120, 121, 158, 164, 166, 197, 224, 253, 268, 271, 272, 274, 276, 280, 282, 309, 313, 315, 319, 339, 427, 568, 624, 639, 790, 792, 797, 831, 881, 882, 883, 886, 925, 930; III 76, 158, 455, 461; IV 52, 126, 913; ruler of Thebes, IV 246; lord of the Two Lands, II 198; bull of his mother, IV 426; fashioner of all that exists, II 149; fashioner of kings and queens, II 199; thunders in heaven, IV 578; equips all lands, IV 579; owns all ships, IV 580; acting as judge, IV 650–58, 672–73, 676; successor of Re, II 189; physical father of king, II 189; crowning kings, II 228–29; shield of bowmen, III, 581; in oaths, II 121, 318, 422, 452; IV 862; worshiped in Zahi, IV 219; in Nubia, IV 218; in Napata, IV 921, 924, 929, 932; in the city of Wa—, of Northern Syria, II 458; in Byblos, IV 580; Egypt, kingdom of, II 910; throne of, see Index VII; staff of, II 71; statues of, IV 190, 217, 219, 220, 245; Amon-of-the-Way, an image of Amon, IV 569, 586; erasure of name of, see Index VII: Erasure; extermination of cult of, II 306; Booty presented to, IV 126, 128; see also Index VII: Booty, Spoil, Plunder; prisoners presented to, I 13; see also Index VII: Captives, Prisoners, Slaves; associate gods of, III 82; see also Amon-Re, Amon-Re-Iny, Amonrasonther, Amon-Kamephis, Amon-Atum, Ir-Amon; western voyage of, II 885, 888; Feasts of, see Index VII: Feasts; Amenhotep, festival leader of, II 912; oasis of, II 189; Estate of, see Index II: Karnak, temple of Amon; Temples of, see Index II: Karnak, Luxor, Medinet Habu, Western Thebes, Mewetkhent, Napata, Sebûʿa, Kanekeme, Tanis, Zahi. For other references to Amon, see Amon-Re and Index II: Temple of Amon at Karnak.

AMON-ATUM, II 853; III 261.

AMON-KAMEPHIS, II 225 n. b; IV 63.

AMONRASONTHER, III 555 n. e.

AMON-RE, II 88, 127, 142, 157, 305, 328, 338, 365, 384, 402 n. c, 418, 460, 601, 606, 662, 791, 792, 834, 904; III 27, 77, 137, 195, 206, 504, 512, 515, 517, 520, 556 n. a, 583, 597, 600, 621, 648; IV 7, 10, 14, 33, 42, 44, 56, 71, 75, 77, 90, 103, 104, 108, 137, 411; IV 726, 751; king of gods, II 73, 310, 370, 389, 638, 844, 878, 885, 926; III 223, 479, 504, 517; IV 4, 10, 15, 16, 26, 27, 28, 29, 31, 32, 49, 52, 57, 58, 80, 105, 110, 128, 143, 183, 184, 185, 186, 222, 225, 230, 236, 383, 384, 424,

463, 477, 489, 491, 494, 495, 496, 497, 510, 511, 522, 523, 528, 531, 534, 539, 541, 563, 564, 566, 580, 586, 593, 594, 609, 610, 611, 615, 616, 617, 622, 626, 632, 633, 634, 635, 637, 638, 639, 640, 641, 647, 652, 653, 654, 659, 660, 665, 668, 671, 672, 673, 677, 698, 705, 706, 707, 708, 721, 736, 740, 762, 770, 777, 795, 988H; lord of gods, II 256; IV 401; the begetter, II 288; the self-begetter, IV 186, 653; 654, 671, 722; lord of life and health IV 580; Hatshepsut, daughter of, II 225, 314; divine offerings for, II 159; see also Index VII: Offerings, and IV 160 ff.; presider over Karnak, II 196, 281, 568, 905; III 150, 285, 519; IV 740, 889, 988D; lord of Thebes, I 484; II 159, 196, 225, 265, 278, 281, 425, 439, 568, 573 603, 606, 614, 627, 630, 646, 654, 656, 797, 886, 888, 889, 890, 896, 905; III 82, 105, 110, 116, 119, 136, 150, 152, 156, 215, 216, 217, 219, 223, 256, 285, 290, 433, 436, 453, 503, 510, 512, 517, 519, 522; IV 15, 126, 130, 184, 458, 652, 653, 704, 706, 722, 740, 854, 886, 889, 900, 924, 926, 931, 988D; lord of the lands, IV 566; lord of the highlands and mountains, IV 458; residing in Nubia, IV 900; lord of "Thrones-of-the-Two-Lands," IV 369; temple of, in the backlands of Fayûm, IV 369; lord of Yered, IV 368; lord of heaven, II 219, 253, 278, 312, 325, 934; III 517; IV 78, 80, 128, 184; lord of earth, II 253. For further references, see Amon.

Amon-Re-Harakhte, III 370.

Amon-Re-Harakhte-Atum: lord of the two lands of Heliopolis, III 371.

Amon-Re-Iny: ruler of Thebes, IV 12.

Amon-Re-Osiris, III 206.

Anath, III 84, 467; IV 105.

Antheret: Hittite divinity, III 386.

Anubis, II 192 n. c, 212; lord of the ⌜cave⌝, I 394; lord of Rosta, III 17; lord of designs in Neru, IV 296; lord of Rekreret, I 540; lord of Sep, IV 368; lord of Tazoser, IV 1029; souls of, I 403; feast of, see Index VII: Feasts, "birth of Anubis;" temples of, see Index II: Neru, Rekreret (in Siut), Sep, Rosta.

Anuket: mistress of Elephantine, IV 991; gifts to, I 500; temple of Satet, Anuket, and Khnum, built by Sesostris I, I 500; giving symbol of life to Sesostris III, I 643; mistress of Nubia, I 644; II 794 n. a; "feast of Nubia" of, II 798; voyage of, II 798.

Apis, IV 960; the Living Son, IV 1011; son of Ptah, IV 309, 781, 791; son of First of Westerners, IV 780; son of Osiris, IV 976, 986; sacred cattle of, IV 332; feast of, see Index VII: Feasts, "Running-of-the-Apis;" temple of, the Serapeum in Memphis, see Index II; burial of, in the Serapeum, I 22; IV 771, 778, 780, 786, 791, 884, 917, 918, 961, 977, 986, 1010. See also Osiris-Apis.

Astarte, IV 105.

Aton, I 66 n. e; II 946, 959, 960, 961, 972, 983, 984, 985, 987, 988, 990, 991, 992, 993, 994, 995, 996, 999, 1000, 1001, 1002, 1003, 1006, 1007, 1010, 1011, 1012, 1015; III 19, 72, 144, 270, 281; IV 62; lord of lords, II 1007; lord of radiance, II 1011; ruler of the Two Lands, II 1007; attributes of, II 991, 992; displacing the name of god, II 987; cult of, introduced by Ikhnaton, II 932; faith of, II 932, 943, 949, 979; hymns of, II 979, 984, 991, 992, 999–1001, 1007, 1010–11; landmarks of, II 969; oblation to, II 952, 958; temples of, see Index II: Akhetaton, Heliopolis, Thebes.

Atum (original sun-god of Heliopolis), I 625; II 91, 192 n. c, 226, 228, 299, 318, 412, 630, 907; III 246, 265, 270, 278, 281, 597; IV 31, 38, 42, 56, 57, 62, 94, 130, 182, 252, 254, 382, 401, 704, 817, 869, 872, 921; going down in the west, II 318; Heliopolis, city of, III 576; lord of the Two Lands of Heliopolis, I 500; II 221, 224, 635, 643, 896; III 159, 245, 288, 548, 600; IV 183, 247, 248, 249, 280, 284, 289, 383; of Khereha, IV 869; great house of heaven of, IV 357; throne of, see Index VII; earthly reign of, II 91; begetter of Pharaoh, II 91; succeeded by Re, II 222; the old man, IV 972; kings crowned by, II 221, 222, 226, 227; gifts to, I 500; temple built to, in Heliopolis by Sesostris I, I 503; lord of the great house, I 504; bull of the gods, I 504; ancient writings of, I 756; mountain of, II 917.

Atum-Harmakhis: statue for (=the Sphinx), II 815.

ATUM-KHEPRI: lord of Heliopolis, IV 732, 872; chapel of, in the temple at Heliopolis, IV 732.

ATUM-RE-HARAKHTE, IV 183, 248, 249, 280, 284, 289, 383.

B

BAAL, III 86, 122, 144, 312, 326, 338, 463; IV 46, 49, 62, 72, 75, 77, 80, 96, 104, 106, 246; servant of, III 630.

BAST, IV 463; mistress of Bubastis, IV 734; mother of, I 485; mistress of Berset, IV 369; of the South, I 396 n. c; protecting the land, I 747; in Heracleopolis, IV 973; feast of, IV 973; residing in Thebes, IV 912; image of, IV 912; foes of, II 792.

BES, II 206.

BULL, THE WHITE: endowment of, I 159.

BUTO, II 223; III 28; IV 62; white crown beloved by, II 235; endowment of, I 156, 159; mistress of Dep, I 500; II 224; mistress of Perneser, I 159; of the South, I 167; mistress of Pe, I 500.

BUTO-UPET-TOWE: ritual priest of, III 542.

C

CITY-GOD: loves the ruler, I 403, 404; leads him, I 404.

D

DEDUN, II 173, 279, 646; temple at Semneh, dedicated to, II 167, 170; presider over Nubia, II 170, 171, 176.

E

EIGHT GODS, THE, II 302; IV 848; temple of, in Hermopolis, IV 848.

ENNEAD, THE DIVINE, I 160; II 360; III 612; IV 382, 399; of Abydos, I 764; III 232, 486, 525; of Elephantine, IV 992; of Heliopolis, III 16, 545, 547; IV 250, 261, 262, 265, 269, 304, 869; of Memphis, IV 309, 322; of temple at Redisiyeh, III 173, 190, 195; of Thebes, II 71, 308, 635, 812, 832, 907, 909; III 27, 29, 32, 206 215, 218, 256, 281, 285, 510, 533; IV 9, 13, 128, 624, 768; of the Senut-house, I 165; the great, II 285; of Pakht, II 301.

ESWERE, IV 484.

ESYE (dei of wisdom), I 504, 747; II 316 ntya.

F

FIRST OF WESTERNERS: see Osiris.

G

GODDESS, IV 599; of South and North, IV 352, 363, 364, 383, 470, 731; acting as midwives, II 206.

GODS, II 118, 149; of Thebes, II 73, 224; of the South, II 828; of the South and North, II 217, 219, 224, 800, 812; IV 183, 335, 352, 353, 363, 364, 383, 470, 731; of the deeps, IV 330; oblations for, IV 330; fragrance, of, II 196; odor of, II 196; council of, II 192; of birth, II 206 n. f; city, II, 53; dancing dwarf of, I 351; sent to a foreign land, III 440–47; desecrated by the Syrian usurper, IV 398; magic powers of, IV 455; forbidding practice of magic by men, IV 455; of wax, for magical purposes, IV 454; "Amon-of-the-Way," an image of Amon, IV 569, 586; see also Index V: Beloved of god, Daughter of god, Mistress of god.

"GREAT-ONE-OF-THE-GARDEN," a goddess, IV 914; image of, IV 914; temples of, IV 914.

H

HAPI, I 500; III 289; great in Niles, IV 887; temple of, at Heliopolis, IV 273; see also Index VI: Per-Hapi, and the Nile-god.

HARAKHTE, II 139, 425, 562, 633, 791, 792, 812, 915; III 159, 179, 237, 288, 370, 496, 499, 542, 546, 556 n. a, 560, n. a, 599, 600; IV 38, 463, 477, 510, 702, 703; lord of heaven, III 3; IV 247; great god, III 3; IV 247; lord of earth, III 3; sun of darkness, III 3; only god, III 18; king of the gods, III 18; king, the image of, III 30; lord of Nubia, III 499; worshiped in Amada, II 791; stela for, I 501; worshiped in the city of Wa—, of Northern Syria, II 458; throne of, see Index VII; temple of, in Karnak, II 935; IV 706, 708.

HARENDOTES (Horus, protector of his father, *Ḥr-nḏ-yt-f*), II 95; IV 484;

in the temple of Min at Panopolis, II 181.
HARKEFTI: prophet of, I 533.
HARKHENTIKHET: lord of Athribis, IV 360, 369; lord of Kemwer, IV 875.
HARMAKHIS, II 811, 814.
HARMAKHIS-KHEPRI-RE-ATUM, II 815.
HARSAPHES: lord of Heracleopolis, I 675; divine fathers of, IV 787, 792; lord of Heliopolis, IV 733; chapel of, IV 733.
HARSEKHA, III 404.
HARSIESE, II 192 n. c; III 24, 32; IV 458, 463, 464; "house of Osiris and Harsiese" (=the temple of Osiris at Abydos), IV 357.
HARVEST-GOD, I 483.
HARVEST-GODDESS, III 265.
HATHOR, II 192 n. c, 208, 209, 226, 337; III 19, 210; blade of, IV 784; cow-headed, II 210; cows of, II 210; daughter of Ptah, IV 331; residing in the South of Memphis, IV 331; mistress of Cusæ, I 500; temple of, II 300; of Diospolis Parva, prophet of, IV 726; (of Heliopolis), mistress of Hotep, II 1042; IV 247; mistress of Hotep-em-Hotep, IV 733; chapel of, IV 733; of the house of Atum, III 400; mistress of the Malachite country, I 715, 720, 722, 723, 725, 738, 750; II 450 n. a; IV 409, 784; temple of (in Buto?), IV 784, 956; endowment of, IV 784; mistress of Nun, I 178; mistress of Dendera, I 423H, 500; mistress of heaven, I 738; mistress of Punt, II 252, 255, 288; mistress of Myrrh, II 295; mistress of Royenet, I 216 bis; mistress of the Sycamore; I 165; mistress of Imu, I 351; sovereign of Thebes, II 357; patroness of Thebes, II 224; procession of, II 357; mistress of the valley, IV 913; image of, IV 913; temple of (in Tanis?), IV 956; residing in Zeme, IV 1002; shrines of, in the sun-temple, Sekhet-Re, I 159; in Ro-she, I 159; shrines of, in the pyramid temple: "The-Soul-of-Sahure-Shrines," I 159; endowment of, I 156, 159, 165; IV 784; mine-chambers at Sinai made for, I 723; priests of, I 216, 217; prophetess of, IV 792; temple of, at Aphroditopolis, IV 366.
HAWK, II 115.
HEKET, II 205, 302; goddess of birth, II 206 n. f; frog-headed, II 202; mistress of Hirur, II 205 n. a; white one of Nekhen, II 205 n. a; the deliverer, II 205 n. a.
HEKU: an obscure divinity, II 210.
HERERET, I 396 n. c.
HIGHLAND GODDESS: mistress of the Red Mountain, I 493.
"HIM-OF-THE-HORIZON," II 314.
HORIZON-GOD (*Yʾ ḫwty*), II 141, 325; III 144, 515; IV 331.
HORUS, I 605; II 70 bis, 73 bis, 120, 138, 143, 220, 279, 318, 430; III 28, 173, 194, 229, 259, 266, 270, 497, 590; IV 17, 47, 304, 720, 1011; son of Isis, II 808; III 236, 272; IV 351; the Mighty Bull, IV 351; who has numbered his limbs, I 502; receiving life from Osiris, I 744; beloved of Mat, IV 351; lord of joy, III 136; on the royal standard, II 143; in the gold sign, II 145 bis; throne of, see Index VII; hawk, symbol of, III 285; lord of Alabastronpolis, III 24, 27; lord of Bek, III 284, 285; lord of Bohen, III 643; of Edfu, II 111, 114; III 165, 195, 285; of He, III 496; house of, III 496, 498; lord of Letopolis, II 95; IV 878; of Nubia, temple built for, by Sesostris I in Apollinopolis Magna, I 500; lord of Pe, IV 1017; prophet of, IV 1017; of the South, lord of Perzoz, IV 726; prophet of, IV 726; lord of Sebi, III 20; image of, IV 915; followers of, II 73; III 16; =the king, I 345, 346, 423C, *et passim;* terror of, I 356; worshipers of, I 78 n. a; II 73; Two Regions of, I 441, 448; Two Lands of, I 441; Feasts of, see Index VII: Feasts (worship of Horus, Rekeh); Temples of, see Index II: Athribis, Heliopolis, Apollinopolis Magna, Perzoz, He, Edfu, Letopolis.
HORUS-SOPED, III 155.
HOR-WATIT, II 303.
HRISHEFYT: king of the Two Lands, IV 368; temple of, IV 368.
HU (deity of taste), I 504.

I

IBIS: footsteps of, III 25.
INMUTEF, III 155.

IR-AMON (=the king): road of, II 792.

IRERTI, II 828.

IRSU, III 285.

ISIS, I 441; II 111, 192 n. c, 318; III 28, 173, 194; IV 47, 463, 895, 896; goddess of birth, II 206 n. f; mistress of heaven, IV 458; "mistress of the pyramid," I 177, 179, 180; divine mother, I 178; III 227; the late date of her cult, I 177; "the great one," II 293 n. e; Horus, son of, II 808; III 224, 236; IV 47, 62, 103, 351, 895; temple of, IV 706, 916; called: "The-Great-Ka-of-Harakhte," IV 706; lake of, IV 916.

K

KAMEPHIS, II 831; III 623; the self-begetting sun-god, II 314 n. b; "bull-of-his-mother," II 225, 314.

KEB, II 192 n. c, 285; IV 400; throne of, see Index VII; god of earth, III 116; divine begetter, II 71; controller of minerals and metals, I 726; II 91; inheritance of, IV 942.

KHENT-YAWETEF: endowment of, I 159.

KHEPRI, II 299, 314, 812, 907; III 281, 288, 411; office of, II 595; statue of (=the Sphinx), II 814.

KHEPRI-SET, IV 399.

KHESETI, II 240, 241.

KHNUM, I 747; II 302, 328, 795 n. d; III 203, 265, 404; lord of the cataract, I 317, 500, 611, 615; II 95, 224, 360, 794 n. a, 796 n. j, 844; III 479; IV 655, 969, 991, 1002; II 205, 207, 212; creator of man, II 199, 202; god of birth, II 206 n. f; at the potter's wheel, II 202; the potter, II 203; father of all gods and goddesses, IV 148; binder of the Nine Bows, II 170, 171; smiter of the Shasu, II 170, 171; of Elephantine, II 89; field of Dodekaschoinos belonging to, IV 146; lord of Hirur, I 637 n. a; II 95, 202; dwelling in Abydos, II 95; lord of Sheshotep, IV 366; temples of, see Index II: Elephantine, Semneh, Sheshotep.

KHNUM-HATWERET: temple of, IV 367.

KHNUM-RE, of Elephantine: temple of, IV 925; lord of the cataract, IV 925.

KHONSU, II 216; III 34, 155, 452, 560 n. b, 623; IV 78, 125, 126, 185, 463, 468, 483, 616, 639, 663, 668; of the Theban triad, I 24; II 244; IV 183, 184, 222, 230, 236; priests of, III 341; the two sacred barques of, III 431; residing in Themet, IV 914; image of; IV 914.

KHONSU-IN-THEBES-BEAUTIFUL-REST, III 136, 150, 156, 431, 440, 447; IV 184, 225, 602, 617, 620, 671, 911; Horus, lord of joy, III 136, 150; IV 225; lord of Thebes, IV 602; temple of, in Thebes (Karnak), IV 214, 225, 472, 602, 603, 660; statues of, IV 214; third prophet of, IV 665; image of, IV 911; name of, IV 911; image of, in Karnak temple, IV 204.

KHONSU-NEFERHOTEP, III 370.

KHONSU-RE, IV 624.

KHONSU-THE-PLAN-MAKER-IN-THEBES, III 431, 440, 441, 442, 447; driving out evil spirits, III 443, 444; priest of, 432; in the form of a hawk, III 445; sent to Bekhten, III 440, 445, 446.

KHONSUPEKHROD: image of, IV 909; name of, IV 909; throne of, IV 909.

KHUYET, goddess of the temple of Khentikhet in Athribis, IV 874.

M

MAT (goddess of truth), II 154, 938; III, 18, 19, 150, 556 n. a, 560 n. b; IV 458, 463; prophet of, I 531; II 352, 936; III 556, 560; daughter of Re, II 939; beloved of Horus, IV 351; mistress of heaven, II 939; ruler of gods, II 939; presider over the palace, II 939; temple of, in Karnak, IV 660.

MEFDET: feast of birth of, I 115.

MENHYT, III 88.

MENMARE, III 172.

MES: endowment of, I 159.

MESKHENET, II 207, 302; III 400; goddess of birth, II 206 n. f; directing the midwives, II 206.

MIN, I 441, 500; II 30; IV 463; "Lofty of the Two Feathers," II 302; lovely like, IV 49; lord of Panopolis, II 181; temple of, II 181; feasts of, II 181; ithyphallic, I 296; II 104, 302 n. a, 889 n. a; august god, I 437; lord of Coptos, I 296, 443, 605, 779, 780; wine offered before him, I 435; III

282; lord of the highlands, I 437, 441, 443, 707; III 282; IV 458; offering of, to Mentuhotep IV, I 437; creator of the pure, costly stone of the Hammamat Mountain, I 442; Hammamat, the highlands of, I 442; head of the Troglodytes, I 443; guarding the expedition to Hammamat, I 448, 707; his forms appeared in a rain storm, I 451; image of "chief-of-heaven," IV 916; shadow of, put on the temple door, II 104, 302 n. a, 889 n. a; likeness of, in year of terror, II 792, 918; divine offerings for, II 567; feasts of, see Index VII: Feasts (Birth of Min, Peret-Min); temples of, see Index II: Coptos, Panopolis.

MIN, HORUS, AND ISIS: triad of, IV 365.

MIN-AMON, IV 26; residing in Bohen, III 77, 79, 159, 161; temple of, III 74, 77, 247; endowment of divine offerings for, III 77, 159; temple-personnel of, III 78; store house of, III 78; slaves of, III 78; of Luxor, IV 909.

MIN-HARSIESE, IV 465.

MIN-HOR OF COPTOS, I 675.

MIN-SI-ESE, III 76, 158.

MONTU, I 468, 471; II 192 n. c, 412, 844; III 86, 94, 141, 152, 224, 285, 307, 312, 319, 457, 479, 490; IV 37, 40, 41, 46, 49, 50, 51, 54, 56, 62, 65, 72, 75, 78, 91, 92, 98, 104, 105, 110, 124, 477, 496, 628, 721, 921, 945; bull of the mighty arm, IV 880; god of Hermonthis, II 352, 828, 831; IV 477; prophets of, II 352; lord of Erment, IV 547; house of, IV 547; lord of Thebes, I 510; II 224, 430; III 84, 147, 308, 326; IV 912; residing in Thebes, IV 82, 103; temple of, in Karnak, IV 660.

MONTU-RE, lord of Thebes, IV 886; prophet of, IV 660.

MOON-GOD, III 486; Thoth, the, III 643.

MUT, II 288, 353, 814, 835; III 34, 256, 371, 452, 500 bis, 560 n. b, 623; IV 57, 78, 80, 126, 185, 463, 468, 483, 489, 616, 623, 634, 649, 663, 702; mistress of Ishru, II 353, 357, 380, 627, 891; III 136, 370; IV 184, 623, 671; the great Bast, III 150; ruler of Karnak, III 150; mistress of amiability, III 150; grants the going in and out in the nether-world, II 353; procession of, II 357; the great sorceress, reared for the dominion of the two regions of Horus, I 441; great-in-Magic, I 468; belonging to the Theban triad, II 244; IV 183, 184, 222, 230, 236; temple of, in Ishru, built by Senmut, II 351; IV 660; the sistrum-bearer, IV 733; image of, in Karnak temple, IV 204; eye of Re, IV 899; of Napata, IV 897, 899; queen of Nubia, IV 898; temple of, in Napata, IV 897–99; mistress of the Nine Bows, II 891; mistress of heaven, III 136; IV 898, 899; queen of all gods; III 136; IV, 899; mistress of Ba (in Hauran), IV 716 n. b.

MUT-HATHOR, mistress of Thebes, II 622.

MUT-KHENT-EBUI-NTERU, IV 369; temple of, IV 369.

N

NEFERTEM, of the Memphis triad, IV 320; defender of the Two Lands, IV 183; protector of the Two Lands, IV 305, 306; statue of, in Medinet Habu temple, IV 191.

NEHEBKAU, a serpent-divinity: house of, IV 971; Nehebkew, II 302.

NEHEMEWI, II 302.

NEIT, I 609; II 630; III 28; houses of, I 609; IV 982; temples of, II 358; mistress of Sais, IV 830; prophet of, IV 830.

NEKHBET: endowment of, I 156, 159; the white one of El Kab, II 828; III 100; mistress of Perwer, I 159; mistress of heaven, I 741; III 28; IV 62; temple at El Kab dedicated to, III 504.

NEPHTHYS, I 500; II 192 n. c; III 28; goddess of birth, II 206 n. f.

NIBMARE: Lord of Nubia, II 894; sole lord, II 900; worshiped as god, II 897.

NILE-GOD: II 210, 212 (?); father of gods IV 296, 886, 888; books of, IV 296, 297, 347; explanation of, IV 296 n. e; oblations for, IV 296, 303, 347; statues of, IV 302, 349, 395, 738; the two, of North and South, II 888.

NILE-GODDESS: statues of, IV 303, 349, 395.

NINE GODS, in Khereha, I 500; see also Ennead of Memphis.

NUBTI: presiding over the Southland, IV 880.

NUN, II 887, 888; IV 62, 189, 308, 888; great council of, IV 330; shrine of, II 607; river of, in Heliopolis, IV 870; costly stones, the products of, III 448 n. b; cavern of, at Elephantine, IV 925.

NUT, II 192 n. c, 285; son of (=Osiris), I 759; II 318, 813, 900; III 84, 139, 144, 148; IV 49, 854; stars in the body of, II 164; Set, son of, III 539, 542.

O

OMBITE GOD (=Set), III 583.

ONOURIS, IV 458, 484; of the tall plumes, IV 365; in Thinis, I 500; IV 365; temple of, see Index II, under Thinis; highpriest of, II 818; son of Re, III 261.

ONOURIS-SHU, IV 355.

OSIRIS, II 91, 92, 192 n. c; III 173, 194, 232, 259, 266, 272, 280, 281, 486, 529; IV 46, 182, 304, 382, 400, 675, 683, 684, 685, 686, 687, 1011, 1024; giving burial, II 358; first of Westerners, I 500, 509, 608, 613, 665–67, 669, 758–61, 763, 765, II 96, 98, 186; III 528; IV 1018, 1021; Apis, son of, IV 780; ruler of the West, III 17; presider over the West, III 17; great, mighty one residing in Thinis, I 666; Lord of Abydos, I 500, 666, 669, 684, 758–59, 765; II 96, 98, 186, 367, 840; III 259, 528; IV 365, 484; secret of, II 180; districts of, III 260; mortuary endowments presented to, II 839, 840; lord of Rosta, I 177, 179, 180; lord of Tazoser, IV 187, 357; the great god of the dead, I 9; king of Upper and Lower Egypt, I 759; the great god, I 330, 338, 684, II 98; lord of heaven, I 338; (*Ḫnty ymntyw*), I 349; lord of life, I 684; lord of eternity, I 613, 762; II 293; ruler of eternity, III 17; IV 424; soul living with, II 378; sacred barge of, I 762, 763, II 183; throne of, in the house of gold, I 764; see also Index VII; coming forth from the body of Nut, I 759; appearance of, in procession, I 763; ennead of, I 763, 764; oblation-tables of, I 764; symbol of, II 874; son of, III 270; skin of pure electrum, III 176; ceremonies at feast of, in Abydos, I 669; dead kings called, III 266, 272; IV 499, 593, 642; burial of, applied to funerals of men, III 212; IV 499, 593, 637–47, 668; of Busiris, IV 484; of Coptos, IV 458.

OSIRIS AND HARSIESE: house of, in Abydos, IV 357.

OSIRIS-APIS: temple of (=Serapeum), IV 965.

OSIRIS-WENNOFER, I 669; lord of Tazoser, III 17; temple of, in Karnak, IV 958K.

P

PAKHT, mistress of Benihasan, III 249; traversing the Eastland, II 301; ways of, are storm-beaten, II 301; ennead of, II 301.

PERE-HARAKHTE, IV 496.

PTAH, II 804, 900; III 25, 173, 179, 237, 371, 428, 537, 554 n. d, 555 n. e, 615; IV 94, 204, 320, 351, 625, 702, 791, 857, 868; of the Memphis triad, IV 183, 305, 306; "Ptah South-of His-Wall," II 164, 613, 619, 620, 812, 836, 885; III 77, 159, 370, 510, 600; IV 183, 305, 306, 307, 313, 315, 331, 336, 337, 338, 342, 346, 347, 383, 463, 496, 781, 857, 866, 928; lord of the white wall, IV 336; lord of "Life-of-the-Two-Lands," II 611, 929; III 23, 77, 159, 370, 600; IV 183, 305, 306, 307, 337, 338, 342, 346, 347, 383, 463, 496, 628, 977; "beautiful-faced," II 601, 611, 790; IV 47, 62, 307, 331, 382, 401; "lord of truth," II 619; father of the gods, IV 307; ready-horned, IV 307; lofty-plumed, IV 307; Memphis, city of, IV 310; temple in, I 167, 241, 288, 720; II 929; III 537; IV 183, 323–30, 337–39; companions of, III 400; priestesses of, III 400; two high priests of, at Memphis, I 212; had built with his fingers the ancient temple of Upwawat at Siut, I 403; creator of handicrafts, III 288; furnishing the temple-plan, IV 625; workshop of, IV 28; wine offered to, II 612; speaking, in the form of his statue, III 582; blessings of, III 394–414; IV 132–35; feast of, II 614; III 23, 77, 159; lord of Thebes, IV 526, 528; temple of, in Karnak, II 157 n. e, 611, 614, 790; IV 526, 528, 960;

proceeding to the treasury of the South, II 614; throne of, see Index VII.

PTAH-NUN: father of the gods, IV 330.

PTAH-SOKAR, IV 928; statue of, in Medinet Habu temple, IV 191.

PTAH-TATENEN, II 641; III 397, 399, 411, 555 n. e, 556 n. a; IV 135; stronghold of, III 576.

Q

QUEEN OF THE LAND (a protecting goddess): district ("bend") of, I 401.

R

RAM-GOD: lord of Mendes, III 542; chief priest of, III 542.

RAYET, II 325.

RE, II 98 bis, 120, 141, 144 bis, 198 n. j, 314, 407, 422, 792, 999, 1013; III 18, 19, 172, 265, 270, 272, 281, 285, 287, 289, 319, 374, 517, 590, 598, 616; IV 256, 353, 382, 460, 836, 870, 958J; bestower of the red crown, II 229; hawk-headed, III 2; originally a king of Egpyt, II 187; became father of every Egyptian king, II 187, 222; succeeded by Amon, II 189; successor of Atum, II 222; Saosis mother of, IV 251, 278; two mothers of, II 318; in oath, II 121, 318, 422, 452; as crowner of Pharaoh, II 142; confers his own titles on Pharaoh, II 143 ff.; lord of gods, IV 259; lord of Heliopolis, III 546; lord of the eastern bend, IV 479; offerings to, at early morning, IV 256, 258; known by the Puntites, by Libyans, III 611; throne of, see Index VII; musician (fem.) of, III 542.

RE-ATUM, IV 62, 401; gritstone mountain of, II 917; the All-Lord, IV 249; the creator, IV 249; of Thebes, III 623; Great Seer of, III 623.

RE-ATUM-KHEPRI, III ex 6

RE-HARAKHTE, III 246, 280; IV 183, 248, 249, 280, 284, 289, 383; temple of, at Heliopolis, II 642; IV 732.

RE-HARAKHTE-ATUM, IV 732.

RE-SEBEK, III 556 n. a.

REKHET (goddess), I 609.

RENENET, II 302; III 265.

RENUTET, II 814.

RESHEP, IV 40.

RESI-INEBEF (=Ptah), IV 305, 322; meaning of, IV 305 n. a.

S

SAFT: shrine of, II 889 n. a.

SAOSIS: mistress of Heliopolis, IV 247, 278; mother of Re, IV 278; of the Heliopolis triad, mistress of Hotepet, IV 183; mistress of Hetep, IV 248, 278; temple of, in Heliopolis, IV 278.

SATET: mistress of Elephantine, I 615, 646, 650; II 360, 794 n. a; IV 991; giving the symbol of life to Sesostris III, I 646; temple of, IV 991.

SEBEK, III 554 n. d, 560 n. b; lord of Silseleh, III 208; temple at, III 208; Horus dwelling in Fayûm, IV 369, temple of Shedet, IV 369; lord of Mesha, IV 368; temple of, IV 368, lord of Neshit-Crocodilopolis, IV 366; temple at, I 709; IV 366; of Peronek, IV 547.

SED: feast of, I 113.

SEFKHET: keeping records, II 212, 231; writing the names of kings, II 230; counts the numbers, II 274, 279.

SEKHMET, I 747; II 226, 829; III 117, 360, 598; IV 90, 320, 655, 928; of the Memphis triad, IV 183, 305, 306; limbs of, II 52; presider (fem.) over Khas, II 814; beloved of Ptah, IV 183, 305, 306, 628; house (?) of, IV 445; mistress of Rehesu, IV 878; house of, IV 878; mistress of Sais, IV 878; house of, IV 878.

SEM: endowment of, I 159.

SEP: highway of, to Khereha, IV 870.

SEPA: endowment of, I 156.

SEREK-GODDESS, II 209.

SERPENT-GODDESSES, IV 194, 268, 333, 356, 407.

SESHAT: goddess, I 109; feast of, I 115.

SET, II 318; III 28, 155; IV 38, 47, 75, 79, 91, 103, 108; portion of, II 70, 120; years of, II 220; god of Kom Ombo, II 828; lord of Oxyrrhyncus, IV 368; temple of, IV 368; son of Nut, III 539, 542; high priest of, III 542; temple of, at Sesu, IV 369.

SHU, II 192 n. c; III 245, 608 n. f; IV 62, 103, 105; Memphis abode of, IV 857; son of Re, IV 355; throne of, see Index VII; Onouris-shu, IV 355.

SNEFRU: lord of the highlands, I 722.

SOKAR: in Shetyt, I 288; in Rosta, II 814; lord of Sehez, IV 855; temple of, in Mer-Atum (Medûm), IV 855; feast of, see Index VII: Feasts.

SOKAR-OSIRIS, II 904.

SOLE-LORD, II 900.

SOPED, II 337; giving the symbol of life to the king, I 617; lord of the East, I 722, 750; IV 1014; divine votress of, IV 784; Horus-Soped, III 155.

SUN OF THE NINE BOWS, II 987.

SUN-GOD: of Kheta, III 386; of Ernen, III 386, 391 bis.

SUTEKH, III 326, 338, 374, 386, 391, 419, 423, 491, 590, 599, 600; IV 43, 104, 105, 578; lord of heavens, III 386, 391; lord of the oasis, IV 726; prophet of, IV 726; Urshu, feast of, IV, 726; giving legal decisions, IV 727, 728; son of Nut, IV 726; temple of, in Ombos, IV 359; temple of, in the Residence city of Ramses III, IV, 362; of Khesesep, III 386; of Seres, III 386; of Aleppo, III 386; of Rekhsen, III 386; of Sekhpen, III 386; of Tehenu, III 611; of Kheta, III 386; of Ernen, III 386; of Zepyerened, III 386; of Perek, III 386.

T

TATENEN, III 179, 399, 411, 608; IV 9, 304, 307, 308, 335, 382, 401; father of the gods, III 411; IV 307, 308; source of artificer's materials, II 91; Ram, lord of Mendes, III 400; double plume of, IV 62.

TEFNUT, II 192 n. c; III 245; Tafnut, IV 254, 988J.

TESKHER: Hittite divinity, III 386.

TEWERET, II 206.

THOTH, II 95, 147, 193, 211, 230(?), 635, 664, 915; III 18, 19, 25, 281, 288, 404; IV 31, 46, 90, 105, 458, 460, 630, 730, 734, 921; lord of Hermopolis, IV 733, 848; dwelling in Hermopolis, temple of, in Hesret, the sacred quarter of Hermopolis, IV 356, 848; leader of the gods, II 95; keeping records, II 231, 275; balances of, II 280; IV 256; ape, sacred animal of, IV 33, 256; lord of divine words, IV 496; records of, III 448, n. b; takes the place of Horus, in the titulary of Khufu, I 176; founder of the ancient temple of Upwawet at Siut, I 403; writing of, I 531; accustomed to justice, I 531, 618; lord of Khmunu, records in writing, II 274; lord of Karnak, III 136; presiding over Hatibti, IV 916; image of, IV 916; divine boat of, I 669; eye-amulet for, IV 373, 386; temple of, at Pauzy, IV 368; the moon-god, priest of, III 643.

TRIAD: of Heliopolis, IV 183, 247, 248; of Memphis, 183, 305, 306, 320; of Thebes, II 224; IV 128, 222, 230, 236, 463.

U

UPWAWET: lord of Siut, I 394 bis, 395, 403, 541; IV 358; the dead smell the earth before, I 613; plan of, I 396; ancient temple of, in Siut, I 398, 403; procession of, I 540, 669; champion of his father (Osiris), I 669; opening the way before Osiris, I 763; lord of Tazoser (cemetery of Abydos), I 767; of the North, II 95; of the South, II 95; IV 358; temple of, in Siut, I 390, 403; IV 358; feast of Birth of Upwawet, I 150; going forth of Upwawet, I 669.

W

WENNOFER, I 669; II 815; III 240, 271, 279, 525; IV 972; ceremony of "That Day of the Great Conflict," I 669; lord of Tazoser, III 17, 234; soil of, III 260; sovereign of eternity, III 272, 278.

WERERET: mistress of Punt, II 288; mistress, great in sorcery, II 288; mistress of all gods, II 288.

WES, IV 912.

WESET, IV 912.

Y

YAMET, goddess: feast of, I 98.

YOH (=Thoth as moon-god), II 896.

Z

ZEBUI: lord of Aphroditopolis, IV 366; temple of, IV 366.

INDEX II

TEMPLES

NOTE.—All temple inscriptions are listed in Indices VI and VII.

Abu Simbel—

GREAT TEMPLE OF RAMSES II, III 449–57, 495–99.

SMALL TEMPLE OF RAMSES II, II 500, 501; dedicated to Queen Nefretiri, III 500.

Abusir—

SUN-TEMPLE OF NUSURRE, I 252 n. a, 423H n. a.

Abydos—

TEMPLE OF OSIRIS, I 534; II 185; IV 365, 1020; restored by Sesostris I, I 534; cleansed by Khenzer, I 784; lower story of, I 784; upper story of, I 784; called: "house of Osiris and Harsiese," IV 357; temple "of First of Westerners," IV 1020.

—Barque of, I 534, 613, 668, 669, 746; II 92; names of, I 669; chapel of, I 668, 669; rudder of, I 613.

—Divine offerings of, IV 676, 1021; altars of, I 746; IV 357, 686, 1020, 1021; amulets of, IV 1020; feasts in, I 665 n. b; lake of, IV 1020; secrets of Osiris in, I 746; oblation-table of, I 787; offering-tables of, I 534; IV 676, 1020; table vessels of, IV 357; furniture of, II 185; stairway of the lord of Abydos, I 528, 673, 684; II 52; wall of, IV 357, 1020; *Wpg* of, IV 1020.

—Shrines in, I 787; IV 1020; portable shrine in, I 667; names of, I 667, 787.

—Statue of Osiris in, I 668, 672, 759; II 92, 95; palace of, I 669; regalia of, I 668; tomb of, before Peker, I 669; cultus image, II 92; called: "protector of the oil tree," I 785; statue of the king in, IV 357; statue of Thutmose III in, II 186; divine offerings for, II 186; lands of the royal domain for, II 186.

—Temple archives of, IV 1022.

—Officials of, IV 357; high priests of, Nebwawi, II 179, 181; lay-priests of, I 668, 765, 783.

—Palace of Ramses III in, IV 357.

—Estate of: arbors of, IV 1021; ferry-boat of, IV 1024; barge of, I 762; IV 916, 1023; cattle of, IV 676, 1021; garden of, IV 676, 682, 687; gardener of, IV 682; gold house of, I 746, 764; income of, IV 683–87; lands of, IV 681, 687, 1021; necropolis of, IV 1020; see also Index VI, Tazoser; people of, IV 357, 365, 676; slaves of, IV 680, 682, 687, 1021; storehouse of, I 783; treasury of, IV 683–86; vineyards of, IV 1021.

"HOUSE OF MENMARE," mortuary temple of Seti I; begun by Seti I, III 174, 225, 226, 263; completed by Ramses II, III, 266; columns of, III 263; statue of, III 263; divine offerings of, III 263.

MORTUARY TEMPLE OF RAMSES II, III 524–29; built of limestone, III 525; dedicated to Wennofer, III 525; garden of, III 527; granary of, III 526; shrine-chamber, III 529; store house of, III 526; portals of, III 528; magazine of, III 527; endowment of, III 526, treasury of, III 527.

Akhetaton—

TEMPLE OF ATON, II 956, 975, 982; broad hall of, II 1018; dedicated to Aton, II 956; chamber of, II 1017.

- Endowment of, II 952, 954, 958, 966.

—Aton-house of Aton, II 987.

—High priests of, II 982, 985; "great seer" of, II 982, 983, 985, 987, 988.

TEMPLE OF "SHADOW-OF-RE" OF THE KING, II 1018.

TEMPLE OF "SHADOW-OF-RE" OF QUEEN TIY, II 956, 1016, 1017, 1018.

TEMPLE OF "SHADOW-OF-RE" OF THE KING'S DAUGHTER, II 1017.

Amâda (read Amada)—

TEMPLE, III 606 n. a.

Aphroditopolis—

TEMPLE OF HATHOR, II 3 n. b; IV 366, 369; people of, IV 366, 369.

TEMPLE OF ZEBUI, IV 366; people of, IV 366.

Apollinopolis Magna—

TEMPLE OF HORUS OF NUBIA, built of sculptured stone in the nome of Apollinopolis Magna by Sesostris I, I 500.

Arsinoe—See Crocodilopolis.

Athribis—

TEMPLE OF HORUS, II 919; called temple of Harkhentikhet (=Horus), IV 360, 369, 874; restored by Ramses III, IV 360; dedicated to Horus, IV 360, 369, 874; and Khuyet, a goddess, IV 874; walls of, IV 360; decrees for, IV 360.

—Estate of: herd of, IV 360, 369; divine bulls of, IV 470; inspectors of, IV 360; lake of, II 919; flowers of, II 919; prophets of, IV 360; slaves of, IV 360.

Babylon—See Khereha.

Benihasan—

CLIFF TEMPLE OF PAKHT, II 296; III 249; restored by Hatshepsut, I 15; II 296 n. c, 298, 300; and by Thutmose III, II 296; called Speos Artemidos by the Greeks, II 296; modern name: Stabl Antar, II 296 n. c; dedicated to Pakht, II 301; offering-table of, II 301; chest of linen in, II 301.

—Priest of, I 624; II 301.

Berset—

TEMPLE OF BAST, IV 369; herd of, IV 369; people of, IV 369.

Bet-el-Walli (read Bet-el-Wâli)—

TEMPLE OF RAMSES II, III 458–77; built in the rock, III 458 n. b; forecourt of, excavated in the rock, III 458 n. b.

Bista—

TEMPLE, IV 956.

Bohen—See Wadi Halfa.

Bubastis—

TEMPLE OF BAST, IV 734; *sḥ*-vessel presented to, IV 734.

TEMPLE OF AMON, IV 751; jubilee-hall of, IV 748, 751.

Buto—

TEMPLE OF BUTO, IV 956; shrine in, I 156.

TEMPLE OF HATHOR OF THE MALACHITE, IV 956.

Coptos—

TEMPLE OF MIN, I 776, 778, 780; IV 365; treasury of, I 778.

—People of, IV 365; scribe of, I 776; inspection of, I 777; priest of, I 776; deposition of a priest of, I 778; lay-priests of, I 776, 777; prophet of, IV 465.

—Sacred property of, I 779; temple income of, I 780.

—Garden of, II 567; maidens for, II 567; pleasant trees in, II 567; vegetables of, II 567.

Crocodilopolis—

HOUSE OF SEBEK, I 709; IV 366, 818, 882; statutes of, I 709; Horus dwelling in, IV 369; people of, IV 366; with inscription of Amenemhet III in, II 233.

TEMPLE OF AMON-RE, IV 369; name of, IV 369; people of, IV 369.

Cusæ—

TEMPLE OF HATHOR, II 300; was in ruins, II 300; restored by Hatshepsut, II 300.

Dêr el Bahri—

TEMPLE CALLED "MOST-SPLENDID," II 375; colonnade of, II 191; doors of, II 375; chapel of Amon in, II 375; floor of, II 375; palace of the god in, II 375.

—Great Seat, the "Khkhet," in, II 375; doors of, II 375.

—Shrine of Thutmose II, II 127; of ebony, II 127; dedicated to Amon-Re, II 127.

—Temple-garden, II 264, 295; equipment, II 265; Punt in, II 295.

Derr (=**Miam**)—

TEMPLE OF RE, III 503; IV 474, 479; chapel of Ramses II in, III 503; dedicated to Harakhte, III 503; name of, III 503; statue of Ramses VI in, IV 479; domains assigned to, IV 479–83.

Drah-abu-ᵓn-Neggah—

MORTUARY TEMPLE OF AMENHOTEP I,

II 45 n. b; called "house of Zeserkere," II 45 n. b.

Edfu—

TEMPLE OF, II 112; dedicated to Horus, II 111; door-keeper of, see Index V; statue of Ahhotep in, II 113, 114.

Elephantine—

TEMPLE OF KHNUM: endowed by Ramses III, IV 146–50; field of, IV 146; ships of, IV 147; people of, IV 147; prophet of, IV 150; honey-collectors of, IV 149; herd of, IV 150.

TEMPLE OF ANUKET AND SATET, I 500; II 798; IV 991, 992, built by Sesostris I, I 500; endowment of, IV 992; storehouses of, IV 992.

El Kab—

TEMPLE OF AMENHOTEP III, III 558 n. d.

TEMPLE OF RAMSES II, III 505; dedicated to Nekhbet, III 505.

Fayûm—See Crocodilopolis.

Hatweret—

TEMPLE OF KHNUM, IV 367; people of, IV 367.

He—See Hem.

Heliopolis—

TEMPLE OF ATUM, I 498; II 643; IV 183, 872, 955; Hathors of, III 400; called house of Atum-Re-Harakhte, IV 256, 262, 281, 284; rebuilt by Sesostris I, I 498–506.

—House of Re, II 642; III 547; IV 250, 252, 266, 735, 871; the "Great House," III 547; house of Re-Harakhte, IV 296, 732; called, dwelling of the gods, I 504; seat of eternity, III 545.

—Encircling wall of, II 642; IV 250; doorway of, II 643; name of, II 643; forecourt of, IV 259, 269; court of, IV 266; doorkeepers of, IV 266; dewat-chamber of, IV 871; sanctuary of, IV 251; great seat in, IV 251; double doors of, IV 251; dedicated to mother of Re, IV 251; mysterious seat of, IV 262.

—Vessels of, IV 269, 732, 735; barque of, III 542; balances of, IV 256; altars in, IV 256, 735; *dw*-altars, IV 735; offering-tablets of, IV 735.

—Colossi in, IV 252.

—Obelisk of Sesostris I in, I 503.

—Pool of Kebeh in, IV 296; oblations to the Nile-God in, IV 296.

—Shrines of, IV 250; of Atum and Tefnut, IV 254; double doors of, IV 254; divine fathers of, see Index V.

—Sphinxes in, IV 732.

—Statues in, IV 268; statues of gods in, IV 250; statue of Re in, IV 253, 268; amulets of, IV 253.

—Stelæ in, IV 255.

—Chapel of Ramses III in, IV 277, 281, 283; name of, IV 277; equipment of, IV 277; people of, IV 281; under charge of the "Great Seer," IV 281.

—Chapel of Atum-Khepri in, IV 732.

—House of Atum in (palace), IV 256, 262; temple treasury located within, IV 256; groves in, IV 262.

—Divine offerings in, IV 256; endowment of, I 156, 159, 165, 166; IV 256; royal gifts to, IV 284–88, 732, 735; decree on administration of, IV 255.

—Officials of, IV 281; priests (*w*ᶜ*b*) of, IV 250; chief ritual priest of, IV 871; high priests of, see Index V; great seer of, see Index V; personnel of, IV 266.

—Estate of, IV 280 82; domains of, IV 265; cattle of, IV 280, 282; cattle-yards of, IV 260; fattening-houses of, IV 260; galleys of, IV 280, 282; gardens of, IV 262, 280, 282, 288; shedeh, IV 262; flower, IV 264; granary of, IV 250, 267, 878; groves of, IV 262, 264, 280, 282, 288; harbor of, IV 266; herds of, IV 251; income of, IV 283; lake of, I 503; IV 261, 264; lands of, IV 251, 265, 281, 282; olive lands of, IV 263, 288; gardeners of, IV 263, 288; people of, IV 281; poultry yard of, IV 265; property of IV 251, 280; ships of, IV 270; slaves of, IV 266; storehouses of, for feasts, IV 257; slaves of, IV 257; storehouse for temple income, IV 258, 270; oblation storehouses in, IV 259; towns of, IV 280, 282; transport-ships of, IV 282; treasury of, IV 250, 256, 266, 270; vineyards of, IV 262; workshops of, IV 280, 281.

TEMPLE OF SAOSIS, IV 278; called: Hetep, Hathor, mistress of, IV 247, 248; and Hotepet, Saosis, mistress of, IV 183; location of, IV 278; barge of, IV 278; name of, 278; property of, IV 278; settlement in, IV 278.

TEMPLE OF ATON, II 1018; called: "Exaltation-of-Re-in-Heliopolis," II 1018.

HOUSE OF HAPI, IV 273; oblations for, IV 273.

TEMPLE OF HORUS, IV 271; name of, IV 271; walls of, IV 271; grove of, IV 271, 272; gardeners of, IV 272; court of, IV 272; oblations in, V 272.

TEMPLE OF RE IN NORTH HELIOPOLIS, IV 274–76, 281, 283; name of, IV 274; restored by Ramses III, IV 276; forecourt of, IV 274; equipment of, IV 274.
—Chief inspector of, IV 281; scribe of, IV 281.
—Gardens of, IV 274; herds of, IV 275; 283; names of, IV 275; people of, IV 281.
—Château of, IV 281.

Hem ($\underline{H}$ ᵓ*m*)—

TEMPLE OF HORUS, III 496, 498 (in both places read $\underline{H}$ ᵓ*m* for $\underline{H}$ ᵓ, as a subsequent collation of the original at Abu Simbel shows).

Heracleopolis—

TEMPLE OF HARSAPHES, IV 972; forecourt of, IV 970; hall of, IV 971; colonnade of, IV 970; doors of, IV 970.
—Lake of, I 111; IV 972.
—Chief prophet of, IV 792; prophet of Neit of, IV 792; sistrum-bearer of, IV 792; divine fathers of, see Index V.

NER: temple in Heracleopolis, IV 968; restored by Hor, IV 968.

TEMPLE OF BAST, IV 973.

Hermonthis—

TEMPLE OF MONTU, II 389; IV 547, 912, 915; built by Senmut.

TEMPLE OF ATON, II 1018; called: "Horizon-of-Aton-in-Hermonthis," II 1018.

Hermopolis—

TEMPLE OF THOTH IN THE SACRED QUARTER OF HESRET, IV 356, 367, 848; court of, IV 356; people of, IV 367; wall of, IV 356; *sḥ*-vessel in, IV 733.
—Dwelling house of Thoth in, IV 356.
—Chapel of Ramses III, built within the court of Thoth's temple, IV 356, 367; dedicated to Thoth, IV 356; people of, IV 367.

TEMPLE OF THE EIGHT GODS, IV 848.

HOUSE: "The love of Thuthotep abides in the Hare nome," I 706.

Kanekeme—

TEMPLE OF AMON, IV 216; built by Ramses III, IV 216.

Karnak—

GREAT TEMPLE OF AMON, II 157, 389, 794, 1040; III 224; IV 183, 184, 222, 405, 494, 495, 671, 706, 736, 887, 926, 945, 949, 958I, 988D, H, J; name of, II, 157; originally built of brick, II 157; rebuilt by Thutmose III, of sandstone, II 157, 794; completed by Amenhotep II, II 794; repaired by High Priest Amenhotep, IV 488 n. c, 489, 494.
—Works of, II 775; chief of, see Index V.
—Walls of, II 794; IV 914; inclosure wall of, II 164, 794; IV 654.
—Endowment of, II 163, 793; dues for, II 557, 559; IV 489; gifts to, IV 230–35, 736, 949; equipment of, II 29.
—Forecourt of, IV 195, 495, 531; Lateran obelisk in, II 627; vase stand in, IV 199; name of, IV 495.
—Jubilee-court of, I 49; IV 707, 764; built by Sheshonk I, IV 707; name of, IV 708; colonnade of, IV 707; pylon of, IV 707.
—Court of, IV 198, 207, 496, 497; planted with sycamores, IV 210.
—Great house in, IV 904.
—Upper gate of, II, 835; IV 958L.
—Bubastite gate of, IV 701, 756 n. a.
—Flagstaves of, II 776; III 94.
—Doorways of, II 154, 564, 601, 794 n. b; great doors of, II 376, 755, 794; gate of, II 309, 376; IV 889; name of, II 154, 309; IV 889; see also Portals; stelæ at, IV 205; upper portal of, II 835.
—Pylon (interior), II 155, 243; erected by Thutmose III, II 155; of Sheshonk I, IV 707; see also Index VII: Pylons.
—Colonnaded hall of Thutmose I, II 100, 103, 104; of Thutmose III, II

599; IV 767; columns of, II 32, 600, 795; IV 889; renewed by Thutmose III, II 600; by Shabaka, IV 889.
—Halls of, II 165, 304; IV 528, 563, 654, 764, 889; built by Thutmose III, II 560; name of, II 560, 599 n. f; IV 753; rebuilt by Amenhotep, IV 489; hall of the sacred chamber, built by Amenhotep II, II 795.
—Central hypostyle of, II 603; IV 701; built by Thutmose III, II 603; architect of, II 605, 772, 775.
—Holy of Holies of, II 153, 155, 795; hall of, II 795; built by Thutmose III, II 153; name of, II 153; statue of Ramses III in, IV 201 n. c.
—Pavement of silver of, II 755; IV 205, 671, 672.
—Chambers of, II 165.
—Chapel of, II 798A; IV 736.
—Shrines in the Karnak temple, II 156; of Thutmose III, II 376, 775, 776; names of, I 375, 376; of Nun, II 606; of Ramses III, IV 197, 198, 201; in eastern end, II 607; shrine inscribed by Amenemhet, I 484.
—Statues of kings in, II 156; statue of Amenhotep III in, II 917; three statues of Amenhotep, son of Hapi, in, II 912, 913, 913 n. c; statue of Amon, IV 736; see also Index VII: Statues; processional image of Amon, IV 737; image of Amon, IV 913.
—Vessels of gold, II 596; costly stones, II 596; electrum, II 596; silver, II 795; bronze, II 795; altar, II 163, 795; IV 736, 900; barge, II 888; IV 209, 211, 563, 575, 586, 904; sacred barque, II 283; IV 611; offering-tables, II 376, 795; oblation-standards, II 795; fire-pans, II 795; oblation-vessels, II 795; oblation-tablets, II 795; IV 199; jars, II 556; amulets, IV 201; censer, IV 736; libation-vases, donated by Intef I, I 421; table, II 353; tablet of victories, II 407; linen: royal linen, II 554; white linen, II 554; *šḫr·w*-linen, II 554; *wm.t*-linen, II 554.
—Sacred pool of, II 559; geese of, II 559; IV 229.
—Palace of high priest of, built by Sesostris I, IV 488; rebuilt by Roy, III 626; IV 488; restored by Amenhotep, IV 489; location of, IV 488.
—Kitchen of, III 624 n. i; refectory, III 624.
—Wine-cellar of, IV 512; prophet of, IV 512.
—Palace of, in the city of the Northland, IV 215; name of, IV 215; built by Ramses III, IV 215; gardens of, IV 215; boulevards of, IV 215; sacred avenue of, IV 215; people of, IV 225.
—House of the Divine Votress of Amon-Re, major-domo of, IV 511, 513, 522; singing women of, IV 521.
—for scribes, priests, *ʿḳ*-priests, high priests, lay priests, ritual priests, *wʿb*-priests, first-, second-, third-, fourth-prophets, high priestesses, divine votresses, see Index V; endowment of lay-priests of, II 618; duties of priests of, II 571; oblation bearers of, IV 515; chief of, IV 515; steward of, II 290, 350; chief steward of, II 359; bakers of, III 624; kneaders of, III 624 n. g; confectioners of, III 624; makers of cakes and loaves, III 624; sacred women of, IV 751.
—for inscriptions in, see Index VI: Karnak.
—Gold-house of, II 751; IV 491; double gold-house, II 751.
—Granaries of, II 43, 63, 343, 350, 806; IV 207, 217, 227, 497, 906; double granary of, II 43, 343; overseer of, II 43, 343.
—Storehouse of, II 332, 402, 554, 645, 646, 751, 759, 929; III 111, 119, 138, 152, 351, 453; IV 227, 497, 550; overseer of, II 352; chief measurer of, II 929; captives assigned for, IV 128; date-storeroom, II 749; metals and stones in, II 558; slaves of, II 555; IV 200; storehouse of dues, IV 489; storehouse for feast of Appearance, IV 200; equipment of, IV 200.
—Treasuries of, IV 211, 217, 227, 489, 497; white house of, II 748, 806; treasures of, II 748, 806.
—in Middle Kingdom, I 421, 484; IV 488.
—under Ahmose I, II 29–32, 34.
—under Amenhotep I, II 44.
—under Thutmose I, II 100, 103–5.
—under Hatshepsut, II 243–45, 304–21, 345–62.
—under Thutmose III, II 150–66, 376, 407, 560, 599, 608, 624, 625, 775, 776, 794; IV 753, 767.
—under Amenhotep II, II 781 ff., 794, 795, 798A, 803–6.
—under Thutmose IV, II 627, 830 ff.

Great Temple of Amon—
—under Amenhotop III, II 888, 889, 899–903, 917.
—under Ikhnaton, II 932, 941.
—under Seti I (Great Hypostyle), III 222–24; name of, III 222; columns of, III 510.
—under Ramses II (Great Hypo-style), III 509-13; name of Ramses IV in, III 510, 512; IV 665; servant of, IV 665.
—under Ramses III, dedicated to Amon, IV 197; name of, IV 197; monolithic shrine of, IV 197, 198; image of Amon in, IV 198; doorways of, IV 197; cultus utensils of, IV 199; sacrificial tablet of, IV 199; offering-tablet of, IV 199.
—Estate of, IV 222–45; captives for, II 918; IV 121, 208, 213; cattle of, II 354, 555, 912; IV 212, 222; overseer of, II 354, 912; IV 212; scribes of, IV 212; inspectors of, IV 212; shepherds of, IV 212; overseers of the horses of, IV 212; large cattle of, IV 225; small cattle of, IV 226; garden of, II 571; a Punt made in it, II 295; loan-cows, from Zahi, II 555; from Kush, II 555; gardens of, in South and North, II 352, 354, 561; IV 222, 226; of Kanekeme, IV 216; gold countries of, III 647; grain of, II 748, 749; IV 206; clean grain, II 561; groves of, IV 226; herds of, IV 212, 224; honey for, II 748; lakes of, II 164; IV 213, 488 n. c, 489; planted, IV 213; southern lake of, IV 489; lands of, IV 190, 222, 223, 226, 948, 950, 954, 957, 958; plowed lands of, II 561; fields of, II 354, 561; milk for, II 555; peasants of, II 554; overseer of, II 554; in South and North, II 561; 555; peasant-serfs of, II 354, 554; chief of, II 354; people of, IV 223, 225; ship of, IV 209; transports of, IV, 211, 226; galleys of, IV 211, 222, 226; archers of, IV 211; captains of, IV 211; towns given to, IV 222; of Egypt, IV 226; Kharu, IV 226; Kush, IV 226; Retenu, II 557; vineyards of, II 386; IV 213, 216; chief of, II 386; things of, IV 222 227; workshops of, II 775; IV 222, 226.
—after the Empire, priests, IV 488 n. c, 489, 494; Twenty-second Dyn., IV 701, 708, 756 n. a, 764; Ethiopians, IV 889; Mentemhet, IV 901–916; Saites, IV 935 ff., 988A ff.

Temple of Mut in Ishru, II 350, 380, 627; IV 489, 901 n. b; Mut, mistress of, II 357, 380, 891; built by Senmut, II 351; inspection of, IV 660; restored by Mentemhet, IV 910; doors of, IV 910; hall of, IV 910; columns of, IV 910; offering-tables of, IV 910; *sḥ*-vessel in, IV 733; shrine in, II 380.
—Garden of, planted with trees, IV 489; lake of, IV 910; storehouse of, IV 910; slaves in, IV 225.

Temple of Aton, II 932, 941; name of, II 932, 942; granary of, II 932; scribe of, II 932; overseer of the granary of, II 932.

Temple of Khonsu-in-Thebes-Beautiful-Rest, IV 214, 609, 610, 611, 624, 626, 912; begun by Ramses III, IV 214; additions to, by Ramses IV, IV 472; by Ramses XII, IV 602–3; completed by Hrihor, IV 609–26; inspected by Menkheperre, IV 660; barque of, IV 611 n. f; colonnade of, IV 622; court of, IV 614, 619; flagstaves of, IV 626, 632; forecourt of, IV 621; great seat of, IV 214 n. e; great place of, IV 610; hall of, IV 214 n. e; name of, IV 602, 610; broad hall of, IV 625; name of, IV 625; hypostyle of, IV 614; image of Khonsu in, IV 913; offering-tables of, IV 610; portal of, IV 626; pylon of, IV 621; built by Paynozem I, IV 632; shrine in, IV 609; sphinx in, IV 649 n. c; statues in, IV 214.
—Income of, IV 227–29; people, IV 225; slaves, IV 225.

Temple of Ptah, II 790; IV 526, 528, 913; originally built of brick, II 157 n. e, 611; inspected by Menkheperre, IV 660; restored by Thutmose III, I 14; II 157 n. c, 611, 614; by Seti I, II 612; called house of the "Beautiful-of-Face," II 790.
—Endowment of divine offerings for, II 620; doors of cedar, II 615.
—Image of Ptah in, IV 913; name of, IV 913.
—Vessels of, II 615; clothing, II 615; linen, II 615; ointments, II 615; offering-tables, IV 913.
—Seat of Ptah, II 615.
—Lay priesthood of, II 620.

Temple of Montu, lord of Thebes, IV 660, 912; offering-tables of, IV 912; lake of, IV 912.

Temple of Mat, IV 660.

Temple of Harakhte, II 935; IV 706,

708; names of, II 935, 940, 942, 959, 984; high priest of, II 934; master of secret things of, IV 706, 708.

TEMPLE OF BAST, IV 912.

TEMPLE OF OSIRIS-WENNOFER, IV 755 n. c, 958K; barque of, IV 958K; portable image of, IV 958K; barge of, IV 958K.

SMALL TEMPLE OF RAMSES III, IV 195; dedicated to Amon, IV 195; name of, IV 195; income of, IV 227–29; doors of, IV 195; people of, IV 223; treasury of, IV 195; herd of, IV 223.

SOUTHERN KARNAK TEMPLE: dedicated to Amon, IV 196; built by Ramses III, IV 196; people of, IV 223; herd of, IV 224; income of, IV 227–29.

Khammat (Soleb)—

TEMPLE IN KHAMMAT: built by Amenhotep III, II 890; of sandstone, II 890, 895, 898; pylons of, II 894; portals of, II 890, 895, 898; divine shadow of, II 895; floor adorned with silver, II 890; obelisks of, II 890, 894; flagstaves of, II 894.

Khereha (Babylon)—

TEMPLE OF ATUM, I 165; IV 869, 870; ennead of Atum in, IV 869; lords of, II 814; endowment of the gods of, I 165.

Kom el-Hisn—

TEMPLE, IV 95.

Kummeh—

TEMPLE OF THUTMOSE III, built of "good white stone of Sha," I 510.

Kurna—

'HOUSE-OF-MENMARE," mortuary temple of Seti I, III 114, 210; name of, III 212, 214, 217, 219, 229, 232, 236; begun by Ramses I, 211–13; completed by Seti I, 210; and Ramses II, III 448 n. b. 516–22; used by Ramses II, III 516–22; built of sandstone, III, 114, 216, 217, 220; barque of, III 212; silver-house of, III 213; palace of, III 213; dedicated also to Ramses I, III 521; sphinx in, III 114; list of captured cities in, III 114.

Luxor—

TEMPLE OF AMON, III 187–212; 215–42, 351, 841, 886; III 506–8, 533, 567; IV 223; restored and inspected by Menkheperre, IV 659, 660; built of sandstone, II 886; walls of electrum, II 886; floor of silver, II 886; portals of, II 886; garden of, III 567; towers of, II 886; lake of, III 567 n. c; inclosure wall of, II 887; IV 628; stairway of, IV 909; hypostyle of, IV 742 n. a.

—Barque of, IV 743; great house of, IV 743; portable image of, IV 743.

—Chapel of Thutmose III in, III 506.

—People of, IV 223; herd of, IV 224; income of, IV 227–29.

TEMPLE OF RAMSES II, within the temple inclosure of Amon, III 507.

Mad—

TEMPLE, IV 915.

Medinet Habu—

TEMPLE OF AMON (XVIII Dyn.): begun by Thutmose I, II 637; completed by Thutmose III, II 637–41; names of, II 638; IV 179; restored by Ramses III, IV 179; by Paynozem I, IV 634.

TEMPLE OF RAMSES III, IV 1 ff.; name of, IV 5, 7, 19, 189, 523, 532, 545; built of sandstone, IV 4, 7, 9, 189; gritstone, IV 189; black granite, IV 189; doors of electrum, IV 4, 189; dedicated to Amon, IV 189; divine offerings for, IV 190; wall of, IV 189; with ramps, IV 189; towers, IV 189; portal of, IV 191.

—First court of, IV 12, 13, 14; name of, IV 14; great seat of, IV 14; doorways of, IV 14; doors of, IV 14; inlay figures of, IV 14; pylon of, IV 15, 85–92, 93–99; flagstaves of, IV 15.

—Second court of, IV 6; built of sandstone, IV 7; great seat of, IV 7; festival of Min celebrated in, IV 9.

—Inlay figures in, IV 7, 9; doorposts of, IV 9.

—Images in, IV 9; scarabs in, IV 191; statues in, IV 191.

—Statue of Amon in, IV 190; name of, IV 190.

—Ptah-Sokar in, IV 191.

—Nefertem in, IV 191.

—Pylon of, IV 10, 60, 61; portal of, IV 11; name of, IV 11.

—Chapel of Khonsu in, IV 5; great seat of, IV 5; door of electrum, IV 5; chapels in, IV 191.

—Pavilion of, IV 17, 111 n. a, 192; balcony of, IV 192; columns of, IV 192; doors of, IV 192; doorposts of, IV 192.

—Double façade of, IV 16; colonnade of, IV 16; roof, of, IV 16.

—Château for, IV 194; lake of, IV 194.
—Estate of, IV 190; captives in, IV 190; garden of, IV 189, 194; arbor-areas of, IV 194; granary of, IV 9, 190, 193; herd of, IV 190, 224, 466; income of, IV 227–29; lake of, IV 189; lands of, IV 190; people of, IV 223; property of, IV 140, 190; ships of, IV 19, 193; storehouse of, IV 9; coppersmiths of, IV 533; treasury of, IV 9, 26, 27, 28, 31, 32, 190, 193, 545, 547; treasury chambers of, IV 25.

Medûm—

Temple of Sokar, lord of Sehez, IV 855.

Memphis—

Temple of Ptah, I 167, 241, 288, 720; II 929; III 537; IV 183, 987; Hatkeptah, ancient name of, IV 865, 868; also called temple of "Ptah-South-of-his-Wall," I 167, 241, 288, 720; II 929; IV 183, 311, 319, 321, 322, 342, 866, 928, 1011; restored by Ramses II, III 537; by Ramses III, IV 314.
—Decrees of, IV 321; divine offerings in, IV 320; feasts of, IV 329, 330; gifts to, IV 342–45.
—Court of, IV 311, 327, 330, 333, 335; name of, IV 330; garden in, IV 333.
—Holy of holies of, IV 865; dewat-chamber of, IV 866.
—Shrine of, IV 320; statues in, IV 320; portable shrine of, IV 315; processional image of, IV 315; barque of, IV 315; great seat in, IV 315; statues in, IV 326, 338 n. a; barge of, IV 330; tablets of, IV 317, 318; great seat of, IV 319, 334; table-vessels of, IV 334; mysterious seat of Sokar in, IV 857; house (=palace) in, IV 338, 340; granaries of, IV 314, 325; storehouse of, IV 314, 324, 328; for the feasts, IV 322; treasuries of, IV 340.
—Officials of, IV 324; high priests of, I 211, 212, 239, 258, 283, 286, 287, 288; III 552 n. e; IV 338; sem-priest of, see Index V: Priests; women of, IV 321; administration of, IV 321.
—Estate of, IV 337–39; cattle of, IV 323, 334, 337; cattle yards of, IV 323; fattening-houses of, IV 323; galleys of, IV 328, 337, 339; gardens of, IV 337, 339; groves of, IV 339; herd of, IV 338, 340; income of, IV 340, 341; lands of, IV 337, 339; magazines of, IV 324; people of, IV 338; poultry yards of, IV 323; slaves of, IV 322, 338; towns given to, IV 337, 339; transports of, IV 328, 339; workshops of, IV 337.

Temple of Aton, II 1018; name of, II 1018.

Temple of Amon, III 530.

Temple of Ramses II of Amon, III 412, 530–37; Thoth, III 531; forecourt of, III 412; double façade of, III 412; endowment of, III 413; sphinx in, III 531; Ineb-Sebek, a sanctuary in, IV 315, 330, 333.

Temple of Seti I, III 214 n. d; name of, III 214 n. d.

Temple of Ramses III, IV 311; name of, IV 311, 338, 340.
—Doors of, IV 311; "great seat" of, IV 311; shrine of, IV 312; image of Ptah in, IV 312; towers of, IV 311; personnel of, IV 313.
—Estate of: cattle yards of, IV 313; fattening-houses of, IV 313; gardens of, IV 313; herds of, IV 313; lands of, IV 313; magazine of, IV 313; storehouses of, IV 313; serf-laborers of, IV 313.

Serapeum, I 22; located in "the western desert of Memphis," IV 977; called temple of Osiris-Apis, IV 965; restored by Psamtik, IV 966; Apis buried in, IV 771, 778, 780, 786, 791, 884, 917, 918, 961; troops of, IV 966; stelæ of Pediese, IV 771–74, 778–81; Harpeson, IV 785–92; Bocchoris, IV 884; Senbef, IV 917, 918; Psamtik I, IV 959–62, 963–66; Necho, IV 974–79; Apries, IV 984–88; Amasis, IV 1008–12.

Mer-Atum—See **Medûm**

Mesha—

Temple of Sebek, IV 368; people of, IV 368.

Mesta—

Temple, IV 956.

Mewetkhent—

Temple of Amon, IV 368; people of, IV 368.

Napata—

Temple of Mut, IV 897–99; and of Amon, IV 929; restored by Taharka, IV 897–99; by Tanutamon, IV 929; adytum of, IV 899; cells of, IV 899; halls of, IV 898, 929 bis; doors of, IV 929; herd of, IV 929.

Neru—
TEMPLE OF ANUBIS, IV 296; "books of the Nile-God" presented in, IV 296.
Ombos—
TEMPLE OF SUTEKH, IV 359, 365; restored by Ramses III, IV 359.
—Chapel of Ramses III in, IV 359; name of, IV 359.
—Herds of, IV 359; lands, IV 359; islands given to, IV 359; people, IV 365; slaves, IV 359; treasury, IV 359.
Oryx Nome—
TEMPLE OF KHNUM, lord of Hirur, adorned by Kheti in his city of the Oryx nome, I 637 n. a.
Oxyrrhyncus—
TEMPLE OF SET, IV 368; people of, IV 368.
Panopolis—
TEMPLE OF MIN, II 181; IV 366; prophets of, II 181; people of, IV 366; feasts of, II 181.
—Chapel of Ramses III in, IV 366.
—Harendotes, in temple of Min, II 181.
Pauzy—
TEMPLE OF THOTH, IV 368; people of, IV 368.
Pe—
TEMPLE OF BUTO, I 500.
Per-Manu—
TEMPLE, IV 956.
Perneser—
TEMPLE OF BUTO, I 150.
Pernu—
TEMPLE OF BUTO, I 156.
Perwer—
TEMPLE OF NEKHBET, I 159.
Perzoz—
TEMPLE OF HORUS, IV 726; prophet of, IV 726.
Ramesseum—
RAMESSEUM, MORTUARY TEMPLE OF RAMSES II, at Thebes, III 329, 335, 365, 448 n. b, 514, 515; of sandstone, III 515; nave of, III 515; barque of, III 515; treasury of, III 515; columns of, III 515; granary of, III 515.
Ramses—
TEMPLE OF SUTEKH IN THE RESIDENCE CITY OF RAMSES II, IV 362; grain of, IV 362; granary of, IV 362; herds of, IV 362; people of, IV 369; serf-laborers of, IV 362; treasury of, IV 362.
Redisiyeh—
TEMPLE OF SETI I, III 162 n. c, 172–95.
Rehesu—
TEMPLE OF SEKHMET, IV 878.
Rosta—
TEMPLE OF ANUBIS (see Sphinx), III 230; IV 4.
Royenet—
TEMPLE OF HATHOR, mistress of Royenet, I 219.
Sais—
TEMPLE OF SEKHMET, IV 878, 956.
Sebûʿa—
TEMPLE OF RAMSES II, III 504; dedicated to Amon, III 504.
Semneh—
TEMPLE OF DEDUN, rebuilt by Thutmose III, II 61 n. a, 167; of sandstone, II 167, 176.
—Originally built by Sesostris III, II 167; within the fortress, II 167; of brick, II 167.
—Sacred to Khnum and Dedun, II 167; located inside fortress at Semneh, I 653 n. c; feasts of, I 655, 655 n. b.
Sep—
TEMPLE OF ANUBIS, IV 368; people of, IV 368.
Serreh (Aksheh)—
TEMPLE OF RAMSES II, III 502; name of, III 502.
Sesu—
TEMPLE OF SET, IV 369; people of, IV 369.
Shedebod—
TEMPLE, IV 780.
Sheshotep—
TEMPLE OF KHNUM, IV 366; people of, IV 366.
Silsileh—
ROCK-TEMPLE OF SEBEK, III 208; built by Harmhab, III 552–560.
Siût—
TEMPLE OF UPWAWET AT SIÛT, I 398, 403; IV 358, 366, 367; of ancient foundation, I 398, 403; ancient walls of, I 403; built by Ptah, I 403; founded by Thoth, I 403; restored by Kheti,

I 398, 403; by order of King Merikere, I 403; monument for the souls of Anubis in, I 403; colonnade of, I 403.
—Wall of, IV 358; barge of, IV 358; royal palace in, IV 358, 367; people of, IV 367; storehouse of, IV 358.
—List of official body of, I 550; lay-priests of, I 539, 544.
TEMPLE OF ANUBIS, LORD OF REKRERET, I, 583; *w* ᶜ *b*-priests of, I 540; great *w* ᶜ *b*-priest of, I 572, 583; fire kindled in, on New Year's night, I 573; lay-priests of, I 576.

Soleb—See Khammat.

Sphinx—
HOUSE OF THE SPHINX, I 180; Osiris, lord of Rosta, I 177, 180, 509; Sokar in, II 814; Anubis, lord of, III 17; identical with the temple of the Sphinx, I 180 n. h.
TEMPLE OF ISIS, near the Sphinx, I 177 n. e, 179; IV 706; built by Pesebkhenno, I 177 n. e.

Tanis—
TEMPLE OF AMON, IV 217 n. i, 956; granary of, IV 217; cattle yards of, IV, 217; poultry yards of, IV 217; gardens of, IV 217; herd of, IV 217; statue of Amon in, IV 217; slaves of, IV 217; treasury of, IV 217; divine offering of, IV 217.

Tep-het—
TEMPLE OF RE, I 159, 165.

Tharu—
TEMPLE, IV 956.

Thebes—
SERET-MAT, II 374.
See also Karnak, Luxor, Mad.

Thebes, Western—
For temples on the west side of Thebes, see also Kurna, Dêr el Bahri, Drah abu-'n-Neggah, Medinet Habu, and Ramesseum.
TEMPLE OF THE MEMNON COLOSSI, built by Thutmose III, II 552, n. i; Amenhotep III, I 14; II 883–85; name of, II 918 n. a; located on the west of Thebes, II 883.
—Portals of, II 883; floor of, II 883; flagstaves of, II 883; station of the king in, II 883; lake of, II 883; fish and fowl in, II 883.
—Storehouse of, II 884; slaves of, II 884; captives in, II 884; cattle of, II 884.
MORTUARY TEMPLE OF THUTMOSE IV, II 821, 823; tablet erected in, by Thutmose IV, II 821, 824; fortress of, II 821, 823.
MORTUARY TEMPLE OF AMENHOTEP III, II 904, 905; built of sandstone, II 905; offerings for, II 907, 908; double pylon of, II 906; statues of, II 906; priests of, II 908; obelisks of, II 908; prophets of, II 908.
MORTUARY TEMPLE OF MERNEPTAH, II 856 n. b; III 602 n. d.
CHAPEL OF PRINCE WAZMOSE, II 928.

Thinis—
TEMPLE OF ONOURIS, IV 355, 365, 484; wall of, IV 355, 365; built by Ramses III, IV 355; name of, IV 355; completed by Ramses III, IV 355; estate of, IV 355; people of, IV 365.

Wadi Halfa—
TEMPLE OF HORUS OF BOHEN, built by Thutmose III, III 639 n. a; III 74, 157; endowed by Ramses I, III 17, 18; Seti I, III 159, 160; divine offerings for, III 77, 159; personnel of, III 78, 160; storehouse of, III 78, 160.

Yered—
TEMPLE OF AMON-RE, IV 368; people of, IV 368.

Zahi—
TEMPLE OF AMON, IV 219; name of, IV 219; built by Ramses III, IV 219; statue of Amon in, IV 219.

Of Uncertain Location—
HOUSE (called) "MIGHTY-OF-THE-GODS," I 97.
HOUSE: HOR-REN, I 119.
TEMPLE OF MUT-KHENT-EBUI-ENTERU, IV 369; people of, IV 369.
HOUSE OF ⌜–⌝ OF HORUS: endowment of, I 156.
HOUSE OF ISIS, I 180.
TEMPLE OF HRISHEFYT, IV, 368; people of, IV 368.
TEMPLE (SUN) OF SEPRE: endowment of, I 156.
SAW, temple of, I 103.
TEMPLE OF SEKHET-RE, I 159.
TEMPLE OF SENUT-HOUSE, THE DOUBLE: endowment of, I 141, 159, 165.
TEMPLES, built by Intef I, I 421.

INDEX III

KINGS OF EGYPT

A

—A, predynastic king of Lower Egypt, I 90.

AHMOSE I (XVIII Dyn.): inscriptions of reign of, II 1–37; chronology of, I 66; accession of, I 51; successors of, II 1; siege of Sharuhen by, II 4; ships of, II 7; grandmother of, II 33; service of Thure under, II 62; Phoenician campaign of, II 20; building designs of, II 34; mortuary endowment of, II 840; mummy of IV 645.

—Nebpehtire (=Ahmose I), II 7, 20, 21, 25, 34, 62, 111, 182, 840; IV, 645.

AHMOSE II: See Amasis.

AKHTHOES, I 53.

ALEXANDER THE GREAT, journey to oasis of Amon, II 189.

AMASIS (XXVI Dyn.): inscriptions of reign of, IV 996–1029; chronology of, I 75; IV 935–41, 996–99, 1026–27. Khnemibre (=Amasis), IV 1009.

—Amasis-Si-Neit (Amasis), IV 1000, 1012, 1025.

AMENEMHET I (XII Dyn.): inscriptions of reign of, 463–97; chronology of, I 64, 460–62; Nubian war of, I 8, 472–73, 483; expeditions to Hammamat, I 466–68; to the Sand-dwellers, I 469–71; teaching of, 474–83; insurrection against, I 479–81; coregency with Sesostris I, I 481; reorganization of Egypt, I 482; death of, I 491–92.

—Sehetepibre (=Amenemhet I), I 465, 473, 478, 491, 597.

AMENEMHET II (XII Dyn.): inscriptions of reign of, I 594–613; chronology of, I 64, 460–62, 594.

—Hekenemmat (=Amenemhet II), I 616.

—Nubkure (=Amenemhet II), I 595, 600, 679 bis, 685.

AMENEMHET III (XII Dyn.): inscriptions of reign of, I 707–48 (title of reign overlooked by printer); chronology of, I 64, 460–62; expeditions to Hammamat, I 707–12; to Sinai, I 713–28; temple-inscription at Arsinoe, II 233.

—Nematre (=Amenemhet III), I 673, 708, 713, 718, 719, 721, 728, 747.

AMENEMHET IV (XII Dyn.): inscriptions of reign of, I 749–50; chronology of, I 64, 460–62.

—Makhrure (=Amenemhet IV), I 749, 750.

AMENEMOPET (XXI Dyn.), IV 663; chronology of, I 70.

—Usermare-Setepnamon (=Amenemopet), IV 663.

AMENHIRKHEPESHEF-RAMSES-NETERHEKON: see Ramses V.

AMENHOTEP I (XVIII Dyn.): inscriptions of reign of, II 38–53; chronology of, I 66; Sothic date of, I 46, 51; succession of, I 43; II 1; rewards of Ahmose-Pen-Nekhbet under, II 22; Nubian campaign of, II 39, 41; Libyan war, II 42; Karnak gate of, II 44; career of Ahmose, son of Ebana, under, II 38, 39; career of Ahmose-Pen-Nekhbet under, II 44–46; service of Thure under, II 63; death of, II 45; mummy of, IV 638, 647; tomb of, IV 513, 665, 667, 668, 691, 692, 699.

—Zeserkere (=Amenhotep I), II 25, 39, 41, 42, 51, 63; IV 513, 638, 913.

AMENHOTEP II (XVIII Dyn.): inscriptions of reign of, II 780–809; chronology of, I 66; coregency with Thutmose III, I 66 n. a; II 184 n. d; Asiatic campaigns of, I 16; II 780–98; date of campaigns of, I 66; II 780; Amâda and Elephantine stelæ of, I 16; II 791–98; Karnak chapel of, II 798A; reliefs of, II 781, 791, 798A, 799, 801, 802.

—Okheprure (=Amenhotep II), II 186, 782, 795, 797, 800, 804, 808, 809.

AMENHOTEP III (XVIII Dyn.): inscriptions of reign of, II 841–931; chronology of, I 66; birth and coronation of, I 13; II 187–212, 215–42, 841; Nubian war of, II 842–55; tablet of

victory of, II 856–59; commemorative scarabs of, II 860–68; queens of, II 861-62, 866–67; jubilee celebrations of, II 870–74; building inscriptions of, II 878–910; campaigns of, II 844, 582–85; celebration of the coronation day of, II 849; deification of, II 893, 894; tomb of, IV 556; reliefs of, II 187–212, 215–42, 843, 845, 856, 857, 858.
—Nibmare (=Amenhotep III), II 844 bis, 853, 886, 888, 889, 890, 891, 892, 894, 897, 898, 915, 916, 922.

AMENHOTEP IV: see Ikhnaton.

AMENI: crown prince (=Amenemhet II), I 520.

AMENISRU, II 866 n. c.

AMENMESES (XIXth Dyn.): chronology of, I 67; III 641.

AMENRUD, IV 852 n. c.

APOPHIS, Hyksos king, mentioned in Pap. Sallier, II 4.

APRIES (Hophra) (XXVI Dyn.), IV 1015; inscriptions of reign of, IV 984–95; chronology of, I 75; IV 935–41, 984–85, 1026–27; minimum length of reign of, IV 985; war against Amasis, IV 996–1007.
—Wahib (=Apries), IV 988F.
—Wahibre (=Apries), IV 988, 988F, 990, 1000.

ASHURBANIPAL, IV 405 n. g.

ATHOTHIS (I Dyn.): history of (?), on Palermo stone, I 91 n. b, 93 n. e, 102 n. a.

B

BEKERE: see Tanutamon.

BEKNERANEF (XXIV Dyn.): inscriptions of, IV 884; chronology of, 72 n. d, 73; son of Tefnakhte, IV 884.
—Bocchoris (Bekneranef), IV 884.
—Wohkere (=Bekneranef), IV 884.

BESH, I 81.

BINRE-MERIAMON: see Merneptah.

BOCCHORIS: see Bekneranef, IV 884.

C

CHU-EN-ATEN: see Ikhnaton.

D

DED: see Dedkere-Isesi.

DEDEFRE: chronology of, I 55, 59.

DEDKERE-ISESI (V Dyn.): inscriptions of reign of, I 264–81; length of reign, I 60; titles, I 264–67.
—Dedkhu (Horus-name of Dedkere-Isesi), I 264, 266.
—Ded (Golden-Horus-name of Dedkere-Isesi), I 266.

E

EYE (XVIII Dyn.): inscriptions of reign of, II 1042–43; tomb of, II 989–96; Tiy, wife of, II 989; servants of, II 989; chronology of, I 66.

H

HARMHAB (XIX Dyn.): inscriptions of reign of, III 1–73; chronology of, I 66 n. e, 67 n. g; tomb of, III 1–21; coronation inscription of, III 22–32; wars of, III 33–44; edict of, I 18; III 45–67; legal proceedings in time of, I 66 n. e; wife of, III 22 n. b; reliefs of, III 2, 5–9, 10–13, 15, 18, 20, 34, 37.
—Mernamon (=Harmhab), III 29, 32B.
—Setepnere (=Harmhab), II 573; III 24, 29, 32, 32B, 71.
—Zeserkheprure (=Harmhab), II 573; III 12, 24, 29, 32, 32B, 42, 71.

HATSHEPSUT, chronology of, I 66; divine paternity of, II 188, 190, 192, 196–201, 203–5; pictured in the birth-reliefs as a boy, II 188 n. c; birth of, II 206–8; nursing of, II 210; called king by Khnum and Amon, II 203, 208; Thutmose III called her brother, II 213; maidenhood of, II 223; coronation of, I 150 n. f; II 215–42; wearing king's costume, II 231; expedition to Punt, II 246–295; her temple at Der el-Bahri, II 215–295; pylon-inscription of, II 243–45; restoration of temple of Pakht at Beni-hasan, I 15; II 296–301, and other temples, II 302–3; the two Karnak obelisks, I 16; II 304–21; reliefs of, at Der el-Bahri, II 322–36; daughter of, II 344; vizier of, II 388–90; prominent officials of, II 340–87; usurpation of her monuments by Thutmose I and III, II 126; ebony shrine of, II 126–27; relation with Thutmose III, II 136.
—Khnemet-Amon (=Hatshepsut), II 198, 237, 286, 308, 309, 310, 339.
—Makere (=Hatshepsut), II 201, 208, 213, 230, 238, 239, 245, 253, 264, 269, 271, 274, 280, 285, 286, 288, 308, 309,

310, 314, 329, 339, 344, 350, 357, 365, 368, 370, 377 bis, 380.
—Wosretkew (=Hatshepsut), II 239, 268, 285, 308, 309, 325, 339, 354.

HEKENEMMAT: see Amenemhet II.

HEKMARE-SETEPNAMON: see Ramses IV.

HOPHRA: see Apries.

HRIHOR (XXI Dyn.): inscriptions of reign of, IV 608–26; chronology of I 70; IV 604–7; high priest of Amon, IV 566, 580, 593, 594, 609, 610, 611, 612, 615, 617, 621, 622, 624, 626; vizier, IV 593; king, IV 607, 620, 622–26; building of the temple of Khonsu, IV 611–26; reliefs of, IV 611–14, 621, 626.
—Siamon-Hrihor (=Hrihor), IV 620, 623, 626.

I

IKHNATON (XVIII Dyn.): inscriptions of reign of, II 932–1018; chronology of, I 66, 67 n. g; temple of Harakhte in Thebes, II 931–35; vizier of, II 938–48; landmarks of Tell el-Amarna, II 949–72; the Tell el-Amarna tombs, II 977–1018; change of name, II 932; Aton-faith of, II 932, 943, 949, 979; queen of, 943, 958, 959, 961; daughters of, 958, 961; estate of, II 1004; reliefs of, II 933.
—Amenhotep IV (=Ikhnaton), I 66; II 934, 939.
—Chu-en-Aten, III 2.
—Neferkheprure-Wanre (=Ikhnaton), II 934, 942, 950, 971, 981, 983, 987, 991, 992, 994, 999, 1001, 1002, 1003, 1004, 1007, 1010, 1012.
—Wanre (=Ikhnaton), II 975, 984, 993, 995, 1003, 1013.

IKHNERE-SETEPNERE: see Siptah.

INTEF I (XI Dyn.), (Horus-Wahenekh): inscription of reign of, I 421–23; his tomb-stela, I 421; chronology of, I 63, 415–18, 529; the conquests on the northern frontier of Thebes, I 422–23; king of Thebes, I 421–23; chief treasurer of, I 423A–F.
—Intefo, IV 514; pyramid of, IV 514; hound of, IV 514.
—Wahenekh (Intef I), I 423, 423B, 423D 423F, 529.

INTEF II (XI Dyn.), (Horus-Nakhtneb-Tepnefer): inscriptions of reign of, I 23A–G; chronology of, I 63, 415–18; chief treasurer of, I 423A, 423G; son of Intef I, I 423G.
—Nakhtneb-Tepnefer (Intef II), I 423 G.

INTEF III (XI Dyn.): chronology of, I 63, 415–18, 424; vassal of Mentuhotep II, I 424, 425.

INTEF (Nubkheprure), (XIII Dyn.): pyramid of, IV 515.

INTEFO: see Intef I.

INTEFO (Sekhemre-Upmat): pyramid of, IV 516; stela of, IV 516.

ITY (VI Dyn.): inscription of, I 61 n. a, 386–87; pyramid of, I 387.

K

KAIECHOS (I Dyn.): cult of "Running-of-Apis," I 114 n. a.

KASHTA, IV 940.

KEMOSE: queen of, II 33; pyramid of, IV 519.
—Uzkheperre (=Kemose): pyramid of, IV 519.

KHAFRE (IV Dyn.): inscriptions of reign of, I 188–209; chronology of, I 54, 55, 59, 190; son of, I 190; referred to, II 815.

KHANEFERRE: chronology of, I 55, 60.

KHASEKHEMUI (II Dyn.): birth of, I 86, 136.

KHAYU: predynastic king of Lower Egypt, I 90.

KHEKURE: see Sesostris III.

KHENZER (XIII Dyn.): inscriptions of reign of, I 781–87; cleansing of the temple of Abydos, I 783–87.
—Nematre-Nekhere (=Khenzer), I 786.

KHEPERHEZRE-SETEPNERE: see Sheshonk I.

KHEPERHEZRE-SETEPNERE: see Takelot II.

KHEPERKERE: see Sesostris I.

KHEPERKHARE-SETEPNAMON: see Paynozem I.

KHNEMET-AMON: see Hatshepsut.

KHNEMIBRE: see Amasis.

KHUFU (IV Dyn.): inscriptions of reign of, I 176–187; mentioned, I 189, chronology of, I 54, 55, 59; his relief at Wadi-Maghara, I 176; history of, on the Palermo stone, I 86; his full name, I 176; his Horus-name, I 176,

180; sphinx and temple of, I 177; daughter of, I 180; pyramid of, I 180.
—Khnum-Khufu ("Khnum protects me"), full name of Khufu, I 176, 176 n. c.

M

MAKERE: see Hatshepsut.

MAKHRURE: see Amenemhet IV.

MEKH, predynastic king of Lower Egypt, I 90.

MENEKHIB: see Psamtik II.

MENES (I Dyn.): accession of, I 53, 58, 79, 88; history of, on Palermo stone (?), I 91, n. b.

MENKHEPERRE: see Thutmose III.

MENKHEPRURE: see Thutmose IV.

MENKUHOR (V Dyn.): inscription of, I 263; length of reign of, I 60; titles of, I 263.
—Menkhu (Horus-name of Menkuhor), I 263.

MENKURE (IV Dyn.): inscriptions of reign of, I 210–12; chronology of, I 54 bis, 55, 59, 254, 255; title of, I 211; mentioned, I 213, 217; educated Ptahshepses, I 256.

MENMARE: see Seti I.

MENMARE-SETEPNEPTAH: see Ramses XII.

MENPEHTIRE: see Ramses I.

MENTUHOTEP I (XI Dyn.): inscriptions of reign of, I 423H; chronology of, I 63, 415–18, 423H; wars of, I 423H.
—Nibhotep (=Mentuhotep I), I 423H.

MENTUHOTEP II (XI Dyn.): inscriptions of reign of, I 424–26; chronology of, I 63, 415–18, 425; chief treasurer of, I 425–26; first great king of the Theban line, I 426; pyramid of, IV 520.
—Nibhepetre (=Mentuhotep II), pyramid of, IV 520.
—Nibkhrure (=Mentuhotep II), I 426; name to be read Nibhepetre, p. 344, add.

MENTUHOTEP III (XI Dyn.): inscriptions of reign of, I 427–33; chronology of, I 63, 415–18, 427; mortuary temple of, IV 520 n. b.

MENTUHOTEP IV (XI Dyn.): inscriptions of reign of, I 434–59; Hammamat inscriptions, I 434–53; sarcophagus of, I 448; expedition of, I 447; vizier of, I 438, 445; chronology of, I 63, 415–18, 434; mother of, I 450.
—Nibtowere (=Mentuhotep IV), I 437, 440, 441, 446, 450, 455, 456.

MERERI: see Pepi I.

MERIAMON-HORUS-PESIBKHENNO: see Pesibkhenno II.

MERIAMON-OSORKON: see Osorkon I.

MERIAMON-OSORKON: see Osorkon III.

MERIAMON-PAYNOZEM: see Paynozem I.

MERIAMON-PEDIBAST: see Pedibast.

MERIAMON-PEMOU: see Pemou.

MERIAMON-PIANKHI: see Piankhi.

MERIAMON-RAMSES: see Ramses II.

MERIAMON-SHESHONK: see Sheshonk I.

MERIAMON-SHESHONK: see Sheshonk III.

MERIAMON-SHESHONK: see Sheshonk IV.

MERIAMON-SIBAST-OSORKON: see Osorkon II, IV 747.

MERIAMON-SIBAST-SHESHONK-NUTERHEKON: see Sheshonk III.

MERIAMON-SIESE-PEMOU: see Pemou.

MERIAMON-SIESE-TAKELOT: see Takelot II.

MERIAMON-YEWEPET: see Yewepet.

MERIKERE (King of Heracleopolis), I 398, 399; titles of, I 399, 403; restoration of the temple of Upwawet, I 403.

MERNAMON: see Harmhab.

MERNEPTAH (XIX Dyn.): inscriptions of reign of, III 569–638; chronology of, I 67, n. b; accession of, III 578; Libyan-Mediterranean invasion against, III 572–617; prominent officers of, III 618–38; reliefs of, III 594, 597, 628.
—Binre-Meriamon (=Merneptah), III 575, 607, 610, 635.
—Merneptah-Hotephirma (=Merneptah), III 575, 588, 598, 600, 607, 610, 631, 633, 634, 638.

MERNEPTAH: see Seti I.

MERNEPTAH-SIPTAH: see Siptah.

MERNERE I (VI Dyn.): inscriptions of reign of, I 316–36; chronology of, I 61; inscriptions at the First Cataract, I 8, 316–18; sarcophagus of, I 321; pyramid of queen of, I 321–22;

expeditions to the Negro tribes, I 333–36.
MERNERE II (VI Dyn.): chronology of, I 61.
MIEBIS (I Dyn.): name last on Palermo stone, I 103 n. b, 148 n. c.

N

NAKHTNEB-TEPNEFER: see Intef II.
NAMLOT: king, IV 814, 830, 833, 849, 882; prince of Hatweret, IV 820.
NEBE: see Psamtik I.
NEBKHEPRURE: see Tutenkhamon.
NEBPEHTIRE: see Ahmose.
NECHO (XXVI Dyn.): IV 1028; inscriptions of reign of, IV 974–80; chronology of, I 75; IV 935–41, 974–75, 1026–27.
—Uhemibre (=Necho), IV 976, 980, 1028.
NEFEREFRE (V Dyn.): chronology of, I 255, 261.
NEFERHOTEP (XIII Dyn.): inscriptions of reign of, I 753–72; restoration of the temple of Osiris at Abydos, I 755–65; decree concerning the necropolis of Abydos, I 766–72.
NEFERIBRE: see Psamtik II.
NEFERIRKERE (V Dyn.): inscriptions of reign of, I 242–49; chronology of, I 55, 60, 254–56, 260, history on Palermo stone, I 163-67; vizier of, I 243–48.
NEFERKERE: see Pepi II.
NEFERKERE: see Shabaka.
NEFERKERE-SETEPNERE: see Ramses IX.
NEFERKHEPRURE-WANRE: see Ikhnaton.
NEFERTEM-KHURE: see Taharka.
NE⌈HEB⌉: predynastic king of Lower Egypt, I 90.
NEMATRE: see Amenemhet III.
NEMATRE-NEKHERE: see Khenzer.
NESUBENEBDED (XXI Dyn.) (=Smendes): inscriptions of reign of, IV 627–30; living at Tanis, IV 564, 565, 566, 574; wealthy ship-owner, IV 574; ruler of the Northland, IV 581, 582; king, IV 627–30; chronology of, I 70; IV 604–7; restoration of the wall of Luxor, IV 627-30.
—Smendes (=Nesubenebded), IV 564 n. c.
NETERIMU (II Dyn.): reign of, on Palermo stone, I 117.
NIBHEPETRE: see Mentuhotep II.
NIBHOTEP: see Mentuhotep.
NIBKHRURE: see Mentuhotep II.
NIBMARE: see Amenhotep III.
NIBMARE-MERIAMON: see Ramses V.
NIBTOWERE: see Mentuhotep IV.
NUBKHEPRURE-INTEF: inscription of, I 773–80; insurrection in time of, I 773–74; deposition of the count of Coptos, I 775-80; pyramid of, IV 515.
NUBKURE: see Amenemhet II.
NUBTI: a Hyksos king, III 542.
NUSERRE (V Dyn.): inscriptions of reig uof, I 250–62; chronology of, I 54 ter, 55, 60, 167 n. a; relief of, I 250; titles, I 250; sun-temple of, at at Abusir, I 252 n. a, 423H n. a.

O

OKHEPERKERE: see Thutmose I.
OKHEPERNERE: see Thutmose II.
OKHEPERRE: see Sheshonk IV.
OKHEPRURE: see Amenhotep II.
OPEHTISET (=Nubti): a Hyksos king, with whom a new era began, III 549.
OSORKON I (XXII Dyn.): inscriptions of reign of, IV 729–37; records of Nile levels under reign of, IV 695; chronology of, I 71; IV 694–95; temple gifts of, IV 729–37; wife of, IV 739, 740.
—Meriamon-Osorkon (I), IV 740.
OSORKON II (XXII Dyn.), IV 771, 774; inscriptions of reign of, IV 742–51; records of Nile levels under reign of, I 43 n. b; IV 696–97; chronology of, I 71, 71 n. a; IV 694–95; flood inscription of, IV 742–44; reliefs of, IV 749–50, 757–70.
—Osorkon (II) Siese-Meriamon, IV 743.
—Usermare-Setepnamon (= Osorkon II), IV 743, 774.
OSORKON III (XXIII Dyn.), IV 830, 872; inscriptions of reign of, IV 795; records of Nile levels under reign of, IV 794; chronology of, I 72, 72 n. d; IV 793–94; living in Bubastis, IV 878; son of, IV 794.
—Meriamon-Osorkon (III), IV 795.

P

PAYNOZEM I (XXI Dyn.): inscriptions of reign of, IV 631–49; chronology of, I 70; IV 604–7; high priest of Amon, IV 631–42; king, IV 642–49; temple buildings of, IV 632–35; restoration of mummies by, IV 636–47.
—Kheperkhare-Setepnamon (=Paynozem I), IV 645, 649.
—Meriamon-Paynozem (I), IV 659.
—Paynozem-Meriamon (=Paynozem I), IV 645, 649, 652, 660.

PEDIBAST (XXIII Dyn.): records of Nile levels under reign of, IV 794; chronology of, I 72.
—Meriamon-Pedibast, IV 794.

PEFNEFDIBAST, IV 814. The Demotic, from a recent observation of Spiegelberg, shows we should read Pefthewowebast (*Pf-ṯ᾿w-ʿwy-B᾿stt*).

PEMOU (XXII Dyn.): inscriptions of reign of, IV 778–81; records of Nile levels under reign of, IV 698; chronology of, I 71; IV 694–95, 778.
—Meriamon-Pemou, IV 780.
—Meriamon-Siese-Pemou, IV 698.
—Usermare-Setepnamon (=Pemou), IV 698, 780.

PEPI I (VI Dyn.): inscriptions of reign of, I 295–315; chronology of, I 61; expedition of, I 295, 297–98; queen of, 310; army of, I 311–12; war against Sand-dwellers, I 311–14; campaign in Southern Palestine, I 315.
—Merire (=Pepi I), I 298, 302

PEPI II (VI Dyn.): inscriptions of reign of, I 337–85; chronology of, I 61; queen-mother of, I 339, 341; queens of, I 344; vizier of, I 347–49; letter of, 350–54; grandees of his reign: Pepi-nakht, I 355–60; Khui, I 361; Sebui, I 362–74; Ibi, I 375–79; Zau, I 380–85.
—Neferkere (Pepi II), I 340, 382.

PESIBKHENNO I (XXI Dyn.): chronology of, I 70; IV 604–7.

PESIBKHENNO II (XXI Dyn.): chronology of, I 70; IV 604–7; daughter of, IV 740.
—Meriamon-Horus-Pesibkhenno (II), IV 740.

PIANKHI, I 22; stela of, IV 796–883; reliefs of, IV 814, 815.
—Meriamon-Piankhi, IV 816, 817, 834.

PSAMMUS (XXIII Dyn.?), I 72 n. d; IV 812; inscriptions of reign of, IV 935–73.

PSAMTIK I (XXVI Dyn.), IV 978; chronology of, I 75; IV 935–41; stela of adoption, I 23; IV 935–58; the Serapeum stelæ, IV 959–66.
—Nebe (=Psamtik I), IV 945.
—Wahibre (=Psamtik I), IV 943, 945, 958D, 960, 978.

PSAMTIK II (XXVI Dyn.), IV 987, 988A, C, E, I; inscriptions of reign of, IV 981–83; chronology of, I 75; IV 935–41, 984–85, 1026–27.
—Menekhib (=Psamtik II), IV 988C.
—Neferibre (=Psamtik II), IV 982, 988C.

PSAMTIK III (XXVI Dyn.): chronology of, I 75.

PTOLEMY EUERGETES II, II 912.
— - PU: predynastic king of Lower Egypt, I 90.

R

RAMESSIDS: tombs of, in the "valley of the kings," IV 473, 490, 491.

RAMSES I (XIX Dyn.): inscriptions of reign of, III 74–9; chronology of, I 67; coffin of, IV, 667.
—Menpehtire (=Ramses I), III 76, 77, 78, 213, 373, 521; IV 667.

RAMSES II (XIX Dyn.): inscriptions of reign of, III 251–568; chronology of, I 67 n. a; length of reign of, IV 471; lost calendar of, I 43 n. b; date of campaigns of, I 43; erasure of inscriptions of Hatshepsut, II 192 n. d, 193; restoration of temple at Der el-Bahri, II 192 n. d; coregency with Seti I, III 268; mortuary temple in Abydos for Seti I, III 251–81; the well of Akita, III 282–93; the Asiatic war, III 294–391; treaty with the Hittites, I 18, 36; III 367–91; subsequent relations with the Hittites, III 392–447; Nubian wars of, III 448–91; buildings of, III 492–542; jubilees of, III 543–60; birth of, III 400; youth of, III 267; marriage of, III 415–24, 428, 432–47; sons of, III 350, 362, 456, 474, 477, 482; daughters of, III 482 n. c; coffin of, IV 665, 691; tomb of, IV 545, 594; mummy of, IV 642; reburial of, IV 665; obelisks of, III 392, 543 n. c, 567; reliefs of, III 255–539.

Ramses II—
—Meriamon-Ramses (II), III 271, 281, 285.
—Ramses-Meriamon (=Ramses II), III 317, 336, 360, 365, 370, 375, 376, 377, 379, 380, 381, 382, 383, 384, 386, 389, 390, 433, 486, 501, 504, 507, 520, 522, 527, 548, 553, 554, 556, 560.
—Usermare-Setepnere (=Ramses II), II 192 n. d; III 259, 271, 279, 281, 285, 306, 317, 336, 360, 365, 370, 373, 375, 378, 381, 382, 384, 385, 389, 433, 442, 447, 502, 507, 552, 553, 554, 556, 560; IV 524, 545, 642, 665.

RAMSES III (XX Dyn.): inscriptions of reign of, IV 1–456; inaccurate publications of I 29; chronology of, I 69; length of reign of, I 48; accession of, IV 63; calendar of, I 43 n. b; IV 139–45; buildings of, IV 1–34 (see also Papyrus Harris *passim*); first Libyan war of, IV 35–58; northern war, IV59–82; second Libyan war, IV 83–114; Syrian war, IV 115–135; Nubian war, IV 136–38; endowment of temples, IV 146–50, 231–35, 284–88, 342–45, 372–81; Papyrus-Harris, IV 151–412; harem-conspiracy, IV 416–53; practice of magic, IV 454–56; mummy of, IV 640, 641; reliefs of, IV 25, 29–34, 45–57, 69–82, 99–114, 117–30, 132–35, 137–38, 184, 246, 305.
—Usermare-Meriamon (=Ramses III), IV 37, 49, 55, 62, 75, 79, 94, 103, 105, 106, 110, 122, 126, 128, 130, 182, 230, 248, 249, 284, 289, 290, 297, 306, 307, 342, 346, 347, 352, 353, 364, 372, 383, 397, 455, 491, 523, 545, 547, 640.

RAMSES IV (XX Dyn.): inscriptions of reign of, IV 457–72; chronology of, I 69, 69 n. a; first expedition to Hammamat, IV 457–60; second expedition to Hammamat, IV 461–68; completion of the temple of Khonsu, IV 472; reliefs of, IV 458, 463.
—Hekmare-Setepnamon (=Ramses IV), IV 463, 472.
—Ramses-Hekma-Meriamon (=Ramses IV), IV 246, 304, 351, 382, 411, 412.
—Ramses-Meriamon (=Ramses IV), IV 463, 472.
—Usermare-Setepnamon (=Ramses IV), IV 246, 304, 351, 382, 411, 412.

RAMSES V (XX Dyn.): inscriptions of, IV 473; chronology of, I 69; tomb of, IV 473.
—Amonhirkhepeshef-Ramses-Neterhekon (=Ramses V), IV 473.
—Nibmare-Meriamon (=Ramses V), IV 473.

RAMSES VI (XX Dyn.): inscriptions of reign of, IV 474–83; chronology of, I 69; tomb of Penno, IV 474–83; reliefs of, IV 476, 477.

RAMSES VII (XX Dyn.): inscriptions of reign of, IV 484–85; chronology of, I 69; scribe of, IV 485; reliefs of, IV 484.
—Ramses - Menthirkhepeshef - Meriamon (=Ramses VII), IV 484.
—Usermare-Ikhnamon (=Ramses VII), IV 484.

RAMSES VIII (XX Dyn.): chronology of, I 69.

RAMSES IX (XX Dyn.): inscriptions of reign of, IV 486–556; chronology of, I 69, 69 n. a; high priest of Amon in reign of, IV 486–98; tomb-robberies in time of, IV 499–556; reliefs of, IV 493.
—Neferkere-Setepnere (=Ramses IX), IV 510.
—Ramses-Meriamon (=Ramses IX), IV 510.

RAMSES X (XX Dyn.): chronology of, I 69; coregency with Ramses IX, IV 544.
—Uhem-mesut (=Ramses X), IV 545.

RAMSES XI (XX Dyn.): chronology of, I 69.

RAMSES XII (XX Dyn.): inscriptions of reign of, IV 557–603; chronology of, I 69; report of Wenamon, IV 557–91; affairs in the South, IV 595–600; building the temple of Khonsu, IV 601–3, 609–15; restoration of mummies, IV 592–94.
—Menmare-Setepneptah (=Ramses XII), IV 596, 609, 611, 612.
—Ramses (XII)-Khamwese-Meriamon-Nuterhekon, IV 596, 609.

RAMSES-HEKMA-MERIAMON: see Ramses IV.

RAMSES-KHAMWESE-MERIAMON-NUTERHEKON: see Ramses XII.

RAMSES-MENTHIRKHEPESHEF-MERIAMON: see Ramses VII.

RAMSES-MERIAMON: see Ramses II.

RAMSES-MERIAMON: see Ramses IV.

RAMSES-MERIAMON: see Ramses IX.

RAMSES-SIPTAH: see Siptah.

S

SAHURE (V Dyn.): inscriptions of reign of, I 236–41; chronology of, I 54 bis, 55, 60, 254–56; history on Palermo stone, I 159–62; titles of, I 236; privy councilor of, I 259.

SAKERE (XVIII Dyn.): chronology of, I 66.

SEBEKEMSAF (Sekhemre-Shedtowe): queen of, IV 517; pyramid of, IV 517, 528.

—Sekhemre-Shedtowe (=Sebekemsaf), IV 517; queen of, IV 517; pyramid of, IV 517, 528.

SEBEKNEFRURE (XII Dyn.): chronology of, I 64.

SEBEKTOWE: see Shabaka.

SEHETEPIBRE: see Amenemhet I.

SEKA: predynastic king of Lower Egypt, I 90.

SEKENENRE-TAO: see Tao.

SEKENENRE-TAOO: see Taoo.

SEKHEMRE-KHUTOWE (XIII Dyn.): inscriptions of reign of, I 751–52.

SEKHEMRE-UPMAT: pyramid of, IV 516.

SENEKHKERE, I 420 n. f.

SESHMUTOWE: see Sesostris II; I 616.

SESOSTRIS I (XII Dyn.): inscriptions of reign of, I 498–593; chronology of, I 64, 460–62, 487–88; coregency of, I 487; building inscription of, I 14, 498–506; Nubian expeditions, I 510–12, 518–21; appointments of, I 627; buildings of, IV 489.

—Kheperkere (=Sesostris I), I 501, 512, 520, 525, 529, 598, 784; IV 489.

SESOSTRIS II (XII Dyn.): inscription of reign of, I 614–39; chronology of, I 64, 460–62; coregency of, 614.

SESOSTRIS III (XII Dyn.): inscriptions of reign of, I 640–700; chronology of, I 64, 460–62; conquest of Nubia, I 10; queen of, I 655 n. b; made god, II 169; hymn to, I 17; treasurer of, I 9, 661–70.

—Khekure (=Sesostris III), I 644, 647, 650, 652, 663, 672, 675, 686; II 170, 171 174, 175.

SETEPNERE: see Harmhab.

SETI I (XIX Dyn.): inscriptions of reign of, III 80–250; chronology of, I 67; Karnak inscriptions of, III 80–156; other temple inscriptions, III 162–98; building inscriptions, III 199–250; wars in Asia, III 80–119; in Libya, III 120–56; queen of, IV 555; her tomb, IV 555, 593; restoration of monuments by, I 13, 15; II 312; reliefs of, III 80–156, 163, 165, 203; obelisk of, III 544; tomb of, IV 545, 642, 665, 666, 667; mummy of, IV 639, 661; coffin of, IV 666, 691.

—Menmare (=Seti I), II 612, 878; III 82 n. b, 83, 86, 88, 100, 101, 105, 110, 116, 122, 132, 134, 136, 143, 144, 146, 150, 154, 155, 160, 169, 171, 175, 179, 195, 223, 260, 263, 267, 270, 271, 272, 280, 289, 373, 541; IV 545, 555, 593, 642, 661, 665, 666, 667.

—Merneptah (=Seti I), III 266, 272.

—Seti-Merneptah (=Seti I), II 312, 856; III 86, 88, 94, 100, 122, 132, 134, 143, 144, 146, 150, 154, 169, 175, 195, 270, 271, 541, 545, 547, 645; IV 665, 666, 667.

—Uhem-Mesut (=Seti I), III 94, 101, 108, 169, 223.

—Hartema (=Seti I), III 96, 122, 132.

SETI II (XIX Dyn.): chronology of, I 67; succeeding Siptah, III 641; viceroy of Kush, III 639, 640, 642, 643, 646, 647.

SETI-MERNEPTAH: see Seti I.

SETNAKHT (XX Dyn.): chronology of, I 69; rule of, IV 399; death of, IV 400.

—Setnakht-Mererre-Meriamon (=Setnakht), IV 399.

—Userkhare-Setepnere-Meriamon (=Setnakht), IV 399.

SETNEH, an ancient king, I 166.

SHABAKA (XXV Dyn.): inscription of reign of, IV 889; records of Nile levels under reign of, IV 886; chronology of, I 74; IV 885.

—Neferkere (=Shabaka), IV 886.

—Sebektowe (=Shabaka), IV 886.

SHABATAKA (XXV Dyn.): record of

Nile levels in reign of, I 43; IV 887; chronology of, I 74; IV 885.

SHEPSESKAF (IV Dyn.): chronology of, I 54 bis, 55, 59, 254, 255, 257; daughter of, I 257; son-in-law of, I 54, 257; pyramid of, I 151;

SHEPSESKERE: chronology of, I 55, 60.

SHESHONK I (XXII Dyn.), I 26, 49; IV 787, 792; inscriptions of reign of, IV 699–728; records of Nile levels under reign of, IV 695; chronology of, I 71; IV 694–95; quarrying at Silsileh, IV 701–8; buildings in Karnak temple, IV 701–24A; campaign in Palestine, IV 709–24; rebellion in the oasis in reign of, IV 729; reliefs of, IV 702, 709–18.

—Kheperhezre-Setepnere (=Sheshonk I), IV 700, 703, 724.

—Meriamon-Sheshonk (I), IV 700, 704, 705, 721, 724.

SHESHONK II (XXII Dyn.): chronology of, I 71; IV 694–95.

SHESHONK III (XXII Dyn.): inscriptions of reign of, IV 756–77; records of Nile levels under reign of, IV 698; chronology of, I 71; IV 694–95, 778; annals of high priest Osorkon, IV 756–70.

—Meriamon-Sheshonk (III), IV 698.

—Meriamon-Sibast-Sheshonk- (III) Nuterhekon, IV 774.

—Usermare-Setepnamon (=Sheshonk III), IV 698, 774.

SHESHONK IV (XXII Dyn.): inscriptions of reign of, IV 782–92; records of Nile levels under reign of, IV 698; chronology of, I 71; IV 694–95.

—Meriamon-Sheshonk (IV), IV 698.

—Okheperre (=Sheshonk IV), IV 784, 791.

—Usermare-Meriamon (=Sheshonk IV), IV 698.

SIAMON: Tanite king, IV 663; chronology of, I 70; IV 604–7.

SIAMON-HRIHOR: see Hrihor.

SIPTAH (XIX Dyn.): inscriptions of reign of, III 639–51; chronology of, I 67; viceroys of Kush in time of, III 639, 643, 646; queen of, IV 400 n. c; reliefs of, III 647, 648.

—Ikhnere-Setepnere (=Siptah) III, 648, 650.

—Merneptah-Siptah (=Siptah), III 650.

—Ramses-Siptah (=Siptah), III 642, 643.

SMENDES: see Nesubenebded.

SNEFRU (III Dyn.): inscriptions of reign of, I 168–75; mentioned, I 176, 189, 731; chronology of, I 54 bis, 55, 56, 58, 86; placed in III Dynasty by Palermo stone, I 86; became god of the Sinai region, I 168, 722; commemorated by roads and statues in the Delta, I 168, 493; regarded as god, I 722; founder of mining, I 168; smiter of barbarians, I 169; dispatched a fleet to bring cedar from Lebanon I 89; gates of, I 148; his relief at Wadi Maghara, I 169.

T

TAHARKA (Tirhaka) (XXV Dyn.), IV 942, 962; inscriptions of reign of, IV 892–918; records of Nile levels under reign of, IV 888; chronology of, I 74; IV 885; fleeing before Ashurbanipal, IV 405 n. g, 917; Piankhi, father of, IV 892; death of, IV 919.

—Nefertem-Khure (=Taharka), IV 888.

TAKELOT I (XXII Dyn.): inscriptions of reign of, IV 738–40; records of Nile levels under reign of, IV 695; chronology of, I 71, 71 n. g; IV 694–95; queens of, IV 696, 792.

TAKELOT II (XXII Dyn.), I 35; IV 777; inscriptions of reign of, IV 752–55; chronology of, I 71; IV 694–95; coregency with Osorkon II, IV 697.

—Kheperhezre-Setepnere (=Takelot II), IV 762.

—Meriamon-Siese-Takelot (II), IV 753, 762.

TAKELOT III (XXIII Dyn.): chronology of, I 72, 72 n. d; coregency with Osorkon III, I 72 n. d.

TANUTAMON (XXV Dyn.): inscription of, IV 919–34; coregency with Taharka, IV 920; conquest of the Delta IV 927–34.

—Bekere (=Tanutamon), IV 921, 934.

TAO (Sekenenre): pyramid of, IV 518.

—Sekenenre-Tao, pyramid of, IV 518. an officer of, II 7; queen of, II 33.

TAOO (Sekenenre): pyramid of, IV 518.

—Sekenenre-Taoo, pyramid of, IV 518.

TETI (VI Dyn.): inscriptions of reign of, I 282–94; chronology of, I 61.

TEYEN: predynastic king of Lower Egypt, I 90.

THESH: predynastic king of Lower Egypt, I 90.

THUTMOSE I, II 25, 74, 114; inscriptions of reign of, II 54–114; chronology of, I 66; rewards of Ahmose-Pen-Nekhbet, under II 23; coronation decrees of, I 18, II 54–60; full titulary of, II 56, 69; feast of coronation of, II 60; service of Thure under, II 64; Tombos inscription of, II 67–73; fortress on Tombos, built by, II 72, 121; Nubian frontier of, II 67; comparative dates of Asiatic and Nubian campaigns, II 67, 79; tribute of South and North, II 70; boundaries of, II 73; clearing of cataract canal by, II 75–76; Nubian campaign of, II 67–77, 80, 84; Asiatic campaign of, II 73, 81, 85, 125; obelisks of, II 86-89; first jubilee of, I 66 n. g; II 89; works at Abydos of, II 90–98; tomb of, II 105; old age of, II 64; death of, II 108; still living under Thutmose II, II 121; usurpation of monument of Hatshepsut by, II 126; succession of children of, II 135.

—Okheperkere (=Thutmose I), II 25, 64, 70, 75, 80, 84, 87, 88, 114, 121, 194, 196, 224, 238, 311, 317, 478, 778.

THUTMOSE II (XVIII Dyn.), II 25; inscriptions of reign of, II 115–27; chronology of, I 66; rewards of Ahmose-Pen-Nekhbet under, II 24; service of Thure under, II 65; biography of Ineni, II 115, 118; accession of, II 116; death of, II 118; Nubian war of, II 119–22; first campaign of, campaign against Shasu, II 123–24; campaign in Syria (now known to belong to Thutmose I), II 125; usurpation of monument of Hatshepsut by, II 126; death of, II 363, 368; mummy of, IV 637.

—Okhepernere (=Thutmose II), II 21, 24, 25, 65, 116, 122, 124, 125, 127, 332 n. d, 389, 390, 595; IV 637.

THUTMOSE III (XVIII Dyn.); later inscriptions, of reign of, II 391–779; (for earlier inscriptions, see Thutmose III and queen); chronology of, I 66; length of reign of, I 48; II 592; Sothic date in reign of, I 43, 46, 51; service of Thure under, II 66; coronation of, II 131 ff., 594; power in Syria before his campaigns, II 137, 184; receives homage of all foreign princes, II 148; capture of Joppa, I 24; campaigns in Syria, I 43; II 391–540; offerings from conquests of, II 541–72; buildings of, II 131 ff., 593–643; Nubian wars of, II 644–54; hymn of victory of, II 655–62: annals of, I 3 bis, 13, 14, 66 n. h; II 391–540; vizier of, I 20; II 663–762; prominent officials of, II 763–79; called a brother of Hatshepsut, II 213; ascension to heaven of, II 222; death of, II 592; son of Thutmose II, II 595; wife of, II 779; son of, II 780; coregency with, II 184 n. d; mortuary temple of, II 552 n. i; statues of, II 164, 165, 186; obelisks of, I 16; II 563, 571, 626–36, 776; temple at Medinet Habu, II 637–41; reliefs of, II 450 n. a, 543–46, 645, 646, 653, 655.

—Menkheperre (=Thutmose III), II 21, 25, 146, 154 ter, 157, 174, 176, 179, 185, 186, 213, 332, 332 n. d, 370, 383, 387, 392, 407, 441, 451, 458, 584, 592, 635, 642, 650, 654, 656, 750, 752, 755, 758, 761, 779, 794, 832; III 58; IV 628.

THUTMOSE III AND QUEEN (XVIII Dyn.): inscriptions of reign of, II 128–390.

THUTMOSE IV (XVIII Dyn.): inscriptions of reign of, II 810–40; chronology of, I 66; youth of, II 813–15; accession of, I 24; II 812; Asiatic campaign of, II 816–22; Nubian campaign of, II 823–29; buildings of, II 830–38; obelisk of, I 16; II 830; mummy of, II 15; sphinx stela of, I 15; II 810–15; palace in Abydos, II 839.

—Menkheprure (=Thutmose IV), II 812, 821, 825, 832, 834, 836, 837, 838, 840; III 32B; IV 539.

THUTMOSES, feud of the, II 128–30.

TIRHAKA: see Taharka.

TUTENKHAMON (XVIII Dyn.): inscriptions of reign of, II 1019–41; chronology of, I 66; restoration of inscriptions by, II 897, 1019; reliefs of, II 1021, 1028, 1035.

—Nebkheprure (=Tutenkhamon), II 897, 1036, 1041.

—Tutenkhaton (Tutenkhamon), II 1019.

U

UHEMIBRE: see Necho.

UHEM-MESUT, see Ramses X.

UHEM-MESUT: see Seti I.

UNIS (V Dyn.): length of reign of, I 60; Sabu, official of, I 282, 283.

USEKHARE-SETEPNERE-MERIAMON: see Setnakht.

USERKAF (V Dyn.): inscriptions of reign of, I 213–35; chronology of, I 54 bis, 55, 60, 231, 255; history on Palermo stone, I 153–58; coronation-feasts of, I 258.

USERKERE (VI Dyn.): chronology of, I 61; probably identical with Ity, I 61 n. a.

USERMARE-IKHNAMON: see Ramses VII.

USERMARE-MERIAMON: see Ramses III.

USERMARE-MERIAMON: see Sheshonk IV.

USERMARE-SETEPNAMON: see Amenemopet.

USERMARE-SETEPNAMON: see Osorkon II.

USERMARE-SETEPNAMON: see Pemou.

USERMARE-SETEPNAMON: see Ramses IV.

USERMARE-SETEPNAMON: see Sheshonk III.

USERMARE-SETEPNERE: see Ramses II.

UZKHEPERRE-KAMOSE: see Kamose.

W

WAHENKH: see Intef I.

WAHIB: see Apries.

WAHIBRE: see Apries.

WAHIBRE: see Psamtik I.

WANRE: see Ikhnaton.

WAZENEZ: predynastic king of Lower Egypt, I 90.

WOHKERE: see Bekneranef.

WOSRETKEW: see Hatshepsut.

Y

YEWEPET: high-priest of Amon, IV 607, 700, 705; called "king," IV 814, 830, 868; of Tentremu, IV 878.
—Meriamon-Yewepet, IV 794.

Z

ZESERKERE: see Amenhotep I.

ZESERKHEPRURE: see Harmhab.

ZET (XXIII Dyn. ?), I 72 n. d; IV 812.

ZOSER (III Dyn.): gift to Khnum, I 24, 201; chronology of, I 58; terraced pyramid of, I 170.

INDEX IV

PERSONS

A

AABU, I 707.

ABRAHAM: visit to Egypt of, I 620 n. d; III 10.

ABRAM: field of, IV 715.

AFRICANUS, I 72 n. e; IV 884.

AHHOTEP I: mother of King Ahmose I, parentage of, II 33; age of, II 49, 52; restoration of Princess Sebekemsaf's tomb by, II 112; Yuf, favorite of, II, 109–14; Edfu estate belonging to, II, 113.

AHMOSE (officer of Ikhnaton): inscription of, II 1004–8; tomb of, II 1004.

AHMOSE: queen of Thutmose I, Yuf, favorite of, II 114; coition with Amon, II 194, 195, 203; confinement, II 204–5; birth of Hatshepsut, II 206, 210.

AHMOSE (son of Ebana), biography of, II 1–16, 38, 39, 78–82.

AHMOSE (Saite general), IV 1013, 1014.

AHMOSE-NOFRETERE, queen of Ahmose I, II 26, 34.

AHMOSE-PEN-NEKHBET, biography of, II 17–25, 40–42, 123–24, 344.

AHMOSE-SEPIR, pyramid of, IV 519.

AHMOSE-SITKAMOSE, queen, IV 644.

AHUBEN: father of Psamtik, the priest, IV 1029.

AHENESH, chief of Me, IV 815, 868, 878.

AMENEMHAB: inscription of, II 578–92; biography of, II 574–78; tomb of, II 574 n. g; adventures of, II 574–75.

AMENEMHAB, peasant, IV 539.

AMENEMHET, I 518.

AMENEMHET (= Ameni): inscription of, I 515–23; biography of, 515, 516; titles of, I 518; three expeditions of, I 519–21; administration of, I 522; character of, I 523; also called Ameni, I 518 n. a; son of Khnumhotep I, I 515.

AMENEMHET, inscription of, I 730–32.

AMENEMHET (official of Amenemhet III): inscription of, I 707–9; expedition to Nubia, I 707; titles of, I 707; expedition to Hammamat, I 709.

AMENEMHET, third prophet of Amon, II 931.

AMENEMHET, vizier of Mentuhotep IV: tablet of, I 444–48; titles of, I 438, 442, 445; expedition of, I 442–47.

AMENEMHET-AMENY, II 689 n. d.

AMENEMOPET, first prophet, IV 480.

AMENEMOPET: tomb of, II 671 n. e; tomb-inscription of, II 671 n. e.

AMENEMOPET, viceroy of Kush, III 204 n. b, 477 bis.

AMENEMUYA, son of Ramses II, III 362.

AMENEMYENET, IV 524.

AMENEMYENET, brother of Neferhotep, III 73.

AMENHIRKHEPESHEF, son of Ramses II, III, 350, 456, 482.

AMENHIRUNAMEF, son of Ramses II, III, 467, 471, 474, 477.

AMENHOTEP, bodyguardsman of Thutmose IV: inscription of, II 818.

AMENHOTEP, high priest of Amon, I 69 n. a; IV 487, 489, 494, 495, 498, 523, 531, 534; inscriptions of, IV, 488–98.

AMENHOTEP, son of Hapi: inscriptions of, II 911–27; deification of, II 911–12; promotions of, II 914–17; mortuary temple of, II 921–27; also called Huy, II 924.

AMENHOTEP, treasurer, IV 495.

AMENHOTEP, viceroy of Kush, brother of Huy, II 1028.

AMENHOTEP, workman, IV 526.

AMENI (= Amenemhet), I 518 n. a; inscription of, I 515–23.

AMENI, father of Sisatet, I 671.

AMENI, magnate of the south: inscription of, I 649–50.

AMENI (under Amenemhet III): rock-inscription of, I 721–23.

AMENIRDIS I, IV 940, 946.
AMENIRDIS II, IV 940.
AMENISENEB, I 716.
AMENISENEB: inscriptions of, I 781–87; titles of, I 782; commission to, I 783–84; rewards of, I 785–87.
AMENKEN: inscriptions of, II 801–2; tomb of, II 801.
AMENKHA, IV 449.
AMENMOSE, IV 466.
AMENNAKHT, scribe, IV 526, 529.
AMENOPET: district of, IV 539; house of, IV 539.
AMENUSERE, I 777.
AMU, father of Mentuhotep, the general, I 512.
ANI, II 977.
ANI, III 634.
ANUBISEMONEKH, father of Methen, I 171, 172.
APOPHIS, a Hyksos king, II 4.
ARTATAMA, king of Mitanni, II 866 n. h.

B

BABA, father of Ahmose of El-Kab, II 7.
BAHU, herdman, IV 481.
BAY, III 647, 648.
BEDEL, king of Dor, IV 565.
BEHKESI, I 365.
BEK, architect of Ikhnaton: inscription of, II 973–76; reliefs of, II 974, 976.
BEK, king's-scribe, IV 668.
BEKET, architect of the tomb of Khnumhotep II, I 639.
BEKET, matron: daughter of a count, I 622; mother of Khnumhotep II, I 622, 639; titles of, I 628.
BEKETATON, daughter of Ikhnaton, II 1016.
BEKI, IV 547.
BEKI, IV 665, 667.
BEKNEKHONSU: inscription of, III 561–68; statue of, I 20; III 561 n. d; titles of, III 563; career of, III 564, 565.
BEKNEKHONSU, IV 466.
BEKNEKHONSU, IV 665.
BEKNENEF, prince, IV 830.
BEKNEPTAH, captain, I 343.
BEKNEPTAH, chief commander of Heracleopolis, IV 777.
BEKNUREL, chief of police, IV 512.
BEKUREL, queen of Seti I, IV 555.
BENTRESH, III 436, 438, 443.
BERKET-EL, rich shipowner of Sidon, IV 574.
BINEMWESE, IV 443.
BUPENAMONKHA, slave, IV 682.
BURDED, I 351, 353.
BUTEHAMON, scribe, IV 640.
BUYUWAWA, a Libyan, IV 787, 792.

C

CORNELIUS GALLUS, I 459 n. c.

D

DEBHEN: inscription of, I 210–12; tomb of, I 210–12.
DED, king of Libya, III 579; IV 43.
DENE, slave, IV 682.
DENEREG, II 114.
DIODORUS, IV 884 n. a.
DISNEK, wife of Idu-Seneni, I 338 ter.
DUSHRATTA, king of Mitanni, II 866 n. h.

E

EBEK, slave, IV 682.
EFNAMON, prophet, IV 692.
EGEM, Hittite chief of archers, III 337.
EHATINOFER, workman, IV 551.
EHENEFER, a negro slave, IV 539.
EKPTAH, slave, IV 680.
EMKU, father of Ameniseneb, I 782.
EMUIENSHI, sheik of Upper Tenu, I 494.
ENEBNI, nobleman, II 213; statute of, II 213.
ENEFSU, IV 550.
ENEKHHOR, commander, IV 878.
ENEKHHOR, priest, IV 958B.
ENEKHNEFERIBRE, II 896 n. d.
ENEKHNES-MERIRE I, wife of Pepi I and queen-mother of Mernere I, I 344; titles of, I 345.
ENEKHNES-MERIRE II, wife of Pepi I and queen-mother of Pepi II, I 341, 344, pyramid of, I 341; titles, I 346.

ENEKHNESNEFERIBRE, divine consort, IV 988A, C, G, H, I; stela of, IV 988A–J; statue of, IV 988I n. a.

ENEKHWENNOFER, father of Senbef, IV 918.

ENEN, II 931.

ENENKHET, I 360.

ENKHETESI, mother of Psamtik the priest, IV 1029.

ENKHOFNAMON, prophet, IV 665, 667, 689.

ENKHU, vizier, I 783; stelæ of, I 783 n. d; statue of, I 783, n. d.

ENROY, wife of Teshere, IV 553.

ENWAW, charioteer, III 635.

EPERDEGEL, III 632.

ERO—EKH, IV 682.

ERREM, IV 455.

ESHEHEBSED, IV 438.

ETI: inscription of, I 457–59; stela of, I 457; biography of, I 457–58; titles of, I 459.

ETI, wife of chief of Punt, II 254, 258.

F

FETONEMUT, Singer of Amon-Re, IV 641.

G

GERBETES, Hittite chariot-warrior, III 337.

GILUKHIPA, queen of Amenhotep III, II, 866 n. h; see also Kirgipa

H

HAPI, IV 537, 539.

HAPI, father of Amenhotep: II 912; burial of, II 920; written Hapu, II 924, 925.

HAPI, mother of Khui, I 675.

HAPU: inscription of, I 614–16; inspection of the fort of Wawat, I 616.

HAPU, vizier of Thutmose IV, II 665.

HAPUSENEB, vizier under Hatshepsut: inscriptions of, II 388–90.

HAREMSAF, chief of works, IV 706, 708.

HARHOTEP, II 110.

HARKHEB, high priest of Amon, IV 952.

HARKHUF: inscriptions of, I 325–36, 350–54; nobleman of Assuan, I 325; titles of, I 326, 332; home-life of, I 328, 331; tomb of, I 325, 329, 330; journeys of, I 333–36, 356; father of, I 333; son of, I 336 n. a; letter to, I 350–54; rewards of, I 352.

HARMINI: stela inscription of, II 47, 48.

HARMOSE, gardener, IV 682.

HARNAKHT: inscription of, I 717, 718; surname of, I 718.

HARNEPE—R—, IV 682.

HARNETAMEHU, surname of Harnakht, I 718.

HARNURE: inscription of, I 733–38; biography of, I 733–34; expedition to Sinai, I 735–38.

HARPESON, high priest of Heracleopolis, IV 787, 792.

HARPESON, prophet of Neit, IV 787, 792.

HARSIESE I, high priest of Amon, IV 698.

HARSIESE II, high priest of Amon, IV 698, 794.

HARSIESE, Sem-priest, IV 779.

HARSIESE, slave, IV 682.

HATEY, II 932.

HATEY, III 32C, 513.

HATSHEPSUT-MERETRE: statue of, II 802.

HEKIB, "beautiful name" of Pepinakht, I 356.

HEKNEFRUMUT: see Enekhnesneferibre.

HEMUKHROW, I 343.

HENEMI, I 343.

HENHATHOR, son of Nekonekh: scribe, I 218, 221; prophet, I 221; chief heir of Nekonekh, I 225.

HENKU: tomb-inscription of, I 280–81; nomarch of the Cerastes-Mountain, I 281; brother of, I 281.

HENOFER, mother of Senmut, II 358.

HENPTAH I, high priest of Heracleopolis, IV 787, 792.

HENPTAH II, high priest of Heracleopolis, IV 787, 792.

HENTTOWE, queen of Paynozem I, IV 649.

HENU: inscription of, I, 428–33; titles of, I 428; expedition to Red Sea, I 429; equipment of his army, I 430; improvement of the Red Sea territories, I 431; shipbuilding at Red Sea, I 432; quarrying at Hammamat, I 433.

HENUT, mother of Kheye, I 750.
HENUT, mother of Sebek-hir-hab, I 725.
HENUTENAMON, IV 448.
HENUTENUTER, mother of Tewhenut, IV 727.
HENUTSEN, daughter of Khufu, I 180; king's-confidante, I 185.
HEPI, treasurer of the God, I 342.
HEPZEFI: inscriptions of, I 535–93; prince of Siut, I 535; contracts of, 539–93; titles of, I 537–38; statue of in temple of Anubis at Siut, I 540.
HERETIBSUTEN, IV 774.
HERNOFER, divine votress, IV 784.
HERODOTUS, I 23, 24, 75 n. h, 180 n. i; II 792 n. d; III 56 n. c, 171 n. b; IV 989, 998.
HERUNOFER, father of Penno, IV 482.
HETAMENTHENOFER, prophet, IV 660.
HETEB, queen of Alasa, IV 591.
HETEPHIRES, king's-confidant, I 196.
HETIHENKER, chief of Libya, IV 784.
HEZETHEKNU, wife of Nekonekh, I 216, 217, 218, 221, 224.
HIRMAMONPENE, inspector, IV 593.
HOR, II 229 n. e.
HOR: commander of Heracleopolis, IV 967; statue of, IV 967; inscription of, IV 968–73.
HORI, IV 957.
HORI, deputy, IV 531.
HORI, inscription of, III 82 n. b.
HORI: king's-messenger, III 645; son of Ubekhu, III 650.
HORI, king's-scribe, IV 485.
HORI, scribe, IV 465.
HORI, standard bearer, IV 423, 426, 453.
HORI, standard bearer, IV 531.
HORI, temple scribe, IV 281.
HORISHERE, scribe, IV 526, 529.
HOTEP, son of Kam, I 187.
HOTEPHIRYAKHET: tomb-inscriptions of, I 251–53; priest at Abusir, I 251; judge, attached to Nekhen, I 252; eldest of the hall, I 253; his intercession, I 252; given a sarcophagus by the king, I 253.
HUI, II 929.
HUI, III 210.
HURABES, prince, IV 878.
HUY, beautiful name of Amenhotep, son of Hapu, II 924.
HUY, chief, IV 338.
HUY (of Amarna), inscription of, II 1014–16; tomb of, II 1014; reliefs of, II 1014, 1016.
HUY, overseer of herds, IV 338.
HUY, viceroy of Kush: inscription of, II 1019–41; tomb of, II 1019; family of, II 1026, 1040; reliefs of, II 1022–24, 1028, 1035, 1039, 1040.
HUY, IV 524.

I

IBDU, commander, I 303.
IBE, steward of Nitocris, inscription of, IV 958A–M.
IBEB, father of Amenemhet, I 707.
IBEBI, I 282, 283; see Sabu-Ibebi.
IBI, probably the son of Zau of Abydos: inscriptions of, I 375–79; biography of, I 375; titles of, I 376–77; wife to, I 375; son of, I 376, 380; career of, I 377–78; tomb of, I 378; mortuary endowment, I 379.
IB-PSAMTIK-MENEKH (=Nesuhor), IV 990.
IBSHE, I 620 n. d.
IDI, I 466 n. c.
IDU, also called Seneni: inscription of, I 338; tomb of, I 337; wife of, I 338.
IFRER, father of Nesuhor, IV 990.
IHE, nomarch of the Hare nome, I 688 n. a.
IHI, statue of, I 165.
IHU, treasurer of the god, I 298, 299.
IHY, I 387.
IKHAMON, slave, IV 680.
IKHERNOFRET: inscription of, I 661–70; biography of, I 9, 661; commission to Abydos, I 665–66; royal letter to, I 664; the drama of Osiris, I 669; temple of Osiris, I 667–68; titles of, I 664; mother of, I 670; relatives of, I 670.
IKHI, nobleman of IV Dyn., I 183.
IKHI, ship-captain: son of the preceding, I 301; father of, I 301.
IKHI, treasurer of the god (VI Dyn.): I 298, 299; inscription of, I 301.
IKHNOUBET, daughter of Nekonekh, I 230.

IKUDIDI: inscription of, I 524–28; titles of, I 526; prayer of, I 526; expedition of, I 527; tomb of, at Abydos, I 528; home of, at Thebes, I 527.

IKUI, father of Intef the nomarch, I 491.

INHOTEP, inscription of, I 388–90.

IMI, mother of Mentuhotep IV, I 450.

IMSU, I 529; great grandfather of, I 529.

IMTES, queen of Pepi I, I 310; legal proceedings against, I 310.

INENI: biography of, II 43–46, 99–108, 115–18, 340–43; career under Amenhotep I, II 44–46; under Thutmose I, I 99–108; under Thutmose II, II 115–18; under Thutmose III and Hatshepsut, II 340–43.

INHAPI queen, tomb of, IV 665, 666, 667.

INI, chief judge, I 373.

INI, inscription of, III 198.

INI, steward, IV 546.

INTEF, inscriptions of, I 466–68, 466 n. c.

INTEF, nomarch: inscription of, I 420; biography of, I 419; ancestry of I 419 n. c; mortuary stela of, I 419–20; founder of the Theban line, I 419; son of, I 419; statue dedicated to, I 419; titles of, I 420; father of, I 419; also called "Intefo" (Intef the great), I 419 n. d.

INTEF, palace-overseer, I 390.

INTEF, ship-captain, I 365.

INTEF, the Herald: inscription of, II 763–71; titles of, II 763; duties of the royal herald, II 764, 767; character of, II 768; tomb of, II 763 n. e.

INTEFYOKER: inscription of, I 529, 423 n. a; lineage of, I 529.

IPI, ship-captain, I 387.

IRAMON, artisan, IV 539.

IRBASTUZENUFU, daughter of king Amenrud, IV 852 n. c.

IRETERU, prophetess of Hathor, IV 787, 792.

IRHORO (=Neferibre-nofer), IV 981.

IRI, father of Harkhuf, I 333.

IRI, royal attendant, I 369, 370, 371.

IROI, IV 445.

ISESI, I 351, 353.

ISIS, wife of Ramses III, IV 523, 543.

J

JOSEPHUS, II 912 n. b.

K

KA, I 731.

KAM, governor, I 187.

KARA, IV 423, 426.

KARU, watchman, IV 550.

KEDENDENNA, IV 423, 443, 446.

KEKSIRE, mortuary priest, I 218.

KEM, father of Hori, III 645.

KEMETH, Hittite chief of warriors, III 337.

KEMI, mother of Neferhotep, I 755.

KEMWESE, water-carrier, IV 539.

KENNEBTIWER, king's-confidant, I 197.

KENOFER (Zaty-), crown prince, I 389.

KEPER, king of Meshwesh, IV 90; captured by Ramses III, IV 97, 109; fettered, IV 103.

KEPES, queen of Takelot I, IV 792.

KERES, stela inscription of, II 49–53.

KEROME, king's-daughter, IV 755.

KEROME, queen of Sheshonk I, IV 792.

KEROMEM, queen of Takelot I, IV 696, 747, 760.

KERPES, IV 432.

KEWKEW, IV 948.

KEY, cattle-overseer, IV 224.

KEY, father of Thuthotep, I 692 n. c.

KHAMHET: inscription of, II 819; titles of, II 872; tomb of, II 819, 870, reliefs of, II 819, 870, 871, 872.

KHAMMALE, IV 434.

KHAMMALE, chief, IV 466.

KHAMOPET, IV 433.

KHAMOPET, IV 532.

KHAMPET, II 929, 930, 931.

KHAMTIR, deputy of the army, IV 466.

KHAMTIR, overseer, IV 466.

KHAMWESE, prophet of Amon, IV 795.

KHAMWESE, son of Ramses II, III 350, 362, 474, 482, 552, 553, 554, 557, 558.

KHAMWESE, vizier, IV 511, 513, 522, 523, 531, 532, 540, 543, 585, 586.

KHARU, IV 523, 532.

KHAY, captain of infantry, III 630 632.

KHAY, vizier, III 556, 559, 560.

KHEBUHATHOR, son of Nekonekh, I 218, 221.

KHENEMSU KHENTKHETIHOTEP, rock-inscriptions of, I 713–16.

KHENTEMSEMETI, inscription of, I 607–613; titles of, I 608; honors of, I 609; temple-inspection by, I 610–12; stela of, I 613.

KHENTISUTHATHOR, I 218, 221.

KHENTKHETIHOTEP, see Khenemsu.

KHENTKHETWER: inscription of, I 604–5; expedition to Punt of, I 605.

KHENU, inferior scribe, I 299.

KHENUKA, a nobleman: inscription of, I 231–35; his titles, I 220, 222; mortuary priest of, I 213.

KHERPESAR, Hittite scribe, III 337.

—KHET, I 343.

KHETASAR, king of Kheta, I 18; III 371, 372, 373, 374, 375, 391.

KHETI I, nomarch of Siut: inscription of, I 398–404; biography of, I 398–99; ancestry of, I 398, 400; career of, I 401, 404; old age of, 402; restoring the temple, I 403; titles of, I 400.

KHETI II: inscriptions of, I 405–414, 426 (?); biography of, I 405–6, 426; wealth and generosity of, I 408; digging the canals for Siut, I 407; monuments of, I 409, 426; army of, I 410; fleet of, I 411; tomb of, I 412; childhood of, I 413; grandfather of, I 414; mother of, I 414, 426(?).

KHETI, nomarch of Oryx nome, I 637 n. a; temple of Khnum, I 637 n. a.

KHETI, wife of Khnumhotep II, I 633.

KHEYE, I 750.

KHNEMHOTEP, *ḫrp-sḥ*, I 361; expedition to Kush and Punt, I 361.

KHNUM-ENKHEF, I 343.

KHNUMHOTEP I: inscription of, I 463–65; biography of, I 463; titles of, I 464; career of, I 465; grandfather of Khnumhotep II, I 464; made count of Menet-Khufu, I 465; of the entire Oryx nome, I 625–26; sons of, I 627; daughter of, I 628.

KHNUMHOTEP II: inscription of, I 619–39; biography of, 619–21; titles of, I 622; tomb of, I 623; count of Menet-Khufu, I 624, 629; grandfather of I 625–26; uncle of, I 627; mother of, I 628; buildings of, I 630, 637–39; honors of, I 631; sons of, I 632–33; ancestry of, I 625–26, 634–36; official staff of, I 623; wife of, I 633.

KHNUMHOTEP III: son of Khnumhotep II, I 620 n. a, 633; made ruler of Menet-Khufu, I 620 n. a; titles of, I 633; mother of, I 633; his son(?), I 620 n. a; ruling in (?), I 620 n. a.

KHNUMHOTEP, the treasurer: inscription of, I 617–18; titles of, I 618.

KHONSUHETNETERNEB, priest, III 432.

—KHUF, I 343.

KHUFU, I 387.

KHUI, I 361.

KHUI, father of the queen of Pepi I, I 344; of Zau, I 349.

KHUI: inscription of, I 674–75; titles of, I 675.

KHUI, judge, I 299.

KHUNI, master of bath, I 336.

KHUU, father of Nenekhseskhnum, I 305.

KINEN, I 776.

KIRGIPA: wife of Amenhotep III, II 867; daughter of Satirna of Naharin, II 867; harem ladies of, II 867; chief of harem of, II 867.

KISUTHATHOR, son of Nekonekh, I 218, 221.

L

LEMERSEKENY, commander, IV 821.

M

MAHARBAAL, IV 423, 443, 446.

MAHU, II 809.

MAI, IV 423, 426, 452.

MAI: tomb of, II 997; inscription of, II 997–1003; titles of, II 997; hymn of, II 999; prayer of, II 1003.

MAKERE, queen of Osorkon I, IV 740.

MANETHO, I 24, 53, 61 n. b, 62 n. d, 78 n. a, 79 n. a, 86; II 296, 912.

MASAHERET, high priest of Amon, IV 647.

MATKHA, daughter of Shepseskaf and wife of Ptahshepses, I 257.

MATNEFRURE, queen of Ramses II, III 417.

MEHETNUSEKHET, wife of Sheshonk, IV 676, 679, 684, 685, 686, 687, 787, 792.

MEHETNUSEKHET, IV 958C, M.

MEHI, son of Senezemib, I 274–277.

MEKETATON, daughter of Ikhnaton, II 961.

MEKHU, father of Sebni, I 363; expedition to Nubia, I 363; death of, I 364; embalment of body of, I 370; burial in Nekheb, I 373.

MEKMEL, Syrian prince, IV 566.

MEN, captain, son of Mut, I 606.

MEN, father of Bek, II 975, 976.

MENGEBET, ship-captain, IV 565.

MENKHEPERRE, high priest of Amon, IV 650, 652, 653, 654, 655, 657, 658, 660, 661, 663, 668, 671; inscriptions of, IV 650–61.

MENKHEPERRESENEB: inscriptions of, II 772–76; offices of, II 772–74; reliefs of, II 773, 774.

MENKHET, mother of Meri, I 508.

MENMARENAKHT, overseer, IV 546.

MENTEMHET, prince of Thebes, IV 901, 904, 949, 951; inscription of, IV 901–916; buildings of, IV 902, 909–916; wife of, IV 951; relief of, IV 903, 909.

MENTEMTOWE, IV 423, 426.

MENTEMWESE, IV 692.

MENTHIRKHEPESHEF, chief of police, IV 512.

MENTUHOTEP (general): inscription of, I 510–14; titles of, I 512; relief of, I 514; son of, I 512; degradation of, I 514.

MENTUHOTEP: inscriptions of, I 530–34; copied by, I 530; titles of, I 531; character of, I 532; building operations of, at Abydos, I 534.

MER, mortuary priest, I 218.

MERASAR, king of Kheta, III 373, 391.

MERETATON, daughter of Ikhnaton, II 961; temple of, in Akhetaton, II 1017.

MERERI, scribe of the marine, I 390.

⌜M⌝ERET-⌞NEIT⌟, mother of King [Miebis ?], I 103.

MERETUBEKHET, IV 957.

MERI: inscription of, I 507–9; titles of I 508; builder of the pyramid-chapel of Sesostris I, I 509; son of Menkhet, I 508.

MERI, deputy of Wawat, IV 481.

MERIAMON, son of Ramses II, III 350, 362.

MERIAMON-SHESHONK, high priest of Amon, grandson of Sheshonk I, IV 740.

MERIBAST, IV 487.

MERIPTAH, II 923, 929, 930, 931.

MERIRE I: inscription of, II 982–88; wife of, II 984; office of, II 985; tomb of, II 982, 1018;

MERIRE II, II 981.

MERIRE, scribe, II 1043.

MERIRE-MERIPTAH-ONEKH I, chief architect of Pepi I: inscription of, I 299; titles of, I 298, 299; son of, I 298.

MERIRE-MERIPTAH-ONEKH II, son of the preceding, ritual priest, I 298.

MERIRE-ONEKH, I 343.

MERIRE-ONEKH, commander, I 303.

MERMOSE, viceroy of Kush, II 855; inscription of, II 851–55.

MERNUTERSETENI, eldest son of Weshptah, I 243.

MER-PTAH-SI-HAPI, mother of Teperet, IV 1000.

MERSEGER, queen to Sesostris III, I 655 n. b; II 171.

MERTHOTH, prophet, IV 665.

MERTITYÔTES, royal favorite of Snefru, Khufu, and Khafre, I 54, 55; stela-inscription of, I 188–89; titles, I 189.

MERTUSAMEN, IV 446.

MERU, hereditary prince, I 370.

MERWER, IV 551.

MERYEY, king of Libya, III 579, 586, 610, 612, 615; IV 43.

MESEDSURE, IV 428, 429.

MESHESHER, king of Meshwesh, IV 90.

MESHKEN, king of Libya, IV 43.

MESSUI, IV 445.

METELLA, king of Kheta, III 374, 375, 377.

METENU, father of Sebeko, I 716.

METHDET, III 632.

METHEN: inscriptions of, I 170–75; biography of, I 170; activity in the Delta, I 170; ruler of Fayum and Anubis nome, I 170; died in reign of Snefru, I 170; son of Anubisemonekh I 171; and Nebsent, I 176; career of,

I 172; honors and gifts to, I 173, 175; offices, I 174; family of, I 175.

METHREM, a Hittite, III 337.

MEYA, III 32B.

MINEMHET, I 776, 780.

MINHOTEP, I 776.

MINHOTEP, II 800.

MITSHERE, IV 523.

MONTU—, son of Ramses II, III 362.

MUSEN, chief of Me, IV 787, 792.

MUT, mother of Men, I 606.

MUTEMUYA, IV 486.

MUTEMUYA, queen of Thutmose IV, II 866 n. h.

MUTNEZMET, wife of Harmhab, II 1043; III 22 n. f.

MUTNOFRET, queen of Ramses II, III 255.

N

NAKHT I, eldest son of Khnumhotep I, I 627; ruler of Menet-Khufu, I 627.

NAKHT II, eldest son of Khnumhotep II, I 632; ruler of the Jackal nome, I 632.

NAKHTAMON, III 633.

NAKHTAMON, artificer, IV 466.

NAKHTAMON, butler, IV 466.

NAKHTAMON, charioteer, IV 466.

NAKHTEMHET, IV 528.

NAKHTEMMUT, IV 539.

NAMLOT I, chief of Me, IV 676, 679, 683, 685, 686, 687, 787, 792; statue of, IV 678, 680.

NAMLOT II, high priest of Heracleopolis, IV 787, 792.

NEATESNAKHTE, mother of Senbef, IV 918.

NEBAMON, overseer, IV 517.

NEBET, mother of the queen of Pepi I, I 344; of Zau, I 349.

NEBETHAPI, IV 682.

NEBETU, wife of Thutmose III, II 779.

NEBETYOTEF, mother of Ameniseneb, I 782.

NEBNESHI, IV 787, 792.

NEBSENT, mother of Methen, I 175.

NEBUNNEF, III 255-57; inscription of, III 256.

NEBWAWI: biography of, II 177–78; statue of, II 178–83; stela of, II 184–86; career of, II 179–86; offices of, 180–83, 185–86.

NEBZEFAI, IV 445.

NEFERHER, of Bista, IV 957.

NEFERHET, stela of, II 839 n. d.

NEFERHOR, king's-messenger, III 643.

NEFERHOR, scribe of the archives, III 643.

NEFERHOTEP, king's-butler: inscription of, III 68–73; reliefs of, III 69, 73.

NEFERHOTEP, tomb of, III 68 n. c.

NEFERHOTEPES, king's-mother, I 241.

NEFERHOTEPUR, I 776.

NEFERIBE-NOFER, overseer of magazine, IV 981; statue of, IV 981–83.

NEFERKERE EM-PER-AMON, king's-butler, IV 495, 511, 513, 522, 531.

NEFERNEFRUATON-NOFRETETE, queen of Ikhnaton, II 959, 984, 991, 1010, 1015.

NEFERPERET, chief treasurer under Ahmose I, II 28.

NEFRETIRI, queen, IV 479.

NEFRETIRI, queen of Ramses II, III 482 n. c, 499, 500, 501.

NEFRURE, eldest daughter of Hatshepsut, II 344, 362, 363, 364.

NEFRURE, queen of Ramses II, III 435.

NEFRUSEBEK, IV 968.

NEHI, viceroy of Kush: temple-inscription at Semneh of, II 651; pillar-inscription of, II 412-13; grotto-inscription of, II 652; confusion with Thure, II 61.

NEHRI, I 628; married to Beket, I 628; son of, I 636; Khnumhotep II, son of, I 622, 631, 633, 634, 639; ruled as a babe, I 636; ka-house in Mernofret, I 635.

NEHRI, father of Key, I 692 n. c, 692 n. a.

NEHSI, II 290.

NEKENNEBTI, king's-confidant, I 194.

NEKE-ONEKH, I 343.

NEKHTHARNESHENU, chief of Me, IV 878.

NEKONEKH, a nobleman: inscriptions of, I 213–30; titles and offices of, I 213; 216, 230; wife of, I 216, 224; children of, I 214, 228–30; tomb of, I 215; testamentary enactments of, I

216–22; will of, I 223–25; priest of Hathor I 219; enactments for the mortuary priesthood of, I 226, 227; mortuary statues of, I 228–30.

NEKRI, II 1 n. c.

NEKUPTAH, I 387.

NEKURE, prince, I 190–99.

NEKURE, son of preceding, I 195.

NEMATHAP, queen (?), I 173.

NENEKH-KHENTIKHET, ship-captain, I 266.

NENEKHSEKHMET: inscription of, I 237–40; chief physician of Sahure, I 238; his tomb, I 238; its false door, I 238–39.

NENEKHSESKHNUM, commission to, I 305; son of, I 305.

NENESBAST, mother of Pefnefdineit, IV 1025.

NESHENUMEH, slave, IV 682.

NESIKHONSU, wife of Paynozem II, IV 689.

NESIMUT, queen, IV 555.

NESIPAI, IV 689.

NESITETAT, slave, IV 682.

NESNEKEDI, chief of Me, IV 830.

NESSUHATHORYAKHET, son of Nekonehk, I 218, 221.

NESSUMONTU: stela inscription of, I 469–71; career under Amenemhet I and Sesostris I, I 469–71.

NESTENT, queen of Namlot, IV 844.

NESUAMON, IV 547.

NESUAMON, chief of police, IV 545, 548, 552.

NESUAMON, high priest of Amon, IV 487.

NESUAMON, king's-butler, IV 495, 511, 513, 522, 523, 526, 528, 531, 533, 540.

NESUAMON, master of hunt, IV 539.

NESUAMON, priest, IV 551.

NESUAMON, prophet, IV 531.

NESUAMON, scribe, IV 486.

NESUAMON, Sem-priest, IV 541.

NESUBAST, prophet, IV 726, 728.

NESUBENEBDED, high priest of Amon, IV 794.

NESUHOR, IV 652.

NESUHOR, governor, 990, 993: statue-inscription of, IV 989–95.

NESUMIN, IV 948.

NESUMONTU, IV 547, 749.

NESUPEHERNEMUT, prophet, IV 660.

NESUPEKESHUTI, scribe, IV 665, 668, 689, 692.

NESUPTAH, prince of Thebes, IV 901, 904, 908.

NESUPTAH, chief of prophets, IV 950.

NEWSETREKENYE, IV 784.

NEZEMIB, a private citizen: inscription of, I 278–79.

NIBAMON: inscription of, II 777–79.

NIBMARE-NAKHT, vizier, IV 523, 535, 546.

NITOCRIS, daughter of Taharka, I 61 n. c.; IV 942, 958D; adopted by Psamtik I, IV 943, 945; beautiful name of, IV 943; divine votress, IV 942, 946, 958D, M, 988D; death and burial of, IV 988G.

NOFER, watchman, IV 551.

NOFRETETE, queen of Ikhnaton, II 961.

NUBHOTEP, wife of Zezemonekh, I 186.

NUBKHAS, queen, IV 517, 528, 538.

O

ONENEY, IV 452.

OSORKON, high priest of Amon, IV 698, 753, 755, 760, 769, 770, 777.

P

PAHRI, grandson of Ahmose, son of Ebana, II 3; titles of, II 3 n. c.

PAKAUTI, king's-scribe, IV 485.

PATONEMHAB, III 22; tomb of, III 22 n. a; high priest of Re, III 22 n. a.

PAY, steward, IV 224.

PAY—, overseer, IV 638.

PAYBEK, IV 550, 551.

PAYERNU, IV 423.

PAYKAMEN, IV 547, 548.

PAYNEFERHIR, chief overseer, IV 637.

PAYNEHSI, IV 547.

PAYNEHSI, IV 682.

PAYNEHSI, viceroy of Kush, IV 597.

PAYNOFER, scribe, IV 512.

PAYNOZEM, scribe, IV 527.

PAYNOZEM II, high priest of Amon, IV 663, 668, 671, 672, 688, 689; inscriptions of, IV 662–67.

PAYONEKH, high priest of Amon, IV 631, 632, 633, 634, 635, 637, 638, 639, 641.

PE'AOKE, inscription of, II 839–40.

PEBEKKAMEN, IV 427, 428, 429, 430, 439, 440, 444, 454.

PEBES, IV 423, 426, 452.

PEBES, prince in Per-Hapi, IV 878.

PEBES, scribe, IV 526, 529.

PEDIAMENEBNESTTOWE, third prophet of Amon, IV 953.

PEDIAMENESTTOWE, ritual priest, IV 881.

PEDIAMON, chief of workmen, IV 668.

PEDIAMON-NEBNESTTOWE, IV 852 n. c.

PEDIESE, chief of Me, IV 774, 779; relief of, IV 779.

PEDIESE, prince of Athribis, IV 868, 874, 875, 879.

PEDIHARSOMTOUS, prophet, IV 878.

PEFNEFDIBAST, high priest of Ptah, IV 774, 781.

PEFNEFDIBAST, ruler of Heracleopolis, IV 852; decendants of, IV 852 n. c.

PEFNEFDINEIT, chief physician, IV 1017, 1025; statue-inscription of, IV 1015–25.

PEFROI, IV 423, 426.

PEHENUI, IV 550.

PEHETI, father of Nesubast, IV 726, 728.

PEKAMEN, coppersmith, IV 532.

PEKENU, IV 784.

PEKHARU, coppersmith, IV 523, 532.

PEKRUR, hereditary prince of Per-soped, IV 932.

PELUKA, IV 439.

PEMERIAMON, steward, IV 546.

PEMERKHETEM, III 634.

PEMOU, IV 815, 878; prince of Busiris, IV 878.

PEN, II 682.

PENAMON, III 633.

PENAMON, butler, IV 584.

PENAMON, scribe, IV 647.

PENANUKET, IV 541.

PENDUA, IV 430.

PENE—, IV 682.

PENEBIK, scribe, IV 512.

PENHUIBIN, IV 442, 455.

PEN-NEKHBET, called Ahmose: see Ahmose-Pen-Nekhbet.

PENNO, II 1041.

PENNO: inscription of, IV 474–83; titles of, IV 474; tomb of, IV 474–83.

PENRENUT, IV 423.

PENTEWERE, IV 444, 447.

PENTEWERE, chief of Me, IV 878.

PENTEWERE, scribe, copyist of Papyrus Sallier III, III 315.

PEPI-NAKHT: inscriptions of, I 355–60; titles of, I 356; character of, I 357; expeditions to Nubia, I 358–59; expedition against Asiatics, I 360.

PENITHOWE, steward, IV 338.

PERAMSES, vizier, III 542.

PERE, IV 442.

PERE, scribe, IV 450.

PEREHIRUNAMEF, son of Ramses II, III 456, 482.

PEREHU, chief of Punt, II 254, 258; family of, II 254.

PEREKAMENEF, IV 445.

PEREMHAB, IV 423,

PEREMHAB, captain, III 634.

PEREMHAB, deputy, III 634.

PERENNEFER, III 73.

PEREPEWYOT, officer, IV 593.

PERSEN: tomb-inscription of, I 241; title of, I 241.

PESE'EKE, IV 784.

PESER, father of Amenemapet, III 477 bis.

PESER, mayor of Thebes, IV 513, 526, 527, 528, 531.

PESIBKHENNO, high priest of Amon, IV 688.

PETEWNTEAMON, IV 431.

PETHENEF, prince, IV 815, 878.

PETHUT, chief of Me, IV 787, 792.

PETKHEP, princess (=queen) of Kheta, III 391; born in the land of Kezweden, III 391.

PETPETDEDES, priestess of Harsaphes, IV 787, 792.

PEWER, slave, IV 682.

PEWERO, mayor of Western Thebes, IV, 511, 512, 522, 527, 528, 535.

PEYES, IV 444, 445, 451.

PEYES, Hittite charioteer, III 337 bis.

PEYNOK, IV 429.
PIRSUN, IV 443, 446.
PIYAY, III 644.
PLINY, IV 878 n. e.
PREMHAB, see Patonemhab.
PSAMTIK, chief of militia, IV 968.
PSAMTIK, priest, IV 1029; mortuary stela of, IV 1026–29.
PSENMUT, IV 957.
PTAH, nobleman of IV Dyn., I 182.
PTAHHOTEP, brother of Senbef, IV 918.
PTAHMOSE, deputy, IV 338.
PTAHSHEPSES: inscription of, I 254–62; importance thereof on chronology, I 54 bis, 55, 254, 255; education of, I 256, 257; marriage of, I 257; career of, I 258–62.
PTAHWER, inscription of, I 728.
PUEMRE: inscriptions of, II 379–87; statue of, II 380; tomb of, II 382; relief of, II 385.
PUREM, commander, IV 821.
PURME, commander, IV 881; probably identical with Purem, *q. v.*
PUTOKER, I 466 n. c.
PUTOWE, IV 948.

R

RAHENEM, wife of Ibi, I 375.
RAMOSE, father of Senmut, II 358.
RAMOSE, king's-scribe, II 1043.
RAMOSE, messenger, III 372.
RAMOSE, of Amarna, II 947 n. a.
RAMOSE, the vizier: inscription of, II 936–48; titles of, II 936; tomb of, II 936–47; reliefs of, II 938, 941, 944; burial of, II 947.
RAMSES, son of Ramses II, III 456, 482.
RAMSES-ESHAHAB, III 496, 498.
RAMSES-ESHEHAB, scribe, IV 465.
RAMSES-KHEMENTER-BAY, III 647, 648.
RAMSESNAKHT, III 633.
RAMSESNAKHT, high priest and first prophet of Amon, I 69 n. a; IV 466, 487, 489, 494, 495.
RAMSESNAKHT, scribe, IV 466.
RAY, chief treasurer of Thutmose III, II 450 n. a.
RE, attendant, II 1043.
RE-AM, brother of Henku, I 281; titles of, I 281.
REBESNEN, III 337.
REBEYER, king of Aleppo, III 337.
REDEDET, mother of the first kings of the V Dyn., II 198 n. j.
REKHMIRE, vizier of Thutmose III: ancestry of, II 663; office of, II 665. tomb of, I 20; II 663; inscriptions of, II 663–762; reliefs of, II 712, 714, 717, 747, 752, 753, 756, 761, 762.
REKHPEHTUF, king's-messenger, III 642.
RENSENEB, I 752.
ROME, high priest of Amon, III 621, 628.
ROY, frontier official, III 630.
ROY, high priest of Amon, III 623, 626; inscription of, III 618–28; titles of, III 623; reliefs of, III 626 n. c, 628.
ROYENET, II 7.
ROYENET, mother of Bek, II 975.
RUMA, IV 442.

S

SABU, also called Ibebi: inscriptions of, I 282–86; titles of, 283–86; career of, I 283–286; son of, I 287.
SABU, also called Thety: inscription of, I 287–88; office of, I 288; son of Sabu-Ibebi, I 287.
SABU "the black," I 287 n. b.
SATIRNA, king of Naharin, II 867; Artatama, father of, II 866 n. h; Dushratta, son of, II 866 n. h; Gilukhipa (=Kirgipa), daughter of, II 866 n. h, 867.
SEBEKDIDI-RANEFSENEB, rock-inscription of, I 719–20.
SEBEKEMSAF (*sic!* for Sebekemsas, wife of one of the XIII Dyn. Intefs), queen Ahhotep restores tomb of, II 109–112.
SEBEKENEKH, father of Nehri, I 636.
SEBEK-HIR-HAB, rock-inscription of, I 725–27.
SEBEKHOTEP, I 665 n. b.
SEBEK-KHU, called Zaa: inscription of, I 676–87; biography of, I 677–79; Asiatic campaign of, I 680; honors of, I 681–82; titles of, I 683; tomb of, I 684; career of, I 685–86; campaign in Nubia, I 687.
SEBEKNAKHT, II 931.
SEBEKO, I 716.

SEBNI: inscriptions of, I 362–74; biography of, I 362–64; death of father of, I 365; expedition to Nubia, I 366–70; king's letter to, I 371; honors and reward of, I 372.

SEHETEPIBRE: inscription of, I 743–48; titles of, I 745; tomb of, I 746; instruction of, I 747–48.

SEKHEMKERE, prince, I 54, 55.

SEMEN, II 822.

SEMRETES, a Hittite, III 337.

SENBEF, hereditary prince, IV 918.

SENEB, son of Enkhu, I 783.

SENEBTEFI, I 723.

SENEKH: inscription of, I 454–56; titles of, I 455; career of, I 456.

SENEZEM, chief scribe, I 343.

SENEZEM, leader of recruits, I 343.

SENEZEMIB, vizier: inscriptions of, I 268–77; career of, I 270; royal letters to, I 271, 273; son of, I 274.

SENISENEB, mother of Thutmose I, II 58.

SENMUT: biography of, II 345–68; architect of Hatshepsut, II 304, 345; took part in the Punt expedition, II 290, 346; statues of, I 20; II 345, 349–58, 363–68; tomb of, II 348; titles of, II 354; tombstone of, II 348.

SENUONEKH: inscriptions of, I 231–35; priest under Userkaf and Sahure, I 231; tomb of, I 231; endowment of mortuary priests of, I 232–35.

SENY, IV 485.

SEPLEL, king of Kheta, III 373, 377.

SEPTHER, brother of the Hittite king, III 337.

SESI, official titles of, I 299.

SETAU, high priest of Nekhbet, I 69 n. a; IV 414–15; tomb at El Kab, IV 414–15.

SETEMHAB, IV 19.

SETEPNERE, son of Ramses II, III 362.

SETI, son of Ramses II, III 350, 362.

SETI, viceroy of Kush, afterward King Seti II, III 642, 643, 646, 647.

SETI, vizier, III 538, 539, 542.

SETIMPERAMON, IV 436.

SETIMPERTHOTH, IV 435.

SETNAKHT, artisan, IV 537, 541.

SHEDMEZER, IV 445.

SHEM-BAAL, III 632.

SHEPNUPET I, daughter of Osorkon, IV 940.

SHEPNUPET II, daughter of Piankhi, IV 940, 946; (=Nitocris), IV 943, 945.

SHEPSESHATHOR, priest, I 218, 221.

SHESHONK, chief of Me, IV 675, 677, 683, 687, 787, 792; stela of, IV 675–87.

SHESHONK, hereditary prince, IV 774.

SHUTTARNA, king of Mitanni, II 866 n. h; see also Satirna.

SIAMON, I 777.

SIAMON, king's-son, IV 646.

SIHATHOR: inscription of, I 599–603; title of, I 599; commissions of, I 600; expeditions of, I 602–3.

SIMONTU: inscription of, 594–98; childhood of, I 597; career of, I 598; death of, I 595; birth of, I 596.

SIMUT, II 931.

SINOURIS, I 785.

SINUHE: tale of, I 486–97; biography of, I 486–89; titles of, I 490; death of Amenemhet, I 491–92; flight to Palestine, I 493–94; return to the court of Egypt, I 495–97.

SIRENPOWET, nomarch of Elephantine, I 510 n. b.

SISATET: inscriptions of, I 671–73; relatives of, I 676–71.

SISEBEK, prophet, IV 1017.

SI[T], mother of Kheti II, I 414 and n. a.

SITAMENI, mother of Ikhernofret, I 670, 671.

SITAMON, daughter of Amenhotep III, II 912.

SITKAMOSE, queen, IV 644; mummy of IV 644.

SITRE, I 426.

SITYOH, II 612.

SOMTOUS-TEFNAKHTE, nomarch of Heracleopolis, IV 944.

STIRA, I 716.

STRABO, III 51 n. b.

SUDIAMON, IV 672, 673.

SULE, scribe, IV 466.

SUTE, II 299 n. e.

SUTEKHMOSE, III 632.

SUTIMOSE, IV 647.
SYNCELLUS, I 72 n. e; IV 884 n. d.

T

TA, vizier, IV 414.
TADUKHIPA, queen of Amenhotep IV, II 866 n. h.
TAKELOT, chief of Me, father of Pediese, IV 774; chief of Meshwesh, IV 779, 781.
TAKELOT, high priest of Amon, IV 698, 794.
TAKELOT, Sem-priest, son of Pediese, IV, 774.
TARTESEB, royal Hittite messenger, III 371, 372.
TEDENETNEBAST, princess, IV 795.
TEDER, Hittite chief of warriors, III 337.
TEDIESE, IV 682.
TEDIMUT, slave, IV 682.
TEFIBI, nomarch of Siut: inscriptions of, I 393–97; kind rule of, I 395; war with the South, I 396; mortuary prayer of, I 394; titles of, I 395; son of, ruling while a minor, I 395; father of Kheti I, I 403 bis.
TEFNAKHTE, chief of the West, IV 818, 819, 830; chief of Sais, IV 859, chief of Me, 838, 854, 880; father of Bocchoris, IV 884.
TELAMON, IV 539.
TEMEKHONSU, queen of Osorkon I, IV 792.
TENR, wife of Merire I, II 984.
TENTAMON, IV 564, 565, 574, 581, 582.
TENTSEHERYE, mother of Weshtehet, IV 784.
TENTSEPEH, divine mother, IV 792.
TENTSEPEH, priestess of Harsaphes, IV 787, 792.
TENTSEPEH, king's-daughter, IV 787, 792.
TENTSEY, IV 695.
TENTTO, a singer, IV 589.
TEPERET, king's-confidante, IV 1000.
TEPIRAMENEF, IV 682.
TERE, sister-wife of Pediese, IV 774.
TERGEN, Hittite officer, III 337.
TERGENENES, Hittite charioteer, III 337.
TERGETETETHES, Hittite chief of archers III 337.
TESENETHOR, mother of Nesuhor, IV 990.
TESHERE, priest, IV 547, 550, 553.
TESITNAKHT, tomb of, robbed, IV 499.
TETI, I 777.
TETI, IV 547.
TETI, mother of Thutnakht, I 689.
TETISHERI, grandmother of Ahmose I, II 33, 36.
TEWHENUT, mother of Nesubast, IV 727, 728.
TEWOSRET, queen of Siptah, IV 400 n. c.
TEYEDER, Hittite chief of bodyguard, III 337.
TEYNAKHTE, IV 452.
THANENI, campaign-recorder of Thutmose III, II 392; tomb of, II 392; inscription of, II 820; referred to, II 451 n. d; titles of, II 820.
THARA, III 633.
THAROY, coppersmith, IV 532.
THAY, II 1043.
THEKEREM, III 632.
THEMER, king of Libya, IV 43.
THENEKEMET, priestess of Harsaphes, IV 787, 792.
THENTI, tomb of, at Giseh, I 182 n. a.
THESHEN, eldest son of Zezemonekh, I 186.
THESPEREBAST, king's-daughter, IV 771, 774.
THETHI, I 361.
THETHI, nobleman, I 184; master pyramid builder, I 301.
THETHIST (treasurer, X Dyn.): inscription of, I 423A–G; stela of, I 423A n. a; titles of, I 423C; career of, I 423D.
THEWETHES, king of Tenes, III 337.
THURE, viceroy of Kush, II 54–55; temple-inscription of, at Semneh, II 61–66; rock-inscriptions of, on Sehel, II 75–76; rock-inscription of, at Assuan, II 77.
THUTEMHAB, III 437.
THUTEMHAB, commander, IV 367.
THUTHOTEP: tomb-inscriptions of, I

688–706; ancient family of, I 688, 692–93; his great statue, I 694–706.

THUTIY, attendant, III 632.

THUTIY, general under Hatshepsut and Thutmose III, I 24; II 275; inscription of, II 369–78; tomb of, II 369 n. c; titles of, II 371.

THUTMOSE, III 32C.

THUTMOSE, chief scribe, IV 281.

THUTMOSE, major-domo, IV 672, 673.

THUTNAKHT, I 689.

THUTREKHNEFER, IV 423, 443, 446.

THUYA, mother of Tiy, II 862, 867.

TIY, great queen of Amenhotep III, II 861, 862, 904, 1014, 1016; parents of, II 862, 864, 865, 867, 869; pleasure lake of, II 869; Zerukha city of, II 869.

TIY, queen of Ramses III, IV 427, 447.

TIY, wife of Eye, II 989; nurse of Ikhnaton, II 989.

TUTU: inscription of, II 1009–1013; tomb of, II 1009.

U

UNI: inscriptions of, I 292–94; 306–315, 319–24; biography of, I 6; childhood of, I 292–94; offices of, I 293; judge, I 307; equipment of tomb of, I 308; superior custodian, I 309; prosecution of the queen, I 310; war against the Bedwin, I 311–14; against Palestine, I 315; governor of the South, I 320; expedition to the Ibhet quarry, I 42, 321; to Elephantine, I 322; to Hatnub, I 323; to the Southern Quarries, I 324.

URAMON, prophet, IV 512.

USERKHEPESH, chief workman, IV 526, 528.

USERMARE-NAKHT, prophet of Min, IV 465.

USERMARE-SEKHEPERSU, butler, IV 466.

UZAHOR, governor of the door of south countries, IV 980.

UZAI, I 343.

UZARENES, wife of Mentemhet, IV 951.

UZMUTENKHOS, queen of Osorkon II, IV 792.

UZPTAHENKHOF, high priest of Heracleopolis, IV 787, 792.

W

WAYHESET, prophet, IV 726, 727, 728; stela of, IV 725–28.

WEBKUHATHOR, son of Nekonekh, I 218, 221.

WENAMON, envoy to Syria, I 18; report of, IV 557–91.

WENNOFER, divine father, IV 668.

WENPEHTI, weaver, IV 552.

WEREN, IV 437.

WERET, mother of Meya, III 32B.

WERET, Syrian prince, IV 566.

WERMER, king of Libya, IV 43.

WESHPTAH, vizier of Neferirkere: tomb-inscription of, I 243–48; untimely death of, I 246; his ebony coffin, I 247; buried by the king, I 248; beside the pyramid of Sahure, I 249.

WESTEHET, chief caravaneer, IV 784; relief of, IV 783.

WOSER, vizier, uncle of Rekhmire, II 663, 665; tomb of, II 671 n. e; tomb-inscription of, II 671 n. e.

Y

YAKHETIRNI, I 387.

YARSU, a Syrian chief, IV 398.

YATA, mother of Ptahwer, I 728.

YATU, I 723.

YATU, mother of Amenhotep, II 912; burial of, II 920.

YEKERIB, I 343.

YENINI, IV 440.

YEWELOT, high priest of Amon, IV 794; will of, IV 795.

YUF, stela inscription of, at Edfu, II 109–114.

YUH, III 32C.

YUI, judge, III 32B.

YUROI, IV 515.

YUYA, father of Tiy, II 862, 867; tomb of, II 861 n. c.

Z

ZAA, surname of Sebek-khu, I 676, 683.

ZAKAR-BAAL, prince of Byblos, IV 566, 567.

ZATY, I 343.

ZATY, called Kenofer, crown prince, I 389.
ZAU, son of Zau-Shemai: inscription of, I 380–85; biography of, I 380; titles of, I 381; burial of his father, I 382; tomb of, I 383; prayer of, I 384; succession of, I 385.
ZAU, vizier, brother of queen of Pepi I, I 347; relief of, I 344; titles of, I 348; his five brothers of the same name, I 347.
ZAU-SHEMAI, son of Ibi, I 380, 382, 383.
ZEAMONEFONEKH, of Mendes, IV 878.
ZEAMONEFONEKH, prince, IV 815, 830.
ZEDI, divine father, IV, 547, 553.
ZEDKHIYU, prince in Khentnofer, IV 878.
ZEDTI, IV 957.
ZEKHONSEFONEKH, high priest of Amon, IV 650, 668, 689, 691, 692.
ZEMI, son of Harkhuf, I 336 n. a.
ZEPER, III 630.
ZEPTÁHEFONEKH, prophet, IV 699.
ZEZEMONEKH, treasurer of the god, I 186 bis.
ZOSERSUKHONSU, scribe, IV 640.

INDEX V

TITLES, OFFICES, AND RANKS

A

ADMINISTRATOR, IV 525, 671, 676; Methen, I 173, 174.

ADVANCED SEAT, OF: Thethi, I 423C, 423D, Amenemhet, I 445.

ADVOCATE OF THE PEOPLE: Mentuhotep, I 533.

ANNOUNCER, second in rank in the temple, I 550.

ARCHITECT: see Chief of works.

ARTIFICER, I 262, 285, 447; II 92, 436; IV 488 n. c; rank of, III 271.
Chief artificer, Nakhtamon, IV 466.

ARTISAN, III 275; IV 539, 541, 551; 600, 858.
—Assistant artisan, I 298, 301.

ARTISTS, I 447.

ASSISTANT (*ḫry-ᶜ*): Neferperet, II 28; Bek, II 975; Thutmose, III 32C; Beknekhonsu, III 566; Amenhotep, IV 489.

ATTACHED: to Dep, Mentuhotep, I 512.
—to the Double House, Sabu-Ibebi, I 284, 285; Merire-Meriptah-Onekh, I 298, 299; Sesi, I 299.
—to the king: Ptahshepses, I 258–61; Sabu-Ibebi, I 283.
—Attached to Nekhen: Uni, I 293; Kknumhotep I, I 464; Amenemhet, I 518; Mentuhotep, I 531, 533; Senmut, II 352; Ramose, II 936; Khay, III 556; see also, Judge.
—Attached to the pyramid: Enekhnes-Merire I, I 345; Enekhnes-Merire II, I 341, 346.

ATTENDANTS, II 53, 474; III 69; IV 124, 402, 405, 407; Sinuhe, I 490; Re, II 1043; Thutiy, III 632; Nakhtamon, III 633.
—Chamber attendant: Uni, I 293; Harkhuf, I 332.
—Commander of attendants, *q. v.*
—Feast-day attendant, Sabu-Ibebi, I 284, 285, 286.
—King's attendant, Iri, I 369; Zaa, I 687; Mai, II 997; Neferhotep, III 70.

AUTHORITIES, THE GREAT, of South and North, IV, 460.

B

BELOVED, KING'S, III 102; Sabu-Ibebi, I 285; Thethi, I 423C; Sinuhe, I 490; Khnumhotep, I 618; Khui, I 675; Enebni, II 213; Ahmose, II 1004; Harmhab, III 16.
—of Buto, Dedkere-Isesi, I 264.
—of god, Merikere, I 399.
—of Khnum, Mernere, I 317.
—of the lord of Coptos, Pepi I, I 296.
—of Upwawet, Mother of Kheti II, I 414.
—Title of queen, Enekhnes-Merire II, I 341.

BUTLER, IV 409, 466, 522, 524, 543, 585; Pebes, IV 423, 426, 452; Kedendenna, IV 423; Maharbaal, IV 423; Payernu, IV 423; Thutrekhnefer, IV 423; Mesedsure, IV 428; Weren, IV 437; Peluka, IV 439; Yenini, IV 440; Nebzefai, IV 445; Henutenamon, IV 448; Nakhtamon, IV 466; Penamon, IV 584.
—Butlers of the palace, IV 402.
—Constituting a lower court, IV 443, 446, 448, 449, 450.
—King's butler, III 371; IV 54, 55, 67, 77, 497, 511, 598; Neferhotep, III 70; Ramses-eshahab, III 496, 498; Usermare-sekhepersu, IV 466; Amenhotep, IV 495; Nesuamon, IV, 495, 511, 513, 522, 526, 528, 531, 533, 540; Neferkere-em-Per-Amon, IV 495, 511, 513, 522, 531; Ini, IV 546; Pemeriamon, IV 546.

C

CAPTAIN: Merire-onekh, I 343; Nekeonekh, I 343; Yekerib, I 343; Khnum-enkhef, I 343; Hemukhrow, I 343.
—of archers, III 484, 587, 631; IV 405, 552; Perehirunamef, III 482; Binemwese, IV 443.
—of infantry, IV 65; Khay, III 630, 632; Penamon, III 633; Peremhab, III 634.
—of gendarmes of Coptos, II 774.
—of marines, IV 407.

Captain—
—of police, Oneney, IV 452.
—Fleet-captain, II 750.
—Ship captain, IV 211, 572; Nenekh-Khentikhet, I 266, 276; Ikhi, I 301; Intef, I 365; Ipi, I 387; Men, I 606; Nibamon, II 779; Mengebet, IV 565, 566.
CARAVAN-CONDUCTORS, I 312, 334, 336; Harkhuf, I 332, 334; —khuf, I 343; Merire-onekh, I 343; Neke-onekh, I 343; Pepi-nakht, I 356; Enenkhet, I 360.
—Chief caravaneer: Weshtehet, IV 784.
CHIEFS (in Egypt), II 172, 385, 1023; III 405; IV 65, 281, 398, 468, 489, 873, 875; Thutiy, II 372; Perekamenef, IV 445; Osorkon, IV 777.
—of archers: Enebni, II 213; Peramses, III 542; Seti, III 542.
—of the army, Ramses II, III 288.
—Builders, IV 858.
—of the chamber, IV 437; Pebekkamen IV 427, 428.
—of chiefs: Sheshonk, IV 675, 677; Namlot, IV 678, 683, 687.
—of the royal council halls, Ahmose-Si-Neit, IV 1000 n. a.
—of a district: Zeptahefonekh, IV 699; Wayeheset, IV 726; Khamwese, IV 795.
—Fowler, Harnahkt, I 718;
—of gendarmes, Ini, III 198.
—of foreign gendarmes, Seti, III 542.
—of police, IV 522; Beknurel, IV 512; Menthirkhepeshef, IV 512; Nesuamon, IV 545, 548, 552.
—of police of the necropolis, in Western Thebes, Pewero, IV 511, 512, 522, 527.
—of the harbor, Somtous-Tefnakhte, IV 944.
—of harem-ladies, II 867.
—of the highland (a necropolis official), I 584, 585.
—of the house of Pharaoh, Senebtefi, I 723.
—of irrigation, Wayheset, IV 726.
—of king's estate, Senmut, II 386.
—of the land: Senmut, II 357; Harmhab, III 25, 26.
—of militia in Busiris, Psamtik, IV 968.
—of the New Towns, I 354; see also Governor of.
—of all nobles of judicial office: Amenemhet, I 438.
—of oblation-bearers of House of Amon: Yuroi, IV 515.
—of the palace: Ahmose-Si-Neit, IV 1000; Pefnefdineit, IV 1017.
—of the peasantry, III 322.
—of the peasant-serfs of Amon: Senmut, II 354.
—of the people (*rḫy.t*), II 236, 238.
—of the phyle, Nesuptah, IV 908.
—of the priestly phyle of Abydos: Ameniseneb, I 782, 787.
—of quarry service, II 935; Amonmose, IV 466; Beknekhonsu, IV 466.
—of the sailors: Ahmose, son of Ebana, II 80.
—of sculptors: Bek, II 975; Men, II 976.
—Sistrum-bearer of Harsaphes, Tentsepeh, IV 787, 792; Thenekemet, IV 787, 792; Petpetdedes, IV 787, 792.
—of the stable: Amenhotep, II 818; Ini, III 198; Pemerhketem, III 634.
—of the court stables, IV 466.
—of strongholds: Sisebek, IV 1017.
—of the temples: Ahmose-Si-Neit, IV 1000 n. a.
—of temple-palace: Huy, IV 338.
—of the White House: Ameni, I 722.
—of works, I 646; II 384; III 264, 271; Senezemib, I 271–73; Merire-Meriptah-onekh, I 298, 299; Amenemhet, I 442, 445; Mentuhotep, I 531; Simontu, I 598; Ineni, II 43, 106; Rekhmire, II 757; Hui, III 210; Hatey, III 513; Ramses-nakht, IV 466; Amenhotep, IV 491; Haremsaf, IV 706, 708.
—of chiefs of works: Senmut, II 368.
—of works of Amon: Intef, II 775.
—of works in the "Eternal Seat": Meya, III 32B.
—of the king's work: Amenhotep, II 912, 917; Ramose, II 936; Mai, II 997.
—of works in the Red Mountain: Bek, II 975; Men, II 976.
—workmen: Userkhepesh, IV 526.
—of workmen: Pediamon, IV 668; see also under Commander, Deputy Door-keeper, Fan-bearer, Favorites, Inspector, Judge, Justice, Measurer, Mayor, Physician, Priest, Prophet, Mortuary priest, Ritual priest, Scribe, Steward.
—Chiefs of Heracleopolis, Karnak, two lands and two towns of the Oasis, Sais, Two Lands, the West, see Index VI.
—Chiefs of Kush, Libya, see Index VI.
—Assistant chief of the chamber, Eshehebsed, IV 438.

Chiefs—
—The Great Chief of Me: Musen, IV 787, 792; Pethut, IV 787, 792; Sheshonk, IV 675, 677, 678, 680, 787, 792; Namlot, IV 676, 678, 683, 685, 686, 687, 787, 792; Takelot, IV 774, 779; Pediese, IV 774, 779; Hetihenker, IV 784; Akenesh, IV 815, 868; Zeamonefonekh, IV 815, 830; Sheshonk, IV 830; Nesnekedi, IV, 830, 878; Tefnakhte, IV 838, 854, 880; Pethenef, IV 878; Pemou, IV 878; Nekhtharneshenu, IV 878; Pentewere, IV 878; Pentibekhenet, IV 878.
—The Great Chief of Meshwesh: Takelot, IV 779, 781; Pediese, IV 781.

CHIEFTAINS, IV 111, 129.

COMMANDANT: regulations of, II 298; chief of: Khamale, IV 466.
—Commandant of Coptos, Kinen, I 776; of fortress, II 718, 719; III 586; of Tharu: Peramses, III 542; Seti, III 542; of infantry, IV 466; of ruler's table, II 695; of towns, III 484.
—Great commandant of the residence city: Zaa, I 683.

COMMANDER, IV 824, 825; Inushefenu, IV 366, 367.
—of the army, II 864; III 264, 332, 484; IV 819, 821; Ibdu, I 303; Yakhetirni, I 387; Zaty-Kenofer, I 389; (Crown Prince) Sesostris I, I 492; Mentuhotep, I 512; Renseneb, I 752; Ramose, II 947 n. a; Mai, II 997, 1002; Ramses, III 482; Inushefenu, IV 366, 367; Thutemhab, IV 367; Peyes, IV 445; Paynozem (I), IV 643; Purem, IV 821; Lemersekeny, IV 821; Enekhor, IV (830), 878; Purme, IV 881; Ahmose, IV 1014.
—in chief of the army, IV 109, 121, 124 n. b; Amenmose, II 811; Harmhab, III 4, 16; Amenhirkhepeshef, III 350, 482; Hrihor, IV 609, 612; Menkheperre, IV 652, 653, 654, 655; Paynozem, IV 671; Yewepet, IV 700, 705; Osorkon, IV 753, 760, 762; Yewelot, IV 795; Somtous-Tefnakhte IV 944.
—of the whole land: Kheti I, I 398 (Herakleopolitan kingdom); Ramses (III), IV 400.
—of the army of Heracleopolis: Namlot, IV 787, 792; Uzptahenkhof, IV 787, 792; Henptah, IV 787, 792; Harpeson, IV 787, 792; Hor, IV 968.
—of attendants, Zaa, I 687.
—of commanders, Amenemhet, I 445.
—of followers, Amenemhet, I 707.
—of infantry, III 484.
—of Middle Egypt, Kheti II, I 410.
—of the official body of the king, I 445.
—of recruits, Mentuhotep, I 512.
—on the river, Senekh, I 455.
—of sailors, Enenkhet, I 360.
—of strongholds, I 312; Ibi, I 377; Zau, I 381, 384.
—of the stronghold of granary, Ibi, I 379.
—of the troops: Merire-onekh, I 303; Amenemhet, I 707; Thaneni, II 820; Mermose, II 852.
—of troops in the highlands, Senekh, I 445.
—of the troops of a village, II 852.
—in chief of the troops of Oryx nome, Amenemhet, I 519.
—of works upon the mountain, Uzahor, IV 980.
—chief commander of the army of Heracleopolis, Bekneptah, IV 777.
—naval commander, I 211, 276; Amenemhab, II 591.

COMPANION, I 334, 336, 355; II 1008; III 270; IV 611, 652; Uni, I 307; Senmut, II 352, 361, 366; Thutiy, II 371; Amenemhab, II 579; Nehi, II 652; Rekhmire, II 713; Intef, II 763.
—of the feet: Amenhotep, II 818; Harmhab, III 20; Rekhpehtuf, III 642.
—of Horus (queen's title): Enekhnes-Merire I, I 345; Enekhnes-Merire II, I 346.
—of the palace, I 312; Amenemhet, I 731.

—Companions, I 246, 312, 755, 757, 758, 761; II 236, 292, 335, 353, 873, 935, 993; III 20, 484; IV 52, 54, 71, 77, 147, 398, 460, 494, 629, 765, 958 D, 988H; counted by the herald, II 767; permitted to "enter in" to his majesty, IV 460.
—of the court, II 290, 292.
—of Ptah, III 400.
—Female companions, III 267.
—of the king, I 201; IV 958D, 966, 1004.
—Sole companion, I 505; Kam, I 187; Re-am, I 281; Uni, I 293, 309;

Merire-meriptah-onekh, I 298, 299; Nenekhseskhnum, I 305; Iri, I 333; Harkhuf, I 326, 332, 336, 352; Khuni, I 336; Pepi-Nakht, I 356 bis; Enenkhet, I 360; Sebni, I 364; Mekhu, I 365, 368, 370; Ibi, I 377 bis; Zau, I 381, 384; Tefibi, I 395; Kheti I, I 395; Kheti II, I 395, 426; Henu, I 428 bis; Eti, I 459 n. a; Khnumhotep I, I 464; Intef, I 467; Idi, I 466 n. c; Putoker, I 466 n. c; Sinuhe, I 490; Mentuhotep, I 512; Mentuhotep, I 533; Simontu, I 596; Khnumhotep II, I 631; Nakht II, I 632; Khnumhotep III, I 633; Kheti, I 637 n. a; Ikhernofret, I 664; Neferperet, II 28; Keres, II 52; Thure, II 170 n. c (?); Nehsi, II 290; Senmut, II 350; Puemre, II 385; Nehi, II 652; Rekhmire, II 713; Intef, II 763, 767; Amenhotep, II 912; Ramose, II 936; Mai, II 997, 1002; Amenhotep, II 1040; Harmhab, III 8, 16, 20; Somtous-Tefnakhte, IV 944; Neferibre-nofer, IV 981; Nesuhor, IV 995; Ahmose-Si-Neit, IV 1000; Pefnefdineit, IV 1017.

Conductor: of overseers, Amenemhet, I 444.
—of the palace, Amenemhet, I 445.

Confidant, King's: I 298; IV 873; Thethi, I 184; Nekennebti, I 194; Nekure, I 195; Hetephires, I 196; Kennebtiwer, I 197; Nekonekh, I 216, 217, 224; Khenuka, I 220, 222; Nonekhsesi, I 230; Kheti I, I 403; Kheti II (?), I 413; Ikudidi, I 527; Khnumhotep II, I 622; Ibe, IV 958G.
—Real confidant of the king: Sinuhe, I 490; Men, I 606; Khentemsemeti, I 609; Senmut, II 352; Harmhab, III 20; Khnumhotep, I 618; Khui, I 675; Sebekdidi, I 720.
—Confidant of the princes of the king: Kheti II, I 413.

Confidante, King's: Henutsen, I 185; Nekennebti, I 199; Hezethekenu, I 217, 218, 221, 224; Ikhnoubet, I 230; Teperet, IV 1000.

Consort, Divine: see Divine consort.

Councilor, II 666.

Counselor, Khnumhotep, III I 663.

Count, I 312, 336, 414; III 484; Uni, I 293, 320; Harkhuf, I 326, 332, 336; Zau, I 348; Khui, I 349; Pepi-Nakht, I 356; Thethi, I 361; Khui, I 361; Sebni, I 364, 372; Mekhu, I 370; Ibi, I 377; Zau, I 384; Tefibi, I 391, 395; Kheti I, I 391; Kheti II, I 391; Intef, I 419; Amenemhet, I 438, 445; Khnumhotep I, I 464, 625, 626; Intef, I 467; Mentuhotep, I 512; Amenemhet, I 518; Crown Prince Ameni, I 520; Crown Prince Sesostris (II), I 521; Mentuhotep, I 531, 533; Hepzefi, I 537–39, 541, 544, 549, 554, 559, 568, 571, 572, 576, 579, 582, 589; Simontu, I 596; Khentkhetwer, I 605; Nehri, I 628; Khnumhotep II, I 622, 624, 629, 631, 639; Nakht II, I 632; Kheti, I 637 n. a; Ikhernofret, I 664; Sebek-khu, Zaa, I 683; Thutnakht, I 689; Sehetepibre, I 745; Minemhet, I 776; Ahmose-Pen-Nekhbet, II 20; Ineni, II 43; Keres, II 52; Nehsi, II 290; Senmut, II 350, 354, 362, 366; Thutiy, II 371; Puemre, II 383, 385; Hapuseneb, II 389; Nehi, II 652; Rekhmire, II 713, 754, 757; Intef, II 763, 767, 775; Minhotep, II 800; Khamhet, II 872; Amenhotep, II 912; Ramose, II 936; Mai, II 997, 1002; Huy, II 1036; Amenhotep, II 1040; Harmhab, III, 8, 16, 20; Beknekhonsu, III 563; Amenhotep, IV 495; Namlot, IV 787, 792; Uzptahenkhof, IV 787, 792; Henptah, IV 787, 792; Harpeson, IV 787, 792; Henptah, IV 787, 792; Harpeson, IV 787, 792; Uzahor IV 980; Neferibre-nofer, IV 981; Nesuhor, IV 995; Pefnefdineit, IV 1017.
—Appointment of, by the king, I 385; given as a mortuary honor, I 385 n. c.
—Daughter of count, Beket, I 622.
—Son of count: Amenemhet, I 519; Khnumhotep II, I 629.
—Counts of Abydos, Coptos, Middle Egypt, Thinis, see Index VI.

Countess: Beket, I 628.

Cup-Bearer of the King: Sabu-Ibebi, I 285.

Custodian, IV 992.
—of the domain of Pharaoh, I 382; Pepi-nakht, I 356;
—Inferior custodian of the domain of Pharaoh, Uni, I 294;
—Superior custodian of the domain of Pharaoh, the four, I 309; Uni, I 300, 310, 312.

D

DARLING: Zau, I 381; Khnumhotep, I 618.
DAUGHTER OF THE GOD (queen's title): Enekhnes-Merire II, I 346.
"DAUGHTER, THE GREAT—": Nitocris, IV 942; Shepnupet II, IV 946; Amenirdis I, IV 949.
DEPUTY, III 371; collecting dues, III 51, 54; Methen, I 172, 174; Mahu, II 809; Peremhab, III 634; Ptahmose, IV 338; Hori, IV 531.
—of the army, IV 466; Amenemhab, II 809; Khamtir, IV 466; the two of, collecting dues, III 54.
—of fortress: Penno, II 1041.
—of the harem: Amenkha, IV 449.
—of the king: Harmhab, III 17.
—of nomes: Methen, I 172.
—of Kush, II 1041.
—of Wawat, IV 480; Penno, IV 474, 477, 482, 483; Meri, IV 481; see also Treasurer.
—Chief deputy, IV 466; scribe of, IV 466.
DEVOTED TO HORUS: Mertityotes, I 189.
DIGNITARIES OF THE KING, II 236, 238, 290, 292, 335, 343.
DISTRICT OFFICIALS, II 717, 729; recorders of, II 717, 729.
DIVINE CONSORT: Ahmose-Nefretiri, II 34; Ahhotep, II 110; Hatshepsut, II 344, 360, 361, 362; Nefrure, II 364; Nitrocris, IV 942, 943, 988D; Mehetnusekhet, IV 958M, Enekhnesneferibre, IV 988D, G, H; ornaments of, IV 988H; steward of, IV 958B.
DIVINE FATHER (priestly title of low rank, also king's father-in-law) II, 97; 292, 302, 925; III 270, 958D; inspection of, I 610; acting as judge, III 65; Puemre, II 383; Eye, II 989, 992, 993; Senbef, IV 918; Psamtik, IV 1029.
—Divine father of Amon, IV 988H, J; Neferhotep, III 71; Perennefer, III 73; Beknekhonsu, III 566; Roy, III 623; Zedi, IV 547; Zekhonsefonekh, IV 668, 689, 691, 692; Nesupekeshuti, IV 668, 689; Wennofer, IV 668, 692; Efnamon, IV 692; Haremsaf, IV 706, 708.
—of Harsaphes: Musen, IV 787, 792; Pethut, IV 789, 792; Sheshonk, IV 787, 792; Namlot, IV 787, 792.
—of Sekhetre: Enekhwennofer, IV 718; Senbef, IV 718; Ptahhotep, IV 718.
DIVINE HAND (=divine votress), IV 414.
DIVINE MOTHER: Tentsepeh, IV 792; Kerome, IV 792; Temekhonsu, IV 792; Kepes, IV 792.
DIVINE VOTRESS, IV 942.
—of Amon-Re, IV 511, 513, 521, 522; Nitocris, IV 942, 945, 958D, M, 988G; induction into office of, IV 958D, 986H; ornaments of, IV 958H.
DOOR-KEEPER: of judgment-hall, II 711.
—of the temple of Edfu: Yuf, II 112.
—Chief of the door-keepers in the temple of Hathor, Pese'eke, IV 784; see also "Keeper of the door."
DWELLERS IN THE PLACE OF THE HAND (priestly title), II 97.

E

ELDEST OF THE ⌈—⌉ CHAMBER, Uni, I 307.
—"Eldest of the hall" of the temple of Amon: Wenamon, IV 563.
ENVOY: Wenamon, I 18; see King's messenger.
EPER, IV 466.
EPRU, IV 281.
EXALTED ONES, I 413.
EXCELLENT: Enebin, II 213.

F

FAN-BEARERS, II 1014; III 41, 94, 332, 651; IV 76, 124; Mentuhotep, I 514; Amenhotep, II 912; Merire I, II 988; Eye, II 989, 992; Ahmose, II 1004; Huy, II 1029; Harmhab, III 16, 17; Meya, III 328; Amenemopet, III 204 n. b; Amenhirunamef, III 467, 471, 477; Seti, III 542; Piyay, III 644; Seti, III 646, 647.
—Chiefs of fan-bearers, II 935.
"FATHER OF THE TWO LANDS": title given to Harmhab, III 26.
—Great father (=teacher), Senmut, II 364.
FAVORITE, II 994, 996; were a prey to the terror of Heracleopolis, I 401.
—of Horus: Simontu, I 596; Harmhab, III 17.
—of the king: Mertityôtes, I 55, 189; Senezemib, I 270; Harkhuf, I 332; Zau, I 381; Kheti II, I 409, 413;

Thethi, I 423 ter, 423E; Henu, I 428; Amenemhet, I 442, 445; Meri, I 508; Mentuhotep, I 512; Mentuhotep, I 531; Khnumhotep, I 618; Khui, I 675; Sebekdidi, I 720; Senmut, II 352; Thutiy, II 371; Intef, II 767; Rekhpehtuf, III 642; Amenhotep, IV 498; Ahmose-Si-Neit, IV 1000 n. a.
—Chief of favorites, Nesikhonsu, IV 689.
—Favorite of the king (lady's title): Nebet, I 349.
—Favorite of the Two Goddesses (one of the oldest of the Pharaoh's five titles, designating him as the protégé of Buto, serpent-goddess of the North, and Nekhbet, vulture-goddess of the South, the patron-goddesses of the kingdom; it stands second in the Pharaoh's fivefold titulary), I 169; II 120 *et passim.*

Fellow of the King, in counseling, Mentuhotep, I 531.

First under the King: Sesi, I 299; Nenekhseskhnum, I 305; Thethi, I 423C.

Following the King, II 993; Thethi, I 423C; Enebni, II 213; Eye, II 993; Ahmose, II 1008; Harmhab, III 20.

Foremen, I 697; foreman of the: Ineni, II 343; Senmut, II 352.
—of the Tomb, Beket, I 639.

G

General: Thutiy, I 24; Harmhab, III 16.
—of the army, II 925.

Girdle, Fastening of (a rank?): Uni, I 294; Simontu, I 597.

God (=king), I 262, 273 *et passim.*
—Great god, I 169, 176, 236 *et passim;* writing of, I 264.

Golden Horus (one of the five royal titles), I 250 *et passim.*

Governor, III 322, 323; Kam I 187.
—of Dep, Methen, I 172, 174, 201; Sinuhe, I 490; Mentuhotep, I 512; Sisebek, IV 1017.
—of the door of the southern countries; Uzehor, IV 980; Nesuhor, IV 990, 995.
—of the eastern highlands: Khnumhotep I I 625; Khnumhotep II, I 622, 624.
—of foreign countries: Pepi-nakht, I 356; Seti, III 542; Peramses, III 542.
—of the gold countries of Amon: Seti (II), III 647.
—of the gold country of Coptos, II 774.
—of the palace: Nenekhseskhnum, I 305; Mentuhotep, I 533.
—of the pyramid city: Zau, I 348; Pepinakht, I 356.
—of the new towns: Nekonekh, I 216.
—of the northern countries, III 484.
—Governor of the residence city, III 484; IV 777; Amenemhet, I 438, 442, 445; Crown Prince Sesostris (II), I 521; Nehri, I 628; Enkhu, I 783; Hapuseneb, II 389; Rekhmire, II 675, 754; Amenhotep, II 923; Ramose, II 936, 937 n. a, 940; Seti, III 542; Peramses, III, 542; Khay, III 556, 560; Ta, IV 414; Khamwese, IV 511, 513, 522, 523, 531, 532, 540, 543; Nibmarenakht, IV 546; Pay nozem I, IV 634; Paynozem II, IV 668.
—Governor of the South, IV 753; Uni, I 293, 320 bis; Harkhuf, I 326, 533; Sebni, I 364; Ibi, I 377; Amenemhet, I 445; Putoker, I 466 n. c; Thutnakht, I 689; Osorkon, IV 765, 767, 777; Namlot, IV 787, 792; Uzptahenkhof, IV 787, 792; Henptah, IV 787, 792; Harpeson, IV 787, 792; Mentemhet, IV 904, 949.
—Governor of the Southern Countries, III 484; Thure, II 170 n. c (?); Nehi, II 651, 652; Huy, II 1029; Amenhotep, II 1030; Amenemopet, III 204 n. b; Seti (II), III 646.
—Governor of Elephantine of the South, II 172.
—Real governor of the South: Nenekhseskhnum, I 305; Ibi, I 378.
—Governor of the two doors in the northern countries: Ahmose, IV 1014.

Grain Registrar: Simontu, I 598.

Grandees, II 292 bis; III 264, 484.
—of the palace, head of: Thethi, I 423C, 423E.

Great in Possessions (queen's title): Enekhnes-Merire I, I 345; Enekhnes-Merire II, I 346.

Great Lord, see Lord.

Great One of the King of Lower Egypt: Amenemhet, I 445; Sehetepibre, I 745.

Great Ones, of Heracleopolis, I 401.

GREAT PILLAR IN THE NOME OF THEBES, Eti, I 459.
GREAT SEER, IV 281; Merire I, II 982, 983, 985, 987, 988.
—of Re-Atum in Thebes, Roy, III 623.
GREATEST OF THE GREAT: Senmut, II 355; Harmhab, III 20.
GREAT-HEARTED, Thethi, I 423C.
GUARDIAN, KING'S: Neferibre-nofer, IV 981.

H

HARBOR-MASTER, IV 572.
HEAD OF THE TWO LANDS, Harmhab, III 27.
HEIR OF A RULER: Kheti I, I 400.
HERALD, II 925 n. a; duties of, II 52, 764, 767; departments of office of: manager of court and palace ceremonies, II 764, 767; communications to the people by, II 764, 767; communications from the people to, II 764, 767; messenger of the judgment-hall, II 764, 767; communication to foreign lands by, II 764, 767.
—of the judgment-hall, Intef, II 763.
—King's herald, II 9, 11; Intef, II 763, 767, 768; Penrenut, IV 423; Neferkere-em-Per-Amon, IV 495, 511, 513, 522, 531; Ini, IV 546.
—Queen's herald: Keres, II 50, 52.
HIGH PRIEST, see Priest.
HIGH-VOICED: Henu, I 428.
HONORED BY HIS CITY-GOD: Ibi, I 378.
—by the king, Sabu-Ibebi, I 283, 284, 285, 286.
HORUS (the oldest of the Pharaoh's five titles, and the one identifying him with the sun-god; it stands first in the fivefold royal titulary), e. g., II 120 *et passim*.
HORUS, GOLDEN (third title of the Pharaoh in his fivefold titulary; the Greek rendering *ἀντιπάλων ὑπέρτερος* suggests that the gold-sign (*nb*) on which the Horus-hawk stands, is but a symbol for Set, whose name is written with this sign. The Horus-hawk surmounting the symbol of Set would then mean, "Horus Victor over Set." But against this is the early literal rendering of the gold-sign, in II 145), e. g., II 120 *et passim*.
—*ḥry ydb:* Mentuhotep, I 533.

I

IMI-KHENTIT: Tutu, II 1009.
INSPECTORS, II 1026; IV 208, 360, 361, 407, 466, 652, 671, 676, 751, 958G; impost from, IV 225; laws on, III 58.
—of the cattle of Amon, IV 212.
—of the fields, II 437; III 275; IV 149.
—of the necropolis, IV 511, 512, 517, 522, 525, 533, 593.
—of the harem, IV 455; Petewnteamon, IV 431; Kerpes, IV 432; Khamopet, IV 433; Khammale, IV 434; Setimperthoth, IV 435; Setimperamon, IV 436; Errem, IV 455.
—of the highlands, III 192.
—Chief inspector: Perehotep, IV 281; Hori, IV 281; Nesupekeshuti, IV 665, 668.

J

JUDGE: Anubisemonekh, I 171; Methen, I 172; Hotep, I 187; Zaty, I 343; —khet, I 343; Zau, I 348; Sinuhe, I 490; Ramose, II 936; Yui, III 32B; Khay, III 556, 560; receiving bribes, III 64.
—Attached to Nekhen, I 310; Hotephiryakhet, I 252; Sesi, I 299; Khui, I 299; Uni, I 307, 309; Harkhuf, I 332; Pepi-nakht, I 356; see also "Attached to Nekhen."
—Chief judge, I 307; IV 777; Senezemib, I 271, 273; Ini, I 373; Amenemhet, I 445; Mentuhotep, I 531.
—Field judge: Methen, I 174; son of Henutsen, I 185; see also "High-voiced."
—Judging the people and the inhabitants, Amenemhet, I 445.
—Justice, chief: Zau, I 347, 348; Ramose, II 936; Khay, III 556, 560.
—Chief of the six courts: Nenekhseskhnum, I 305; Henu, I 428; Amenemhet, I 445; Rekhmire, II 713, 754.

K

KEEPER OF THE DOOR OF THE SOUTH: Zau, I 380; Intef, I 420; Henu, I 428; Amenemhet, I 445.
—of the door of the highlands, Khnumhotep III, I 633.
—of the house of rolls, III 264.
—of the wardrobe of the temple (fourth in rank), I 550, 559; in charge of the wicks, I 560, 566.
—of the wide hall of the temple (sixth

in rank), I 550; see also Door-keeper, Storeroom-keeper.

KENBETI, II 719, 720, 722, 723, 727, 733, 734, 738, 745.

KHETKHET-OFFICERS, III 66.

KING, EGYPTIAN: divine birth of, II 122, 187, 189 *et passim;* choice of, by oracle, II 134–36; offers incense, II 139; station of, in temple ritual, see Station of the king; as Bull, Lion, Panther, see Index VII; mourning for nomarch, Kheti II, I 414.

—Names of, see Horus, Golden Horus, Two Goddesses, King of Upper and Lower Egypt, Son of Re.

—Titles of: the double lord, III 285; enduring in monuments, I 441 *et passim;* excellent god, I 441 *et passim;* fashioner of beauty, I 423B; I 423G *et passim;* first in thrones, I 441 *et passim*; good god, I 492 *et passim;* great in love, I 441 *et passim;* "Great Pillar," I 420 n. d *et passim;* heir of Horus in his Two Lands, I 441 *et passim;* living forever, I 437, 440, 450, 456 *et passim;* living like Re forever, 423B, 423F 423G I 441, 443 *et passim;* lord of joy, I 441 *et passim;* mighty in fear, I 441 *et passim;* son of Hathor, I 423H; Sun of Egypt, IV 79, 82, 127; "who makes his Two Lands to live," I 420, and n. f, *et passim;* shade of the whole land, I 399 *et passim;* "Star of the South," I 511; White Bull, I 511 *et passim;* king among the Bedwin, Sinuhe, I 490.

KING OF LOWER EGYPT, I 95, 145; III 175; appearance of, I 105, 114, 121, 123, 127, 129, 131, 134, 140, 141, 143, 150, 167.

KING OF UPPER EGYPT, I 90; III 175; appearance of, I 99, 105, 116, 119, 121, 134, 140, 141, 143, 150, 167; magnates of, I 445, 745.

KING OF UPPER AND LOWER EGYPT (early title of the Pharaoh, the fourth in his fivefold titulary: assumed by by Menes as ruler of both kingdoms), e. g., II 120 *et passim.*

KING'S CHILDREN, I 246, 256, 413; II 813; IV 54, 55 63, 77, 92, 124, 523, 524, 525, 528.

KING'S CONCUBINES, IV 844.

KING'S DAUGHTER, IV 844, 849; Ahmose-Nefretiri, II 34; Sebekemsaf, II 112; Nefrure, II 344; Hatshepsut, II 360; Sitamon, II 912; Meretaton, II 961, 1017; Meketaton, II 961; Amose-Sitkamose, IV 644; Makere, IV 740; Kerome, IV 755; Thesperebast, IV 771, 774, 781; Tentsepeh, IV 787, 792; Tedenetnebast, IV 795; Nestent IV 844; Nitocris, IV 942; Amenirdis I, IV 946; Eneknesneferibre, IV 988C, D, H.

KING'S ELDEST SON, I 66 n. g; Ameni, I 520; Zaty-Kenofer, I 389; Amenmose, II 811; Amenhirkhepeshef, III 482; Nesuhor, IV 990.

KING'S HOUSE, see Index VII.

KING'S MOTHER, IV 523, 525, 528, 696, 895; Neferhotepes, I 241; Enekhnes-Merire I, I 345; Enekhnes-Merire II, I 341, 346; Tetisheri, II 33, 36; Ahhotep I, II 52, 111; Seniseneb, II 58; Ahmose, II 196; Mehetnusekhet, IV 792; Tentsey, IV 695, 787, 792; Kerome, IV 696, 787, 792.

KING'S SISTER, IV 844, 895; Ahmose-Nefretiri, II 34; Sebekemsaf, II 110; Hatshepsut, II 360.

KING'S SON (of his body), III 102, 124; IV 109, 121; Nekure, I 190, 193; Ameni, I 520; Kinen, I 776; Thutmose (IV), II 815; Ramses (II), III 132; Khamwese, III 350, 362, 474, 482, 552, 553, 554; Meriamon, III 350, 362; Seti, III 350, 362; Amenhirkhepeshef, III 350, 456, 482; Montu, III 362; Amenemuya, III 362; Setepnere, III 362; Ramses, III 456, 482; Perehirunamef, III 456, 482; Amenhirunamef, III 467, 474, 477; Siamon, IV 646; Yewepet, IV 705; Meriamon-Sheshonk, IV 740; Osorkon, IV 753; Sheshonk, IV 774; Yewelot, IV 794; Nesubenebded, IV 794.

—Viceroy of Kush: Thure, II 64, 170 n. e; Enebni, II 213; Nehi, II 651, 652; Mermose, II 852, 855; Huy, II 1023, 1025, 1026, 1029, 1036, 1038; Amenhotep, II 1030, 1038. Amenemopet, III 204 n. b, 477 bis.

—of Kush, III 289, 291, 292; IV 476; Huy, II 1023, 1025, 1029, 1036, 1038; Amenhotep, II 1030, 1038; Ini, III 198; Amenemopet, III 477 bis; Seti (II), III 642, 643, 646, 647; Hori, III 650; Paynehsi, IV 597; Hrihor, IV 615.

King's Son—
—of Ramses, Zeptahefonekh, IV 699.
KING'S WIFE, IV 523, 525, 528, 844, 849; Enekhnes-Merire I, I 345; Enekhnes-Merire II, I 341, 346; Sebekemsaf, II 110; Ahmose, II 196, 197; Nebetu, II 779; Nefretiri, IV 479; Isis, IV 523; Nesimut, IV 555; Bekurel, IV 555; Nestent IV 844.
GREAT KING'S WIFE: Tetisheri, II 33, 36; Ahmose-Nefretiri, II 34; Ahhotep, II 110, 111, 113; Merseger, II 171; Ahmose, II 214; Hatshepsut, II 214, 232, 344, 360; Tiy, II 862, 864, 865, 867, 869, 1014, 1015, 1016; Nefernefruaton-Nofretete, II 959, 961, 984, 991, 995, 1010, 1015; Matnefrure, III 417; Nefrure, III 435; Nefretiri, III 500 bis, 501; Nubkhas, IV 517; 538; Ahmose-Sitkamose, IV 644; Kerome, IV 696, 760.

L

LAW-GIVER: Mentuhotep, I 531.
LAY-PRIEST, see Priest.
LEADER, IV 55, 123, 124; Hrihor, IV 612; Paynozem II, IV 668; Meriamon-Sheshonk, IV 740; Osorkon, IV 760.
—of the archers of Pharaoh: Paynehsi, IV 597.
—of the army: Intef, II 767; Yewepet, IV 705; Meriamon-Sheshonk, IV 740.
—of bowmen, III 581.
—of the crew of recruits: Henemi, I 343; Senezem, I 343; Amenemhet, I 731.
—of chariotry, IV 54, 71, 92, 397.
—of infantry, IV 54, 71, 92, 397.
—of the feasts of Amon: Meya, III 32B.
—of the king's workmen, III 173.
—of leaders, III 484.
—of the Magnates of South and North, Mentuhotep, I 533.
—of the palace: Thutiy, II 377.
—of the palace-hall: Kam, I 187.
—on the two sides, II 925.
LOCAL GOVERNOR OF DEP, see Governor.
LORD OF CHARIOTRY: Ramses (II), III 267.
—of infantry: Ramses (II), III 267.
—of the double gold-house: Ikhernofret, I 664.
—of the double silver-house: Ikhernofret, I 664.
—of gods, II 288, 294 *et passim*.
—of the palace, II 72; Simontu, I 596.
—of reverence: Khentemsemeti, I 613.
—of truth, royal title of Snefru, I 169.
—of the Black Land: Mentuhotep, I 532.
—of the Red Land: Mentuhotep, I 532.
—of Nekheb: Uni, I 293; Pepi-nakht, I 356; Ini, I 373; Ameni, I 518.
—of Nekhen, I 201.
—of the South, I 359.
—of the Two Lands (a royal title), I 250 *et passim*.
—of the two regions, Merikere, king of Heracleopolis, I 399.
—of Kadesh, II 585, 590.
—of the Lebanon cities, taken as captive, II 436.
—king, the double lord, III 285.
—mother of Kheti II acted as lord of Siut, I 414.
—great lord of the Cerastes Mountain: Ibi, I 377; Zau, I 381.
—of the Hare nome, Nenekhseskhnum, I 305.
—of Middle Egypt, Kheti I, I 403.
—of Nekheb: Khentemsemeti, I 609; Royenet, II 7; Baba, II 7; Ahmose, son of Ebana, II 7.
—of the Oryx nome: Khnumhotep I, I 464, 626; Ameni, I 518; Kheti, I 637 n. a.
—of the South, Hapuseneb, II 389.
—of the Theban nome, Intef, I 420.
—of the royal wardrobe, Mentuhotep I 533.

M

MAGNATES, IV 124, 566.
—of the palace, II 64.
—of the king of Upper Egypt: Amenemhet, I 445; Sehetepibre, I 745.
—of the South: standing in the two aisles before the vizier, II 675, 712; Ameni, I 650.
—of the South and North: Senmut, II 335.
—leader of magnates, I 533.
MAJESTY, I 211 *et passim*.
MAJOR-DOMO, IV 598; Thutmose IV, IV 672, 673.
—of the house of the Divine Votress of Amon-Re: Neferkere-em-Per-Amon, IV 511, 513, 522, 531.
MARSHAL, IV 944.
—of the two thrones, III 484; Nenekhseskhnum, I 305; Thutnakht, I 689.

Marshal—
—Court marshal, III 69.

Master of the Bath: Khuni, I 336.
—of the Double Cabinet: Khnumhotep, I 618; Sisatet, I 672 n. a, 673; Khenemsu, I 713, 716; Sebeko, I 716; Ameni, I 722; Sebek-hir-hab, I 725, 726; Ptahwer, I 728; Amenemhet, I 731; Harure, I 735.
—of the footstool of the palace: Uni, I 320 bis.
—of the harbor, IV 572.
—of horse: Peramses, III 542; Seti, III 542.
—of the horses of the king: Eye, II 989, 992; Perehirunamef, III 482.
—of the hunt: Nesuamon, IV 539.
—of the judgment-hall: Khentkhetwer, I 605; Ahmose, II 1004; Ahmose-Si-Neit, IV 1000.
—of the royal weapons: Enebni, II 213.
—of the king's writings: Mentuhotep, I 533.
—of the palace: Senmut, II 352.
—of all people: Senmut, II 357.
—of the privy chamber, sitting on the right of the vizier, II 675.
—of all secrets, I 755.
—of secret things: Senezemib, I 270; Sabu-Ibebi, I 285; Nenekhseskhnum, I 305; Mentuhotep, I 533 bis, 534; Ikhernofret, I 668; (to this office belonged the duty of clothing the god at his processions, I 745).
—of secrets of heaven, earth, and the nether world: Roy, III 623.
—of the secret things of the king: Ahmose-Si-Neit, IV 1000 n. a.
—of the secret things of the king's wardrobe: Khentemsemeti, I 608.
—of the secret things of the palace: Ramose, II 936.
—of secret things of the temple, third in rank, I 550: Sehetepibre, I 745; Haremsaf, IV 706, 708.
—of the secret writings of the temple: Senmut, II 355; Rekhmire, II 748.
—of the suite, Mai, II 997.
—of the throne: Ahmose-Si-Neit, IV 1000 n. a.
—of all wardrobes: Zau, I 348; Mentuhotep, I 533; Rekhmire, II 713; Ramose, II 936; Senbef, IV 918.
—Master-builder, I 212, 289, 298; III 484; IV 629; Merire-meriptah-onekh, I 298, 299; Thethi, I 301.
—Master-workmen, IV 466.

Mayor: official head of a town or city, under the Empire, the successor of the count (*ḥ ꜣ ty-ꜥ*) of the OK and MK., II 53, 692, 699, 701, 721, 722, 729, 735, 739, 742, 743, 768, 927 bis, 1041; III 82 n. b; IV 147, 533.
—Tribute from, II 708; taxes from, II 717.
—of Nekhen: Harmini, II 47, 48.
—of Thebes: Amenmose: IV 466; Peser, IV 513, 526, 527, 531.
—of Western Thebes: Pewero, IV 511, 512, 522, 527, 528, 535.
—Chief mayor, III 484.

Measurer, Chief, Hui, II 929.

Member of the Court, Sabu-Ibebi, I 283, 285, 286.

Meri-nuter, see Priest.

Messengers, I 429; II 667, 926; III 616; IV 42, 582, 585, 586, 678, 843, 880, 944.
—of Amon: Wenamon, IV 570, 586, 590, 591.
—of the king's house, II 692, 710.
—of the vizier, II 675, 676, 680; duties of, II 682.
—of Bekhten, III 436.
—circuit messenger, II 692.
—divine messenger, said of a portable statue, IV 586.
—king's messenger, I 492; II 120, 206, 207, 254, 255, 260, 261, 262, 337, 371, 423, 651; IV 408; duties of, III 642; Intef, I 467; Amenhotep, II 1030; Harmhab, III 13, 20; Ramose, III 372; Rekhpehtuf, III 642; Neferhor, III 643; Hori, III 645; Ubekhu, III 650; Hori, IV 485; Ahmose, IV 1014.
—of Kheta, Terteseb, III 371, 372; second messenger of Kheta, III 371.

Mistress of All Gods: Wereret, II 288.

Mountaineer (necropolis official), I 584, 585.

N

Nehebkauf (="who controls his ka's") in the upper country: Eti, I 459; also applied to a well-known mortuary divinity, I 459 n. b.

Nobles, I 6, 307, 349; II 236, 238, 288, 289, 353, 368; III 101; IV 52, 54, 55, 65, 123, 124, 281, 425, 427, 428, 429, 430, 431, 432, 433, 434, 435, 436, 437, 438, 439, 440, 441, 442, 444, 466, 495,

511, 513, 517, 521, 522, 524, 531, 533, 534, 765, 944, 1018.
—Conducted by the herald, II 767; of court of examination, IV 425, 427, 428, 429, 430, 431, 432, 433, 434, 435, 436, 437, 438, 439, 440, 441, 442, 444, 456; of judicial office, chief of, *q. v.*; of Elphantine, I 6; of Kheta, III 419.
—Great nobles: Hrihor, IV 612.
—Nobleman: Uni, I 42; Kheti I, I 400.
—Noblest of the noble: Senmut, II 355.
NOMARCHS, I 312, 398; functions of, I 398; Methen, I 172, 174; Kheti, I 398.
—of Heracleopolis: Somtous-Tefnakhte, IV 944.
—of Hermonthis: ancestors of Intef, I 419 n. c.
—of Thebes: Intef, I 419.
NURSE: Eye, II 989.
—of the god (=Pharaoh) in the private chamber: Khentemsemeti, I 609.

O

OBLATION-BEARERS, IV 515; chief of, see under Chief.
OFFICER, II 667, 987; III 51, 52, 54, 55; IV 40, 52, 65, 71, 124, 147, 149, 593.
—of the army, III 340; IV 70.
—of cavalry, III 584.
—of the court, II 236.
—of court fishermen, IV 466.
—of the gendarmes, II 927.
—of the infantry: Tefnakhte, IV 452.
—of marines, III 197.
—Navy officer: Amenemhab, II 579, 591,
—*Sdm-w*-officers.
OFFICIAL BODY OF THE KING, I 429; commander of, I 445.
OFFICIAL STAFF (=local court), consisting of divine fathers, III 65; prophets of the temple, III 65; officials of the court, III 65; priests of the gods, III 65; connivance of, III 58; remittance of impost from, III 63; bribery of, III 64.
OFFICIALS, I 165, 206, 281, 307; II 335, 384, 666, 667, 935, 990, 993, 1002, 1039; III 10, 12, 59, 61, 101, 271, 272, 322, 323; IV 71, 281, 283, 338, 409, 525, 958H; duties of, II 666, 667, 668; III 58.
—of the court, III 65, 437.
—of the treasury: Harnakht, I 718.
—of Nubia, III 643.
—District officials: see District officials.
—Frontier officials, III 629, 636; impost from, IV 225.
—*hsb*-official, II 881.
—*kf*ʾ*-yb*-officials, II 708.
ORDERLIES, IV 281.
—of his majesty, III 450; Nekri, II 1 n. c.
OVERSEER, III 210; IV 583; Behkesi, I 365.
—of the administration of divine offerings: Sesi, I 299.
—of the bounty of the king's field of offerings: Kam, I 187.
—of cattle, II 1041; IV 150.
—of the cattle of Amon, IV 212, 547, 548; Senmut, II 354, 356; Amenhotep, II 912; Pay, IV 224.
—of the castle of Pharaoh, III 57.
—of commissions: Methen, I 173.
—of craftsmen, chief of: Intef, II 775.
—of the crown-possessions, I 312.
—of the fields of Amon: Senmut, II 354.
—of flax: Methen, I 172.
—of the gardens of Amon: Senmut, II 352, 354, 356.
—of the gold-house, III 484; Keres, II 52.
—of the double gold-house: Mentuhotep, I 533; Thutiy, II 371.
—of the granary, II 872; IV 498; Henu, I 428; Ineni, II 43; Nebamon, IV 517; Menmarenakht, IV 546; Paynehsi, IV 597.
of the double granary: Mentuhotep, I 533; Intef, II 768.
—of the granary of Amon: Senmut, II 350, 367.
—of the double granary of Amon: Ineni, II 43, 343.
—of the granary of the temple of Aton: Hatey, II 932.
—of the granaries: Hrihor, IV 615.
—of grain: Henku, I 281.
—of every handicraft: Thutiy, II 371.
—of the royal harem: Huy, II 1014; Peynok, IV 429; Mesedsure, IV 430.
—of herds, IV 466; Hori, III 82 n. b; Huy, IV 338; Penhuibin, IV 455; Beknekhonsu, IV 466.
—of the highland, I 589.
—of the horn of the cattle of Amon, IV 212.
—of horn and hoof: Henu, I 428.
—of horn, hoof, and feather, III 486; Sehetepibre, I 745.

Overseer—
—of hundred, II 617, 700; reporting to the vizier, II 676, 708.
—of land, II 686.
—of the ka-house, seventh in rank in the temple, I 550.
—of the king's hall: Nibamon, II 778.
—of the king's house: Thutnakht, I 689.
—of the king's records: Zau, I 348.
—of the necropolis of Siut, I 582, 584, 585.
—of palace: Intef, I 390.
—of the palace-baths: Kam, I 187.
—of the two pleasure-marshes: Sehetepibre, I 745.
—of royal property: Sehetepibre, I 745.
—of the provision magazine: Methen, I 172.
—of the pyramid: Thethi, I 184.
—of the ⌜ ⌝ of Sekhmet: Iroi, IV 445.
—of the silver-house, II 987; III 484; Keres, II 52.
—of all works of the house of silver: Senmut, II 352.
—of the double silver-house, Mentuhotep, I 533, Thutiy, II 371.
—of stone-work: Uzai, I 343.
—of the storehouse, fifth in rank in the temple, I 550.
—of the storehouse of Amon: Senmut, II 352, 356.
—of that which is and that which is not: Henu, I 248.
—of that which heaven gives, earth creates, and the Nile brings: Amenemhet, I 438.
—of the temples: Henu, I 428; Hapuseneb, II 389.
—of the temples of Neit: Senmut, II 358; Mai, II 997, 1002.
—of *š t ꜣ y:* Wayeheset. IV 726.
—of ten, I 276.
—of the treasury, II 925; Meriptah, II 923; Meya, III 32B; Thutmose, III 210; Piyay, III 644; Pay, IV 638.
—of the gold treasury, Pefnefdineit, IV 1017.
—of the western highlands, Mentuhotep, I 533.
—of the White House, II 1020; IV 495, 511, 512, 522; Henu, I 428; Ramose, II 947 n. a; Huy, II 1014; Setemhab, IV 19, 20; Mentemtowe, IV 423, 426; Pefroi, IV 423, 426; Pere, IV 442; Khamtir, IV 466; Menmarenakht, IV 546; Zekhonsefonekh, IV 668, 689, 691, 692; scribe of ——, IV 512, 522.
—of the double White House, I 505.
—of works in the mountain of Gritstone: Harmhab, III 17.
—of works in the temples: Minhotep, II 800.
—of workmen, II 383.
—Chief overseer: Yekerib, I 343; Khnum-enkhef, I 343; Hemukhrow, I 343.
—Chief overseer of the estate, II 925.
—Chief overseer of the White House: Payneferhir, IV 637.
—Chief overseer of works in the temple of Amon: Beknekhonsu, III 564, 566, 567.
—Conductor of overseers: Amenemhet, I 445.
—Gang-overseer of the crown possessions in the Oryx nome, I 522.

P

PHARAOH, see King.
PHYSICIANS: chief, I 246; Nenekhsekhmet, I 238, 240; Pefnefdineit, IV 1017.
PILLAR, of his mother (a priestly office), II 133, 240; III 155 n. b; Prince Thutmose (III), II 138.
—of the South: Sehetepibre, I 745.
PILOT, II 252.
—of the people: Mentuhotep, I 531.
POLICE, captain of, *q. v.;* chief of, *q. v.*
POSSESSED OF LOVE: Ibi, I 378.
PREFECTS OF EGYPT, Roman, Mommsen's theory of, I 28.
PRIEST, II 766; III 413; IV 124, 468, 906, 927, 1025; see also Prophet; Divine father; Shepseshathor, I 218, 221; Tetheri, IV 547, 550, 553; Nesuamon, IV 551; acting as judges, III 64, 65.
—of Amon, 925; III 624.
—of Edfu: Yuf, II 112, 113.
—of Horus: Khnumhotep, II, I 624.
—of Khnum: Khentemsemeti, I 609.
of Khonsu-the-Plan-Maker-in-Thebes; Khonsu-hetneterneb, III 432.
—of Min, Neferhotepur, I 776.
—of Pakht, II 301; Khnumhotep II, I 624.
—of goddess Seshat, I 109.
—of Thoth: Neferhor, III 643.
—of the northern crown: Khentemsemeti, I 609.
—of the southern crown: Khentemsemeti, I 609.

Priest—
—Priestesses of Ptah, III 400.
ᵓ *ḳ* -PRIEST OF KARNAK: Hariesese, IV 753.
CHIEF PRIEST OF THE RAM-GOD: Seti, III 542.
GREAT-PRIEST OF ANUBIS, I 572.
HIGH PRIEST OF AMON, I 22; II 925; IV 539, 574, 587, 747; revolt by, IV 486; succession of, I 69 n. a; III 622, 626; title carried by divine consort, Enekhnesneferibre, IV 988D, G, H; Rise as King, IV 25–34, 139–45, 151–79, 189–226, 218–19, 224, 236–37, 405, 486–98, 592–94, 601–3, 608–626; see also "First prophet of Amon."
—Meriptah, II 929, 930, 931; Nebunnef, III 255, 257; Beknekhonsu, III 563, 565, 566, 568; Rome, III 618, 621; Roy, III 618, 623, 626; IV 487; Beknekhonsu, III 618; IV 487; Ramsesnakht, IV 487, 489, 494, 495; Nesuamon, IV 487; Amenhotep, IV 487, 489, 494, 495, 523, 531, 532, 534; Hrihor, IV 566, 580, 593, 594, 609, 610, 611, 612, 615, 617, 621, 622, 624, 626; Payonekh, IV 631, 632, 633, 634, 640, 641; Paynozem I, IV 631, 632, 633, 634, 637, 638, 639, 640, 642; Zekhonsefonekh, IV 650; Masaheret, IV 647; Menkheperre, IV 650, 652, 653, 654, 655, 657, 658, 659, 660, 661; Nesubenebded, IV 662; Paynozem II, IV 663, 668, 671; Pesibkhenno, IV 688; Yewepet, IV 607, 700, 705; Harsiese, IV 698; Osorkon, IV 698, 753, 755, 760, 762, 769, 770, 777; Meriamon-Sheshonk, IV 740; Harsiese, IV 698, 753, 794, Takelot, IV 698, 794; Yewelot, IV 794, 795; Nesubenebded, IV 794; Harkheb, IV 952.
—of Aton, Merire I, II 982, 985; see also "Great seer."
—of Nekhbet: Setau, IV, 414.
—of Onouris: Amenhotep, II 818.
—of Osiris: Nebwawi, II 179, 181.
—of Ptah at Memphis, IV 338; Ptahshepses, I 258; Sabu-Ibebi, I 283, 286; Sabu-Thety, I 287; Khamwese, III 552 n. l; Takelot, IV 781; Pediese, IV 781; Pefnefdibast, IV 774; ; the two, of Memphis, I 211, 212, 239, 288; sacred possessions and duties of, I 288.
—of Re, at Heliopolis, Patonemhab, III 22 n. a; the two, I 165.
of Set: Seti, III 542.
—High priestess of Amon, IV 414 n. c.
LAY-PRIESTS (*Wnwt*= or "hour-priests," laymen who served periodically in the temples), IV 906, 958D.
—of Amon at Karnak, II 353; IV 926, 988H, J; at Tanis, IV 217.
—of the temple of Anubis, I 576, 580.
—of Min at Coptos, I 776; complaint by, I 777.
—of Osiris at Abydos, I 668, 783; II 97; III 263.
—of Upwawet, lord of Siut, I 539, 544, 547, 554.
MERI-NUTER PRIEST: Khui, I 349; Putoker, I 466 n. c; Mentuhotep, I 533; Rekhmire, II 713; Ramose, II 936; Huy, II 1036; Khay, III 556, 560; Enekhhor, IV 958 B.
MORTUARY PRIEST (*k*ᵓ-servant), I 201, 204, 205, 538; II 908, 996; III 271; Mer, I 218; Keksire, I 218; of Senuonekh, I 232–35; of Senezemib, I 274.
—of Menet-Khufu, endowment of, I 630; duties of, I 630.
—of Siut, duties of, I 538, 562; in charge of the statue of Hepzefi, I 542, 544, 555, 562, 574; kindling the fire on News Year's night, I 562.
—Mortuary priests divided into phyles, I 274; chief of, see Index V.
—Mortuary lay-priests, III 277.
—Assistant mortuary priest, I 202.
—Inferior mortuary priest, I 202.
—Chief mortuary priest, Ptah, I 182.
RITUAL PRIEST (*ḥry-ḥb*), I 246; II 97, 239, 766; III 31, 78, 160; Re-am, I 281; Merire-Meriptah-onekh II, I 298; Isi, I 333; Harkhuf, I 326, 332, 336; Pepi-Nakht, I 356; Sebni, I 364; Mekhu, I 365, 370; Putoker, I 466 n. c; Neferhotep, III 72; duties of, II 239; tenth in rank in the temple, I 550.
—of Amon, IV 988H.
—of Buto-Upet-Towe: Seti, III 542.
—Chief ritual priest, I 370; IV 871, 958D; Zau, I 348; Pediamenesttowe, IV 881; "stretched the cord" at the ceremony of laying the foundation-stone for the temple in Heliopolis, I 506.
SEM-PRIEST: Zau, I 348; Mentuhotep, I 533; Ikhernofret, I 668; Sehetepibre, I 746; Hapuseneb, II 389 Rekhmire, II 713; Ramose, II 936 Khamwese, III 552, 553, 554; Roy,

III 623; Nesuamon, IV 541; Senbef, IV 918.
—of Ptah. Khamwese, III 557; Takelot, IV 781; Pediese, IV 781; Takelot, IV 774; Harsiese, IV 779; Tefnakhte, IV 830.

w ᶜ b-PRIEST, II 97 bis, 283; III 31, 78, 160; IV 250, 958D, F, 1018; regulations of, IV 250.
—of Amon, Beknekhonsu, III 565; IV 988H.
—of Heliopolis, IV 250.
—of Siut, I 538, 563, 564; endowment of, I 538; Hepzefi, I 552.
—Great *w ᶜ b*-priest of Amon, Harsiese, IV 753.

wtb-PRIEST (or *wḏb;* perhaps better *šm ꜣ;* see Schaefer, Mysterien, Sethe, *Untersuchungen* IV, 63); Ikhernofret, I 668.

PRIESTHOOD, later, I 24.

PRIESTHOOD OF HATHOR, I 216.

PRIEST-KINGS, I 22.

PRINCE, II 185, 993, 1006; III 174, 287, 290, 291, 322, 325, 422, 466, 471, 613; IV 71, 77, 92, 147, 208, 238, 343, 360, 397, 402, 460, 494, 497, 583, 818, 819, 821, 822, 830, 868, 873, 881; august office of, II 669; supplies for, furnished by the herald, II 767; Sekhemkere, I 54; Tefibi, I 394; Mentuhotep, I 533; Kheti, I 637 n. a; Senmut, II 350; Harmhab, III 13, 27; Amenhirunamef, III 467, 471; Paynozem II, IV 668.
ḥ ꜣ ty-ᶜ, only from Nubian time on (in Empire "mayor," *q. v.*, and before Empire, "count," *q. v.*): Pethenef, IV 815, 878; Pemou, IV 815, 878; Zeamonefonekh, IV 878; Akenesh, IV 878; Nektharneshenu, IV 878; Hurabes, IV 878; Zedkhiyu, IV 878; Pebes, IV 878; Ahmose-Si-Neit, IV 1000 n. a.
—of Esneh: Pahri, II n. 3b.
—of the greatest of companions: Harmhab, III 20.
—of the king: confidant of, *q. v.*
—of the palace, Zau, I 381.
—of Thebes, Nesuptah, IV 904; Mentemhet, IV 904, 948.

CROWN PRINCE, see King's eldest son.

HEREDITARY PRINCE (*rp ᶜ -ty*), III 102, 124; IV 110, 121, 124 n. b, 304; 347; administration of law executed by, III 25; Zau, I 348; Khui, I 349; Meru, I 370; Tefibi, I 391, 395; Kheti I, I 391; Kheti II, I 391; Intef, I 419, 420; Amenemhet, I 438, 442, 445; Khnumhotep I, I 464, 625, 626; Intef, I 467; Putoker, I 466 n. c; Sinuhe, I 490; Mentuhotep, I 512; Amenemhet I 518; Crown Prince Ameni, I 520; Crown Prince Sesostris (II), I 521; Mentuhotep, I 531, 532; Hepzefi, I 537, 538, 539; Simontu, I 596; Khentkhetwer, I 605; Nehri, I 628; Khnumhotep II, I 622, 624, 631, 639; Nakht II, I 632; Ikhernofret, I 664; Sebek-khu-Zaa, I 683; Sehetepibre, I 745; Ahmose-Pen-Nekhbet, II 20; Neferperet, II 28; Ineni, II 43; Keres II 52; Nehsi, II 290; Senmut, II 350, 354, 362, 366; Thutiy, II 371; Puemre, II 383, 385; Hapuseneb, II 389; Nehi, II 652; Rekhmire, II 713, 717, 729, 748, 754, 757; Intef, II 763, 767, 775; Minhotep, II 800; Khamhet, II 872; Amenhotep, II 912, 923, 924, 925; Ramose, II 936, 937 n. a; Mai, II 997, 1002, Huy, II 1036; Amenhotep, II 1040; Harmhab, III 8, 16 bis, 20, 25, 27; Ramses (II), III 132, 267; Amenhirunamef, III 474, 477; Amonhirkhepeshef, III 482; Seti, III 542; Peramses, III 542; Khay, III 556, 560; Beknekhonsu, III 563, 568; Roy, III 623; Seti (II), III 646 n. i; Ramses (III), IV 400; Amenhotep, IV 495; Hrihor, IV 612; Sheshonk, IV 774; Beknenef, IV 830; Pediese, IV 868, 874, 875, 879; Senbef, IV 918; Pekrur, IV 932, Uzahor, IV 980; Neferibre-nofer, IV 981; Nesuhor, IV 995; Pefnefdineit, IV 1017.

HEREDITARY PRINCESS: Beket, I 628; Ahmose-Nefretiri, II 34; Hatshepsut, II 360; Nefernefruaton-Nofretete, II 959; Enekhnesneferibre, IV 988 I.

PRINCESS OF KHETA: Petkhep, III 391.
—of Kush, II 1035.

PRIVY COUNCILOR, I 505; Ptahshepses, I 259; Harkhuf, I 332, 336; Harmhab, III 16, 20.
—of the right hand: Senmut, II 358.
—of the treasurer of god: Idi, I 466 n. c.

PROPHETS (a priestly office), I 165, 217, 349; III 77, 103, 160; IV 360, 466, 906, 908, 958D, F; in charge of the sacred writings, II 353.
—of the temples, acting as judges, III 65.
—regulation of, II 754.

Prophets—
—of Abydos, I 535, 746.
—of the house of King Amenhotep: Pe ͨ enkhew, IV 512.
—of Amon, IV 753, 988H, J; Prince Thutmose (III), II 138; Senmut, II 351; Intef, II 775; Nesuamon, IV 531; Enkhofnamon, IV 665, 689; Khamwese, IV 795; Nesuptah, IV 904.
—of Anubis: Mentuhotep, I 533.
—of the gods of Buto, Zaü, I 348.
—of dues: Harhotep, II 110.
—of Harkefti: Mentuhotep, I 533.
—of Harsaphes: IV 747.
—of Hathor of Diospolis Parva: Wayeheset, IV 726.
—of Horus: Mentuhotep, I 533.
—of Horus of Letopolis: Pediharsomtous, IV 878.
—of Horus of the South, lord of Perzoz: Wayeheset, IV 726.
—of Horus, Amenhotep, chief of, II 912.
—of Isis: Ahmose-Si-Neit, IV 1000.
—of Khnum, IV 150.
—of "Khonsu-the-Plan-Maker-in Thebes": Khonsuhetneterneb, III 432.
—of Mat: Mentuhotep, I 531, 533; Senmut, II 352; Ramose, II 936; Khay, III 556.
—of Min-Harsiese: Usermare-Nakht, IV 465.
—of Montu: Nesupehernemut, IV 660; Hetamenthenofer, IV 660.
—of Neit: Harpeson, IV 787, 792; Tefnakhte, IV 830.
—of Ptah, III 413; Sabu-Ibebi, I 284; Senbef, IV 918.
—of Sebek of Peronekh: Paynehsi, IV 547.
—of Sokar: Sabu-Ibebi, I 284; Sabu-Thety, I 288.
—of Soped: Ahmose, IV 1014.
—of Sutekh, lord of Oasis: Wayheset, IV 726; Nesubast, IV 726.

CHIEF PROPHET, IV 908.
—in Heracleopolis: Namlot, IV 787, 792; Uzptahenkhof, IV 787, 792; Henptah, IV 787, 792; Harpeson, IV 787, 792; Henptah, IV 787, 792.
—of Horus, lord of Sebi: Harmhab, III 20.

CHIEFS: of the prophets, IV 466.
—of Thebes: Nesuptah, IV 950.
—of North and South: Ramose, II 936.
—in Hermopolis: Thutiy, II 371.
—in temple of Min, at Panopolis: Nebwawi, II 181.
—of Montu of Hermonthis: Senmut, II 352.
—First prophet of Amon (=high-priest of Amon): Meriptah, II 931; Beknekhonsu, III 565 n. c; Roy, III 623 n. e; Ramses-nakht, IV 466; Amenemopet, IV 480.
—Second prophet of Amon, Enen, II 931; Beknekhonsu, III 565; Roy, III 623.
—of dues: Yuf, II 112.
—Third prophet of Amon: Amenemhet, II 931; Beknekhonsu, III 565; Roy, III 623; Zeptahefonekh, IV 699; Pediamennebnesttowe, IV 953.
—of Khonsu: Merthoth, IV 665, 691; Efnamon, IV 492.
—Fourth prophet of Amon: Simut, II 931; Nesupehernemut, IV 660; Hetamenthenofer, IV 660; Mentemhet, IV 904, 949, 951.

INFERIOR PROPHET: Ini, I 373; Idi, I 466 n. c.
—of the pyramid-city: Uni, I 307.

MORTUARY PROPHET, II 908; III 271.

SUPERIOR PROPHET, I 312, 349; III 484; a procession due to, I 569; highest in rank in the temple, I 354, 550; Intef, I 420; Putoker, I 466 n. c; Hepzefi, I 538–39, 544, 549, 554, 559, 568, 572, 576, 582, 589; Thutnakht, I 689.
—of all gods: Seti, III 542.
—of Hathor: Nekonekh, I 216.
—of Min: Intef, I 467; Putoker, I 466 n. c.
—of Upwawet, lord of Siut, I 550, 551; Tefibi, I 395; Kheti I, I 395; Kheti II, I 395, 426; Hepzefi, I 568.

PROPHETESS OF HATHOR (in Heracleopolis): Ireteru, IV 792.

Q

QUEEN: see King's wife, Great king's wife; table-scribe of, III 58.

TITLES OF:
—Very favored: Enekhnes-Merire I, I 345; Enekhnes-Merire II, I 346.
—Very amiable: Enekhnes-Merire I, I 345; Enekhnes-Merire II, I 346.
—Queen of the land: see Index I.

QUEEN-MOTHER, IV 895; Tiy, II 1016.

R

RECEIVER OF INCOME: rank of, II 675.

RECORDER OF THE DISTRICT, II 717, 719, 720, 724, 727, 728, 736, 737, 738, 741, 745.
—of district officials, II 717, 729.
—of the troops: Harmhab, III 20.

REGISTRAR OF GRAIN, I 598.

REVERED: Nenekhsekhmet, I 240; Re-am, I 281; Harkhuf, I 336; Meri, I 508; Imsu, I 529; Simontu, I 598.
—by the god: Zau, I 348.
—by the great god, Henutsen, I 185; Pepi-nakht, I 356; Ikudidi, I 526.
—by Hathor: Hezethekenu, I 216; Ikhnoubet, I 230.
—by Ptah: Ptahshepses, I 262; Sabu-Ibebi, I 285.
—by Osiris: Uni, I 293, 324.

RITUAL PRIEST: see Priest.

RULER, an unprecise rendering of the unprecise *ḥḳ*ꜣ, which signifies, ruler, prince, nomarch, I 400 n. a; III 175; IV 818 *et passim;* Methen, I 174.
—in the Cerastes-Mountain: Henku, I 281.
—of fields: Methen, I 174.
—of Southern Perked: Methen I, 172, 174.
—of towns, IV 398.
—of the "New Towns": Nehri, I 628.
—of rulers: Kheti I, I 400.
—heir of a ruler: I 400.
—palace ruler: Methen I, 172, 174.

S

SANDAL-BEARER, Uni, I 320 bis.

SATISFYING THE KING: Intef, I 420 *et passim.*

SCRIBE: I 5; II 385, 766; IV 581, 784.

SCRIBES, II 53, 717, 986; IV 52, 466, 652, 671, 676, 958G; Anubisemonekh, I 171; Ptah, I 182; Zaty, I 343; —khet, I 343; Imsu, I 529; Thutiy, II 275; Ineni, II 343; Thutiy, II 371; Intef, II 767; Hatey, II 932; Merire, II 1043; Hui, III 210; Amenhirkhepeshef, III 350; Neferhor, III 643; May, IV 423; Amennakht, IV 526; Nesupekeshuti, IV 665.
—of the army, II 925; IV 466.
—of the army-lists: Sule, IV 466.
—of the deputy of the army: Ramsesnakht, IV 466.
—of the archives: Neferhor, III 643; Piyay, III 644; Peremhab, IV 423; Mai, IV 426, 452.
—of computation: Intef, II 763.
of the crown-possessions: Hori, IV 465.
—of the district, II 719, 723, 725, 726, 727, 729, 731, 738, 740, 744; IV 529.
—of the domain: Penno, IV 482.
—of the harem: Simontu, I 598; Pere, IV 450.
—of the great harem: Simontu, I 598; Pendua, IV 430.
—of the hieroglyphs, I 755.
—of the king's records: Henhathor, I 218, 221, 225; Khenu, I 299; Seti (II), III 647.
—of rolls of Pharaoh, IV 498.
—of the marine: Mereri, I 390.
—of the mayor, II 721; IV 529.
—of the necropolis, IV 530; Horishere, IV 526, 529; Pebes, IV 526, 529.
—of the Theban Necropolis: Buteham-on, IV 640.
—of the pryamid-phyle: Pepi-nakht, I 356.
—of the recorder, II 719, 720, 727, 729, 736, 737, 738, 741, 745.
—of recruits: Thanem, II 820; Harmhab, III 17.
—of the sacred book: performed the "stretching of the cord" at foundation ceremonies, I 506.
—of the house of Sacred Writings, IV 460; Messui, IV 445; Shedmezer, IV 445; Ramses-eshehab, IV 465.
—of the temple: eighth in rank in the temple, I 550; Neferhotepur, I 776; Perehotep, IV 281; Hori, IV 281; Zosersukhonsu, IV 640; Penamon, IV 647.
—of the altar: ninth in rank in the temple, I 550.
—of the cattle of Amon, IV 212.
—of the House of Amon, III 624; IV 531; Merithoth, IV 665.
—of the Sacred Treasury of Amon: Siamon, I 777.
—of the overseer of the treasury: Paynozem, IV 527.
—of the assistant treasurer: Yuf, II 114.
—of the vizier, II 675, 712; Seneb, I 783; Penebik, IV 512, 522; Nesupekeshuti, IV 668.
—of the White House: Peluka, IV 439; Penamon, IV 647.
—of the overseer of the White House of Pharaoh, IV 511.

CHIEF SCRIBE: Senezem, I 343; Thutmose, IV 281.

Chief Scribe—
—of the king's writings: Senezemib, I 271, 273.
—of the king, III 291.
—of the provision magazine: Methen, I 172.
—of the vizier, II 670; IV 511.
—of the overseer of the White House: Paynofer, IV 512, 522.

FIELD SCRIBE, II 717.
—of the waters of Abydos, I 529.
—of Horus of Edfu: Denereg, II 114.

INFERIOR SCRIBE: Hotep, I 187; Sesi, I 299.

KING'S-SCRIBE: Nonekhsesi, I 230; Amenhotep, II 915; III 50, 102, 332; IV 121, 124 n. b, 491; Simontu, I 596, 598 bis; Thaneni, II 820; Mermose, II 855; Khamhet, II 872; Amenhotep, II 914, 924, 925; Khampet, II 929, 930, 931; Eye, II 989, 992; Ahmose, II 1004; Amenhotep, II 1038, 1040; Ramose, II 1043; Harmhab, III 8, 16, 17; Meya, III 32B; Thutemhab, III 437; Amenhirunamef, III 467, 471, 477; Peramses, III 542; Seti, III 542; Piyay, III 644; Seti (II), III 647; Setemhab, IV 20; Pakauti, IV 485; Hori, IV 485; Neferkere-em-Per-Amon, IV 495, 522; Nesuamon, IV 511, 513, 523, 526, 528, 531, 533, 540; Pemeriamon, IV 546; Bek, IV 668.
—of the army, II 923; Paynehsi, IV 597.
—of the Hittite king, III 337

SACRED SCRIBE, III 437; IV 958D, 988H.

SEAL-SCRIBE, Amenemhet-Ameny, II 686 n. d.

SUPERIOR KING'S-SCRIBE: Amenhotep II 916;
—Table scribe: Ani, II 977.
—of harem, III 58.
—of queen, III 58.

SEALER OF CONTRACTS IN THE HOUSE OF AMON: Ineni, II 43.

SEER, THE GREAT: see Great seer.

SEM-PRIEST: see Priest.

SERVANT: royal, I 307; Thethi, I 423D.
—of the royal harem of the queen: Sinuhe, I 490.
—of Neit: Khentemsemeti, I 609.
—of the royal toilet, Khentemsemeti, I 609.
—real servant, Meri, I 508; Khentemsemeti, I 608.

SHADE-BEARERS, II 1014; III 40; see also Sunshade-bearers.

SHEIK OF THE HIGHLANDS: Ibshe, I 620 n. d.
—of the Red Land, I 423 D, 429.
—of Upper Tenu, I 494.
—of villages, II 692, 699, 701, 768.
—Tribute from, II 708.

SISTRUM-BEARER OF HARSAPHES, chief of, *q. v.*

SMALL LORD, I 458, 459.

SMITER OF ALL COUNTRIES: Sahure, I 236, 250, 267.

SON OF RE (fifth title of the Pharaoh in his fivefold titulary; it was introduced at the close of the Fifth Dynasty on the triumph of the Heliopolitan priests of Re, the sun-god), e. g., II 20 *et passim;* origin of title of, II 187.
—"Son of Re" put within the cartouche, I 423H, n. b.

SON OF A RULER: Kheti I, I 400, 401, 402.
—of a daughter of a ruler: Kheti I, I 400.

STANDARD-BEARER, III 208; IV 70; Pe'aoke, II 839; Kara, IV 423, 426.
—of the infantry, Hori, IV 423, 426, 453.
—of the marines: Hori, IV 531.

STEWARD, III 484; IV 491; Henu, I 428; Ikudidi, I 526; Thutiy, II 275; Khampet, II 929, 930; Sebeknakht, II 931; Ramose, II 1043; Ramses-nakht, III 633; Penithowe, IV 338; Ini, IV 546.
—Collecting taxes, III 55.
—in charge of herds, IV 224.
—of Amon: Semut, II 290, 350, 352, 353, 354, 357, 366; Piyay, III 644; Pay, IV 224.
—of the court: Pemeriamon, IV 546.
—in Egypt: Senekh, I 455.
—of estates of Pharaoh, II 871; Ahmose, II 1004.
—of Horus: Penno, IV 474.
—of the House [of Shadow-of Re]: Huy, II 1014.
—of the king's daughter: Amenhotep, II 919.
—of the king's wife: Nibamon, II 779.
—of the palace: Nekonekh, I 216, 217, 224.
—of the storehouse of the leader of works: Khui, I 675.

Steward—
—of the southern city (=Thebes): Thutmose, III 32C.

CHIEF STEWARD, II 706. Senmut, II 351, 361; Intef, II 768; Harmhab, III 20; Pefnefdineit, IV 1017, 1025.
—of Amon, Senmut, II 354, 356.
—of the divine consort: Ibe, IV 958B, G.
—of the king: Senmut, II 354, 357.
—of the king's mother: Keres, II 52.
—of the princess: Senmut, II 362.

STOREROOM KEEPER: Yatu, I 723.
—of the palace, Kheye, I 750.

STRETCHING THE MEASURING CORD, I 506; Amenemhet, I 445.

STRONG OF BOW, Kheti II, I 410.

STRONG-VOICED: administrative position, having to do with lands, Methen, I 172.

SUBJECT OF THE KING: Thethi, I 423D.

SUBORDINATE OF THE KING, Thethi: I 423D.

SUNSHADE-BEARERS, IV 56, 70, 72, 76, 109, 110, 123, 124, 405 n. g; see also Shade-bearers.

SUPERIOR OF SUPERIORS: Senmut, II 368.

SUPERINTENDENT OF GRANARY, II 925.
—of the royal domain: Neferhotep, III 70.

SUPERVISOR, Uni, I 294.
—of everything of the whole land, Amenemhet, I 438.
—of fields in Thinite nome: Imsu, I 529.
—District supervisor, II 708.

T

TEACHER: see Great Father.

TOWN-RULERS, II 717, 721, 723, 729.

TREASURER, II 708; Sebekdidi, I 720; Sebekhotep, I 723.
—of the god: Hepi, I 342; Burded, I 351, 353; Thethi, I 361; Khui, I 361; Zaty-Kenofer, I 389; Khnumhotep, I 618; Zezemonekh, I 186; Theshen, I 186; Ikhi, I 298, 299, 301; Ihu, I 298, 299; Harkhuf, I 336; Khenemsu, I 713, 716; Amenemhet, I 731; Harure, I 735, 736; privy councilor of, *q. v.*
—Two treasurers, I 212.
—of the palace, III 484.
—of Pharaoh, I 447; Amenhotep, IV 495.
—Assistant treasurer, II 114; Eti, I 459; Meri, I 508; Sihathor, I 603; of the chief treasurer: Sebekdidi, I 720; Sebekhotep, I 723.
—Chief treasurer, I 646; III 484; Thethi, I 423C; Kheti II, I 426; Henu, I 428; Mentuhotep, I 532, 533; Beket, I 637; Ikhernofret, I 664, 672; Neferperet, II 28; Khenemsu, I 713, 716; Ptahwer, I 728; Neferperet II 28; Nehsi, II 290; Ray, II 450 n. a; Meriptah, II 929, 931; Ramses-Khenenter-Bay, III 647; Nesupekeshuti, IV 689; of the Theban necropolis: Merithoth, IV 665; daily reporting to the Pharaoh II 678; to the vizier, II 679; ranks of, II 675, 678; in charge of the gold-house, II 706.
—Deputy of the chief treasurer: Ameniseneb, I 716; Sionouris, I 785; see also under Official.

TUTOR, royal: Senmut, II 364; Neferibre-nofer, IV 981; see also Great Father.

V

VICEROY OF KUSH, I 18; residence of, II 54, 62; earliest known, II 61; appointment of earliest known, II 64; territory of, extending from Nekhen to Napata, II 1022, 1025; investiture of, II 1020; two of them holding office at the same time, II 1027, 1028; see also King's son, and King's son of Kush.

VIZIER, I 307; II 925; III 69, 324, 333, 470, 484; IV 76, 110, 147, 150, 511, 517, 522, 524, 527, 543, 547, 777, 873; Senezemib, I 271, 273; Khety, II 689 n. d; Zau, I 347, 348; Amenemhet, I 438, 442, 445; Crown Prince Sesostris (II), I 521; Mentuhotep, I 531; Enkhu, I 783; Hapuzeneb, II 388, 389; Woser, II 663, 665; Rekhmire, I 20; II 663, 665, 666, 748, 754; Hapu, II 665; Amenhotep, II 923; Ramose, II 936, 937 n. c, 940; Seti, III 542; Peramses, III 542; Khay, III 556, 559, 560; Ta, IV 414; Khamwese, IV 511, 513, 522, 523, 531, 532, 540, 543; Nibmare-nakht, IV 523, 535, 546; Hrihor, IV 593; Paynozem (I), IV 634; Paynozem (II), IV 668.
—Archives of, IV 534; impartiality of, II 668.
—Departments in office of: judiciary, II 675, 681, 685–86, 688–91, 700, 704, 705; treasury, II 676, 680, 706, 708; war, army, II 593–95, 702; war, navy, II 687, 710; interior, II 677, 687,

697, 707; agriculture, II 698, 699; general executive, II 692, 701,-703; advisory, II 678, 679, 682, 684, 696, 709, 711.
Duties of, II 666, 670, 671–711; reporting daily to Pharaoh, II 678; to the chief treasurer, II 679; taking counsel from Pharaoh, II 678, 694, 697; receiving daily report from the chief treasurer, II 679; mustering of king's body-guard, II 693; garrisons for residence city, II 694; garrison for court, II 694; gives regulations for the council of the army, II 695; in charge of herds, IV 224; judgments reported to, II 681; "hears" criminal cases, II 683; decides real-estate cases, II 686, 689–91; keeps registers of wills and gifts, II 688–89; appointments by, II 697, 698, 699, 700, 703, 705.
—Reports to: from the treasury, II 676, 679; fortresses, II 676, 702; the king's house, II 676; the court, II 676; overseers, II 677; district officials, II 687, 708; mayors, II 692, 708; village sheiks, II 692, 708; great council, II 706; navy officers, II 710; doorkeeper of judgment hall, II 711; concerning rising of Sirius, II 709; concerning high Nile, II 709.
—Hall of, II 666, 681, 682, 688 n. d, 695, 696, 712, 713, 717, 729; importance of, II 666; "hearing" in, II 670; arrangement of the sitting in, II 675, 712.
—Chief scribe of, II 670; scribes of, II 675, 712; records of, II 684; messenger of, II 675, 676, 680, 685.
—Vizier: of the South, IV 224.
—Deposition of vizier, IV 361.

VOTRESS: of the goddess, III 391.
—of Amon-Re, IV 511; see also Divine votress.

W

WARRIOR OF THE RULER: Ahmose, son of Ebana, II 39.

WATCHMAN, III 616; IV 266.
—of the temple of Amon: Paykamen, IV 548; Karu, IV 550; Nofer, IV 551.

WEARER OF THE ROYAL SEAL, I 312, 505; III 264; Harkhuf, I 326, 332, 336; Zau, I 348; Pepi-nakht, I 356; Sebni, I 364; Mekhu, I 370; Ibi, I 377; Zau, I 381; Tefibi, I 391, 395; Kheti I, I 391; Kheti II, I 391, 426; Henu, I 428 bis; Eti, I 459; Khnumhotep I, I 464; Intef, I 467; Idi, I 466 n. c; Sinuhe, I 490; Mentuhotep, I 512; Amenemhet, I 519; Mentuhotep, I 531, 533; Simontu, I 596; Khentkhetwer, I 605; Ikhernofret, I 664; Sehetepibre, I 745; Renseneb, I 752; Minemhet, I 776; Neferhotepur, I 776; Ahmose Pen-Nekhbet, II 20; Neferperet, II 28; Keres, II 52; Thure, II 170 n. c (?); Nehsi, II 290; Senmut, II 350, 351, 361; Thutiy, II 371; Puemre, II 385; Nehi, II 652; Rekhmire, II 713; Intef, II 763, 767; Ramose, II 936; Mai, II 997, 1002; Harmhab, III 16, 20; Ramses-Khementer-Bay, III 647; Neferibre-nofer, IV 981; Nesuhor, IV 995; Ahmose-Si-Neit, IV 1000; duty of, III 264, 287.

WORSHIPERS OF HORUS, I 78 n. a.

INDEX VI

GEOGRAPHICAL

A

ʿnt-district of, II 744; scribe of, II 744; products of, II 744.

ABD EL-KURNA: (hill of Western Thebes), mortuary temple of Seti I, see Index II.
—Temple inscription: by Ramses II, III 488 n. b.
—Tomb inscription: by Ineni, II 43–46, 99–108, 115–18, 340–43, 648; Puemre II 383–87; Rekhmire, II 666–762; Menkheperreseneb, II 773–76; Amenken, II 801–2; Khamhet, II 819, 871–72; Hatey, II 932; Ramose, II 936–47.
—Tombs of: Ineni, II 43 n. c; Puemre, II 382 n. c; Amenken, II 801 n. d; Khamhet, II 819, 872; Hatey, II 932; Rekhmire, II 663 n. d; Menkheperreseneb, II 772 n. a; Ramose, II 936 n. b; Neferhotep, III 68 n. c.

ABU SIMBEL: great temple of Ramses II, III 449, 495.
—Small temple of Ramses II, III 500, 501.
—Stela of Ramses II, III 392, 394–414; 415–24; cf. IV 132–35.
—Temple inscription by Ramses II, III 449–57, 496–99, 500–1; Rekhpeh tuf, III 642.

ABUKIR, IV 405 n. g.

ABUSIR: city of Sun-barques at, I 167, n. a, 251; tomb of Weshptah, I 242 n. a; of Hotephiryakhet, I 251; temple of Nuserre, I 252 n. a, 423H n. a.

ABYDOS: city of Thinite nome I 349, 396 nn. d, h, 529; II 692; III 281; IV 485, 675, 676, 678, 679, 1019, 1023.
—Nome of, IV 1020; fields of, IV 1021; desert of, IV 1023; district of, II 738; scribe of, II 738; tower in, III 260; IV 357; "Eternity of the Kingdom," a district south of, IV 681; canal of, I 763; III 261.
—Bends (=promontories) of: "Lord of offerings," I 684; "Mistress of Life," I 684; region of eternity, III 436.
—Cemetery of: see Tazoser.
—Pool of, IV 681.
—Palace of, IV 1019; palace of Thutmose IV in, II 839; royal residence in, of Sesostris III, I 665 n. b; of Ramses III, IV 357.
—Fortress of, III 82 n. b.
—Temples of: see Index II.
—Feasts of: monthly, I 663 n. b; half-monthly, I 665 n. b; beginning of seasons, I 668; great feast of Osiris, I 669.
—Mortuary chapel of Tetisheri, II 36.
—Tombs of, III 266; tomb of Tetisheri, II 36.
—Count of, IV 1024; mayor of, III 82 n. b.
—Priestly phyle of, I 782; prophets of, contracts for remuneration of the, I 536, 746, 765.
—Officials of: field scribe of the waters of, I 529; recorder of, II 738; scribe of the recorder of, II 738; kenbeti of, II 738.
—Gods of: see Index I under Osiris, Anubis, Upwawet, Wennofer, First of the Westerners.
—Statues for gods of, II 95.
—Products of, II 738.
—Temple inscriptions: by Seti I, III 227–43; Ramses II, III 251–81; 485–86.
—Inscription on Mastaba-tomb of Uni, I 271 n. a; tomb of Ikudidi, I 524–28; memorial tablet of Ikhernofret, I 661 n. d.
—Stelæ of Enekhnes-Merire, I 344 n. a; Ikudidi, I 524 n. d; Mentuhotep, I 530 n. c; Sihathor, I 599 n. e; Khentemsemeti, I 609 n. a; Sisatet, I 671 n. e, 673; Sebek-khu, I 676 n. c; Sehetepibre, I 743 n. c; Neferhotep, I 753 n. a, 766 n. b; Ameniseneb, I 781 n. a, 786 n. i; Ahmose I, II 33 n. f. Harmini, II 47 n. c; Thutmose I, II 90 n. g; Nebwawi, II 184 n. c; Neferhet, II 839 n. d; Hori, III 82 n. b; Ramses IV, IV 469–71; Hori, IV 484–85; Sheshonk, IV 669 n. d.

ADAMAH: city in Naphtali, IV 714 n. b.

ADDAR: city in Judah, conquered by Sheshonk I, IV 716.

ADEL: city in Palestine, IV 712 n. c.

ADORAIM: city in Judah, conquered by Sheshonk I, IV 712 n. f.

AJALON: city of Israel, in Dan, conquered by Sheshonk I, IV 712.

AKHETATON, II 949, 957, 958, 1000; founded by Ikhnaton, II 960; deeded to Aton, II 954, 966; made the capital, 955.
—Boundaries of, II 961–64, 966-69;
—Landmarks (=stelæ) of, II 949–72; area of, II 965.
—Mountains of, II 962, 963, 964, 965, 966, 969, 971, 972, 994, 1003, 1013; highland of, II 1008.
—Pavilion in, II 960; houses of, II 978; gardens of, II 978; palaces of, II 978; temples of, II 978; storehouse of, II 1015; tombs of, II 977–1018.

AKHMIM: called district of the city of Min, II 740; in the Panopolite nome, I 529; location of, I 423 n. a, 529.
—Officials of: nomarch, Intefyoker, I 423 n. a; scribe of, II 740.
—Products of, II 740.

AKITA: Nubian country, written Akati, IV 477; gold in, III 286; lacking in water, III 286, 289; road to, III 291; well dug for, III 292.

AKKO: captured by Seti I, III 114.

ALABASTRONPOLIS, IV 818 n. g; Harmhab, nomarch of, III 20 n. c; Horus, lord of, III 24, 27.

ALASA: land of, IV 591; captured by Seti I, III 114; invaded by the Northerners of the Isles, IV 64; Heteb, queen of, IV 591; crews of, IV 591.

ALEPPO, I 3; land of, III 319, 320, 321, 322; ally of Kheta, III 312; located north of Tunip, III 319; under the Hittites, III 386; Wan, west of, II 582; prisoners from, II 798A; Rebeyer, king of, III 337; Sutekh, god of, III 386.

AMÂDA: stela of Amenhotep II, II 791 n. f; temple of, III 606 n. a.

AMOR, CITY OF, IV 117; citadel of, IV 117; fortress of, IV 117; banner of, IV 117.

AMOR, LAND OF: Kadesh in, III 141, 310, 340; Deper in, III 356; shore of, III 310; captives of, IV 39, 129; chief of IV 39, 117, 127, 129; seed of, IV 39; the Northerners of the Isles camp in, IV 64.

ANDROPOLIS, IV 1004,

ANTIOCH, II 582 n. c.

ANUBIS: nome of (XVII), ruled by Methen, I 170, 173.

APHRODITOPOLIS: nome of, II 327; IV 818 n. h, 948; two mountains of, III 510; northern frontier of the South in time of Uni, I 311, 320; also in time of Tefibi, I 396 n. h; in time of Intef I, I 423; just north of the Thinite nome, I 423 n. a; across the river from Akhmim, I 423 n. a; made the door of the North by Intef I, I 423; serpent and feather signs of nome of, I 423 n. a.
—Gods of: Zebui, lord of, IV 366; temple of, IV 366; Hathor, temple of, IV 366.

APOLLINOPOLIS MAGNA: nome (II) of Upper Egypt, temple of Horus of Nubia, built by Sesostris I, I 500.

ARAINA: city of or near Naharin, battle at, II 496, 498.

ARAM: district of, III 634.

ARANAMI: city on east side of Orontes, south of Kadesh, III 310.

ARASA: field of, in Wawat, IV 482.

AREK: Nubian region, captured by Amenhotep III, II 845 n. f.

ARKO: island of (near third cataract), inscription of Thutmose I, II 67 n. a.

ARRAPACHITIS: country of, II 512; IV 131; tribute of, II 512.

ARSINOE: temple inscription of Amenemhet III, II 233.

ARUNA (city south of Megiddo), II 421, 425, 426, 427; road of, II 422; conquered by Sheshonk I, IV 713.

ARVAD: land of, III 306; ally of Kheta, III 309, 312; a city of Zahi, II 461; captured by Thutmose III, II 461; by Ramses II, III 306, 366; invaded by the Northerners of the Isles, IV 64.
—Products of: grain, II 461, 465; pleasant trees, II 461; gardens, II 461; fruit, II 461; wines, II 461; winepresses, II 461; groves of, II 465.

ASIA, I 728; marshes of, II 321; eastern boundary of Egypt, II 321; strongholds of, IV 141; tribute from, II 385.

ASIA, ends of: tribute from, II 386.

ASIA MINOR, I 25.
ASIATICS, I 620 n. d, 680; II 296, 321, 412, 440, 657, 658, 837, 916; III 7, 9, 10, 12, 84, 118, 139, 141, 144, 151, 165, 457, 479, 484, 486, 490; IV 62, 72, 78, 80, 103, 104, 105, 119, 355, 356, 720, 721, 840, 994.
—in Avaris, II 4, 14, 303; Sharuhen, II 416; Yeraza, II 416; Megiddo, II 441; Negeb, II 580; Wan, II 582; Tikhsi, II 587; Orontes region, II 784; Niy, II 786; Retenu, II 658; IV 219; Kharu, III 101; Ikathi, II 787; of the army of Mitanni, IV 722.
—Campaigns against: by Sahure, I 236; Nuserre, I 250; Isesi, I 267; Pepinakht, I 360 bis; Mentuhotep I, I 423H; Amenemhet I, I 465; Sesostris III, I 681 bis, 707; Ahmose, II 30; Thutmose I, II 101; Harmhab, III 20; Ramses II, III 453, 490; Ramses III, IV 119, 122.
—Chiefs of, III 490; slaves of, for temple of Amon, II 555.
Bringing eye-paint, I 620 n. d; tribute from, II 120; III 453.
—Their abodes destroyed, III 11; famine of, III 11; asking to live in Egypt, III 11; revolt amongst, II 416.
ASKALON: city of, III 355; rebellion of, III 355; captured by Ramses II, III 355; by Merneptah, III 617.
ASSASÎF (Thebes), cliff-tomb of Neferhotep, III 68 n. c.
—Tomb inscription, by Neferhotep, III 70–72.
ASSIUT (see Siut), I 398, 401 n. a.
ASSUAN: field of dodekaschoinos, IV 146.
—Granite quarry of, I 42; II 304, 876.
—Rock inscriptions: by Hapu, I 614–16; Sesostris III, I 653; family of Neferhotep, I 753 n. b; Thutmose I, II 77; Thutmose II, II 119 n. c; Senmut, II 359; Amenhotep III, II 844 n. b; officer of Amenhotep III, II 876; Bek, II 973–76; Seti I, III 202; Ramses II, III 478 n. a.
—Tomb inscription of Harkhuf, I 325, 336.
—Tomb of Harkhuf, I 325.
—Trading post on the Nubian frontier, I 493 n. i.
—See also Suan.
ASSUR: tribute from, II 445, 446, 449; chief of, II 446, 449; captured by Ramses II, III 366 n. c.
—Products of: lapis lazuli, II 446; vessels of *ḥrtt*-stone in colors, II 446; horses, II 449; wagons, II 449; *m-ḫ*ʾ*-w*-skins, II 449; *nḥb*-wood, II 449; kanek wood, II 449; carob wood, II 449; olive wood, II 449; meru wood, II 449; nebi wood, II 449.
ATFIH, IV 818 n. h.
ATHRIBIS: nome of, IV 873; reached by ships from Heliopolis, IV 873; harbor of, IV 873; treasury of, IV 874.
—Gods of: Horus, IV 360, 874, 956; Khuyet, goddess, IV 874.
—Temple of Horus in, IV 360, 956; called Khenti-khet, IV 360, 369, 874.
—Stela of Merneptah, III 596–601.
—Vizier deposed in, IV 361; Amenhotep, lord of, II 912.
ATIKA: copper mines of, IV 408; messengers sent to, IV 408; reached both by land and sea, IV 408.
AUTOMOLOI, IV 989.
AVARIS, II 4, 296; siege of, II 4, 8, 9, 11 n. d; capture of, II 12; of the Northland, II 303.
AYAN, IV 818; see also Tayan.
AYAN: limestone of, I 534, 635, 740; II 27, 44, 103, 302, 339, 345 n. c bis, 380, 390, 603, 604, 799, 800, 875; III 240, 525; IV 7, 216, 355, 356, 358, 970, 979, 982.
—Eper of foreigners of, IV 466. See also Troja and Turra.
—Well in, built by Ramess III, IV 406; foundation of, IV 406; battlements of, IV 406.

B

BA, locality in Hauran: Mut, mistress of, IV 716 n. b.
BAB EL-MANDEB, IV 407 n. c.
BABYLON, III 479; lapis lazuli of, II 446, 484.
BABYLONIA: ancient reckoning of years in, I 81.
BACK-LANDS, II 797.
"BALANCES OF THE TWO LANDS," IV 864; meaning of, IV 864 n. a.
BARBARIANS (*ḫ*ʾ*s.tyw*), I 532; II 303, 427; IV 106; slain by Snefru, I 169; by Uni, I 315.
—Four (Nubian tribes) slain by Sesostris I, I 519; by Thutmose III, II 413.
"BARQUE OF THE SYCAMORE": an estate in the district of Thebu, IV 597.

"BEAUTIFUL-IS-KHAFRE": city in nome of the Cerastes Mountain, I 199.

"BEAUTIFUL REGION," a district northwest of Thebes, IV 795.

BEDWIN, III 10; IV 246; lands of, IV 217.
—Sinuhe, king among the, I 490; "walls of the ruler" made to repulse the Bedwin, I 493; chief of, I 493.
—Slain by Snefru, I 168; by Sahure, I 236; by Nuserre, I 250; running like hounds before Amenemhet I, I 483.
—Southern Bedwin, in the district of Sais, IV 957.

BEHBEIT, in central Delta, IV 818 n. a, 878 n. a.

BEHNESA (Oxyrrhyncus), IV 818 n. b.

BEK: Nubian region, also written Beki, II 852; Horus, lord of, III 284, 285; fortress of, II 852.

BEKEN: Libyan people, slain by Ramses III, IV 405.

BEKHEN: name given the Hammamat region, IV 460, 465, 467; reached from Egypt by ox-carts, IV 467.

BEKHTEN: chief of, III 435, 439, 440, 444, 445, 446.
—Bentresh, second daughter of, was possessed of an evil spirit, III 436, 438, 443.
—Nefrure, oldest daughter of chief of, became queen of Ramses II, III 435.
—Nobles of, III 442; soldiers of, III 442, 444, 446; messenger of, III 436, 437.
—Transportation of Khonsu to, III 442.
—Tribute of, III 435; horses from, III 446.

BEKHU, II 597.

BELMEM: city of Palestine, IV 713 n. f.

BEND, THE GREAT, IV 110.
—of Naharin (=Euphrates), II 479 n. a, 631, 656.
—of the Sea, III 118.

BENIHASAN: temples of, see Index II.
—Tombs of: Khnumhotep I, I 463 n. a; Amenemhet, I 515 n. a; Khnumhotep II, I 119 n. c, 619 n. d.
—Pakht, mistress of, III 249.
—Temple inscription: by Hatshepsut, II 297–303; Seti I, III 249.
—Tomb inscriptions: I 10, 34; by Khnumhotep I, I 465; Amenemhet, I 518–23; Kknumhotep II, I 622–39.

BENJAMIN, CITIES OF, IV 712 n. h.

BERBER DOGS, I 421 n. b.

BERSET: located on the "Water-of-Re," IV 369; Bast, mistress of, IV 369; temple of Bast in, IV 369.

BERSHEH: tomb inscriptions of Thuthotep, I 688–706.

BÊT-EL-WALLI (correct form: Bêt-et-Wâli), temple of Ramses II, III 458.
—Temple inscriptions by Ramses II, III 458–77.

BETH-ANATH: captured by Seti I, III 114; mount of, III 356.

BETH ANOTH: city in Judah, conquered by Sheshonk I, IV 716.

BETH-HORON: city of Israel, in Ephraim, conquered by Sheshonk I, IV 712.

BETH-SHAEL: captured by Seti I, III 114.

BETH-SHEAN: city of Israel, in Manasseh, conquered by Sheshonk I, IV 712.

BETH-TELEM: city of Palestine, IV 713 n. h.

BEWEY: Syrian locality on southern Orontes, III 340.

BEYEN, TOWER OF, IV 867.

BIGEH (*Sn-mw·t*), fortress of, II 718; commandant of, II 718.
—Products of, II 718.
—Rock inscriptions, by Ramses II, III 553.

BISTA: temple of, IV 956; district of, IV 957.

BIT, OASIS OF, IV 867.

BLACK LAND, II 245; III 471; Mentuhotep, lord of, I 532; Thutmose II, king of, II 116; Hatshepsut, ruler of, II 299, 319, 321.

BOHEN (=Wadi Halfa): Min-Amon, residing in, III 77, 159, 248; temple of, III 74; 159; endowment of divine offerings for, III 77, 159; Horus, lord of, III 285, 643.

"BRILLIANT-IS-KHAFRE": city in the Upper nome, I 199.

BUBASTIS: Bast, mother of, I 485; Osorkon III living in, IV 878.
—Temples of, II 846; IV 734, 751; IV 956.
—Inscription of Amenhotep III, II 846–50.

BUSIRIS: nome of, I 159; IV 830 n. a; called Per-Osiris, IV 830, 878; district of, IV 968; city of, IV 485, 830; Osiris, lord of, IV 485; militia of, IV 968.

BUTO: city in nome of Xois, I 156, 174; gods of, I 348; temple of Buto in, IV 956; temple of Hathor of the Malachite in (?), IV 956.

BYBLOS: ships of, II 492; Zakar-Baal, prince of, IV 566, 567; harbor of, IV 569, 591; nobles of, IV 570.
—Journal of former kings of, IV 576.
—Ruled Lebanon, IV 577; fortress of, IV 573; butler of, IV 585; letter scribe of, IV 588, 589.
—Tribute to Egypt never paid by, IV 577; storehouses of, IV 576; agents of, IV 576.

C

CAIRO, MUSEUM OF, IV 1014 n. a, *et passim.*

CANOPUS, IV 405 n. c.

CARCHEMISH: expedition of Thutmose III to, II 583; conquered by Ramses II, III 306; by Ramses III, IV 131.
—Ally of Kheta, III 309; battle at, II 583; invaded by Northerners of the Isles, IV 64.
—Not included in Kheta, III 306; IV 64, 131; located by the waters of Naharin, II 583.
—Prisoners from, II 583.

CATARACT, FIRST, I 24; II 15 n. e.
—Canals dug by Uni, I 324; by Sesostris III, I 643–48; cleared by Thutmose I, II 75–76; by Thutmose III, II 649-50.
—Khnum, lord, I 317, 500, 611, 615; II 95, 224; Khnum-Re, lord of, IV 925.
—Rock inscriptions, by Mernere, I 8, 21, 317 n. a, 318 n. h; Amenhotep III, II 843.

CATARACT, FOURTH: cartouches found at, I 21.

CATARACT, SECOND, I 651.

CERASTES MOUNTAIN: XII nome of Upper Egypt, I 199; rise to power of, I 375; Henku, nomarch of, I 280, 281; hawk, sacred animal of, I 281 n. c: great lords of: Ibi, I 377; Zau, I 381.

CIRCLE, THE GREAT (Okeanos), II 73, 220, 325, 661, 804; III 480; IV 45.

CIRCLE OF THE EARTH, IV 64.

COPTOS, I 7; II 729; road of, I 429; highland of, IV 407; haven of, IV 407; landing place for expeditions to and from Punt, IV 407.
—District of, II 733; gold country of, II 774; highlands of, II 774.
—Min, lord of, I 296, 443; Min-Hor of, I 675; triad of: Min-Horus-Isis, IV 365.
—Officers of: commandant of, king's son, Kinen, I 776; captain of gendarmes of, II 774; governor of the gold country of, II 774; count of, I 776; a culprit, I 777; punishment of I, 778–79; office given to Minemhet, I 778; kenbeti of, II 733; gendarmes of, II 774; priest of Min, scribe of the temple, wearer of the royal seal, Neferhotepur, I 776; army of, I 776.
—Products of, II 733; gold from the highlands of, I 521; II 774.
—Stela of Ramses II, III 427–28.
—Temple of Min: see Index II; house of Min-Harsiese, IV 465.

COW STRONGHOLD: city of, I 174, 187.

CROCODILE NOME: northern boundary of, I 529.

CROCODILOPOLIS: capital of Fayum, IV 818 n. a; House of Sebek in, I 709; IV 366, 818, 882.

CUSÆ (XIV nome of Upper Egypt): Hathor, mistress of, I 500; II 300; temple of, II 300; products of, II 732.

CYPRUS, LAND OF, II 659; see also Isy.

D

DAKHEL (=Southern Oasis): stela of Wayeheset in, IV 725; village of Mut in, IV 725 n. a.

DAMASCUS, II 476 n. b.

DAN: cities of, IV 712 n. b.

DANEON PORTUS, IV 878 n. e.

DED: chief of Me, lord of, IV 830; Pemou, lord of, IV 878.

DELTA, I 22, 25, 170; III 10; IV 189, 780 *et passim;* see North, Northland; marshes of, IV 271; rising of Sothis in, I 45; predynastic kings of, I 78; governed by Amenemhet I, I 482.

DENDERA: district of, II 734; Kenbeti of, II 734; products of, II 734; Hathor, mistress of, I 423H, 500.

DENYEN OF THE ISLES, IV 403; ally of the northerners, IV 64; slain by Ramses III, IV 403; captives of, IV 81, 82, 403.

DEP (Buto): local governor of, I 172, 174, 175 n. a, 512; IV 1017; see also Index V: Governor; Buto, mistress of, I 500; II 224.

DEPER: city of Amor, captured by Ramses II, III 356.

DERDEN, III 306, 349.

DÊR EL-BAHRI, II 187; Temple of: see Index II.

—Cliff tomb of Amenhotep I, IV 668, 690–92.

—Temple inscription: by Thutmose II, II 125; Hatshepsut, II 192, 194, 196–98, 200–1, 203, 205, 208, 213, 214, 216, 219–20, 223–25, 227, 229, 230, 233, 235–41.

—Tomb inscription in, IV 668, 689, 691–92.

DÊR EL-GEBRÂWI: cliff tomb of Henku, I 280; tomb of Ibi, in the southern necropolis of, I 375 n. f.

—Tomb inscriptions by Henku, I 281; Ibi, I 377–79.

DERR (in Nubia, also called Miam): temple of Re in, III 503; IV 474, 479.

DESERT: Methen, local governor in, I 174.

DIOSPOLIS, II 336.

DIOSPOLIS PARVA: recorder of, II 737; scribe of the recorder of, II 737; products of, II 737; Hathor of, IV 726; product of, IV 726.

DOG RIVER, III 297.

DOOR (=Elephantine): "people who were in the door," I 367.

DOOR OF THE COUNTRIES (=Elephantine), IV 980; door of the southern countries, IV 990, 995; Governor of: see Index V.

DOOR OF THE HIGHLANDS: keeper of, I 633.

DOOR OF THE NORTH: Intef I of Thebes made the Aphroditopolite nome the, I 423; see also Two Doors of the Northern Countries.

DOOR OF THE SOUTH (Elephantine), I 367 n. d; keeper of, Zau, I 380; Intef, I 420; see also IV 990.

DOR: city of Thekel, IV 565; Bedel, king of, IV 565; harbor of, IV 566; treasury of, IV 566.

DRAH ABU-'N-NEGGAH: brick pyramid of Intef II in, I 421 n. a.

—Mortuary temple of Amenhotep I in, 45 n. b.

—Tombs of Thutiy, II 369 n. c; Nibamon, II 777 n. e.

—Stela of Intef, I 419 n. a; Intef I, I 421 n. a; Keres, II 49 n. a; Thutiy, II 369 n. c; Nipamon, II 777 n. e; stelæ of Thutiy, II 369–78; Nibamon, II 777–79.

E

EAST LAND, I 159; Eastern land, II 658; applied to God's Land, II 658.

EASTERNERS, II 656.

EDFU: property of Queen Ahhotep in, II 113.

—District officials of, II 721; mayor of, II 721; scribe of mayor of, II 721; recorder of, II 721.

—God of: Horus of, II 111; called beautiful god of, II 828.

—Products of, II 721.

—Stela of Yuf, II 109 n. b.

—Temple of, II 112; tomb of Sebekemsaf in, II 109, 112.

EDOM: the Shasu of, III 638; conquered by Sheshonk I, IV 714.

EGWOWE: cities of, plundered by the Libyans, IV 405; probably identical with Canopus, IV 405 n. o.

EGYPT, I 26, 32, 33, 451, 453; II 39 bis, 98 bis, 294, 314, 341, 460, 462, 900, 1032, 1033; III 38, 50, 84, 101, 107, 112, 136, 144, 148, 152, 155, 265, 270, 281, 285, 374, 375, 378, 381, 409, 411, 435, 479, 489, 580, 581, 585, 590, 591, 592, 608, 612, 614, 616; IV 37, 40, 42, 43, 45, 47, 52, 54, 55, 62, 63, 66, 67, 71, 77, 86, 90, 91, 92, 99, 103, 105, 109, 110, 112, 124, 126, 130, 183, 190, 202, 220, 229, 233, 246, 250, 255, 263, 282, 310, 313, 335, 341, 351, 353, 382, 387, 397, 398, 399, 400, 408, 410, 464, 466, 467, 471, 569, 571, 578, 582, 586, 588, 655, 720, 821, 822, 869; see also Two Lands, Two Regions, Kem, South and North.

—Called daughter of Re, III 612; home of civilization, IV 579.

Egypt—
—Boundaries of, see Index VII: Boundaries.
—Reorganization of, by Amenemhet I, I 482–83; Harmhab, III 31; captured by Osorkon I, IV 740; invasion of, by the Libyans, III 572–617; by the northerners, IV 64, 77; by Meshwesh, IV 88, 95.
—Foes of, south, east and west (Nubians, Asiatic, Libyans), I 423H.
—Classes of, IV 402; see also Index VII; districts of, IV 220; feudal principalities of, IV 746.
—Gods of, III 77, 159, 206; see also Index I.
—Laws of, III 64; see also Index VII.
—Ships of, IV 574, 576, 580, see also Index VII.
—Strongholds of, II 467; IV 141; see also Index VII: Fortresses, Strongholds.
—Temples of, III 585; see also Index II.
—Towns of, given for support of temples, IV 226; see Index VII; waters of, II 420.
—Egyptians, II 267; smitten by Mentuhotep I, I 423H.

EHNAS (=Heracleopolis): nobles of, I 398; see Heracleopolis.

EKBET: unknown people, II 70.

EKERETH: Syrian land of, captured by Ramses II, III 306; ally of Kheta, III 309.

EKETERI, III 312; see also Ekereth.

EKWESH: a northern people in alliance with Libya, invading Egypt, III 574, 579.
—Captives from, III 588, 601.
—Hands of, III 588, 601; who had no foreskins, III 588 bis.
—of the countries of the sea, III 588, 601; slain by Merneptah, III 588.

ELEPHANTINE, II 935; of the South, 172, 717.
—Frontier of the South: in time of Uni, I 311, 320; in time of Tefibi, I 396; of Amenemhet I, I 482; of Thutmose I, II 101.
—the two caves of, III 171; IV 125; quay of, IV 146 n. c; inscription on, IV 146–50.
—Temples of Satet and Anuket, I 500; IV 991, 992; endowment of, IV 992; temple of Khnum, IV 146–50, 925.
—Building of the crown possessions of the South in, I 650.
—Fortress of, I 650, 650, n. e; II 719; doorway of, I 650.
—Governor of, II 172; chiefs of, II 172; nobles of, I 6; nomarch of, Sirenpowet, I 510 n. b; city officers of, II 719; commandant of the fortress of, II 719; recorder of, II 719; scribe of the recorder of, II 719; kenbeti of, II 719; scribe of, II 719; fishermen of, II 650; IV 148; fowlers of, IV 148; honey collectors of, IV 149; natron-gatherers of, IV 148; salt gatherers of, IV 148.
—Gods of, II 798; sailing on the river, II 798; Khnum-Re, lord of, IV 925; Satet and Anuket of, I 500; IV 991, 992; Satet, mistress of, I 615, 646, 649; II 360; offering-tables were given to the southern gods in, by Sesostris I, I 500.
—Products of, II 719; granite from, I 322; IV 679; Hatshepsut's obelisks from, II 327; obelisk of Thutmose I, II 89.
—Stela of Ameni, I 649; Amenhotep II, II 791 n. g; Seti I, III 203–4.

EL-HESSEH: island of, I 317 n. a.

EL KAB (modern name of Nekheb), II 3 n. b; nomarchs of, II 1; Ahmose, son of Ebana, nobleman of, II 7.
—Great lords of: Khentemsemeti, I 609; Royenet, II 7; Baba, II 7; Ahmose, son of Ebana, II 7; Setau, high priest of, I 69 n. a; III 558 n. d; IV 414, 415.
—Temple of Ramses II, III 505; temple of Amenhotep III, III 558 n. d.
—Cliff tombs: of Ahmose, son of Ebana, II 1 n. a; Ahmose-Pen-Nekhbet, II 25 n. f; Pahri, II 3 n. d; Setau, IV 414, 415; tomb of Ini, north of, I 373.
—Nekhbet, the white goddess of, II 828.
—Temple inscription, by Ramses II, III 505, 558.
—Tomb inscription: of Ahmose, son of Ebana, II 6–16, 39, 80–82; of Ahmose-Pen-Nekhbet, II 25; Setau, IV 414.
—Stela, I 741.

EL-KHARGEH: the southern oasis, IV 725 n. a.

ELLESIYEH: grotto inscription, by Nehi, II 652.

EMU: green gold of, II 265; electrum from, II 298, 387.

ENDS, or ends of the earth (lit. "hinder-ends," meaning the extreme

North, always "behind" to the Egyptians, as far as known to them), II 120, 498, 586, 761 n. a, 771; III 34.
ENDS OF ASIA: tribute from, II 386, 891.
ENENES: Syrian land, III 337; archers of, III 337.
ENI: probably the same as Esneh, I 459.
EN-PARAN, IV 716.
EPHRAIM: cities of, IV 712 n. a, 714 n.b.
ERETH: a Hittite fortress, IV 118.
ERKATU: city north of Fenkhu, captured by Thutmose III, II 529.
ERMENT: Montu, lord of, IV 547; temple of, IV 547; see Hermonthis.
ERNEN: Hittite city, sun-god of, III 386, 391 bis; Sutekh, god of the city of, III 386.
ERWEN: Syrian land, ally of Kheta, III 309 n. d, 312.
ESBET: a Lybian people captured by Ramses III, IV 405.
ESHMUNEN (=Khmunu), I 695.
ESNEH: islands of, II 723.
—Prince of: Pahri, II 3 n. b; town ruler of, II 723; scribe of the islands of, II 723; Kenbeti, II 723.
—Products of, II 723.
ETHIOPIANS, I 22; see Kush.
ETI: a canal of the Nile, by Heliopolis, III 576, 870.
EUPHRATES: earliest reference to, II 68, 73; boundary stone set up at, by Thutmose I and III, II 478; crossed by Thutmose III, II 479 n. a; see also Inverted water.
EYE OF RE (=Thebes), IV 906.

F

FARAFRAH: oasis of, III 580 n. c.
FAYÛM, I 170, 174; III 580 n. a; IV 818 n. g.
—Back lands of, IV 369.
—Temple of Amon-Re in, IV 369; Horus dwelling in, IV 369; temple of Sebek of Shedet in, IV 369.
FENKHU: lands of, II 27 n. a, 30, 120, 439, 529; disturbing the boundaries of Thutmose III, II 439; conquered by Sheshonk I, IV 719; of marshes of Asia, III 118; oxen from, II 27.
FIELD OF ABRAM, THE: city in southern Palestine, conquered by Sheshonk I, IV 715.
FOREIGN COUNTRIES: Governors of: see Index V.
FOUR BARBARIAN COUNTRIES, I 519.
—Four eastern countries, I 675.

G

GAD: cities of, IV 712 n. g.
GATE OF IHOTEP: a district, I 312.
GAZA: city of, II 417; Zeper and Roy from, III 630.
GAZELLE-NOSE: land of, I 315.
GEBEL-ABUFODAH, I 401 n. a.
GEBEL BARKAL (Napata): stelæ of, I 22; of Piankhi, IV 796 n. a.
GEBEL MARÂG: near Dêr el-Gebrâwi, north of Assiut, tomb of Zau in, I 380 n. d.
GEBELEL-AHMAR: gritstone quarry of, II 493 n. b, 906 n. a.
GEBELÊN, I 427, 459; quarry of, IV 629.
—Temple fragments of Mentuhotep I from, I 423H.
—Recorder of, II 724.
—Products of, II 724.
—Rock inscription of Hui, III 209–210.
—Pillar inscription, by Nesubenebded, IV 628-30.
—Stela of Eti, I 457 n. d.
GEKET: city of Syria, III 632, 632 n. b.
—Men of: Thutiy, III 632; Thekeran, III 632; Methdet, III 632; Shew-Baal, III 632; Sutekhmose, III 632; Eperdegel, III 632.
GENEBTEYEW: tribute from, II 474.
—Products of: oxen, II 474; calves, II 474; bulls, II 474; ivory, II 474; ebony, II 474; panther skins, II 474.
GEZER: people of Kharu, captured by Thutmose IV in, II 821; revolt by, III 606; subdued by Merneptah, III 606, 617.
GIBEON: city of Israel, in Benjamin, conquered by Sheshonk I, IV 712.
GIZEH: tombs at, I 180 nn. i, j, 268 n. i.
—Stela of Khufu, I 177 n. e.
—Tomb of Thenti, I 182 n.a; mastaba of Thethi, I 184; tomb of Nekure, I 190; of Debhen, I 210; mastaba-tomb of Senezemib, I 268.
—Vase inscription of Hatshepsut, II 214 n. d.

GOD'S LAND, II 288, 900; IV 313, 328, 341, 387, 883.
—Name applied to Naharin, III 434; to countries in the North, III 116; to the eastern land, II 658; to Retenu, II 451, 773, 820, 888; to Punt, II 253, 255, 264, 265, 271, 286; IV 407.
—Marvels of, II 285, 288; III 274.
—Sea of, II 257.
—Treasurer of, II 271, 277.
—Located near Red Sea, I 433; stela of Khnumhotep, executed in—, found at Wadi Gasus ("Sewew"), I 618; costly stones from I 764; III 448 n. b; Hammamat in front of, IV 460; on the way to, IV 463.
—Chiefs of, III 448 n. b; IV 407.
—Products of, IV 270; myrrh tree, II 264; fragrant wood, II 265; malachite, II 450 n. a; cedar from, II 888; southerns of, II 288; trees taken from, II 294, 295; myrrh-sycamores from, IV 333; sweet wood from, II 321.

GOLD COUNTRY OF AMON: Governor of, see Index V.

"GREAT IS KHAFRE": pyramid city of Khafre, I 199, 202.

"GREAT-IS [-THE FAME]-OF-KHAFRE": city of, I 197.

GREECE, I 25.
—Greeks, II 296 n. c; IV 994, 1003.

GREEN, THE GREAT (=Sea), II 660, 877.

H

HAGG-KANDIL, II 695.

HAMATH, II 584 n. c.

HAMMAMAT, I 433; the august primeval mountain, I 441; the pure, august stone, which Min has made, I 442; the highlands of Min, I 442; in front of God's Land, IV 460.
—Black basalt from, I 675.
—Gods of: Isis, Min, Mut, I 441; Min, Mut, I 468.
—Rock inscriptions of, Isesi, I 7; inscriptions from Middle Kingdom, I 10; quarry inscription of, I 61 n. a; inscription of Ahmose II, I 75 n. h; rock inscriptions of Pepi I, I 295–301; Ity, I 386–87; Imhotep, I 388–90; Henu, I 428–33; Mentuhotep IV, I 434–53; Amenemhet, I 444–48; Senekh, I 454–56; Intef, I 466–68, 466 n. c; Khui, I 674–75; Amenemhet, I 707–9; Ramses IV, IV 457–60; 461–68.
—HAPHARAIM: city of Israel, in Issachar, conquered by Sheshonk I, IV 712.

HAPI: city of Delta, IV 818.

HARABAT: town by the well of, III 84.

HARE NOME, I 700–6; IV 821, 948.
—Location of, I 626; youths of, I 700, 703; army of, IV 848; warriors of, I 701.
—Hermopolis (=Khnum-Eshmunen): chief city of, I 688; IV 840; priests of, I 702.
—Cemetery of, at Bersheh, I 688; at Shekh Saᶜîd, I 688.
—Harbor of, IV 833.
—Great lords of: Nenekhseskhnum, I 305; Nehri, I 692 n. c; Key, I 692 n. c; Thuthotep, I 688, 692, 693; Thutnakht, I 689; Ihe (?), I 688 n. a.

HARPOON NOME, I 174.

HATBENU, IV 818, 839.

HATIBTI: Thoth presiding over, IV 916.

HATKEPTAH: ancient name of the temple of Ptah at Memphis, IV 316.

HATNUB (alabaster quarry in the desert behind Amarna): location of, I 695.
—Alabaster from, I 7, 305, 323, 696; II 45, 302, 375, 546 n. b.
—Expedition to, by Uni, I 323.
—Rock inscription by Nenekhseskhnum I 7, 305.
—Hieratic graffiti from, I 695 n. b.

HAT-SEHETEPIBRE: residence city of Nehri, I 628; probably identical with Ithtowe, the residence city of Amenemhet, I, I 628 n. c.

HATSEKHEM (Diospolis parva), II 762.

HATSETENI, IV 818.

HATSHO, IV 102; location of, IV 102 n. d; fortress of, IV 107.

HATURT-AMENEMHET: mayor of, II 735; products of, II 735.

HATWARET: see Avaris and *Ḥ·t-wᶜr·t*.

HATWERET: in XVI nome of Upper Egypt, IV 820; Namlot, prince of, IV 820.
—Khnum, lord of, IV 367; temple of, IV 367.

HAUNEBU (peoples of the distant North in the Mediterranean): conquered by Henu, I 447; by Harmhab, III 34; Ramses III, IV 130.
—Hands of, II 120; people of, II 70.

Haunebu—
—Impost of, II 953; tribute of, II 953.
Hauran: Mut worshiped in, IV 716 n. b.

HE: a Nubian land, I 602; islands around, I 602; see also Hem.

HEBENU, IV 820 n. b.

HEBREWS, IV 281 n. e.

HEFAT, I 459.

HEH (=Semneh), I 652.

HEIGHT-OF-WAN: see Wan.

HEKA, I 103.

HELIOPOLIS, II 628; III 28, 32, 271, 545; IV 263, 265, 471, 870, 871; nome of, IV 955; land of, IV 257, 262; the two lands of, IV 183 *et passim*.
—Middle district of, IV 957; names of, IV 957.
—Besieged in the Libyan-Mediterranean invasion, III 612, 613.
—Kings crowned in, by Atum, II 221, 222.
—Sand hill of, IV 870.
—Canal of, IV 266, 278, 394.
—Harbor of, IV 873; pool of Kebeh, IV 870; river of Nun, IV 870.
—Cleansed by Thutmose III, II 642; Thutmose IV, II 812; Ramses III, IV 250.
—Offering ceremonies of, II 562.
—As place of future punishment, III 180.
—Temple model of, III 240.
—Temples of Atum-Re (=Harakhte), Aton, Horus, Saosis, Hapi, Re (in north Heliopolis): see Index II.
—Two pylons in, III 246; two obelisks in, III 246; two pairs in, III 246; London obelisk, II 632–33; New York obelisk, II 634–36; obelisk of Seti I, III 544.
—Amenhotep II, divine ruler of, II 782, 796, 797, 806; Harmhab, sovereign of, before becoming king of Egypt, III 4; Ramses III, ruler of, IV 5, 37, 62, 94, 105, 182, 215, 217, 218, 219, 423.
—Lords of, III 16, 614; table of, III 16.
—High priest of Re: Patonemhab, III 22 n. a; Sem-priests of, II 389.
—Gods of, III 245, 246, 545; IV 183, 247, 248; Atum, lord of: see Index I; Re, lord of: see Index I; Harsaphes, lord of, IV 733; Horus, III 1; Osiris, III 1; Isis, III 1; Nephthys, III 1; Hathor, III 1; IV 247; ennead of, III 16, 545, 547; IV 250, 261, 262, 265, 269; triad: of Atum, Saosis, Re-Harakhte, IV 183, 247, 248; spirits of, I 155, 159, 165, 167; II 314.
—Obelisk inscriptions, by Thutmose III, II 633, 635–36; Ramses II, III 545–48.
—Stela of Thutmose III, II 642.
—Northern Heliopolis, IV 721; temple of Re in, IV 274–76.

HELIOPOLIS, SOUTHERN (at Erment, south of Thebes), II 906 n. a, 934; IV 721, 768.

HEM (read so instead of He): Horus of, III 496, 498; temple of, III 496, 498.

HEMY: in the Delta, wine of, IV 734.

HENEM: city in Palestine, IV 713 n. e.

HEPEN: pool of, III 100.

HERACLEOPOLIS, IV 968; kingdom of, invasion of, by Thebans, I 396 n. d; insurrection within, I 398; consisting of the Northland and Middle Egypt, I 407 and n. b; end of (Dynasties IX and X), I 416; defended by the princes of Siut, I 422; conquered by Intef I of Thebes, I 422; finally overthrown by Mentuhotep I, I 423H.
—District of, IV 948.
—City of, I 401, 403; besieged by Tefnakhte, IV 818; by Pianchi's army, IV 825; streets of, IV 968.
—Merikere, king of, I 399; Tefnefdibast, ruler of, IV 852.
—Army of, IV 777, 787, 792, 868; Commander of, Commander in chief of, see Index V.
—Great ones of, I 401; Somtous-Tefnakhte, nomarch of, IV 944; Hor, chief of, IV 968.
—Temple of Harsaphes of, I 111; IV 792, 956, 968, 970, 971–72; temple of Bast, IV 973.
—Gods of: Harsaphes, lord of, I 675; IV 792; Divine father of: see Index V.

HERACLEUM, IV 405 n. g.

HERENKERU: city in southern end of Libanon, under the rule of Kadesh, II 436; plundered by Thutmose III, II 436; called a city of Retenu, II 557; impost of, II 557.

HERMONTHIS, III 615; nomarchs of, the Intefs, I 419 n. c; recorder of,

II 727; scribe of the recorder of, II 727.
—District of, II 727; scribe of, II 727; kenbeti of, II 727.
—Temples of: see Index V; throne of Amon in, II 314.
—Montu, god of, II 352, 828; see Index I; prophets of Montu, II 352.
—Products of, II 727.
—See also Erment.

HERMOPOLIS (Khmunu), IV 842, 848, 948; captured by Pianchi, IV 833, 842.
—Hermopolis (*wnw*), IV 833, 843 bis.
—Hesret, a sacred quarter of: Thoth, presider over, II 95, 147; IV 356; temple of Thoth in, IV 356, 848; Thoth, lord of, IV 848.
—Prophets of, II 371; chief of, II 371.
—Royal palace of, IV 849; granary of, IV 851; treasury of, IV 849; magazines of, IV 849; stables of, IV 850; colossus of, I 695.

HERMOPOLIS PARVA, IV 830 n. b.

HERUR: see Hirur.

HERYPEDEMY, IV 867.

HES: Libyan people, slain by Ramses III, IV 405.

HESEBKA (XI nome of Lower Egypt), IV 830, 878.

HESEN: stronghold in the Harpoon nome, I 174.

HESRET (a sacred quarter of Hermopolis), II 95, 147; IV 356; lord of, III 25.

HESWER: city in the Saitic nome, Methen palace-ruler of, I 174.

HIGHLAND (upper lands back from the river, along the foot of the cliffs), II 80, 113, 114.

HIGHLANDS: captured by Mentuhotep I, I 423H; cleared of Troglodytes by Henu, I 429 n. g; beasts of, I 436; mountain of Hammamat, the highlands of Min, I 442; commander of troops in, I 455.
—Extending southward to Thau and northward to Menet-Khufu, I 456.
—Source of ebony, II 127; gold from, II 373; III 195; electrum from, II 374.
—Door of: see Door of the Highlands.
—Inspectors of: see Index V.
—of Akhetaton, II 1008; of Coptos, II 774.
—The eastern, governors of: see Index V.
—The western, I 533; overseers of, see Index V.

HILL COUNTRY (=First Cataract), I 318.
—Hill countries, the two, II 297.

HIPPONON, IV 818 n. e.

HIRUR (Herur) (town by Benihasan): Khnum, lord of, I 637 n. a; II 95; Heket mistress of, II 205 n. a.

HORIZON OF HORUS: a part of the Oryx nome, I 619; on the east of the river, I 625; up to the eastern highlands, I 625; detached as a separate principality, I 619; Menet-Khufu, chief city of, I 619.

HORNS OF THE EARTH: in the South, II 101, 120, 631, 652; III 115, 118, 204 n. b, 588 n. c, 600; on the Nubian border, IV 102; mountain of, IV 102; in Asia, II 412.

HOTEP (sacred quarter of Heliopolis): Hathor, mistress of, II 1042.

HOU, city of, I 401 n. a.

HOUSE OF HATHOR: recorder of, II 728.

"HOUSE-OF-MENKHEPRURE": district of Memphis, II 1043.

"HOUSE-OF-MENMARE-MERIAMON": town west of Memphis, IV 338, 340.

"HOUSE-OF-OKHEPERKERE": district of Memphis, II 1043.

"HOUSE-OF-PTAH": district of Memphis, II 1043.

"HOUSE-OF-RAMSES-MERIAMON": see Ramses, ctiy of.

"HOUSE-OF-THE-NORTH": city of, I 125.

HUA, HEIGHT OF: a Nubian region, II 849, 850; captives from, II 850.

HYKSOS: their neglect of the Egyptian temples, I 15; II 296; chronology of, I 65; war with, I 24, 774; II 4 n. a; length of reign, I 52; expulsion of, II 1, 4; resumption of building after, II 26; they ruled in ignorance of Re, II 303.
—Era begun by, III 538, 542.
—Kings of: Opehtiset-Nubii, III 538, 542; Paophis: see Index III.

I

IBHET: Nubian region: revolt of, II 852; capture of, II 853.

Ibhet—
—Archers of, II 854; servants of, II 854; captives of II 854.
—Campaign in, by Amenhotep III, II 852–55.
—Cattle of, II 853.
—Harvest of, II 852.
—Quarry of, I 321, 322.

IBRIM: mayor of, IV 474.
—Cliff tomb of Penno in, IV 474 n. a.
—Tomb inscription, by Penno, IV 476–83.

IDEHET: two wells dug in, by Henu I 431.

IHETEB: a well dug there by Henu, I 431.

IKATHI: city near Niy in Syria, Egyptian infantry in, II 787; revolt of, II 787; captured by Amenhotep II, II 788; booty from, II 788.

IKEN, Nubian city, I 652.

IKHERKIN: Nubian land, I 510.

ILION, III 312 n. c.

ILLAHÛN: at the mouth of Fayûm, IV 818, 853.

IMERES: city of, I 173.

IMU: Hathor, mistress of, I 351.

IMUKEHEK: probably a Libyan region, war of Amenhotep I in, II 42.

"INVERTED WATER" (=the Euphrates), II 73; IV 407; the sea of (=Indian ocean), IV 407 n. c; fleet of Ramses III sailing thereon to the land of Punt, IV 407.

IREM: Nubian region.
—Captured by Hatshepsut, II 26; Thutmose III, II 494; Amenhotep III, II 845 n. f.
—Chiefs of, II 267; son of chief of, II 494.

IRSHU: sacred quarter of Mut in Karnak; see Index II: Karnak, Temple of Mut.

IRTHET: negro tribe, I 311, 317, 334 bis, 336; chief of, I 324, 336 bis.

IRTHETH: negro land, I 334.

ISEUM (=Neter), modern Behbeit, IV 818 n. a, 878 n. a.

ISIDIS OPPIDUM (=Neter, modern Behbeit), IV 818 n. a.

ISLANDS, IV 830, 873, 880, 882.

ISLE OF SNEFRU, I 312, n. d, 492.

ISLES: Northerners of the, IV 75; invading northern Syria, IV 64; camping in Amor, IV 64; intending to attack Egypt, IV 64, 77.

ISLES, (the Greek Islands): II 73; isles in the midst of the sea, II 1006; IV 880.

ISRAEL: desolated by Merneptah, III 615; captured by Sheshonk I, IV 712.
—Towns of, IV 712.

ISSACHAR: cities of, IV 712 nn. c, f.

ISY (=Cyprus), II 659; captured by Thutmose III, II 493, 511; Ramses II, III 366 n. c.
—Prince of, II 511; chief of, II 521.
—Tribute of, II 493, 511, 521.
—Products of: copper, II 493, 521; lead, II 493, 521; lapislazuli, II 493; crude copper, II 511; ivory, II 493, 521; horses, II 511.

ITFIT (see also Atfih): recorder of, II 741; scribe of the recorder of, II 741; products of, II 741.

ITHTOWE: between Medûm and Memphis, IV 818, 856.

J

JACKAL NOME: location of, I 626, 632.
—Ruler of, Nakht II, I 632.

JACOB-EL, IV 131.

JONIANS, III 312 n. c.

JOPPA: capture of, I 24; II 577.

JORDAN, IV 716.

JOSEPH-EL, IV 131.

JUDAH: kingdom of, IV 713 n. d.

K

KADER: city in land of Pemehtem, in Syria, captured by Seti I, III 94.

KADESH, I 3; III 310, 311, 322, 325, 336; extent of its dominion, II 420.
—Located in the land of Amor, III 141, 310; of Zahi, III 318.
—District of, II 531; Syria, a dependency of, II 420; ally of Kheta, III 309, 312.
—Captured by: Thutmose III, II 465, 585; Amenhotep II, II 798A; Seti I, III 141 bis; Ramses II, III 306.
—Siege of, II 589; great battle at, III 306–312, 317–27; assault on, II 590.
—Highland of, III 308, 318.
—Cities of, captured by Thutmose III,

II 531; groves of, II 465; harvest of, II 465.
—Prince of, II 589; lords of, II 585, 590; chief of, II 420, 430, 435, 596, 773.
—Tribute from, II 773.
—Prisoners of, II 585, 798 A.
—Booty from, II 435, 436, 532, 585; chariot, II 435; suit of bronze armor, II 435; meru wood, II 435; chairs, II 436; staff, II 436; statue, II 436; clothing, II 436.

KANA: captured by Thutmose III, II 529.

KANEKEME (in the Delta): a vineyard of Amon, IV 216; temple of Amon in, IV 216.

KARBANITI (Kerben), IV 405 n. g.

KARNAK, II 43, 63, 80, 105, 383, 390, 606, 832, 833, 834, 835, 837, 838, 881; III 27, 28, 215, 216, 220, 261, 511, 512, 517; IV 9, 201, 495, 616, 624, 635, 768, 823, 851, 855, 945, 958C.
—Quay of, I 22; IV 693 n. a, 914.
—Hapuseneb, chief in, II 389; for other officials see Thebes (eastern), and Index II: Karnak, Temple of Amon, and Index V.
—Gods of: see Index I: Amon, Amon-Re, Harakhte, Aton, Mut, Khonsu, Montu, Mat, Horus, Ptah, Osiris-Wennofer, Hathor.
—Temples of: see Index II: Temples of Amon, Mut, Khonsu, Ptah of Thebes, Montu, Bast, Mat, Harakhte, Seti I, Ramses II, Osiris-Wennofer, and Index II: Thebes (eastern).
—Obelisks: of Thutmose I (Nos. 1 and 2), II 86; Hatshepsut (Nos. 1 and 2), II 304, erected by Senmut II 351; Thutmose III, II 624–25; Ramses II, III 543 n. c.
—Statues: of Senmut, II 349; Puemre, I 380 n. e; Amenhotep, son of Hapi, II 912, 913.
—Temple inscriptions: by Thutmose III, II 131–66, 415–37, 439–43, 445–49, 451–52, 455–62, 464–67, 469–75, 747–87, 489–95, 497–503, 507–515, 515–19, 529–40, 654; Hatshepsut, II 305; Amenhotep II, II 798A, 804–6; Seti I, III 82–150, 223–24; Ramses II, III 348–51, 355, 367–91, 509–513; Merneptah, III 574–92; Ramses IV, IV 472; Ramses IX, IV 492–98; Sheshonk I, IV 709–724; Osorkon, IV 753, 756–70 777.
—In temple of Khonsu: inscriptions by Ramses XII, IV 602–3; Hrihor, IV 609–26; Paynozem I, IV 632–33, 649.
—In temple of Ptah; inscription of Thutmose III, in II 611.
—Column inscription: of Thutmose III, II 601; Amenhotep II, II 804–6.
—Obelisk inscriptions: by Thutmose I, II 86–88; Hatshepsut, II 308–321.
—Statue inscriptions: by Senmut, II 350–58; Puemre, II 380–81; Amenhotep, son of Hapi, II 912, 914–20.
—Stelæ of: Ahmose I, II n. d; Thutmose III, II 599 n. d; Thutmose III, II 609 n. e; Thutmose III, II 655 n. b; Amenhotep II, II 781 n. b; Ramses II, III 429–47; Sheshonk I, IV 724A; Kerome, IV 755; Yewelot, IV 795; Psamtik I, IV 935–58; Enekhnesneferibre, IV 988A–J; for other inscriptions, see Thebes, and Index II: Karnak, Temple of Amon.
—Stela in temple of Ptah: of Thutmose III, II 609 n. e; Seti I, III 82.

KAROY: region of Kush, II 889; III 285; region of Napata, II 1020, 1025; gold from, II 889; III 285.
—Tablet erected in, by Amenhotep II, II 800.
—Campaign of Thutmose IV to, II 818.
—Southern boundary of Egypt at, II 862.

KAS (*K*ɔ*š*): Nubian land, I 510; see also Kush.

KASR-ES-SAIYÂD: cliff tomb of Idu-Seneni in, I 337 n. a.

KAU: negro tribe, I 311.

KAY: town of, IV 948.

KEBEH: pool of, in Heliopolis, IV 296, 870.

KEBEH (probably a region of upper Euphrates), II 101.

KEBES: a Syrian locality, III 337; Tergetetethes, chief of archers of, III 337.

KEDEM bordered on Yaa, I 496.

KEFTYEW: land of, II 659; ships of, II 492; vessels of the make of, II 537; tribute of, II 761, 773; classed with "all the Isles in the midst of the sea," II 761 n. a.
—Captured by Thutmose III, II 761; Ramses II, III 366.

Keftyew—
—Chief of, II 773.
KEHEK: captives of, III 588.
—Made into an Egyptian class, IV 402, 410.
KEHENI: near Athribis, IV 873.
KELEKESH: III 306, 349; ally of Kheta, III 309.
KEMED: captured by Seti I, III 114.
KEMWER: lake of, I 493; shore of, IV 724A; Harkhentikhet, lord of, IV 875.
KENEMETYEW, II 808.
KENOFU: pyramid city of Amenemhet I, I 490 n. a.
KERBEN: city of Egypt, IV 405; location of, IV 405 n. g.
KEREKHEN: n. –, Hittite city, III 386.
KEREMIM: captured by Seti I, III 114.
KERET, II 925.
KERPET: city on mount of Bethanath, III 356; conquered by Ramses II, III 356.
KERZET: Hittite city, III 386.
KESHKESH: Syrian land of, ally of Kheta, III 309, 312; captives from, III 428.
KETNE: place in Syria, II 598; captured by Thutmose III, II 598; by Amenhotep II, II 798A; by Ramses II, III 366; prisoners from, II 798A.
KEYKESH: Libyan people, slain by Ramses III, IV 405.
KEZWEDEN: Syrian locality, ally of Kheta, III 309, 312; land of, III 386; dependency of Kheta, III 386; queen of Kheta from, III 391.
KHAFRE: cities of, I 195–98.
KHAFTET-HIR-NEBES: necropolis in western Thebes II 927; goddess, II 70, 339, 606, 655.
KHAMEHEM: captured by Seti I, III 114.
KHAMMAT: modern Soleb, in Nubia; temple of, II 890 894–98; fortress of, II 894, 896, 897; mayor of, II 1041.
KHARU, IV 883.
—Captured by Kadesh, II 420; Amenhotep II, II 798A; Thutmose IV, II 822; Seti I, III 84, 101; Ramses II, III 457; Merneptah, III 617; Sheshonk I, IV 724.
—Sea of (the Mediterranean), IV 565.
—Asiatics of, III 101.
—King's messenger to, III 651.
—Towns of, given for support of temples, IV 226; Gezer, city of, II 821; Tyre, city in, III 630, 633.
—Chiefs of, III 84; Yarsu, chief of, ruling Egypt, IV 398.
—Tribute of, II 1015; IV 724; impost of, IV 229.
—Vases of, called ᵓ-*k*ᵓ-*n*ᵓ vases, II 436; bows of, II 501; prisoners from, II 798A, 821, 884; IV 225; oil of, IV 33; see also Syria.
KHAS: Sekhmet presider over, II 814.
KHASEY: Nubian land, I 510.
KHATITHANA: tribe of, II 789; city of, II 789; captured by Amenhotep II, II 789; belonged to Retenu, II 790.
KHEMKHEM, IV 915.
KHEMMIS: Horus in, II 138, 814; IV 923.
KHENBET: Hittite city, III 386.
KHENT: nome of (XIV), I 159, 165.
KHENT-EBUI-ENTERU: Mut of, IV 369; temple of, IV 369.
KHENTHENNOFER: Nubian region, II 14, 30, 80, 121; III 270, 285; captives from, II 162, 646; Nubian Troglodytes from, II 268, 646; youths (=recruits) of, III 332; under the authority of the viceroy of Kush, II 1026.
—Fine gold from, IV 770.
—Gods of, III 448 n. b; Nibmare, lord of, II 898.
—Nomes of, III 448 n. b.
KHENTIKHET: see under Temples of Athribis: Index II.
KHENTNOFER, IV 878.
KHEREHA (modern Babylon), II 814; cavern of, IV 869.
—Mount of, IV 870; highway of god Sep to, IV 870; located in Per-Hapi, IV 878.
—Nine gods in, I 500; temple of, I 165; lords of, II 814; ennead of Atum in, IV 869.
KHERPENTERES: Hittite city, III 386.
KHESEKHET: Nubian region, II 849.
KHESEP: Hittite city, Sutekh, god of, III 386.
KHETA: field of, a district in Memphis, II 1043.

KHETA: land of, III 34, 374, 375, 380, 381, 383, 384, 386, 387, 388, 389, 390, 391, 410, 415, 479.
—Districts of, III 321.
—Wars with: by Seti I, III 114, 143, 144, 147, 148, 151, 152; Ramses II, III 306–312, 317–27, 392, 448 n. b; by Merneptah, III 617; Ramses III, IV 129.
—the great coalition of prince of, III 309; treaty of Egypt with, I 18, 36; III 367–91; invasion into, by the people of the Isles of the Northerners, IV 64.
—Grain transported by ships from Egypt to, III 580.
—Kings of, III 375 n. c; Seplel, III 373, 377; Merasar, III 373, 391; Metella, III 374, 375, 377; Khetasar, III 371, 372, 373, 374, 375, 391; queen of, Petkhep, III 391; Matnefrure, eldest daughter of King Khetasar, given as queen to Ramses II, III 410, 415, 417; second daughter of Khetasar, III 428.
—Chief of, visiting Egypt, III 421, 424, 426; chiefs of, II 525, 773; III 144, 309, 310, 319, 321, 322, 323, 325, 326, 330, 336, 337, 338, 340, 346, 349, 359, 360, 371, 372, 373, 374, 375, 376, 378, 379, 380, 381, 382, 383, 384, 385, 386, 389, 390, 391, 417, 418, 419, 421, 424, IV 129; Thewethes, III 337; Rebeyer, III 337; Septher, III 337.
—Kheta, the Great: tribute from, II 485, 525, 773; III 151, 421; gifts from, III 420.
—Officers of, III 337; nobles of, III 419; people of, III 421; prisoners from, III 342; regulars of, III 424; warriors of III, 424; chariot warrior of, Gerbetes, III 337; charioteers: Tergen, III 337; Tergenenes, III 337; Peyes, III 337; soldiers of: Semretes, III 337; Methren, III 337; chief of the warriors of, Teder, III 337; chief of the archers of, Tergetetethes, III 337; Egem, III 337; Rebesnen, III 337; scribe of chief of, Kherpesar, III 337; chief of the bodyguard, Teyeder, III 337; king's messengers, Tarteseb, III 371, 372.
—Chariotry of, III 309, 310, 312, 320, 321, 338, 424; infantry of, III 320, 321, 338, 424; army of, III 419, 424.
—City of, III 365; cities of: Ernen, III 386; Zepyerened, III 386; Perek, III 386; Khesesep, III 386; Seres, III, 386; Aleppo, III 386; Rekhsen, III 386; Sekhpen, III 386; Zeyethekhrer, III 386; Kerzet, III 386; Kherpenteres, III 386; Kerekhen, III 386; Khewek, III 386; Zen, III 386; Zen-wet, III 386; Serep, III 386, Khenbet, III 386.
—Fortresses of Ereth, IV 120.
—Gods of, III 386; Sun god, III 386; Sutekh, III 386; Antheret, III 386; Tesker, III 386.
—Products of: silver, II 485; III 420; white precious stone, II 485; *ṯ ͗-gw*-wood, II 485; gold, II 525; III 420; horses, III 420, 428; goats, III 428; large cattle, III 428.

KHEWEK: Hittite city, III 386.

KHMUNU (=Eshmunen, Hermopolis): chief city of the Hare nome, I 688; Thoth, lord of, II 274; see Eshmunen, Hermopolis.

KIKKAR: locality in Palestine, IV 713 n. h.

KINA: brook of, II 428, 430.

KODE: captured by Kadesh, II 420; by Ramses II, III 306; located north of Megiddo, II 434; ally of Kheta, III 309, 321; invaded by the Northerners of the Isles, IV 64.
—All Kode, III 321; not included in the districts of Kheta or land of Naharin, III 321; IV 64.
—Chief of, III 421; visiting Egypt, III 421, 426; folk of, "curly-haired," II 657.

KOM EL-HISN: temple of, IV 956.

KOM OMBO: Set, god of, II 828.

KONOSSO, ISLAND OF: rock inscription by Mentuhotep I, I 423H n. d; Thutmose IV, II 823 n. b; Amenhotep III, II 845.

KUBBÂN: stelæ of Thutmose I, II 54 n. a; Ramses II, III 282–93.

KUMMEH (37 miles above Wadi Halfa): temple of, built of "good white stone" from Shat, I 510.
—Rock inscription by Amenemhet IV, I 749.

KURNA: Temple of Seti I, see Index II.

KURNET-MURRAÎ (west side of Thebes): cliff-tomb of Huy, II 1019 n. a.

KURUSKO (half-way between first and second cataract): inscription of, I 412 n. b.

KUSH: land of, II 121 bis, 122, 858;

III 44, 498; IV 313, 341, 387, 410; passed by Sesostris I's expedition; sailing southward, I 519.
—Campaigns against, by: Pepi II, I 361; Sesostris I, I 510 n. b; Sesostris III, I 647, 650, 653, 661, 672; Amenhotep I, II 39, 41; Thutmose I, II 76–77, 84; Thutmose II, II 119–22; Thutmose III, II 648; Thutmose IV, II 824; Amenhotep III, II 844, 845, 857; Harmhab, III 42; Seti I, III 164 bis; Ramses II, III 285, 392, 471.
—Rebellion of, II 844.
—Colony from, II 824; Troglodytes of, III 490; Negro people of, IV 114; Negro slaves from, II 494, 502, 514, 522, 526; prisoners from, II 857.
—Tribute from, II 891, 1015; III 42, 453, 590, 644; impost of, II 127, 494, 502, 514, 522, 526, 538; harvest of, II 494, 502, 514, 514, 538, 871.
—Towns of, given for support of temples, IV 226.
—Localities of: Pool of Horus, II 845; Karoy, II 889.
—Viceroy of, I 18, called "King's son," II 47; see Index V; first appointed by Thutmose I, II 47; earliest known II 61; appointment of earliest known, II 64; residence of, II 54, 62; called "King's son of Kush," II 1023; see Index V.
—Chief of II 122; III 590; IV 114; chiefs of, II 844, 857, 891, 1035, 1036; III 164; princess of, II 1035; deputy of, see Index V; king's messenger to, III 651.
—Products of: gold, II 522, 526; bulls, II 514; oxen, II 494, 502, 514, 1035; calves, II 494, 502, 514; ivory, II 494, 502, 514; ebony, II 494, 502, 514; ships, II 494, 502, 514, 538; chariot, II 1035, 1039.

L

LEBANON: expedition to, I 146 n. a; capture of Tripolis of, by Thutmose III, II 236; by Amenhotep II, II 783.
—Owned by Byblos, IV 577; claimed by Amon, IV 580.
—Fortress, built by Thutmose III in, II 548; name of, II 548.
—Imposts of, II 483, 510; chiefs of, II 483, 548; III 94; harvest of, II 519; booty of, II 783.
—Products of, II 436; birds of, II 483; wild fowl, II 483; horses, II 783; cedar from, III 94; IV 577.
LETOPOLIS: Horus lord, IV 878; presider over, II 95; prophet of, IV 878.
LEVI-EL, IV 131.
LIBYA: land of, III 581, 586, 611; IV 40; people of, I 423H, 492; III 590; IV 822, 994.
—Invasion by, into Egypt, III 572–617; IV 91; plundering western Egypt, IV 405.
—Conquest of, by Mentuhotep I, I 423H; Amenemhet I, I 492; Ramses II, III 448 n. c; Merneptah, III 574, 584, 591, 594, 598, 608; Ramses III, first war, IV 35–58; second war, IV 83–114.
—Kings of: Ded, III 579; IV 43; Meshken, IV 43; Meryey, III 579, 586, 610, 612, 614; IV 43; Wermer, IV 43; Themer, IV 43.
—Chief of, Hetihenker, IV 783, 784; chiefs of, III 579, 580, 583, 584, 586, 588, 589, 590, 594, 595, 610, 615; IV 114, 127, 783, 784.
—Uncircumcised phalli of, III 587, 588, 601 ter; IV 52, 54; seed of, III 604; IV 91; families of, III 598.
—Chariotry of, III 583; infantry of, III 583; archers of, III 609; bowmen of, III 579; captives from, III 584, 588, 600; IV 52, 54, 57, 78, 79.
LIBYAN NOME, I 159.
LISHT: pyramid of Sesostris I in, I 507 n. b.
LOWER EGYPT: kings of, I 78, 78 n. a, 90; II 287; III 577, 585.
LUKA: ally of Kheta, III 309, 312; ally of Libya, invading Egypt, III 574, 579; uncircumcised (?), III 588.
LUXOR, II 187, 190, 226, 230, 351, 554; III 27, 30; IV 836, 909.
—Wall of, built by Thutmose III, IV 628; restored by Nesubenebded, IV 628–30.
—Feast of, II 809, 887, 888; see Index VII: Feasts, of Southern Opet.
—Obelisk of Ramses II, III 543 n. c, 567.
—Temple reliefs and inscriptions of Amenhotep III, II 187–212, 215–42, Ramses II, III 480–84, 506–8; Menkheperre, IV 659; see also Opet, the Southern.

LYCOPOLIS: XIII nome of Upper Egypt, I 280, 396; jackal, sacred animal of, I 281 n. c.

M

MA'SARA (quarry), I 8; II 26.
—Rock inscriptions, by Neferperet, II 26 n.c. See Ayan.

MACHANAIM: city of Israel, in Gad, conquered by Sheshonk I, IV 712.

MAD: sacred precinct near Karnak, IV 915; bull of, IV 915; house of, IV 915.

MALACHITE COUNTRY, I 161; IV 409; products of: silver, IV 409; gold, IV 409; royal linen, IV 409; mek-linen, IV 409; malachite, IV 409; Hathor, mistress of: see Index I.

MALACHITE FIELD, IV 1003.

MANASSEH: cities of, IV 712 n. d.

MANU, MOUNTAIN OF: western boundary of Egypt, II 321, 905; IV 12, 13, 246.

MARSHES, OF ASIA (exact rendering of the word translated "Marshes" is uncertain, but the lands of the upper Euphrates are meant), II 120, 321, 402, 657; III 480; IV 90.
—Applied to the Kode-folk, II 657; of the lands of Mitanni, II 659; of Fenkhu, III 118.
—Marshes of Asia, II 321; eastern boundary of Egypt, II 321; tribute from, II 385; III 434.
—Marshes of the earth, revolt in, II 416; as far as Naharin, II 631; III 115, 118, 434.

MAZOI: negro tribe, I 311, 317; chief of, I 324; people of, captured by Amenemhet I, I 483; gendarmes of, IV 466.

ME, GREAT CHIEFS OF: Sheshonk, IV 675, 677, 678, 680; Namlot, IV 676, 678, 683, 685, 686, 687; see also Meshwesh and Index V: Chiefs.

MEBER, III 578.

MEHAY: dom palm of, IV 234.

MEDINET HABU: Themet, a region of, IV 634 n. b.
—Pylon inscriptions by Ramses III, IV 61–68, 85–92, 94–99, 101–6, 130, 132–35, 137–38.
—Temple inscription by Thutmose III, II 638–41, Ramses III, IV 4–17, 26–34, 37–58, 70–82, 107–14, 117–29, 140–45.
—Temple of Thutmose III in: see Index II; Temple of Ramses III, IV 1 ff.; see Index II.

MEDÛM, IV 818, 855; see also Mer-Atum.

MEHENET: sacred district of Sais, IV 1011; temple in, IV 982; mysterious linen from, IV 1011.

MEGIDDO, II 439.
—Campaign against, by Thutmose III, II 412–43; by Sheshonk I, IV 712.
—In the land of Retenu, II 402; seized by Kadesh, II 420; brook of Kina south of, II 428; chief of, II 435; Asiatics in, II 441; surrender of, II 434, 441; harvest of, II 437; plain of, II 429; cattle of, II 430; siege of, II 432, 440.
—Spoil of: mares, II 431, 435; foals, II 435; stallions, II 435; chariot, II 435; suit of bronze armor, II 435; bows, II 435; meri wood, II 435; large cattle, II 435; small cattle, II 435; white small cattle, II 435.

MEKHER: negro land, I 334.

MEMPHIS, II 790; III 28, 77, 159, 260, 271, 286, 608, 610, 612, 613, 615; IV 328, 471, 491, 724, 781, 818, 859, 861, 930, 956; beautified by Thutmose IV, II 812; latitude of, I 45; fall of supremacy of, I 53, 56.
—Called "Life-of-the-Two-Lands," IV 977; "the wall," I 372; the white wall, IV 336; a walled city, III 608.
—Besieged in the Libyan-Mediterranean invasion, III 608, 610, 612, 613; besieged by Piankhi, IV 857–64; captured by Piankhi, IV 865; captured by Tanutamon, IV 928.
—Nome of, I 159; hunting on the highlands of, II 813; lions of, II 813; wild goats in, II 813.
—Temples: of Ptah (Hatkeptah), Ramses II, Aton, Amon, Seti I, Ramses III, Serapeum: see Index II.
—Gods of: city of Ptah, IV 310; mysterious seat of Sokar in, IV 857; abode of Shu, IV 857; sanctuary of Ineb-Sebek, IV 315, 330, 333; ennead of: see Index I; triad of: Ptah, Sekhmet, Nefertem; IV 183, 305, 306.
—Dated stelæ of, I 22.
—Quarters of, II 814; districts of: "fiel of-the-Kheta," II 1043; "House-o

Okheperkere," II 1043; "House-of-Menkheprure" II 1043; "House-of-Ptah," II 1043.
—Western road of, IV 338; western canal of, IV 338.
—Harbor of, IV 858, 863; stronghold of, IV 858; treasury of, IV 868; granaries, IV 868, 878.
—High priests of: see Index V: Priests.

MENDES (=Per-Benebded), IV 830, 878; Ptah-Tatenen, as a ram, lord of, III 400; the ram-god, lord of, III 542.
—Nome of, Methen, overseer of, I 173, 174; cities of, I 197, 198.

MENET-KHUFU: northern point of the Highlands, I 456; located in the Benihasan region, I 624 n. a; was the chief city of "Horizon of Horus," I 619; birthplace of Khufu (IV Dyn.), I 619.
—Colonnaded hall, rebuilt by Khnumhotep II, I 637.
—Rulers of: Khnumhotep I, I 465, 625; Nakht I, I 627; Khnumhotep II, I 624, 629.

MER-ATUM: modern Medûm, IV 818, 855; house of Sokar in, IV 855.

MEREM: city in northern Palestine, conquered by Ramses II, III 356.

MERET-SNEFRU: city of, I 165.

MERNEPTAH-HOTEPHIRMA: city of, III 634; located in the land of Aram, III 634; fortress of, III 638; in Theku, III 638; stronghold of, III 633; well of, III 631; pools of Pithom of, III 638.

MERNOFRET: city of, I 635; ka-house of Nehri in, I 635.

MERO—: city of Tikhsi, II 587.

MESA: Syrian land of, conquered by Ramses II, III 306; ally of Kheta, III 309, 312.

MESBET: see Esbet.

MESED, IV 879.

MESEZUT (of the Saitic nome): city of, I 174 n. f.

MESHA: Sebek, lord of, IV 368; temple of, IV 368.

MESHENETH: Syrian locality, captured by Ramses II, III 306; ally of Kheta, III 309.

MESHWESH: a Libyan land, IV 90, 103, 108, 113.
—Captured by: Merneptah, III 580, 598, 608; Ramses III, IV 40, 43, 52, 58, 84, 91, 92, 103, 104, 107, 224, 405.
—Invading Tehenu, IV 87; Egypt, IV 88, 405; in alliance with Temeh, IV 91.
—Kings of: Keper, IV 90, 97; Meshesher, IV 90.
—Chief of, IV 87, 109, 111, 112, 114, 779, 781.
—Army of, IV 90; warriors of, IV 90, 97; men of, IV 111; chiefs of, IV 90; chieftains of, IV 111; leaders of, IV 112.
—Hands of (indicating that circumcision was practiced in), IV 58, 54 (?), 111; seed of, IV 43.
—Captives from, IV 90, 92, 111, 405; impost from, IV 92.
—Feast of "slaying the Meshwesh," IV 145; herd named after conquest of, IV 224.
—Cattle from, III 589; IV 110, 111; herds of, IV 90; horses of, IV 86, 90, 111; asses of, IV 111; copper swords from, III 589; swords from, IV 111; bows from, IV 111; quivers from, IV 111; spears from, IV 111; chariots from, IV 111; see also Me.

MESTA, TEMPLE OF, IV 956.

METENU, IV 818 n. h, 882.

METHER: Nubian country, I 368.

MEWETKHENT: temple of Amon in, IV 368.

MIAM (see also Derr): chief of, II 1037; Horus, lord of, III 285; IV 474; Penno, chief of the quarry service of, IV 474; statue of Ramses VI in, IV 479; domains of, IV 479–83.
—Treasurer of, IV 474; mayor of, IV 474; scribe of the White House of, IV 474.

MIDDLE EGYPT, I 10; boundaries of, in the Middle Kingdom, I 396 n. h; rebellion of, chastised by Merikere, I 400; counts of, I 401, 414; belonging to the Heracleopolitan kingdom, I 396, 401, 407, 413, 414.
—Kheti I, great lord of, I 403; Kheti II, commander of, I 410; Nakht II, forefront of, I 632.

MIGDOL OF RAMSES, IV 77.

MIN: city of, II 740; see Akhmim.

MINIEH: province of, I p. 48.

MIN-SI-ESE, III 76.

MIPER: (in Saite nome) Methen palace ruler of, I 172, 174.

MIRAMAR: stela at, I 281 n. c.

MITANNI, I 3; lands of, II 659, 773.
—Asiatics of the army of, IV 722.
—Called Naharin, II 867.
—Caves of, II 773.
—Chiefs of, II 773, 804.
—Cities of, II 773.
—Kings of: Artatama, II 866 n. h; Shuttarna, II 866 n. h; Dushratta, II 866 n. h.
—Overthrown by Thutmose III, II 773; Ramses III, IV 131.
—Princesses of: Mutemuya, II 866 n. h; Gilukhipa, II 866 n. h, 867; Tadukhipa, II 866 n. h.
—Tribute from, II 804.

MIYU: district of Wawat, IV 480.

MONS CASSIUS, II 582 n. c.

MUT, VILLAGE OF: in Dakhel of the southern oasis, IV 725 n. c.

N

NAHARIN, LAND OF, III 321, 434; not included in the districts of Kheta or Kode, III 321, 344, 346; Mitanni designated as in, II 867; great bend of (=Euphrates), crossed by Thutmose III, II 479 n. a, 631; waters of (=Euphrates), II 583; located between Carchemish and Naharin, II 583; marshes of, II 631; III 115, 118; boundary of, II 871.
—Campaigns to: by Thutmose I, II 81, 85; Thutmose III, II 476–80, 485, 496–503, 532; Amenhotep, II II 800; Thutmose IV, II 817–19; Amenhotep III, II 858; Ramses II, III 365.
—Captured by: Kadesh, II 420; Thutmose III, II 479, 498; Amenhotep II, II 800; Thutmose IV, II 817–19; Amenhotep III, II 858; Seti I, III 114, 115, 118; Ramses II, III 306–312, 317–27, 344.
—Revolt of, II 498; coalition of, with Kheta, III 309; sent auxiliary troops to Kadesh, II 532.
—Tablet erected there by Thutmose I, II 478; by Thutmose III, II 481; boundary stone of Thutmose III placed east of Euphrates, II 478; tablet erected by Amenhotep II in, II 800.
—King of, II 81, 479; princes of, II 480, 819; Satirna, chief of, II 867; Kirgipa, princess of, II 867.
—Populations of, II 858; harem ladies of, II 867.
—Tunip in the land of, III 365; towns of, II 479; settlements of, II 479; prisoners of, II 581.
—Tribute of, II 482, 819; harvest of, II 480; booty from, II 480, 500, 501, 532, 817.
—Products of: oxen, II 482; calves, II 482; bullocks, II 482; bulls, II 482; incense, II 482; sweet oil, II 482; green oil, II 482; fruit, II 482; grain, II 480; horses, II 482; gold, II 482; silver vessels, II 482; chariots II 482; weapons of war, II 482.

NAHR EL-KELB, stela of Ramses II, III 297; see Dog River.

NAPATA, I 22; II 647; IV 895, 923; city of Nubia, II 797; a prince of Tikhsi hanged on its wall, II 797; southern boundary of the territory of the viceroy of Kush, II 1022, 1025; also called Karoy, II 1020, 1025.
—Cliff temple of, IV 897–99, 924; pure mountain of, IV 924, 932; see Gebel Barkal.
—Amon of, IV 921, 924, 929, 932.
—Stela of Tanutamon, IV 919–34.

NAPHTALI: cities of, IV 714 n. b.

NEDYT: flats of, where the enemies of Osiris were ceremoniously slain, I 669.

"NEFERIRKERE-BELOVED-OF-THE-DIVINE-ENNEAD": city of, I 165.

"NEFERIRKERE-BELOVED-OF-THE-SPIRITS-OF-HELIOPOLIS": city of, I 165.

NEFRUS: wall of, IV 820.

*Ng*ʾ*w* (ox), city of, I 493.

NEGEB, IV 715; battle in, II 580; prisoners of, II 580; people of, called Asiatics, II 580.

NEGRO: land of, I 146; II 797; III 285, 457, 490; IV 477, 724.
—Negroes, II 71, 849, 1035; III 448 n. b, 451; IV 338; slain, I 465, 707; chief's children and commanders slain, I 358; prisoners taken, I 538; II 648; chiefs of, I 359; II 648.
—Revolt of, II 826.
—Imported to Egypt for attendants, II 494, 526.
—Captives, III 40, 44, 452; IV 225; servants, II 854; slaves, IV 539.

Negro—
—Negro tribes, I 311, 333–36, 510.
—Products of, I 336; baskets of, II 271; ships, I 652; bulls, I 658; herds, I 652; grain, I 658; trading, I 652; wells, I 658; II 850.
—Negro words: "urum" = black, IV 821 n. g.
—Negresses, II 854.

NEKHEB: ancient name of El Kab, I 293, 373, 609; II 7; Lords of: see Index V; for further references see El Kab.

NEKHEN (= Hieraconpolis): city of, I 201, 252, 293; II 47; northern boundary of the territory of the viceroy of Kush, II 1020, 1022, 1025.
—Lord of: see Index V; district officials of, II 722; mayors of, II 722; Harmini, II 47, 48; kenbeti of, II 722; "Attached to," see Index V; Judge attached to, see Index V.
—Gods of, II 888; Heket, white one of, II 205 n. a; Nekhbet, the white goddess of, III 100.
—Products of, II 722.

NEMYEW: chiefs of, II 267.

NER: temple of, in Heracleopolis, IV 968; restored by Hor, IV 968.

NERU: see Index II.

NETER: in central Delta, Tefnakhte, great prince of, IV 818.

NETHER WORLD, I 378; II 95, 293, 664, 936; III 259, 272, 278; IV 4, 182, 309, 353, 411, 485, 852; the glorious ones entering the, III 17; going in and out of, II 353, 378; IV 187; door of, III 240; gates of, II 378; gods of, III 280; IV 473; water of, III 291, 292; king of, IV 182.

NEW ISLES: domains of Re in, IV 265.

NEW TOWNS: Nekonekh, governor of, I 216; Nehri, ruler of, I 628; chief of, I 354.

NIBMAT: bend of Horus, a district, I 312.

NILE, I 483; III 587; IV 354, 407, 479, 480, 481, 482; flooding ancient landmarks through irrigation, in time of Kheti II, I 407.
—Rising of, in time of Uni, I 42; of Shabataka, I 43.
—Connected with Red Sea, II 248.
—Full Nile, royal title, II 992, 1003; III 486.
—Great, Nile, II 883, 887; III 404; IV 246.
—High Nile, IV 470; to be reported to the vizier, II 709; as epithet of the king, II 994.
—Nile levels, I 22, 95, 97, 98, 99, 100, 101, 103, 104, 105, 106, 107, 108, 109, 110, 111, 112, 113, 114, 115, 119, 120, 121, 122, 123, 124, 125, 126, 127, 128, 129, 130, 131, 133, 134, 135, 136, 137, 138, 139, 140, 141, 142, 143, 144, 146, 147, 148, 152, 157, 159, 165, 749, 752; IV 695, 696, 697, 698, 743, 793, 794, 886, 887, 888.
—Shores of, IV 72; sources of, III 171 n. b; valley of, I 1, 8; III 290.
—"I was a Nile [to my people]," Tefibi, I 395.

NINE BOWS, I 423H; II 72, 120, 148, 656, 792, 828, 836, 887, 1029; III 30, 77, 103, 110, 114, 132, 346, 408, 414, 457, 465, 474, 479, 489, 498, 510, 577, 580, 590, 600, 607, 617; IV 38, 49, 52, 54, 55, 57, 62, 63, 66, 67, 68, 71, 72, 77, 78, 81, 103, 104, 105, 110, 123, 124, 126, 246, 259, 304, 351, 620, 712, 718, 720.
—Chiefs of, III 26; captives from, IV 190.
—Sun of, royal title, II 1037; III 38, 44, 152; IV 122.
—Thebes, mistress of, IV 751; Khnum, binder of, II 170, 171; Mut, mistress of, II 891.

NIY, city in upper Retenu: gifts from, II 125; south of Naharin, II 481; elephant hunt at, II 588; south of Orontes, II 786; walls of, II 786.
—Asiatics of, II 786; prisoners from, II 798A.

NOMADS (Asiatic): strongholds of, overthrown by Nessu-Montu, I 471.

NORTH, the, III 155; IV 47, 72, 130, 359, 864; great lake of, III 479; countries of, III 457; chiefs of, IV 860, 930; gods of, II 217.

NORTH AND SOUTH, I 161, 274, 340; genii of, 206; union of, I 78; numbering of cattle in, I 81; building the wall of, I 146.
—Prophets of, II 936.

NORTH COUNTRIES, III 351; chiefs of, II 1032; captives of, III 351.
—Northern countries: two doors of, IV 1014; Governor of, see Index V.

Northern Isle: probably the same as Isle of Snefru, I 312.

Northerners, I 81; II 656, 797, 835, 887; III 273, 574; IV 722, 845, 934.

Northerners of the Isles: attacking Northern Syria, IV 64; camping in Amor, IV 64; intending to invade Egypt, IV 64; allies of, IV 64.

Northland, I 156, 158, 212, 311, 407; II 224, 341, 355; III 281; IV 189 n. c, 190, 780, 825, 830, 832, 835, 838, 841, 853, 859, 876, 882, 883, 895, 922, 925, 927, 934, 1003.
—Avaris of the, II 296, 303; city of, IV 215.
—Belonging to the Heracleopolitan kingdom, I 407 n. b, 413, 414.
—Wine gardens of Amon in, IV 213; stern-rope of, II 885; Busiris, city of, IV 485; princes of, IV 868, 873.

Nubia (*T*ɔ-*pd·t*), III 31, 179, 479, 500, 501, 502; IV 443, 929, 994, 1014.
—Regions of, I 311, 336, 510; II 843, 845 n. f, 849.
—Campaigns to: by Pepinakht, I 355, 358, 359; Mekhu, I 363, 365; Sebni, I 363, 366, 368; Mentuhotep I, I 423 H; Sesostris III, I 658; Ahmose I, II 5; Thutmose I, II 67–77, 78–80, 84; Thutmose II, II 122; Thutmose III, II 446–48; Thutmose IV, II 826–29; Amenhotep III, II 842–55 Ramses II, III 448 n. b, 457; Ramses III, IV 136–38; Sheshonk I, IV 723.
—Towns of, conquered by Thutmose III, II 645, 646, 647; Napata, city of, II 797.
—Chief of, I 317, 602; II 71, 80; Officials of: see Index V.
—Temple of Amon in, IV 218.
—Gods of, III 290; Horus of, I 500; Anuket, mistress of, I 644; Dedun, presider over, II 170, 171, 176; Nibmare, lord of, II 894, 897; Harakhte, lord of, III 499.
—Impost of, IV 190; reckonings of, III 448 n. b.
—Upper Nubia, products of: gold brought from, I 665; fine white stone of, II 176.
—Inscriptions in, I 8, 10; under the empire, I 21.

Nubian Troglodytes, II 11, 268, 646, 837, 892.

Nubians, I 423H, 658; II 71, 101, 916; sacrificed to Amon, II 645.

Nuges: city in southern Lebanon, ally of Kheta, III 309; under the rule of Kadesh, II 436; called a city of Retenu, II 557; plundered by Thutmose III, II 436; district of, II 490, 508.
—Booty of, II 436, 490, 508; impost of, II 557; products of, II 490.

Nun (the primeval celestial ocean): Hathor, mistress of, I 178; dwellers in, II 95.

O

Oasis: hills of, III 580; district of Toyeh in, III 580; captured by Libya, III 580.

Oasis, northern, III 580 n. c; tribute from, II 385, 386; wine-gardens of Amon in, IV 212; products of, IV 229, 283, 387.

Oasis Dwellers: land of, expedition of Sesostris I to, under Ikudidi, I 527.

Oasis of Amon, II 189.

Oasis of Bit, IV 867.

Oasis Region: tribute from, II 386; Intef, lord of, II 763, 767; Thebans banished to, IV 655, 656.

Oasis, Southern: also called oasis of Dakhel, IV 725 n. a, 726 n. c, 734; and oasis of el-Khargeh, IV 726 n. c, 734; known by ancients as Oasis Major, IV 726 n. c; two towns of, IV 726; two lands of, IV 726; Sutekh, lord of, IV 726; land of, IV 726; rebellion of, IV 726; organization of, IV 726.
Wine and shedeh from, IV 734, 992; tribute from, II 385, 386; wine-garden of Amon in, IV 213.

Okeanos: see Circle, Great.

Ombos: district officials of, II 720; recorder of, II 720; scribe of the recorder of, II 720; kenbeti of, II 720.
—Temple of Sutekh in, IV 359.
—Set, god of, III 583; Sutekh, lord of, IV 359.
—Products of, II 720.

On (=Heliopolis), II 814; two lands of, III 600.

Opet, Southern (=Luxor), II 886; IV 671, 743; restored by Senmut, II 27, 351.
—Ceremony of the voyage to, II 554; feast of, II 591, 809, 887, 888; III 58; IV 671.
—Inclosure wall of, II 887; see also Luxor.

OPHIEION, I 459 n. e; see Hefat.

ORONTES, III 311, 326, 336; ford of, II 784; cattle at the, II 784; booty taken in, II 784, 785; channel of, III 308.

ORYX NOME (XVI of Upper Egypt), I 518; location of, I 619, 626; horizon of Horus, a part of, I 619; bordering on the South to the Hare nome, I 626; North to the Jackal nome, I 626; extending in west to the western highlands, I 626; troops of, I 519, Commander in chief of: see Index V.

—Fields of, I 523, 626.

—Great lords of: Khnumhotep I, I 464, 626; Amen(emhet), I 518, 522 bis; Kheti, I 637 n. a; shepherds of, I 522.

—Temple of Khnum, lord of Hirur, I 637 n. a.

OTHU: captured by Seti I, III 114.

OX (*Ng ͗ w*), city of, I 493.

OXYRRHYNCUS (=Behnesa): XIX nome of Upper Egypt, I 427; IV 818 n. b, 820, 837; district of, IV 948; army of, I 429, 442; boundaries of, I 632.

—Set, lord of, IV 368; temple of, IV 368.

P

PALESTINE: inscriptions in, I 8; civilization of, I 20; campaign in southern Palestine by Uni, I 315; people from, settling in Delta, III 10; conquered by Ramses II, III 471. See also Syria, Kharu Zahi, Retenu.

PANOPOLIS: nome of, north of Thinis, I 529 n. e; Min, lord of, II 181; Min, Horus and Isis of, IV 366; temple of Min in, II 181; IV 366.

PATORIS: nomes of, IV 905.

PAUZY: temple of Thoth in, IV 368.

PE: souls of, I 264; temple of Buto in, I 500; gods of, II 888; Horus, lord of, IV 1017; Buto, mistress of, I 500; royal statue of Sesostris for, I 500; Mentuhotep, lord of, I 512.

PEDES: III 306, 349; ally of Kheta, III 309 n. d, 312.

PEDETISHEW: transporting grain in ships to Kheta, III 580.

PEHER: captured by Seti I, III 114.

PEKANAN: city in Palestine, III 88; plundered by Merneptah, III 617.

—Pekanan: as part of a temple name, according to which Zahi would be a part of Pekanan, IV 219.

PEKER (district at Abydos): feast of, II 94.

PELESET: a Palestine people, conquered by Ramses III, IV 44, 129, 403; chieftain of, IV 129; soldiers of, by land and sea, IV 44; ally of the northerners, IV 64; towns of, IV 71; captives of, IV 81, 82, 129; headdress of, IV 73.

PEMDSHE: (Oxyrrhyncus), IV 818 n. c.

PEMEHTEM: land in Syria; captured by Seti I, III 94.

PENINEYWE, IV 867.

PER-BAST (=Bubastis): residence of Osorkon III, IV 830.

PER-BENEBDED (=Mendes): IV 830; Zeamonefonekh, prince of, IV 878.

PER-BERSET: a Delta city, III 576.

PEREK: Hittite city; Sutekh, god of III 386.

PER-GERER, IV 878.

PER-HAPI: Khereha in, IV 878; Pebes, prince of, IV 878.

PER-HATHOR-RESIT, I 373.

PER-HEBY, IV 878.

PER-HOR: mayor of, II 742; products of, II 742.

PERIRE, III 588, 600; fields of, on the western boundary of Egypt, III 579; district of, III 583.

PERKED, SOUTHERN: Methen, ruler of, I 172, 174.

PER-MANU: temple of, IV 956.

Pr-mr-yw: town of, II 721; town ruler of, II 721; products of, II 721.

PERNEBETPIH, IV 818.

PERNESER: temple of Buto in, I 159.

PERNEZED: capital of Oxyrrhyncus-Behnesa, IV 818, 837.

PERNUB, near Sais, IV 818.

PERONEKH: Sebek of, IV 547.

PER-OSIRIS (=Busiris) IV 830; Sheshonk, chief of Me, lord of, IV 830; Pemou, prince of, IV 878.

PER-PEG, IV 831.

PER-SEKHEMKHEPERRE, near Illahun, IV 818, 853; wall of, IV 853; stronghold of, IV 853.

PERSEPA: Methen, palace-ruler of, I 172.

PERSHESTHET: Methen ruler of, I 172.

PERSIANS: accession of, I 47, 48, 50.

PER-SOPED, IV 878, 956; Pekrur, hereditary prince of, IV 932.

PER-THUTUPREHUI (Hermopolis parva): army of, IV 830, 878; Enekhhor, commander of, IV 878.

PERWEN: Nubian land, I 510.

PERWERSAH: Methen, ruler of, I 174.

PERZOZ: Horus of the South, lord of, IV 726; prophet of, IV 726.

PESEBEK: town of, IV 784.

PETEN, I 493.

PEZEDKU: canal near Avaris, II 9.

PHILAE, I 459 n. e.

PHOENICIA: invaded by Ahmose I, II 4, 19–20.

PITHOM: pools of, III 638; located in Theku, III 638.

PORT OF THE SOUTH: northern frontier city of the South in the time of Tefibi, I 396.

PUNT, II 253, 290; gods of, II 286; known by hearsay to ancestors, II 287; Wereret, mistress of, II 288; called the Red Land, I 429; called God's Land, I 433; II 253, 255, 265, 271, 286; III 116; IV 407; Hathor, mistress of, II 252, 255; called the land of rest, III 116.

—Location of, II 249; in the east, II 892; southern boundary of Egypt, II 321.

—Myrrh terraces of, II 260; ways to, II 285; IV 130; highways of, III 155.

—Expeditions to: by Khufu (?), II 247; Sahure, I 161; II 247; Isesi, I 351; II 247; under Pepi II, by Enenkhet, I 360; II 247; under Pepi II by Thethi, I 361; II 247; Mentuhotep III, I 429; II 247; Amenemhet II, I 605; II 247; Sesostris II, II 247; Hatshepsut, II 246–95, 296, 299; Harmhab, III 37–39; Seti I, III 116; Ramses III, IV 407.

—Chiefs of, II 255, 256, 260, 261, 262, 267; III 37, 38; Perehu, II 254, 258.

—Tribes of: Irem, II 267; Nemyew, II 267.

—A Punt, made in the garden of Amon at Thebes, II 295.

—Puntites, II 288; called "Southerns of God's Land," II 288.

—Tribute from, II 261, 262; III 37; IV 407; gifts from, I 351; slaves from, II 486.

—Products of, II 750; dwarf from, I 351; marvels of, II 265, 266, 271, 272, 274, 277–78, 321, 377, 486, 513; odor of, I 762; II 196, 274; gold from, II 486; gold dust from, III 37; ivory, II 265, 272, 486; shells, II 272; green gold of Emu, II 265; electrum, I 161; II 272; throw sticks, II 272; ebony, II 265, 272, 486; dried myrrh, II 486, 513; fragrant woods, II 265; III 527; myrrh resin, II 265; khesyt wood, II 265; myrrh trees, II 265; cinnamon wood, II 265; myrrh, I 161, 429; II 260, 321; IV 130, 210, 333, 929; ihmut incense, II 265; sonter incense, II 265; incense, IV 130; eye cosmetic, II 265; asses, II 258; apes, II 265; monkeys, II 265; dogs, II 265; southern panther, II 265, 272; panther skins, II 265, 272, 486; small cattle, II 272; oxen, II 486; calves, II 486; bulls, II 486; ostrich feathers, III 37; manna, IV 286, 390.

PUNT RELIEFS: by Hatshepsut in temple at Dêr el-Bahri, II 246 ff.; by Harmhab on his Karnak pylons, III 37.

R

RABBITH: town of Israel, in Issachar, conquered by Sheshonk I, IV 712.

"RAMSES-MERIAMON," city of Ramses, III 261, 371; IV 362, 369, 414; Amon, god of, III 371; Ptah, god of, III 371; temple of Sutekh in, IV 362; people of, IV 369.

—The city of: Palace of, in the city of the Northland, IV 215; name of, IV 215; built by Ramses III, IV 215; gardens of, IV 215; boulevards of, IV 215; sacred avenue of IV 215; people of, IV, 225.

RANOFER: district of, IV 830; Yewepet, king of, IV 878.

RAPHIA, IV 716.

RED LAND, II 245, 297; III 179, 270, 471, 598; expedition to Punt by Henu to bring myrrh from the sheiks of, I 429, 430.

—Mentuhotep, lord of, I 532; pillar of, I 533; Thutmose II, ruler of, II 116; Hatshepsut, ruler of, II 299, 319, 321.
—Chiefs of, executed, II 808; sheiks of, I 423D.

RED MOUNTAIN: quarry of, I 493; II 975, 976; highland goddess, mistress of, I 493; II 297; sandstone from, II 153; gritstone from, II 917 n. c; Chief of works in: see Index V.

RED SEA, I 7, 433; ship-building at, by Enenkhet, I 360; by Henu, I 432; battle at northern end of, I 360; hunting at, I 456; oblation at, I 432; connected with the Nile, II 248.

REDESIYEH: temple of, III 162; built by Seti I, III 172–74; town of, settled by Seti I, III 172; gods of, III 173; stronghold of, III 174.
—Rock inscriptions, by Seti I, III 197–98.
—Temple inscriptions, by Seti I, III 162–95.

REHESU: near Letopolis; Sekhmet, mistress of, IV 878; house of, IV 878.

REHOB: city of Israel, conquered by Sheshonk I, IV 712.

REKHSEN: Hittite city, Sutekh, god of, III 386.

REKRERET: sacred district of Anubis in Siût; Anubis, lord of, I 540, 572, 583.

Rs-nf.t: district of, II 731; scribe of, II 731; products of, II 731.

RESENET: a sacred district of Sais; mysterious linen from, IV 1011.

RESHET: malachite from, II 321.

RESHU: land of, under rule of Hatshepsut, II 299.

RESIDENCE CITY of Ramses III; temple of Sutekh in, IV 362.

RETENU, II 413, 439, 477, 596, 616; III 102, 103, 270, 476, 498; IV 219, 709 n. b; called God's Land, II 451, 820, 888; "Retenu and all the northern countries of the ends of the earth," II 761 n. a; cities of Kharu not included in, II 798A; Lebanon located within, II 548.
—Campaigns to, by: Sesostris III, I 680; Thutmose I, II 81; Thutmose II, II 125; Thutmose III, 1st campaign, II 402, 408–443; 2d campaign, II 444–49; 3d campaign, II 450–52; 4th campaign, II 453; 5th campaign, II 455–62; 6th campaign, II 463–67; 7th campaign, II 468–75; 8th campaign, II 476–87; 9th campaign, II 488–95; 10th campaign, II 496–503; 11th campaign, II 504; 12th campaign, II 505; 13th campaign, II 506–515; 14th campaign, II 516–19; 15th campaign, II 520–23; 16th campaign, II524–27; 17th campaign, II 528–40; Amenhotep II, II 790, 798A; Seti I, III 94, 139, 147; Ramses II, III 392, 448 n. b, 451, 457.
—Princes of, II 413, 471; nobles of, II 790; chiefs of, II 162, 225, 445, 447, 466, 467, 491, 525; III 94, 97, 106, 107, 139, 151, 392, 448 n. b, 451; IV 623.
—Captives from, II 162, 402, 467, 790; III 97, 392, 448 n. b; slaves from, 436, 447, 467, 471, 491, 518.
—Tribute from, II 445, 447, 448, 466, 471, 491, 518, 533(?), 534(?), 761, 820; III 106, 110; presents from, II 1030; dues of, II 596; plunder from, II 790; impost from, IV 28; harvest of, II 473.
—Cities of: Nuges, II 557; Yenoam, II 557; Herenkeru, II 557.
—Products of: gold from, II 447, 471, 491; III 111; chariots, wrought with gold, II 413, 447, 467, 491; gold horn from, II 447; flat dishes from, II 447; silver from, II 447, 491; III 111; malachite from, III 111; lapis lazuli from, III 111; copper from, II 447, 471, 491; vessels of copper from, II 491; lead from, II 471, 491; feldspar from, II 491; colors from, II 491; green stone, II 473, 491; sparkling stone, II 473; costly stone, II 473, 491; III 111; incense from, II 447, 472, 491; dried myrrh from, II 491; plants of, II 451; flowers of, II 452; honeyed wine, II 447; ᶜ*g.t*-wood from, II 447; ivory, II 447; carob wood, II 447; *mrw*-wood, II 447; *psgw*-wood, II 447; fire wood, II 447; cedar, II 838, 888; grain, II 473; clean grain, II 473; barley, II 473; green oil, II 473; wine, II 473; fruit, II 473; oxen, II 491; horses, II 403, 447, 467, 491; asses, II 491; bulls, II 447; bullocks, II 447; small cattle, II 447; calves, II 447, 471, 491.

RETENU, THE LOWER: subject to

Amenhotep II, II 789A; Amenhotep III, II 858; Seti I, III 116; Osorkon II, IV 749.
—Prisoners from, II 798A.

RETENU, THE UPPER, IV 749; subject to Thutmose II, II 125; Thutmose III, II 451; Amenhotep II, II 766, 798A; Amenhotep III, II 858; Seti I, III 112, 116; Ramses II, III 366; Osorkon II, IV 749.
—Prisoners from, II 798A; chiefs of, II 1033; III 112.

RHINOCOLURA, III 51 n. b.

RIDGE: north of the sand-dwellers (southern Palestine), I 315.

RIVER, IV 823, 831; the great (=Nile), III 580; IV 405; the Conopus branch of the Nile, IV 405 n. a.

ROSTA, III 230; Anubis, lord of, IV 4.

ROYENET (=Tehneh), I 213, 218, 221; Hathor of, I 213.

S

Ꜣ-y-wt: land of, north of Kadesh, II 465.

SAFT-EL-HENNEH (=Per-Soped), IV 956.

SAHSETENI, VOYAGE TO, I 112.

SAI, ISLAND OF, II 652.

SAIS, DISTRICT OF, IV 957; southern Bedwin in, IV 957; Mehenet, a district of, IV 982; Resenet, a district of, IV 1011; nome of, Methen, local governor of, I 172, 173, 174.
—Chiefs of: Khentemsemeti, I 609; Tefnakhte, IV 850.
Neit, mistress of, IV 830; Sekhmet, mistress of, IV 878; house of, IV 878, 956.
—Royal statue for, I 500.

SAKKARA, CEMETERY OF, I 289.
—Mastaba-chamber of Methen, I 170 n. c; mastaba of Nenekhsekhmet, I 237; Ptahshepses, I 254; mastaba-tomb of Sabu-Ibebi, I 282; pyramid of Mernere, I 321 n. a.
—Stela of: Nenekhsekhmet, I 237 n. c; Harmhab, III 2.
—Tomb of Harmhab, III 1 n. a.

SAMHUDET: city in the Delta, II 935; IV 878.

SAND DWELLERS: Asiatic, I 311; II 321; III 155; IV 130; five rebellions of, in time of Pepi I, I 314; hacked up by army of Uni, I 313 bis; captives taken by Uni, I 313; their strongholds overturned, I 313; figs and vines destroyed, I 313; numerous troops of, I 313; ridge north of, I 315; slain by Pepi-nakht at the northern end of Red Sea, I 360; expedition against, by Nessumontu, I 471; =Asiatic Troglodytes, I 471; silenced by Mentuhotep, I 532; slain by Thutmose III, II 661.
—Chiefs of, II 70; tribute given by, II 101.

SAND RANGERS, I 493; II 916.

SARBÛT-EL-KHADEM: reached by sea, II 877.
—Rock inscriptions by: Amenemhet II, I 606 n. b; Khenemsu, I 715, 715A; Sebek-hir-hab, I 725 n. d; Ptahwer, I 728; Amenemhet, I 730; Amenemhet IV, I 750; Thutmose III, II 450 n. a.
—Stela of Harure, I 733 n. b; officer of Amenhotep III, II 877.

"SATISFIER-OF-THE-GODS," city of: mayor of, II 1041; fortress of, II 1041; Penno, deputy of, 1041; Mermose, prophet in, II 1041; priest in, II 1041.

SEA, II 220; III 480.
—The great lake of the North, III 479.

SEA, COUNTRY OF THE: Ekwesh of, III 588, 601; Sherden of, IV 129; Teresh of, IV 129.

SEA OF SYRIA (Kharu), IV 565.

SEA PEOPLE, IV 52.

SEBENNYTOS. Akenesh, prince of, IV 878.

SEBI: probably identical with Alabastronpolis, III 20 n. c; Horus, lord of, III 20; Harmhab, chief prophet of, III 20.

SEBÛʿA: temple of Ramses II, III 504.

SEHEL, ISLAND OF, I 642.
—Rock inscription of: Sesostris III, I 642–48; the family of Neferhotep, I 753 n. b; Thure, II 75, 76; Thutmose III, II 649 n. d; Ramose, II 937 n. a; Ramses II, III 553 n. b, 557; Seti (II), III 646.

SEHEZ: Sokar, lord of, IV 855; Menhy of, IV 855.

SEIR: people of, IV 404; a tribe of the Shasu, IV 404; captured by Ramses III, IV 404; tents of, IV 404; cattle of, IV 404.

SEKHEMITE NOME (II of Lower Egypt), I 173, 175.
SEKHEMU: city of, in Xois nome, I 174.
SEKHPEN: Hittite city, Sutekh, god of, III 386.
SEKMEM: city in Syria, I 680.
SEKTU: ships of, II 492.
SEMNEH: southern boundary of Egypt in the time of Sesostris III, I 652; fortress of, I 653 n. c, 752; temple of Thutmose III, I 653 n. c; II 61 n. a, 651.
—Rock inscriptions by Sekhemre-Khutowe, I 751 n. a.
—Stelæ of: Sesostris III, I 651–60; Mermose, II 851–55.
—Temple inscription of Thure, 61 n. a; of Thutmose III, II 167–76; of Nehi, II 651.
SENT, a stronghold: Methen, ruler of, I 172.
SENZAR: battle in, II 584. See Sezar.
SEP: district of, IV 948; Anubis, lord of, IV 368; temple of, IV 368.
SEPED: Libyan people, captured by Ramses III, IV 52–91; seed of, III 91; circumcision practiced among (?), IV 52, 54 (?).
SEREP: Hittite city, III 386.
SERES: Hittite city, Sutekh, god of, III 386.
SERREH: temple of Ramses II in, III 502.
SESU: temple of Set in, IV 369.
SETHU, Negro land, I 336; chief of, I 334, 336 bis.
SEWEW (=Wadi Gasus): on the coast of the Red Sea, opposite Coptos, I 605.
SEZAR (=Senzar): prisoners from, II 798A.
SHABTUNA: city on the west side of Orontes, south of Kadesh, III 310, 319, 324; IV 131.
SHAI: Libyan people, slain by Ramses III, IV 405.
SHARUHEN: flight of Hyksos to, II 4; siege of, II 4, 12 n. g, 13 n. b; revolt in, II 416; captured by Sheshonk I, IV 716.
SHAS-HERET, IV 994.
SHASU (Bedwin of Sinai and vicinity, especially north of it), II 124; Khnum, smiter of, II 170, 171.
—Conquered by Thutmose III, II 517; Seti I, III 86, 88, 101; Ramses II, III 457; Ramses III, IV 129, 403; conquest of, from the fortress of Tharu to Pekanan, III 88.
—People of Seir, a tribe of, IV 404; of Edom, III 638; in army of Kheta, III 319.
—Rebellion of, III 101; captives from, III 108, 457; IV 129; chieftain of, IV 129.
SHAT: Nubian land, I 510; "good white stone" of, temple of Kummeh built of, I 510.
SHATB: modern city just south of Assiut, I 401 n. a.
SHATT ER-RÊGAL (near Assuan): relief of Mentuhotep II in, I 425.
SHEDEBOD, TEMPLE OF, IV 780.
SHEDET: in Fayûm, IV 369.
SHEKELESH: a northern people, invading Egypt, III 574, 579, 595; slain by Merneptah, III 588; ally of the northerners, IV 64; captives from, III 588; IV 81.
SHEKEN: canal of, III 576.
SHEKH SAʿÎD: tombs of the princes of the VI Dyn., I 688; restored by Thutnakt, I 689.
—Tomb inscription of Thutnakt, I 688 n. a.
SHEMESH-EDOM: captured by Amenhotep II, II 783; located in the Lebanon region, II 783; booty from, II 783.
SHEMIK: Nubian land, I 510.
SHEM-RE: city of, I 125.
SHERDEN: a northern people of the sea, IV 129; captives from, III 588, 601; IV 129, 403; rebellious-hearted, III 491; infantry of, IV 72; invading Egypt, III 574, 579; slain by Merneptah, III 588 bis; Ramses III, IV 403.
SHERDEN: a foreign class of mercenary troops, III 307; IV 50, 51, 397, 402, 410.
SHEREM: city in northern Palestine, conquered by Ramses II, III 356.
SHERET-METHEN: city of, I 172, 173.
SHESHOTEP (modern Shatb, south of Assiut): city of, I 401; Khnum, lord of, IV 366; temple of, IV 366.
SHETA: wild cattle hunt in, II 864.

SHET-METHEN: in the Saitic nome, I 173 bis.

SHETYT: Sokar god of, I 288.

SHILOH, IV 131.

SHINAR: captured by Amenhotep III, II 859; Ramses II, III 366 n. c.
—Tribute of, II 484.
—Products of: lapis lazuli, II 484; artificial lapis lazuli, II 484; lapis lazuli of Babylon, II 484; ram's head (artificial) of lapis lazuli, I 484.

SHORE: western (of the Nile?), IV 405; plundered by Libyans, IV 405.

SHUNEH YUSUF, IV 878 n. f.

SHUNEM: city of Israel, in Issachar; conquered by Sheshonk, IV 712.

SIDON: 10,000 ships in harbor of, IV 574.

SILSELEH, IV 706; Sebek, lord of, III 208; rock temple of, III 208; built by Harmhab, III 552–60.
—Sandstone quarry of, I 49; II 935; III 205 n. c; IV 18, 701 n. d.
—Rock inscription, by official of Ikhnaton, II 934–35; Seti I, III 206–8; Ramses II, III 552, 554, 555, 556, 559, 560; Roy, III 627–28; Siptah, III 648; Setemhab, IV 19, 20; Haremsaf, IV 701–8.

SIMYRA: city of, II 476, 528 n. h; captured by Thutmose III, II 465; by Seti I, III 114.

SINAI: peninsula of, I 7, 10, 42, 728; copper mines of, operated in I Dyn., I 168; by Snefru, I 168–69; mine land of, visited by Sihathor, and malachite brought from, I 602; reached by sea, I 718; II 877.
—Gifts of (=mining products), I 353; expedition of Ramses III to, IV 409.

SIÛT, II 729; IV 358, 795; see also Assiut; canal of irrigation dug by Kheti II, I 407; its princes defended the kings of Heracleopolis against Thebes, I 396, 401, 411, 422.
—Princes of: Tefibi, I 393–97; Kheti I, I 398–404; Kheti II, I 405–414; mother of Kheti II "lord" of Siut, I 414; Hepzefi, I 535–93.
—Counts of, I 538, 547, 557.
—Officials of, I 547, 579; recorder of, II 745; scribe of the recorder of, II 745; kenbeti of, II 745.
—Citizens of, I 546, 547, 578, 579.
—Temple of Upwawet, I 398, 403, 541; official body of, I 550; gifts to, I 404, 407; lay priests of, I 539.
—Temple of Anubis, lord of Rekreret, *w*ᶜ*b*-priests of, I 540; great *w*ᶜ*b*-priest of, I 572.
—Necropolis of: overseer of, I 582; official body of, I 584.
—Products of, II 745.
—Tomb inscriptions at, I 10, 391–92; tomb III, I 393–97; tomb IV, I 398–404; tomb V, I 405–414; cliff tomb of Hepzefi, I 535–93.

SOCOH: city of Judah, conquered by Sheshonk I, IV 713.

SOLEB: fortress of, II 894, 895, 897; temple of, II 890, 894–98.

SOMALI COAST, II 249.

SOUTH, II 341; III 155; IV 47, 310, 652, 864, 907, 944.
—Nomes of, IV 857; war with, by Tefibi, I 396; Henu, overseer of the administration of, I 428.
—City of (=Thebes), II 1038.
—Vizier of, IV 224.
—Governor of Uni, I 293, 320 ter; extent of, in time of Uni, I 311; real governor of, Nenekhseskhnum, I 305.
—Great lord of: Hapuseneb, II 389; Lords of: see Index V.
—Magnates of: their rank, II 675; Pillar of: see Index V.
—Affairs of, I 332; boundaries of: in the Middle Kingdom, I 396, 396 n. h; gods of, II 217, 828; granite of, II 315; elephantine of the, II 171; door of: see Door of the South; treasury of, II 614; wine-gardens of Amon in IV 212.

SOUTH COUNTRIES, II 646; princes of, II 887.
—Tribute of, II 652, 1038; impost of, II 652, 653; gifts of, II 271.
—Electrum from, II 654.

SOUTH AND NORTH, I 152, 423D, 451; II 161, 203, 285, 352, 578, 715; III 20, 268, 286, 404; IV 67, 313, 359; captured by Mentuhotep I, I 423H; recruits of, II 332; infantry of, II 429.
—The great authorities of, IV 460; chiefs of, II 871, 872; III 448 n. b; mayors of, II 701, 768.
—Gods of, II 219, 224, 800, 812; IV 183, 335, 352, 353, 363, 364, 383, 470, 731; goddesses of, IV 352, 363, 364, 383, 470, 731.

South and North—
—Tribute of, III 13, 554; harvest of, II 871.
—Fortresses of, II 675.
—Cattle of Amon in, II 912; IV 212.

South and North Countries, II 213; captives from, II 162; expeditions to, II 818.

Southern City (=Thebes), II 706, 826; III 82, 206, 256, 261; IV 414, 467, 708.
—Vizier of, II 675, 717; garrison of, II 694.
—Steward of, III 32C.

Southern Countries, III 285, 480; tribute of, III 116; governor of, II 170; imposts of, II 281; marvels of, II 282; door of, IV 990, 995.

Southern Islands: scribe of, II 726; products of, II 726.

Southern Lake: next to Nomes XX and XXI of Upper Egypt, I 172.

Southerners, II 341, 797, 835, 887; III 204 n. b, 272; IV 722, 845, 934.
—Of God's Land, II 288.

Southland, III 281; IV 190, 819, 880, 905, 907, 922, 934, 948, 958F; bow-rope of, II 885; gods of, IV 34; products of, IV 34.

Sphinx of Harmakhis: district of, I 179.

Suan, I 493; see Assuan.

Succoth, III 638 n. a.

Suhen-em-Opet: castle in Thebes, II 402.

Sycamore: region of, I 493; fields of, II 299; bearing myrrh, II 299.

Syene: in the Delta; wine of, IV 734.

Syria (*Ḫ*ꜣ-*rw*) I 3, 20, 43; IV 313, 341, 383, 387, 410, 582, 883; inscriptions in, I 8; envoy to, I 18; sea of, IV 565, 573.
—Barley from, IV 287, 344, 391; oil from, IV 376; impost of, IV 229, 387; tribute from, IV 724.
—Syrian, III 454, 468; IV 338, 398; crew, IV 574; Syrian chief ruling Egypt, IV 398; slaves of, for temple of Amon, II 555; for temple of Osiris, IV 680.

T

Taanach, II 426; road of, II 421; conquered by Sheshonk I, IV 712.

Tabor, III 356.

Takinash, IV 818 n. c.

Takompso, IV 146.

Tangûr (seventy miles south of the second cataract): inscription by Thutmose I, II 67 n. b; Nubian expedition of Thutmose I to, II 74.

Tanis: called city of the northland, IV 215(?).
—Residence of Ramses II, III 406; Ramses III(?), IV 215, 217 n. i (?); Smendes, IV 564.
—Amon temple of, IV (215, 217(?)), 956.
—Palace of, IV 215.
—Colossus of Ramses II, III 417; obelisk of Ramses II, III 392, 543 n. c.
—Colossus inscription, by Ramses II, III 417.
—Obelisk inscription, by Ramses II, III 392, 448 n. b.
—Stelæ of: Ramses II, III 487–91; Seti, III 538–42; Osorkon II, IV 745–47; Taharka, IV 892–96.

Taroy: Nubian region: fortress of, II 852.

Tayan: Yewepet king of, IV 878.

Tazoser (cemetery of Abydos): Wennofer, lord of, III 17, 234; Upwawet, lord of, I 767, 768; lords of, III 234; located south of Abydos, I 768; addition to, for other tombs, I 771; boundary stelæ set up, I 769; precinct of, III 240; sanctity of, I 770; custodian of, I 770; Anubis, lord of, IV 1029.
—House in, II 36; ennead of, III 218; lord of, III 237.

Tazoser: in western Thebes, IV 91, 309, 382; court of the lord of, IV 4; sacred district of lord of life of, IV 4; place of rest, IV 246.

Tazoser: lords of, III 240; districts of, III 240; nome of, III 240.

Tefrer: lapis lazuli from, III 448 n. b.

Tehenu, II 225, 413; III 134, 457, 600; IV 56, 355, 356; a land to the west, III 116.
—Invaded by Libya, III 579; by Meshwesh, IV 87.
—Captured by Mentuhotep, I 423H; Amenhotep III, II 892; Seti I, III 116, 147; Ramses II, III 448 n. b, 457, 465; Merneptah, III 588, 611, 616, 617; Ramses III, IV 37, 54.

Tehenu—
—Fortress of, II 892.
—Chiefs of, III 116, 132, 139.
—Seed of, IV 87.
—Sutekh gods of, III 611.
—Tribute of, II 321.
—Products of, I 675; ivory, II 321; tusks, II 321.

TEHENUT: nome of, IV 482; domain of, IV 482; located in Wawat, IV 482.

TEHNEH, IV 838; tomb in, I 172; tomb of Nekonekh, I 213; Hathor of, I 213.

TELL EL-AMARNA, I 7, 304, 695; inscriptions of, I 20, 33.
—Cliff tombs of: Ani, II 977; Merire II, II 981; Merire I, II 982–88; Eye, II 989–96; Mai, II 997–1003; Ahmose, II 1004–8; Tutu, II 1009–1013; Huy, II 1014–17.
—Rock inscriptions of, by Ikhnaton, II 949–72.
—Tomb inscriptions by: Ani, II 977; Merire I, II 983–88, 1018; Eye, II 990–96; Mai, II 997, 999–1003; Ahmose, II 1006–8; Tutu, II 1010–13; Huy, II 1015–17.

TEMEH: Libyan land, I 311, 335 bis; IV 91; soldiers of, in the army of Uni, I 311; attacked by the people of Yam, I 335.
—Captives from, IV 92; impost from, IV 92.
—Captured by Merneptah, IV 580, 586, 598, 608; by Ramses III, IV 40, 42, 43, 49, 50, 52, 58, 71, 84, 91, 92, 103, 104.
—Circumcision practiced in (?), IV 52, 54; seed of, IV 50, 58.
—in alliance with Meshwesh, IV 91.
—Timhy stone, from Wawat, IV 373, 389.

TENES: Syrian locality, III 337; Rebesnen, chief of archers of, III 337.

TERERES: Negro land, I 334.

TERESH: a northern people of the sea, IV 129; invading Egypt, III 574, 579; slain by Merneptah, III 588; captives from, III 588, 601; IV 129.

TEREW: a negro people, chief of, IV 114.

TERRACE:
—Cedar, II 32, 94, 103, 611, 614, 755, 794 n. b; IV 904.
—Malachite, I 266, 342.
—Myrrh, II 260, 284, 285, 287, 288, 291 n. a, 294.

TERSES: a Negro people, chief of, IV 114.
—Tetehen (modern Tehneh), IV 838.

THAMUT: district of, II 641.

THARU: city of, II 415; fortress of, III 88, 100, 307, 542 bis, 631.
—Robbers to be sent to, III 51; extortioners sent to, III 54; slave-thieves sent to, III 55; hide-thieves sent to, III 56.
—Temple of, IV 956.

THAU: southern point of the highlands, I 456.

THEBES (=in the original "Thrones of the Two Lands," *nś·wt-t*ꜣ*wy;* or *w*ꜣ*ś·t*, the name of the Theban nome), I 459; II 36, 101, 143, 149, 266, 295, 402, 549, 832, 834, 835, 881, 882, 889, 890, 891, 892, 896, 900, 917; III 23, 30, 144, 154, 165, 260, 261, 271, 436, 507, 515, 566, 580; IV 26, 141, 195, 207, 466, 471, 591, 609, 612, 615, 624, 626, 634, 652, 653, 697, 705, 707, 721, 743, 760, 764, 768, 769, 777, 823, 825, 840, 883, 906, 908, 926, 944, 945.
—Titles of: the mysterious city, IV 187, 220; city of the lord of eternity, III 27; of the hidden name, IV 753; victorious (=Thebes on the east bank), II 329; IV 8, 197, 211, 213, 216, 753, 912; eye of Re, IV 753, 899, 906; mistress of might, IV 912; mistress of temples, IV 753; mistress of the Nine Bows, IV 751.
—Glory of, like a splendid sea, I 423; land of, bequeathed by Intef I to his son, I 423.
—Wall of: the princes of Tikhsi hanged before, II 797.
—Planted with trees by Ramses III, IV 213.
—Exempt from inspection, IV 750, 751.
—Invasion of, in the Heracleopolitan kingdom, I 396 n. d; length of this war, I 415, 420 n. d.
—Intef, founder of Theban line, I 419; Mentuhotep II, first great king of, I 426; Ikudidi of, I 527; Eti, great pillar in, I 459; Intef, nomarch of, I 420.
—Mayors of: Amenmose, IV 466; Peser, IV 513, 526, 527, 531.
—Youths (=recruits) of, II 332.
—Products of, II 730.
—Obelisks of, II 627.

Thebes—
—Gods of, II 73, 224; IV 183; triad of, II 244; IV 128, 222, 230, 236, 463; Hathor, patroness of, II 224; see also Index I.
—Statues of: Senmut, II 363 n. f; Nebnefer, II 928.
—Statue inscriptions by: Nebnefer, II 929–31; stelæ of, Thutmose III, II 609 n. e; Intef, II 763 n. e; Amenhotep III, II 856 n. b, 878–92, 904–910; Amenhotep, II 921; Merneptah, III 602 n. d.

THEBES, THE WEST OF, II 905, 927, 947; III 216, 217, 219, 220, 521, 522, 622; IV 9, 12, 13, 14, 19, 179, 400, 491, 511.
—Mayor of, II 927; Pewero, IV 511, 512, 522, 527, 528, 535.
—District of, II 927; called Khaftet-hir-nebes, II 927; gendarmes of, II 927.
—Necropolis of, II 338, 339; districts of, called: "Place-of-Beauty," part of, IV 523, 525; valley of the kings, 400 n. c, 473, 524; Zeseret, part of, IV 520; "Place of Truth," IV 465; sacred district of "Lord of Life," IV 4, 187; "Beautiful Region" to the northwest, IV 795; fortress of, II 338–39; goddess of, II 338–39; chief of police of necropolis of, Pewero, IV 511; see also Tazoser of Western Thebes.
—Temples of: see Index II: Memnonium, Ramesseum, Mortuary temple of Merneptah, Thutmose IV, Chapel of Wazmose, House of Amon.
—Tomb of Thaneni, II 392; Senmut, II 348 n. a; Amenopet, II 671 n. e; Woser, II 671 n. e; Intef, II 763 n. e.
—Tombstone of Senmut, II 348 n. b.
—Tomb inscription of: Thaneni, II 392; stela of Hatshepsut, II 338.
—For Thebes, east side: see also Karnak, Luxor and Mad, and for Thebes, west side, see also Abd el-Kurna, Drah-abu-ʾn-Neggah, Dêr el-Bahri, Khaftet-hir-nebes, Kurna, Kurnet-Murrai, and Medinet Habu.

THEBU: district of, IV 957; "Barque of the Sycamore," an estate in, IV 957.

THEKEL: in Palestine, IV 567; conquered by Ramses III, IV 44, 77, 403.
—Chieftains of, IV 77, 78, 79, 129.
—Soldiers by land and sea of, IV 44.
—Ally of the northerners, IV 64.
—Captives of, IV 79, 129.
—Dor, a city of, IV 565.
—Ships of, IV 588; mighty sea-people, IV 588.
—Byblos not included under its dominion, IV 590.

THEKNESH, IV 818.

THEKU: frontier city of, III 638; fortress of Merneptah-Hotephirma in, III 638; pools of Pithom of, III 638.

THEMET: a region of Medinet Habu, IV 634; Khonsu residing in, IV 914.

THENEW: Syrian city, prisoners from, II 798A.

THERETI, I 703.

THES(?): a southern boundary of Theban kingdom in time of Intef I, I 423D.

THINIS: nome of, I 349; II 181, 763, 767.
—Location of, I 423 n. a; captured by Intef I of Thebes, I 423; northern boundary of Theban kingdom, I 396 n. h, 423D, 529.
—Cities of: Abydos, I 349, 396 nn. d, h, 529; Thinis, II 763; crown possessions of the South in, I 665 n. b; fortresses of, I 396 n. b, 423.
—Officials of: supervisor of fields of, Imsu, I 529; mayor of, II 739; nomarchs of, Ibi, I 377; Intef, II 763, 767.
—Count of, Intef, II 763.
—Temple of Onouris, IV 355, 365, 484.
—Gods of: Onouris, I 500; Osiris, I 666.

TIKHSI: district of, II 797; battle in, II 587, 797; Mero—, city of, II 587; prisoners of, II 587; Asiatics in, II 587; seven princes of, II 797.

TINAY, CITY OF: chief of, II 537; tribute of, II 537.

TINTTO-EMU: city in Nubia, II 15.

TÔDSHI, IV 818 n. f.

TOMBOS: island of, II 67; inscriptions found there, I 21; fortress at, II 67.
—Rock inscriptions of Thutmose I, II 67–73.

TOMERI (=Egypt), III 490, 616.

TOWÊR: Abydos of, III 260; IV 357.

TOYEH: district of, III 580; in the Oasis region, III 580; captured by the Libyans, III 580.

TOZI, IV 818.

TROGLODYTES, ASIATIC, III 118; the sand-dwellers, defeated by Nessumontu, I 471; smiting of, I 81, 104; II 225; Khufu, smiter of, I 176; the highlands cleared of, by Henu, I 429 n. h; by Sesostris I, I 511; Min, head of, I 443; sarcophagus stone, concealed from, I 451.

TROGLODYTES, NUBIAN, I 654; II 646, 656, 892.

—Bringing tribute, II 120.

—of Khenthennofer, II 268, 646; of Kush, III 490.

—Slain by: Zaa, I 687; Ahmose, II 14; Amenhotep I, II 39; Thutmose I, II 71; Thutmose II, II 121; Thutmose III, II 646, 661; Thutmose IV, II 837; Seti I, II 116, 118; Ramses II, III 285, 490; Sheshonk I, IV 719, 720.

TROJA: limestone quarry of, I 210, 212, 239, 274, 289, 290, 307, 509; II 800, 875; see also Ayan.

TUNIP: city of, III 365; districts of, III 365; located in the land of Naharin, III 365.

—Aleppo, north of, III 319.

—Captured by Thutmose III, II 530.

—Infantry of, II 459; harvest of, II 530; groves of, II 530; chief of, II 773; tribute from, II 534 (?), 773.

—Under rule of Kheta, III 319.

TUPHIUM, I 459 n. e: see Hefat.

TURIN, I 69 n. j.

TURRA: rock inscription, I 181; by Amenemhet III, I 740; Amenhotep II, II 799; Amenhotep III, II 875; see also Troja and Ayan.

TWO DOORS OF THE NORTHERN COUNTRIES, IV 1014; Governor of: see Index V.

TWO HALVES (=Upper and Lower Egypt), I 502; II 318, 805.

TWO HOUNDS (of Mendesian nome), I 174.

TWO LANDS, I 420; II 53, 151, 164, 170, 192 n. d, 198, 208, 225, 235, 266, 271, 285, 286, 305, 309, 315, 319, 325, 328, 341, 352, 361, 374, 376, 377, 412 *et passim;* Amon, lord of, II 198.

—Chiefs of: bound by Mentuhotep I, I 423H; captured by Mentuhotep I, 423H; bowing before Henu, I 428.

—Queen of, II 53.

—King, heir of Horus in his Two Lands, I 441.

Judged by the hereditary prince, I 531.

—Head of: see Index V.

—Chief of the Two Lands, I 423H *et passim.*

TWO MOUNTAINS: costly stones from, III 448 n. b.

TWO REGIONS, I 552; II 116, 176, 341; III 16; IV 304; captured by Mentuhotep I, I 423H; by Amenemhet I, I 465.

—of Horus, II 353.

—Lord of: see Index V.

TYRE, IV 567; captured by Seti I, III 114.

—Chief of: Baalat-Remeg, III 630.

—Upper Tyre, in Kharu, III 633.

U

UHET (=quarry ?): road of, I 335.

ULLAZA: city near Tunip, II 470; location of, II 470; captured by Thutmose III, II 470; by Seti I, III 114; booty from, II 470.

UNESHEK: Nubian region south of Hua, II 850.

UPPER EGYPT, I 25; kings of, I 90; II 287; III 577, 580.

UPPER NOME (XX nome of Upper Egypt), I 199.

UPPER TENU: Emuienshi, sheik of, I 494; see Retenu.

UREM: Nubian region, captured by Amenhotep III, II 845 n. f.

URONARTI: island of, below Semneh, I 654, 655; fortress of, I 654 n. a, 655.

USERMARE-MERIAMON: city in Nubia, IV 102; location of, IV 102 n. a.

USERMARE-MERIAMON: city in Syria, III 308.

UTENTYEW: isles of, II 660.

UTHEK: Nubian country, I 369.

UTHETH: Nubian region, expedition of Sebni to bring back his father, I 367.

V

VALLEY OF THE KINGS' TOMBS: at Thebes, III 32 n. a; IV 400 n. c, 473, 524; tombs of Ramessids in, IV 473 n. a.

W

WA—: city in northern Syria, II 457; plunder of, II 459; storehouse of offerings, II 458.

Wa—
—Gods of: Amon, II 458; Harakhte, II 458.
—Chief of, II 459; *t-h-r*-warriors of, II 459; slaves of, II 460.
—Ships of, II 460.
—Products of: gold, II 459; silver, II 459; lapis lazuli, II 459; malachite, II 459; vessels of bronze, II 459; vessels of copper, II 459; copper, II 460; lead, II 460; emery, II 460.

W ᾽ ḥ-ys ͗ t: recorder of, II 736; scribe of the recorder of, II 736; products of, II 736.
WADI ᶜALÂKI, III 282.
WADI GASUS: stelæ of: Khentkhetwer, I 604 n. b; Khnumhotep, I 617 n. a.

WADI HALFA:
—Temple of Thutmose III, III 639.
—Temple of Horus, III 74; built and endowed by Ramses I, III 54; endowed by Seti I, III 159–61.
—Temple inscription by: Seti I, III 248; Neferhor, III 643; Piyay, III 644; Hori, III 645; 650, 651(?).
—Pillar inscription of Neḥi, II 412–13.
—Stelæ of: Mentuhotep, I 510 n. a; Thutmose I, II 54 n. a; Ramses I, III 74–79; Seti I, III 157–61.

WADI MAGHARA: malachite and copper brought from, I 713; reached by sea, I 718.
—Rock inscriptions of: Snefru, I 168 n. a; Khufu, I 176 n. a; Sahure, I 236 n. a; Nuserre, I 250 n. a; Menkuhor, I 263 n. a; Dedkere-Isesi, I 264 n. a, 265 n. c, 267 nn. e, g; Pepi I, I 302 n. c; Pepi II, I 339 n. e; Khenemsu, I 713 n. i; Harnakht, I 717 n. d; Sebekdidi, I 719; Ameni, I 721; Amenemhet IV, I 750; Hatshepsut and Thutmose III, II 337.

WAG: land between Red Sea and Hammamat, I 433 n. d.

"WALL-OF-HORI," district of Heliopolis, IV 957.

"WALL-OF-PSENMUT," a district of Heliopolis, IV 957.

WALL OF THE SOUTH, II 814; Mut, mistress of, II 814.

WALLS OF THE RULER: made to repulse the Bedwin, I 493.

"WALLS-OF-THE-SOVEREIGN," a name of Memphis, III 615.

WAN, HEIGHT OF: expedition to, II 582; located west of Aleppo, II 582; prisoners of, II 582; Asiatics of, II 582; products of, II 582.

WATER OF RE: a canal, IV 83, 224, 369.

WATET-HOR: tribute of, II 385, 386.

WAWAT: region of, given to temple of Amon, IV 950; the great mountain of, IV 480, 481; water of, II 170; ships to, I 426; fortress of, inspected by Hapu, I 616.
—Expeditions to, by Harkhuf, I 311, 317, 336; Pepi-Nakht, I 358; Sebni, I, 367, 369; Mentuhotep III, I 426; Amenemhet I, I 473–83; Sesostris I, I 510; Thutmose IV, II 826; Merneptah, III 606 n. a.
—Revolt in, II 826; III 606 n. a.
—In charge of mayor of Nekhen, II 47; Penno, deputy of, IV 474, 477, 480; Meri, deputy of, IV 481; Herunofer, IV 482; Bahu, herdsman of, IV 481.
—Impost of, II 475, 487, 495, 515, 523, 527, 539; tribute of, II 48; ships of, II 475, 487, 495, 515, 527; harvest of, II 475, 487, 503, 539; slaves from, II 487; negro slaves from, II 495, 503, 515.
—Gods of, III 448 n. b.
—Products of: acacia wood, I 324; oxen, II 475, 487, 495, 503, 515, 527; calves, II 475, 487, 495, 503, 515, 523, 527; bulls, II 475, 487, 503, 523, 527; gold, II 515, 527, 539; ebony, II [523?]; ivory, II [523?], 527 (?); timhy stone, IV 373, 389.

WAYET: Nubian country, chief of, II 1037.

WERKA: smiting of, I 112.

WESHESH: ally of the northerners, IV 64; slain by Ramses III, IV 403; captives of, IV 403.

WEST: the countries of, III 491; cities of, IV 818; fortress of the, III 586; chief of, Tefnakhte, IV 818, 830.

WEST (=cemetery), II 926; the beautiful, IV 249, 304, 918, 961, 986, 1010, 1029.

WEST SIDE (=Libya), I 492.

WESTERN LAND, II 659; applied to Keftyew and Cyprus, II 659.

WESTERNERS, I 293; II 656.

X

XOIS (Ox nome): nome of, I 156, 159, IV 818; Methen, local governor of, I 172, 173, 174.

Y

YAA: a land in Palestine, on the border of Kedem, I 496; very fruitful, I 496.

YAM: Negro tribe, I 311, 351, 510; chief of, I 324, 336 ter; road to country of, I 333, 334, 335, 352; dancing dwarf from, I 351; a land of spirits, I 351.

YARU: fields of, III 21; plowing in, III 21.

YAT-SEBEK: city of, I 173.

YAWAN, III 312 n. c.

YEHEM: city of Palestine, II 419.

YENOAM: at southern end of Lebanon, under the rule of Kadesh, II 436; called a city of Retenu, II 557; impost of, II 557.

—Captured by Thutmose III, II 436; Seti I, III 90, 114; Merneptah, III 617.

YERAZA: city of the Asiatics, in Judah, revolt in, II 416; conquered by Sheshonk, IIV 714.

YERED: temple of Amon-Re, lord of, IV 368.

YU, LAND OF: under rule of Hatshepsut, II 299.

YUNA: nome of, IV 948.

Z

ZAHI: (primarily western Syria, especially Phoenicia, but applied also more widely), II 497; III 423; IV 72, 141.

—Campaign of Ahmose I in, II 20; of Thutmose III in, II 456–62, 488–95.

—Chiefs, II 392; taken as prisoners, II 392; princes of, II 658.

—Cities of, II 392, 490; Kadesh, city of, III 318; Wa, II 457; Arvad, II 461; Nuges, II 490.

—Egyptian frontier in, IV 65; allied countries of, II 616; highlands of, II 658; gardens of, II 461; groves of, II 392; furnishes supplies for the garrisons in the harbors, II 468, 472, 483, 492; harvest of, II 510, 519.

—Products of, II 461; IV 211; wines of, II 461; grain of, II 46; asses, II 490; heifers, II 490; white goats, II 490; small goats, II 490; horses, II 462, 490; chariots of, II 490; golden vessels, II 490; gold, II 459, 490; silver vessels, II 490; silver, II 459, 490; copper, II 459, 460, 462, 490; black wood, II 490; carob wood, II 490.

—Ships of: Byblos-ships, II 492; Keftyew-ships, II 492; Sektu-ships, II 492.

—Silver vessels of the workmanship of, II 482.

—Temple of Amon in, IV 219.

—Tribute from, II 462, 536 (?); impost of, IV 190, 328.

ZIDPATH-EL: city of central Palestine, IV 713.

ZEFTI: road of, II 421.

ZEN: Hittite city, III 386.

ZEN-WET: Hittite city, III 386.

ZEPYERENED: Hittite city, Sutekh, god of, III 386.

[illegible]: shore of, II 470.

ZERUKHA: city of Queen Tiy, II 869; pleasure lake of, II 869.

ZESERET: a part of the Theban necropolis, IV 520.

ZEYETHEKHRER: Hittite city, III 386.

ZURÎM: city in southern Palestine, IV 714.

INDEX VII

MISCELLANEOUS

A

ABODE, DIVINE, II 152.

ABOMINATION: practice of magic regarded as, IV 454, 455, 456.

ACACIA, IV 226, 282, 387.
—Barges of, IV 916, 1023; canal-boats of, IV 229, 387; cargo-boats of, I 323, 324; kara-boats of, IV 229, 283, 387; tow-boats of, IV 229, 387; transport-boats of, IV 229, 283, 387; warships of, IV 229, 387.
Acacia-wood, from Hatnub, I 323; from Wawat, I 324.

ACCOUNTING: of divine offerings, I 274; of tribute, I 423 D.

ACCOUNTS, I 10, 20.

ACCUSATION, IV 526, 529.

ADDRESS, III 265, 270, 288.

ADMINISTRATION: of canals, IV 266; of the sacred cattle of Apis, IV 332; of temples, IV 202, 255, 317, 321, 354, 360, 363, 665; of temple-women, IV 321; of Egypt, III 26; of law, III 25; of divine offerings, I 299; overseer of, see Index V; see also Index V, Administrator.

ADORNMENTS, IV 1020; of war, III 312, 326; of Re, III 28; of king, IV 876; of Montu, III 319.

ADVANCE-GUARD, II 421.

ADYTUM, II 639, 806; III 240; IV 13, 634, 899; see also Holy of Holies.

AEONS, both, II 317, 759.

AFFAIRS OF THE SOUTH, I 332.

AGENT, IV 576.

AISLE, IV 971.

ALABASTER, II 906; III 529; IV 234, 390.
—Alabaster: of Hatnub, II 302, 375, 546 n. b.
—Alabaster quarry, at Hatnub, I 7, 305, 323, 695 n. b, 696; location of, I 695.
—Articles of alabaster: stela, IV 988A n. b; colossi, IV 191 n. j; great seat, III 525, 529; offering table, I 323 bis; shrine-stair, II 375; statue, IV 302, 988I n. a; altar, II 546 n. b; jar, II 544.

ALLIANCE: defensive, III 378, 380.
—the Hittite, III 306, 309, 312, 336.
—of Libya and Mediterranean peoples, III 574.
—Libyan, IV 35-58.
—Meshwesh. IV 83, 114.
—Northerners, IV 64.

ALLIES, IV 822.

ALLOY, IV 202 n. a, 318 n. a.

ALTAR, I 165; II 35, 149, 163, 298, 795, 974; III 260; IV 256, 357, 686, 763, 823, 958J, 1020, 1021.
—Rank of the scribe of, I 550.
—of temple of Osiris at Abydos, I 787.
—for mortuary offering, II 571.
—Made of alabaster, II 546 n. b; of cedar, I 787; of gold, IV 735; of granite, IV 900; of silver, IV 735, 736, 737.
—Altars, small, of silver, IV 735.
—*dw*-altars, of gold, IV 735.

ALTAR-VESSELS, IV 334.

"AMON-OF-THE-WAY," an image of Amon, IV 569, 586.

AMULETS, II 544; IV 538, 876, 988H, 1011, 1020.
—Eye-amulets, IV 29, 373, 377, 386, 390; of Thoth, IV 373, 386.
—Made of electrum, II 376, 654; of costly stones, II 376; IV 29, 233, 377, 390; of fine gold, IV 253; of gold, IV 201; of Hirset stone, IV 233; of Ketem gold, IV 319; of lapis lazuli, IV 233; of rock-crystal, IV 377; of silver, IV 319, 373, 386.

ANARCHY: in Egypt, IV 398, 764.

ANASTASI 17, stela of Simontu, I 594 n. a.

ANCESTORS, II 287, 293, 377, 611, 628, 805; IV 629, 630, 817, 914.
—Writings of, II 364.
—Offerings for, III 23.
—Regulations for, III 536.

Ancestors—
—Tomb-chambers of, IV 4.

ANCIENT STOCK: Kheti's family of, I 399.

ANIMALS: see Antelope, Apes, Beast, Birds, Bugs, Bull, Bullock, Calves, Cat, Cattle, Cow, Crocodile, Dogs, Fishes, Elephant, Gazelle, Giraffe, Goat, Heifer, Hippopotamus, Horse, Hound, Ibex, Lion, *M-ḥ*ͻ*-w*, Mice, Monkey, Oryx, Oxen, Panther, Serpent, Sheep, Wolf.
—Sacred animals, feeding of, I 281, 281 n. c.

ANNALS, II 151, 310, 940; III 585; IV 460, 756.
—of Thutmose III, II 391–540.

ANTELOPES: for oblation, II 553; IV 768.

APES: from Punt, II 263, 265.
—as taxes from Bigeh, II 718.
—Sacred apes, II 907 bis; III 16; of Thoth, IV 33; 256.
—Thoth apes of gold, IV 256, 735.

APOTHEOSIS: of Sesostris III, II 167; see also Deification.

APPEALS: from local land office to vizier, II 686.

"APPEARANCE" (of a god, in procession), II 158; IV 217; see also Feast.
—Temple as place of, III 217, 218, 224, 508, 522.

APPLES (*dpḥ·t*—), IV 301.

APPOINTMENTS: put into writing, I 274, 780; engraved by artists, I 174; of mortuary priests, I 274.
—of local courts, III 65.
—Made by vizier: see under Vizier.
—Temple appointments, II 928.

ARBOR-AREAS: arbors for temple, IV 194, 264, 1021.

ARCHÆOLOGY: Egyptian, IV 151.

ARCHER, II 213, 900; III 84, 147, 224; IV 71, 74, 118, 397, 842.
—Leader of, IV 597.
—Captain of, III 484, 587, 631; IV 405, 407.
—Chief, III 192; see also Index V; of gold-washing, III 193.
—Assistant chief of, see Index V.
—Naval archers, IV 313; galley archer, IV 407.
—Temple archers, IV 211, 266, 313, 324.
—Mercenary archers, IV 50.
—Archers from Ibhet, II 854; Lybia, III 609; Kheta, III 337; chiefs of, III 337; from Enenes, III 337; chief of, III 337; Tint-to-emu, II 15.

ARCHITECT: see Index V: Builder, Chief of Works, Leader of Works, Master of Works, Overseer of Works.

ARCHITRAVE INSCRIPTIONS, III 222, 226, 502, 513, 514, 602, 603, 621, 626.

ARCHIVES, ROYAL, at Thebes, I 18.
—of Pharaoh, III 643.
—of the ancestors, II 73.
—of the vizier, IV 534.
—State archives: see under Hall of Writing.
—Temple archives: see under House of Sacred Writing.
—Scribes of: see Index V.

ARMLET, II 22, 23, 24.
—of gold, II 64, 545.
—of rock-crystal, IV 303.

ARMOR, coats, scale, II 802.
—Suits of, II 435; III 589; made of bronze, II 435, 500, 501, 534.

ARM-RINGS: of gold, II 585, 587.

ARMS (=weapons), IV 65, 97.

ARMY, IV 678, 832, 837, 854, 858, 859, 861, 863, 864, 879, 1004.
—of Egypt, I 303, 311, 358; II 39, 122 ter, 253, 256, 260 bis, 285, 288, 290, 327, 337, 413, 424, 434, 461, 472, 813, 908, 917; III 20, 141, 224, 320, 324, 325, 340, 422, 423, 455, 461, 489; IV 70, 71, 747, 767, 818, 821, 822, 825.
—Equipment of, I 456; organization of, in time of Uni, I 312; inspection of, by Uni, I 312.
—Affairs of the army, II 429; army drunk, II 462.
—Mustering of, by the vizier, II 693; viceroy of Kush, II 852.
—Council of, II 695; regulation of, II 695.
—Rearguard of, I 680; II 421; advance guard of, II 421; citizens of, I 681; II 53, 864; watch of, II 425, 864.
—Northern wing of, II 426, 430.
—Southern wing of, II 426, 430; center of, II 430.
—Divisions: of Amon, III 308, 310, 332; of Ptah, III 310 n. f, 334, 340; of Re, III 310, 311, 340; two divisions of, III 56.
—Men of, IV 19.
—of the South, I 429, 442; IV 705, 795.
—of the Northland, I 453.
—of Middle Egypt, I 411, 442.

Army—
—of Oryx nome, I 519; of Coptos, I 776; of Heracleopolis, IV 777, 792; of Hare nome, IV 848; of Per-Thut-uprehui, IV 830.
—of the temples, III 31.
—Army-officers, penalty for stealing hides by, III 56; standard-bearer of, III 208; two deputies of, who collected the dues, III 54; chief of: commandants of, commander of, commander-in-chief of, deputy of, general of, leader of, officers of, scribe of, king's scribe of, see Index V.
—Army: of Kheta, III 419; Kush, II 38, 852; Mitanni, IV 722; see also Archers, Bowmen, Cavalry, Chariotry, Citizens, Infantry, Soldiers, Troops, Warriors.

AROMATIC WOOD, IV 329.

ARREARS, I 522.

ARREST, II 702; IV 523, 588.

ARROW, II 785, 865; III 360, 454, 584; IV 50, 70, 75, 77, 96, 823, 845, 1004.
—Libyan, III 584.

ASCENT: Karnak, the august, of the beginning, II 316.

ASIATIC COPPER: see Copper.

ASSEMBLY, II 925 n. a.

ASSES, I 366, 430; III 286; IV 407, 408.
—from Zahi, II 490; from Punt, II 258; from Retenu, II 491, 509; from Wan, II 580; from Hua, II 850; from Libya, III 584, 587; from Meshwesh, IV 111.

ASTRONOMERS: Greek, I 39, 44.

ASTRONOMICAL DATES: in XVIII Dynasty, I 51; in XII Dynasty, I 57.

ASTRONOMY, I 20.

ATMOSPHERE, IV 308.

ATTACK, IV 859.

AUDIENCE, II 955; III 66.
—Audience-hall, I 239, 423E n. d, 501; II 236, 292, 666; III 240.
—Audience, place of, I 320.

AVENUE, SACRED, IV 215.

AXE: of gold, II 23; of silver, II 24.
—Battle-axe, II 802; III 461, 468; IV 118.

B

BACKLANDS, IV 818.

BAGS, II 750.

BAKER, III 624, 625.

BAKING, IV 393.

BALANCES, I 531; II 53, 279, 280, 900, 995; III 288; IV 33, 256, 285, 288, 880.
—of electrum, IV 256.
—Thoth, guardian of, IV 256.

BALCONY, II 985, 989; III 69, 587; IV 42, 52, 70, 76, 124, 408.
—of fine gold, IV 192.

BALE, IV 229, 283, 387.
—*nʿḥ*-bale, IV 371.

BANNER, IV 117.

BANU-FRUIT, IV 378, 395.

BARGE OF A GOD (a large and magnificent craft, in which the god sailed on the Nile, or on the temple lake, at festal celebrations; not to be confused with the portable chapel-barque, *q. v.*), II 304; III 275; IV 65, 407. See also Temple barges below.
—State barge, I 283, 286, 423F; II 373, 596, 797, 809, 838, 864, 869, 997; IV 209, 400; names of, II 373, 596, 797, 809, 838, 864, 869; IV 209.
—Sun barge, IV 209, 278.
—Temple barges, I 261; II 32, 94, 304, 888; III 568; IV 209, 211, 278, 331, 354, 358, 563, 575, 904, 916, 958K, 1023; names of, II 32, 888; IV 278, 563; shrine of, II 888; IV 209, 331; bows of, II 888; IV 331; crowns of, II 888; IV 209; flagstaves of, II 888; obelisks of, II 888; stern of, IV 331; "great house" in, IV 331, 359, 904.
—Barges made of cedar, II 32, 94, 838, 888; IV 278, 331, 904, 916, 1023; of acacia, IV 1023.

BARK, IV 288.

BARLEY, I 496; II 149; III 66; IV 190, 193, 207, 250, 259, 265, 266, 314, 325, 354, 359, 363, 859; from Retenu, II 473; as impost of peasants, IV 229; divine offering, II 562.
—Syrian barley, IV 287, 344, 391.

BARQUE (a portable chapel carried on poles and bearing a shrine, containing the cultus image of the god; it was never placed in the water), I 159, 167, 534, 613, 668, 669; II 92, 318; III 212, 431, 515, 542; IV 91, 315, 353, 611, 743, 958K; bow of, IV 414.
—Barque, celestial, IV 73.
—Barque made of electrum, III 212.

Barque—
—Barque-shrine of fine gold, IV 982.
—Morning barque, II 832; III 281; of Re, II 318; III 16; IV 358, 871; bow of, IV 67.
—Sun-barque, evening, I 167; II 318; IV 331; of Re, II 318, 832; III 16; of Atum, IV 871.

BARS: of copper, IV 408.

BASALT, BLACK: statue of, I 675; obelisks of, III 246.

BASE: of pyramid, IV 517.

BASIN: libation, IV 100 n. a.

BASKET, IV 41, 301, 378.
—Negro, II 120, 271; III 475.

BASTINADO: on feet, IV 548, 549.
—on feet and hands, IV 549, 550, 552, 553.

BATH: master of, I 336; overseer of palace baths, see Index V.

BATHE, IV 823.

BATON (*ḥrp-*): royal, I 646; II 849; official's, II 385; vizier's II 675.

BATTERING RAM, IV 838.

BATTLE, III 141, 455, 461; IV 821, 822, 825, 852; plan of, III 307.
—Battles at Avaris, II 8, 9, 10; at Kadesh, III 306–12, 317–27, 335; with Kheta, III 144, 317–27, 335; on Lebanon, II 783; in Libya, III 120, 123, 584; at Megiddo, II 430; with Meshwesh, IV 90, 103; on the Orontes, II 784; in Naharin, II 479, 499, 581; in Negeb, II 580; in Wan, II 582; in Carchemish, II 583; in Senzar, II 584; in Kadesh, II 585, 589–90; with northerners, IV 73; against Shasu, III 86; in Tikhsi, II 587.
—Sea battle, IV 66.

BATTLE ARRAY, II 426; III 310, 578; IV 43.

BATTLE-AXES, II 802; III 461, 468; IV 118.

BATTLE-CRY, III 44, 479.

BATTLEFIELD, II 578, 579, 792, 818, 916, 918; III 20; IV 49, 106.

BATTLE-LINE, III 86.

BATTLEMENTS, II 894; III 616; IV 117, 355, 356, 357, 358, 406, 859, 861.

BEACH, IV 66.

BEADS: clusters of, IV 377.
—Made of lapis lazuli, IV 343; of rock-crystal, IV 233, 287, 345, 377; of white gold, IV 231.

BEAK: golden, IV 345.

BEANS: shelled, IV 301, 350.

BEASTS, IV 930.
—of the highlands, I 436.

BEATEN WORK, II 436; III 528; IV 14, 189, 191, 202, 203, 268, 285, 319, 326, 334, 343, 732, 733.

BEATING: of witnesses with rod, IV 548, 549, 550, 551, 552, 553, 555.

BEEF: shoulders of, II 571; joint of, IV 565.

BEER: for divine offering, II 620, 621 622, 792, 798; III 77; IV 190, 200, 238, 239, 292, 297, 309, 326, 393, 924, 925, 944, 949, 950, 952, 953, 954, 958 M.
—for evening offering, II 565.
—for food, II 758; III 71.
—for mortuary offering, I 252, 329, 518; II 111 113, 114, 117, 356, 365, 378; III 17; IV 485.
—for oblation, II 553, 571, 960; IV 199, 208, 329, 335, 347, 468.
—for offerings to obelisks, II 563.
—Sweet beer, IV 498.

BEER CELLAR, IV 238.

BEER HALL, IV 451 n. c, 880.

BEGGAR: mercy to, I 479.

BEGINNING (of the world = *pꜣwt*), II 122, 151, 158, 305, 353; III 11, 31, 436; IV 743, 795, 836, 857, 958J, 988J; Karnak, the august ascent of, II 316.
—Feast of, see Feasts.

BEKHEN (a measure), IV 235, 379.

BENI PLANT, IV 380, 395.

BENUT STONE: doorway of, II 643.

BERRIES, IV 295; Seneb, IV 301, 350.

BEWITCHING, IV 455; see Magic, Sorcery.

BILLETS OF EBONY, III 475.

BILLS, I 10, 20.

BIOGRAPHIES: first appearance of, in III Dynasty, I 6, 170; of Uni, I 6; of nobles of Elephantine, I 6; numerous in Middle Kingdom, I 10; see also Indexes III, IV.

BIRDLET, IV 54, 106.

BIRD-POOLS, IV 9; see also Pools.

BIRDS: see Cranes, Doves, Ducks, Fowl, Geese, Hawk, Ibis, Ostrich,

Pedet birds, Sesha birds, Shed birds, Urdu birds, Vulture.
—of Lebanon, II 483.
—Ships of Thekel called birds, IV 588.

BIRTH-HOUSE: of Amon, III 161.

BLACK COPPER, see Copper.

BLACK-WOOD, chairs of, II 490; from Zahi, II 490.

BLADE OF HATHOR, IV 784.

BLASPHEMY, II 237, 343.

BLESSINGS: on observers of treaty, III 388.
—of Ptah, III 394–414; IV 132–35.

BLINDFOLDING OF WITNESS, IV 524.

BLOCK, II 493, 509, 512, 525, 536; IV 231, 234, 245, 285, 288, 390, 391.
—Blocks, august, from Hammamat, for the statues of Mentuhotep III, I 433.
—Block inscription, at Bubastis, of Amenhotep III, II 846–50.
—Death penalty paid at the block, IV 529.

BLOSSOMS, IV 244, 295, 301, 350, 394.

BLUE-FLOWERS, IV 600.

BOATMEN: of the temple, IV 266.

BOATS, IV 229, 283, 387; for king's journeys, I 423F; for transporting obelisks, II 105, 326.
—Divine boat, II 741; of Thoth, I 669.
—See also Canal-boat, Cargo-boat, Ferry-boat, Kara-boat, Tow-boat.

BODY, or belly, as seat of mind, I 246.

BODY-GUARD OF KING, III 310; IV 117, 120, 123; mustered by the vizier, II 693.
—Hittite, III 337.

BOLTS, IV 871, 910.
—for target shooting, II 813.
—of black copper, IV 411.
—of bronze, I 483.
—of copper, I 873; IV 406, 489.
—of tin, IV 929.

BOLTS, LARGE (a measure), I 719, 720, 721.
—of *d*ꜣ-*w*-linen, II 736.
—*pdt*, II 722.
—*Sm*ꜣ.*t* II 722.

BONES: king's, of copper, III 403.

"BOOKS OF THE NILE-GOD," IV 296, 297, 347, 383, 388; explanation of, IV 296 n. e; presented in the pool of Kebeh, in the House of Re-Harakhte in Heliopolis, IV 296; in the House of Anubis, in Neru, IV 296; founded for Ptah in Memphis, IV 347.
—House of books, III 410; see also Day-book.
—Sacred book, II 915; scribe of, I 506; "of the dead," II 807; secrets of, II 915.

BOOTY, II 761; IV 126.
—from Megiddo, II 431; Naharin, II 480, 500, 501, 532, 816; Nuges, II 508; Kadesh, II 532; Lebanon, II 783; Orontes, II 785; Ikathi, II 788.

BORDERS OF EGYPT, I 407; III 580; IV 80, 130, 405.

BOTANY OF EGYPT, IV 151; see also Flowers, Fruit, Grain, Herbs, Plants, Trees, Vegetables, Wood.

BOTTLE: leathern, I 430; of water-skins, I 456.

BOUNDARIES OF EGYPT, II 225, 319, 415, 418, 439, 478, 549, 596, 636, 796; III 82, 86, 94, 107, 112, 118, 155, 165, 360, 421, 428, 474, 476, 479, 575; IV 41, 43, 46, 56, 57, 58, 63, 66, 72, 88, 91, 103, 104, 105, 106, 124, 126, 128, 246, 403, 722; northern, II 321; eastern, II 321; southern, II 321, 862; of the south, I 311, 320, 396 n. h, 423, 652, 657; western, II 321; III 579; in the fields of Perire, III 579.
—Boundaries of fields: registered, settlement of, II 689, 703; unregistered, II 690; of the fields of the sacred cattle of Apis, IV 332; of domains, IV 479, 480, 481, 482, 483.
—Boundaries of nomes, II 703; of the Jackal nome, I 626, 632; Hare nome, I 626; oryx nome, I 626; Oxyrrhyncus, I 632; Akhetaton, II 961-64.
—Boundaries of the Asiatics, III 12; of Askalon, III 355; of the Nine Bows, IV 351; of Naharin, II 871;

BOUNDARY STELÆ, I 766.

BOUNDARY STONE, inscription of, II 1 n. c.

BOUNDARY TABLET, on Euphrates, II 478; in Naharin, II 800; in Karoy (region of Napata), II 800.

BOUQUET, II 974; IV 244, 295, 301, 350, 394.
—of flowers, II 974; IV 244, 295, 350, 394.

Bow, I 682; II 435, 785; III 42, 360, 450, 451, 454, 468, 473, 475, 489; IV 50, 51, 70, 73, 225, 410, 823, 1004; given as taxes, II 718; drawing of, II 792.
—Bows made in Kketa, III 343; Kharu, II 501, 509; Libya, III 584 bis, 601, 609; Meshwesh, IV 111.

Bow (of ship), IV 65, 66, 331, 582; adorned with crowns, II 888; with hawks, IV 331.

Bowl, IV 269; of copper, I 500; of silver, IV 735.
—ꜥ *wy*-bowl, IV 269.

Bowmen: of Egypt, III 577, 578, 584; IV 74; leader of, III 581.
—of Libya, III 579.

Bow-peoples, IV 130.

Bow-rope, IV 863.
—as title of Hatshepsut, II 341; of the Southland, II 885.

Boys, IV 111.

Bracelets, II 22, 23, 24; of gold, II 64, 471; III 69; IV 876; of rock-crystal, IV 303, 349, 377.
—from Retenu, II 471; from Naharin, II 501.

Brand of the Royal House, III 56.

Branding, I 770; III 56, 414; of captives, IV 405.

Bread, IV 382, 467, 565, 925, 944, 949, 950, 951, 952, 953, 954, 956, 957, 958 M; for food, I 336; II 260, 758, 925; III 71, 207, 208; divine offering, II 620; III 71; IV 190, 200, 309, 326; mortuary offering, I 252, 329, II 111, 113, 114, 117, 356, 365, 378, 920; III 17, 526; IV 485; oblation, II 553, 554, 798, 960; IV 208, 329, 335; evening offering, II 565; offering to statue, II 618.
—Fine bread, IV 238, 291, 393.
—of the divine offerings, IV 238, 297, 247.
—Kunek bread, IV 238, 291, 297.
—*p*ꜣ*k*-bread, I 577.
—White bread, II 553; see also Cakes.

Brewery of Pharaoh, III 51, 59.

Bribery: laws on, III 64; penalty for, III 64.

Brick, IV 916, 958M; walls of, IV 489, 914, 1020; temples built of, II 157 n. e, 176, 611, 614; III 517, 520; temple inclosures made of, II 614.
—Mud brick, II 607.

Brick (as a measure), II 521 bis, 534; IV 235, 241, 379, 392.

Bricklayer, II 758, 759; Syrian captives as, II 758 nn. d, g.

Brickmakers, II 759.

Bridge, III 100; IV 861.

Bronze, I 534; II 45, 162, 165, 558; IV 358, 847.
—Mixture of, IV 202, 318, 320, 343, 358.
—in scraps, IV 343.
—Articles made of bronze: corselet, II 447; tablets, IV 231, 318, 343; bolts, I 483; vase, I 500; II 164; IV 538; offering-tables, I 534; II 175; IV 912; temple doors, II 375; III 528; scarab, IV 233; vessels, II 436, 459, 795; III 584; IV 343; shrine doors, IV 320; doorway, III 246; wall (royal title), III 224; helmets from Naharin, II 501; suit of armor from Megiddo, II 435 bis; from Naharin, II 500, 501; from Retenu, II 534(?); spears from Retenu, II 509, 525; from Wan, II 582; swords, II 802; daggers, II 802.
—Articles wrought with, II 490.
—Bronze: from Naharin, II 500; from Retenu, II 518.

Brotherhood, III 373, 375.

Brow, IV 922.

Builders, II 758, 759; IV 275, 858; for Chief of, Master of, see Index V.

Building: of houses, I 147, 328; of Temples, II 33–37, 97, 90–98, 99–106; see also Houses, Palaces, and Index II.

Building Inscriptions: see Inscriptions.

Bull, IV 242, 260, 272, 278, 283, 293, 298, 313, 323, 341, 345, 347, 360, 387, 392, 883, 906; yokes of, I 522; from Negro lands, I 336; army of Tefibi like a, I 396; Kheti II rich in, I 408.
—Bull of Mad, IV 915; divine bulls of Athribis, IV 470; Pharaoh as a bull, II 143, 659, 853; III 117, 144, 147, 285, 360, 372, 455, 489, 507, 608; IV 40, 41, 46, 56, 62, 67, 81, 94, 103, 105, 246, 852; Amon-Kamephis as a bull, II 225, 314, 317; "Bull of his mother," III 24.
—Epithets of, II 659.
—Bulls for mortuary offering, I 540,

542, 556, 559, 584, 591; II 840; III 526; for oblation, I 432, 556, 569; II 553, 554; IV 335, 468, 768, 848, 856, 866, 869, 874, 875; divine offering, II 160, 171, 562, 621; III 413; IV 190.
—Bulls from Egypt, IV 229; Kharu, IV 229; Meshwesh, IV 111; Retenu, II 447, 518; Naharin, II 482; Punt, II 486; Genebteyew, II 474; Wawat, II 475, 487, 503, 523, 527; Kush, II 514.
—*ἰpw*-bulls, IV 242.

Bull Calves, II 553, 554, 562.

Bullocks, IV 9, 190, 260, 272, 313, 323, 335, 341, 345, 360, 958H.
—from Retenu, II 447, 471, 491; Naharin, II 482.
—Bullocks of the bulls, IV 229, 242, 283, 293, 298, 387, 392; of the Nege-bulls, IV 229.

Bunch (a measure), IV 234.

Bundle (a measure), III 77, 159, 207; IV 229, 234, 241, 283, 341, 344, 378, 379, 387, 391, 392, 395, 954.
—*ḥtp*-bundle, IV 350, 949, 950, 952, 953.
—*ḥtp.t*-bundles, IV 301.
—*ḥrš*-bundles, IV 301.
—Sehetep-bundles, IV 295.

Bureau Service, I 295; officials of, I 300.

Burial, II 358, 977, 994, 1003, 1006, 1008; IV 668; offices for, IV 966; coverings for, IV 521, 538.
—Burial (of Osiris), III 910; IV 499, 593, 637–47; of Apis, I 22; IV 771, 778, 780, 786, 791, 884, 917, 918, 961, 977, 986, 1010,

Butter, IV 233, 301, 344, 350, 376.

C

Cabbage, IV 240, 393.

Cabin, IV 840.

Cabinet: double, I 618, 672, 713, 716.
—of the office of the chief treasurer, I 672 n. a, 673.
—of the treasury, I 716.

Cabinet Chamber: plan of rebellion conceived in, I 492.

Cakes, I 336; II 114; III 71; IV 238, 291, 297, 300, 347, 350, 467; makers of, III 624.
—Bull cakes, II 572.
—Dressed-geese cakes, II 572.
—Obelisk cakes, II 572.
—Rahusu cakes, IV 238, 291, 393.
—White-loaf cakes, II 572, 621.
—*sꜣ-tꜣ*-cakes, IV 240, 378, 392.
—*šʿ*-cakes, IV 949, 950, 952, 953, 954.

Calculations: of fields, III 275.

Calendar, Egyptian: introduction of, I 58, early existence of, I 45; oldest fixed date in history, I 45.
—Gregorian, I 40; Julian, I 40; I p. 40.

Calendar of Feasts: of Ramses III, I 43 n. b; IV 139–45.

Calves, I 408; II 139, 149, 160, 723, 733, 739, 740; IV 242, 283, 293, 298, 341, 345, 387, 392, 906, 929.
—for divine offerings, II 458, 793; IV 190; mortuary offering, III 526; oblation, II 960; IV 335, 468, 848, 856, 866, 869, 874, 875.
—Calves: from Kharu, IV 229; Naharin, II 482; Retenu, II 447, 458, 471; Punt, II 486; Genebteyew, II 474; Wawat, II 475, 487, 495, 503, 515, 523, 527; Kush, II 494, 502, 514.

Camp, III 579, 589, 598; IV 64, 870, 873; royal, II 429; III 320, 331, 332, 340.

Canal, II 775; IV 412, 853, 957.

Canal Administration, IV 266.

Canal Boat: of acacia, IV 229, 387.

Canal Wall: of Luxor, IV 628.

Canals of the Delta: Eti, III 576; Sheken, III 576; Water of Re, IV 83, 224; of Heliopolis, IV 266, 278, 394.
—Canal of the first Cataract, II 75; begun by Uni, I 324; cleared by Sesostris III, I 643–45; repaired by same king, I 646–48; names of, I 644; II 650; length, width, depth of, I 647; again cleared by Thutmoses I and III, I 648; II 75, 76, 649–50.
—Canal, for irrigation, in Siut, dug by Kheti II, I 407.
—Canal of Wadi Tumilât, II 248.

Candelabra: of silver, IV 735.

Captives, II 225, 387, 402, 413, 656, 900; III 34, 82, 96, 101, 119, 148, 155, 344, 349, 351, 448 n. b, 597, 598; IV 42, 56, 106, 121, 362, 825, 865.
—Building the temple of Amon, II 758, 759; settled in Egyptian strongholds, IV 403, 405 n. g; distributed to Egyptian families, II 916; as slaves in the temples, II 918; IV 121, 126,

128, 137 n. a, 190, 207, 213; IV 359, 404, 1021.
—Captives from Amor, IV 39, 129; Asiatics, IV 122; Denyen, IV 81, 82, 403; Ekwesh, III 588; Hua, II 850, Ibhet, II 854; Ikathi, II 788; Kehek, III 588; Keshkesh, III 428; Kharu, II 884; Khatithana, II 789; Khenthen-nofer, II 11, 162, 646; adventure with, II 11; Kheta, IV 129; Lebanon, II 783; Libya, III 584, 588, 600; IV 52, 54, 57, 78, 79, 405; Meshwesh, IV 90, 92, 111, 405; Naharin, II 480, 532, III 344; Negros, III 40, 44, 452; IV, 477; Nine Bows, IV 190, 207; Nuges, II 508; Peleset, IV 44, 76, 129, 403; Retenu, II 162, 402, 467, 790; III 97; Sand-dwellers, I 313; II 661; Seir, IV 404; Shasu, III 108; IV 129; Shekelesh, III 588; IV 81; Sherden, III 588, 601; IV 129, 403; Temeh, IV 92; Teresh, III 588; IV 129; Thekel, IV 44, 78, 79, 129, 403; Tintto-emu, II 15; Ullaza, II 470; Weshesh, IV 403; Zahi, II 490.

Caravan, I 312, 332, 334, 336, 343, 352, 356, 360; negro, I 368; conductors of, see Index V.

Caravaneers, III 178 bis, 192, 286.

Carcass, III 88; IV 1004.

Cardinal Points: genii of, II 228, 231.

Cargo, II 266; III 53, 274.

Cargo Boats, I 322, 323; IV 863; of acacia wood, I 323, 324.

Carob Pods, IV 295, 301, 350.

Carob Wood, I 372; IV 391.
—Articles made of carob wood: chairs, II 436, 490; chest, II 755; chariots, II 491; shrine, I 667; staff, II 436; table, II 436, 509.
—Carob wood from Arrapachitis, II 512; Assur, II 449; Retenu, II 436, 447, 491, 509, 525; Zahi, II 490.

Carousing, IV 451.

Carriers, II 287.

Cartouches: found at fourth cataract, I 21.

Cartouche-Vessel: of silver, IV 735.

Carts, Ox, IV 73, 467.

Carved Horns of Oxen, III 475.

Carvers, III 271.

Carvings, IV 489.

Cases: criminal, II 683; real estate, II 686, 689, 690.

Cases: of wrought wood, IV 390.

Caskets: of silver, IV 231.

Cassia Wood, IV 234, 344, 379.

Castle, IV 76; names of, IV 77; royal, I 532; see also Palaces.

Cat: sacred animal, I 281 n. c.

Cattle, I 496; II 736, 829, 884, 887, 984; III 577; IV 229, 235, 242, 275, 280, 282, 283, 336, 337, 339, 341, 342, 345, 360, 362, 363, 364, 370, 372, 379, 383, 384, 387, 423, 470, 676, 821, 958M, 992.
—Importation of, I 146, 147, 281; small cattle and bulls, brought from Negro lands, I 336; numbering of, I 81, 157; raising of, I 408; colors of (=breeds of?), I 408.
—Overseer of cattle, II 1041.
—Cattle of Amon: see Index II: Karnak, Temple of Amon; Inspector of, Overseer of, Scribe of, see Index V.
—Sacred cattle of Apis, IV 332.
—Branded for the royal house, III 56; overseer of, III 57; see also Index V.
—Cattle, curiously decorated, II 1035.
—for divine offering, II 793; III 413; mortuary offering, III 271; oblation, I 432; II 960.
—from Ibhet, II 853; Hua, II 850; Meshwesh, III 589; IV 110, 111, 405; Seir, IV 404; of Egyptian colonists in Kush, II 121.
—Breeds of cattle, I 408 n. g.
—Cattle (*y*ʾ.*t*), IV 242.
—Large cattle, IV 212, 220, 226, 795; from Retenu, II 434, 525; Megiddo, II 435; Zahi, II 462; Kheta, III 428.
—Small cattle, III 276; IV 212, 220, 226, 795, 1021; from Punt, II 272; Retenu, II 434, 447, 471, 518, 525; Megiddo, II 435; Zahi, II 462; Naharin, II 482.
—Wild cattle, III 598; for mortuary offering, II 840; hunt of, II 863–64.
—Black cattle, IV 278.
—Mountain cattle, IV 272.
—Red cattle from Negro lands, IV 724.
—White, small cattle, from Megiddo, II 435.
—Firstlings of the year, II 727; yearlings, II 723, 726, 727, 730, 731, 735, 739, 743; two-year-olds, II 722, 725, 730, 731, 734, 735, 736, 738, 739, 740, 742; IV 242.

CATTLE FODDER, IV 212.

CATTLE FOLDS, I 281, 408.

CATTLE YARDS, IV 9, 217, 260, 313, 323, 330, 859, 958H.

CAUSEWAY, IV 861.

CAVALRY, IV 1004; officers of, III 584.

CAVERN DWELLERS, IV 4.

CAVERNS: of Libya, III 611; of Elephantine, IV 925; of the ennead of Khereha, IV 869.
—Cavern (=tomb), IV 958M.

CAVES, III 134; of Elephantine, III 171; IV 925; Mitanni, II 773.
—Anubis, lord of, I 394.

CEDAR, II 321; IV 226, 234, 245, 282, 345, 379, 385, 391.
—Articles made of cedar: ferry boats, IV 229, 283, 387; barges, II 32, 94, 838, 888; IV 278, 331, 904, 916, 1023; tow boats, IV 229, 387; ships, I 146, 465; II 492; IV 209, 574; palace doors, I 148; shrine doors, II 156; tomb doors, IV 958M; temple doors, II 155, 157, 375, 611, 614, 749 n. b, 903; III 217, 245, 505, 537, 625; IV 11, 355, 356, 357, 358, 362, 910, 970; doors, IV 406, 489; doorposts, IV 406; altars, I 787; flagstaves, II 103; III 94, 537; IV 15; staves, II 718; chests, II 755; mortuary chests, IV 966; panels, IV 929; columns, II 32, 600, 601.
—Cedar (?) from Bigeh, II 718; God's Land, II 888; Lebanon, III 94; IV 577; Retenu, II 838, 888; royal domain, II 157, 903; IV 15, 209, 278, 331, 970.

CEDAR TERRACES: see Terraces.

CEILING: of lazuli, I 483; of electrum, IV 958J.

CELLA, IV 899.

CELLAR: beer, IV 238; wine, IV 512.

CEMETERY, I 202, 208, 209, 238, 243; III 260; IV 182; children of, IV 499; thieves of, 554, 556; see also Necropolis, and Index VI: Abydos, Serapeum, Memphis, Thebes (Western), Tazoser (West), and Highlands.

CENSER, II 93; IV 269; of ebony, I 500; silver, I 500; IV 334; fine gold, IV 334; gold, IV 735, 736.
—Fourfold censer: of gold, IV 735.

CENSERFULS, IV 299, 348.

CENTER: of the army, II 430.

CEREMONIES, III 286, 371, 564; IV 836, 958D, 988J; of Amon-Re, III 206, 256, 436; of Aton, II 994; of erecting the symbol of Osiris, II 874; at feast of Ptah, III 77, 159; of New Moon, II 562, 608; at the voyage to the southern Opet, II 554; of court and palace in charge of the herald, II 764, 767; of investiture, II 1020; IV 958D, 988H.
—Foundation ceremony, I 445, 506, 669; II 152, 157, 608, 614, 795; see also Cord and Measuring-line.
—Mortuary ceremony: benefit of, II 925.
—Temple ceremony, II 826; III 82.

CHAIR, II 802.
—of black wood, from Zahi, II 490.
—of carob wood, from Kadesh, II 436; Zahi, II 490.
—of ebony, from Kadesh, II 436.
—of ivory, from Kadesh, II 436.
—Sedan chair, II 981; vizier's chair, II 675.

CHAMBER, I 307; II 771; IV 849; royal, II 237; Dewat, IV 866, 871; fire III 28; hidden, III 278; Meskhent, III 525; privy, I 256, 286, 290; II 675; quarry, see under Quarry-chamber; sepulcher, IV 540; shrine, III 529; store, III 100; tomb, IV 4, 515, 517; treasure, IV 25.
—for Chamber Attendants, Chief of Chamber, Eldest of the Chamber, see Index V.
—Secret chamber of the mountains, II 946.
—Sacred chamber: in temple of Karnak, II 795; the august dwelling, II 795.
—the sealed chamber (=treasury): sealing of, reported to vizier, II 676, 679.
—Temple chamber, II 164, 390, 1017; names of, II 1017; for oil, II 165.
—Upper chamber of pyramid, I 322; of tomb of Kheti II, I 412.

CHAMPION, II 431; III 400.

CHANNEL OF ORONTES, II 784 n. f; III 325; the inaccessible, II 288.

CHAPEL, II 908; IV 57, 78, 125, 191, 356; IV 732, 733, 736, 737, 755 n. c; of Thutmose III, at Luxor, III 506; of temple of Seti I at Abydos, III 226, 231–34; of Ramses III in temple of Re at Heliopolis, IV 277; of Pesibkhenno, by Great Pyramid, stela of

Eye in, II 1042 n. a; in Thebes, of Prince Wazmose, II 928; of Atum-Khepri, IV 732; of Khonsu, in Ramses III's temple at Medinet Habu, II 5; Ptah-Tatenen at Medinet Habu, II 461; chapel in temple of Medinet Habu, II 641.
—Mortuary chapel, II 36.
—Secret chapel, III 412.
—Tomb-chapels, I 19, 20.

CHAPLETS, IV 876; of gold, II 32.

CHARCOAL, IV 295, 303, 380, 394.

CHARIOT, II 7, 813, 857, 858; III 84, 102, 360, 441, 450, 454, 455, 461, 473; IV 49, 50, 53, 72, 73, 74, 76, 840, 860, 1004.
—Wrought with electrum, II 430, 447 960, 969; wrought with gold, II 413, 435, 447, 501; wrought with gold and silver, II 430, 431, 467, 490, 491, 501, 509, 801; pole of, II 435.
—Chariot: from Assur, II 449; Kheta, III 343; Kush, II 1035, 1039; Megiddo, II 430, 431, 435; Meshwesh, IV 111; Naharin, II 81, 85, 482, 501; Nuges, II 508; Retenu, II 413, 447, 467, 491, 509, 518, 790; Zahi, II 490; Ullaza, II 470; Orontes, II 784, 785; Ikathi, II 788.
—Chariots of carob wood, from Retenu, II 491; of *ṯ*ꜣ-*gw*-wood, II 491.

CHARIOT DRIVERS, IV 405 n. g.

CHARIOT WARRIOR: Hittite, III 337.

CHARIOTEERS (Egyptian), IV 65, 77, 106, 405 n. g; Enwau, III 635.
—First: Perehirunamef, III 482 n. c; Rekhpehtuf, III 642; Hori, III 645; Ubekhu, III 650.
—Charioteer of the court: Nakhtamon, IV 466.
—Charioteers of the chariotry, IV 466.
—Hittite charioteers, III 337.
—King's charioteer, Ini, III 198.

CHARIOTRY: Egyptian, III 267, 307, 311, 325, 327, 342, 365, 380, 428, 578, 583, 587; IV 71, 89, 354, 402, 410, 822; leader of: see Index V; lord of: see Index V.
—Hittite, III 310, 312, 320, 321, 337, 378; Libyan, III 583.
—Syrian, III 309; IV 118.

CHARM: knowledge of, I 378.

CHASTISEMENT: divine, IV 907.

CHÂTEAU, III 588, 600; IV 194, 281.

CHEST, II 376, 802; IV 27, 29, 843.
—Linen, II 301, 719, 721, 722, 723, 726, 727, 730, 731, 744.
—Made of carob wood, I 372; II 755; cedar, II 755; ebony, II 755; ivory, II 755; meru wood, II 755.
—Mortuary chest: of cedar wood, IV 966; ked wood, IV 966; meru wood IV 966.

CHIEF MOUTH, IV 398, 400.

CHILDREN: playing, II 300; length of new-born, I 395; see also education.

CHISEL, III 271; of copper, IV 552.

CHRONOLOGICAL TABLES, I 58–75; IV 607, 693, 812, 940.

CHRONOLOGY, EGYPTIAN, I 38–75, 415–18, 423A, 424, 434, 460–62; IV 604–7, 693–94, 793, 811–13, 885, 935–41; addendum to, I p. 48; length of year discovered in the fifth millennium B. C., I 39; Julian chronology, I 40; Gregorian, I 40; of the XI Dynasty, I 415–18.

CINNAMON, IV 234, 240, 378, 391, 394; from Punt, III 116.

CINNAMON WOOD, IV 287, 300, 344, 348, 378, 391; from Punt, II 265.

CIRCUIT, II 294, 661, 804, 954; IV 818; of Aton, II 795, 1007, 1010; IV 62; of the sun, II 70, 98, 308, 319; IV 40, 71, 249, 623, 988H; of heaven, II 657.

CIRCUIT MESSENGERS, II 692.

CIRCUIT RUNNERS, III 170.

CIRCUMCISION: practiced by the people of Ekwesh, III 588; see also under Hands cut off.

CISTERNS: of the Oasis, IV 726, 727, 728; name of, IV 727, 728.

CITADEL, III 463; IV 117.

CITIZEN, III 61; IV 410.
—Citizen (ᶜ*nḫ*), III 51, 57, 59; IV 397.
—Citizen (*nḏs*), IV 863; duties of, I 536; ka of, II 353.
—Citizen (*šw*ꜣ), II 920.
—Citizens of the army, I 681 bis; II 53, 864; III 57, 59, 206; penalty for stealing hides by, III 57.
—Citizen's cistern, IV 727.

CITIZEN LANDS, IV 755.

CITY OF ETERNITY: tomb of Kheti I, I 402.

CIVILIZATION: Egypt the home of, IV 578.

CLASSES: of people, II 916; IV 190, 197, 251, 278, 402, 403; established by Ramses III, IV 402; consisting of, IV 402.

CLAY, IV 871; for plastering tomb-walls, II 106; field of clay, for bricks, II 758.

CLEANSING: of temples, II 642; of persons, IV 866, 876, 880, 881; see also Index VI: Memphis, cleansing of.

CLIFF, II 966.

CLIFF TEMPLE: at Napata, IV 897–99.

CLIFF TOMB: at Abd el-Kurna, of Rekhmire, I 20; II 663 n. d; Menkheperreseneb, II 772 n. a; Ramose, II 936 n. b; Neferhotep, III 68 n. c.
—Assasîf (Thebes), of Neferhotep, III 68.
—Assiut, of Hepzefi, I 535 n. a.
—opposite Assuan: of Thethi, I 161 n. d; Pepinakht, I 355 n. f; Khui, I 361 n. c; Sebni, I 362 n. f.
—Benihasan: of Amenemhet, I 515 n. a.
—Dêr el-Bahri: of Amenhotep I, IV 668, 690–92.
—Dêr el-Gebrâwi: of Henku, I 280; Ibi, I 375 n. f.
—El Kab: of Ahmose, son of Ebana, II 1 n. a; Pahri, II 3 n. d.
—Gebel Marâg: of Zau, I 380 n. d.
—Ibrim: of Penno, IV 474 n. a.
—Kasr-es-Saiyâd: of Idu-Seneni, I 337 n. a.
—Kurnet-Murraï: of Huy, II 1019.
—Tell el-Amarna: of Ani, II 977; Merire II, II 981; Merire I, II 982–88; Eye, II 989–96; Mai, II 997–1003; Ahmose, I 1004–8; Tutu, II 1009–13; Huy, II 1014–17.
—Thebes: of Thutmose I, II 97; excavation of, II 106; secrecy in excavation of, II 106; Thutmose II, II 389.

CLOTHING, IV 843, 859, 875, 880, 881, 883; changes of, II 588; as mortuary offering, I 252; for embalmment, I 366, 382; presented to the court, I 369; for the gods, IV 335; for taxes, IV. 150, 403.
—Clothing from Kadesh, II 436; see also Garments.
—Clothing the god at his processions: done by the master of secret things, I 745; by queen, II 239.
—Temple clothing, II 615.

CLUSTERS, IV 295, 301, 350, 378; of beads, IV 377.

COALITION: the Hittite, III 309; the Libyan, III 579.

COAT OF MAIL, III 312, 326, 365; IV 99; from the Asiatics on the Orontes, II 785; see also Bronze.

COFFERS, IV 256.

COFFIN, IV 521, 538, 665–67, 852 n. c, 979, 988; name on, IV 499; pit of, IV 972.

COFFIN: of Mekhu, I 368; of Zau, I 382; coffin made of ebony, I 247; of wood, I 382.
—Coffin inscriptions: see under Inscriptions.

COILS OF ROPE, IV 582.

COITION: of god with queen, II 196; III 400 n. c.

COLLARS, II 45; of real malachite, I 534; gold, II 944, 986, 989; III 7, 8, 9, 69, 73; IV 201, 204, 493; of gold, and rock-crystal, IV 373; of gold and costly stone, IV 386, 876.

COLLECTION OF TAXES, III 55, 58, 61, 62; IV 324.

COLLECTORS OF HONEY, IV 149, 266.

COLLUSION: crime of, IV 427, 428, 429, 438, 439, 440, 442, 444, 447.

COLONNADE, IV 622; of temple of Upwawet at Siut, I 403; of temple of Harsaphes at Heracleopolis, IV 970; of temple at Dêr el-Bahri, II 191; of temple of Karnak, II 305, 317, 775; IV 707, 767; of temple of Ramses III at Medinet Habu, IV 16.

COLORS, II 558; from Retenu, II 491, 534(?).

COLOSSUS: in temple of Re at Heliopolis, IV 252; of Medinet Habu temple, IV 191 n. j; at Tanis, of Ramses II, III 417.
—Colossus of Memnon, I 16; II 878, 879, 880, 883 n. e; made of gritstone, II 883 n. e, 906 n. a; temple of Memnon colossi, II 883.

COLPORTEURS, IV 467; districts of, III 172.

COLUMNS, III 510, 512, 513; IV 489, 748, 889.
—Columns made of electrum, III 512, 515; IV 192; cedar, II 32, 600, 601; gold, IV 315; wood, II 614; sandstone, II 795; IV 910; lips of, IV 889.

Columns—
—Column inscriptions: see under Inscriptions.
—Bud columns, III 515.
—Flower columns, III 515.
—Temple columns, I 509; II 614, 795, 805, 917; III 263, 593; IV 315.

COMMAND OF A GOD, II 253; royal, I 271, 273, 354; II 52; III 32B, 67, 586; IV 597, 629, 706, 817, 943.

COMMEMORATIVE SCARABS, II 625, 860.

COMMISSION, I 263, 264, 266, 298, 301, 303, [305], 342, 445, 508; II 985; III 32B, 271; IV 147, 412, 414, 466, 511, 512, 522, 676, 784; to a court, IV 423; overseer of, see Index V.

COMMUNICATIONS, III 291; from people to Pharaoh, II 767; from Pharaoh to people, II 767; to foreign lands, II 767.

COMMUNITY, DIVINE, IV 888.

COMPLAINTS: by the lay priesthood of the temple of Min at Coptos, I 777; by the Mayor of Western Thebes, IV 527; by Wenamon, IV 566.

COMPOSITION OF COURT, IV 426, 531, 546.

COMPUTATION, II 763.

CONCEALED FROM THE PEOPLE, I 404.

CONCUBINES, III 267; king's, IV 844.

CONFECTIONERS, III 624.

CONFIDENTIAL OFFICE: in charge of, Thethi, I 423D.

CONFISCATION OF PROPERTY, I 779; IV 1024.

CONNIVANCE: laws on, III 58.

CONSPIRACY: harem, IV 416–56; crime of, IV 430, 443, 447.

CONSTANTINOPLE OBELISK, II 629–31.

CONTRACT (=treaty), III 386.

CONTRACTS: registered with the vizier II 703; for the remuneration of the prophets of Abydos, I 536; IV 679; of Hepzefi of Siut, I 539–93; for supplies of harbor garrisons, II 483, 510, 519, 535; for endowing divine offerings for Mut-Hathor of Thebes. II 622; for endowment of the lay priesthood of Ptah of Karnak, II 620; for offerings, IV 1022.

CONVEYANCES, I 5; IV 946; see also Wills.

COPPER, I 534; II 155, 558, 666; IV 31, 32, 228, 230, 245, 283, 285, 342, 355, 356, 372, 373, 385, 386, 388, 389, 840, 548, 549, 550, 552, 553, 859, 883, 958G; in scraps, IV 373, 385, 389.
—Objects wrought with, II 157, 376, 794 n. b; III 505, 528; IV 11, 216.
—King's bones of, III 403.
—Articles made of copper: chisels, IV 552; bars, IV 408; shrine doors, IV 198, 254; temple doors, I 483; II 45, 104, 302, 390; III 525; IV 311; vase, I 500; II 164; bowl, I 500; Karnak gate, II 376; offering-tables, IV 911; statue, IV 302, 395; table vessels, IV 190, 354; swords from Meshwesh, III 589; vessels, II 459; bolts, II 813; IV 406, 489.
—Copper from God's Land, III 274; Retenu, II 447, 471, 491, 509, 790; Zahi, II 459, 460, 462, 490, 536(?); Isy, II 493, 521; Sinai, I 713.
—Crude copper: from Retenu, II 509; from Isy, II 511; from Arrapachitis, II 512.
—Asiatic copper, II 45, 104, 614, 755; III 217, 537, 910; offering tables of, II 175.
—Black copper, II 92, 390; IV 245, 284, 285, 342, 373, 385, 389, 732, 734, 736; door-mountings of, II 155; temple doors of, II 375; decorations made of, II 164; bolts of, IV 411; corselet of, IV 373, 389; shrine doors of, II 889 n. a.

COPPER MINES: in Atika, IV 408; at Sinai, I 168.

COPPERSMITH, II 755; IV 523, 524, 532, 533, 534; succession of the craft, IV 532.

COPY OF LETTER, IV 527; of records, IV 535.

CORD, MEASURING, I 445.
—Cord made of palm-fiber, IV 235; of gold and costly stones, IV 386.
—Stretching of the cord at the foundation ceremony, I 506; II 152, 608, 614; feast of, II 157.

CORDAGE, IV 578.

COREGENCY: in XII Dynasty, I 64, 460, 462; of Amenhotep II, I 66 n. a; II 184 n. d; of Ramses IX, I 69 n. c; of Osorkon II, I 71; of Takelot III, I 72 n. d; of Ramses II with Seti I, III 268; see also I 58–75, and Index III.

CORN, II 987; IV 244.

CORNICE, IV 315.
CORONATION, II 151, 594, 849; IV 142, 887, 922, 958D.
CORONATION DECREE: of Thutmose I, I 18; II 131–66; feast of, I 258.
CORONATION INSCRIPTION: of Harmhab, III 22–32.
CORRUPTION OF OFFICIALS, III 58.
CORSELET, III 360.
—Corselets made of black copper, IV 373, 389; bronze, II 447.
—Corselet from Retenu, II 447; from Orontes, II 785.
—Corselets, inlaid, from Naharin, II 501.
CORVÉE, I 320.
COSMETIC, EYE: from Punt, II 265, 272; Naharin, II 501.
COSTUME, II 231; III 34.
COUCHES, IV 875, 876.
COUNCIL: of army, II 695; of gods, II 192; of Nun, IV 330; of understanding, II 914; of war, II 420; III 322.
—the Great Council: reports to the vizier, II 706.
—Local council of a district, II 686.
COUNCIL HALL: royal, IV 100 n. a.
COURSE (of a wall), IV 355, 356, 358, 406, 489.
COURT, ROYAL, I 239, 246, 248, 309, 320, 353; II 107, 151, 205, 232, 236, 238, 255, 260, 292, 371, 620, 622, 675, 706, 769, 1026; III 264, 580, 590; IV 63, 147, 477, 724A, 767, 933, 966; in mourning, I 491; ships of, I 258; garrison of, II 694; officials of, III 65, 437; princes of, III 287; going in and going out of, reported to the vizier, II 676; affairs of, reported by the chief treasurer, II 679; stable of, III 635, 645; chiefs of stables of, IV 466.
—Companions, Members, Nobles, Officers, Officials, Steward of Court: see Index V.
—Temple court, IV 198, 207, 272, 311, 327, 330, 333, 335, 363, 614, 619, 707.
—Peristyle of, at Luxor, III 506.
—Legal court: appointment of, III 65; IV 423; instructions to, IV 424; composition of, IV 426, 531, 546.
—Legal court: great nobles of, IV 425, 427, 428, 429, 430, 431, 432, 433, 434, 435, 436, 437, 438, 439, 440, 441, 442, 444; of butlers, IV 443, 446, 448, 449, 450.
—the great court of Thebes, IV 531, 533.
—Court of examination, IV 425.
—Court = decree of court, II 290.
—Court-marshal, III 69.
—Court-fishermen, IV 466; divisions of, IV 466; officers of, IV 466.
COURTIERS, III 267.
COVERINGS, BURIAL, IV 521, 538.
COW, IV 229, 242, 283, 293, 298, 341, 347, 387, 392.
—for divine offering, IV 190; for oblation, IV 335.
—Cow speaking, I 408.
—Cows from Kharu, IV 229; Retenu, II 471.
—Cows of Hathor, II 210.
—Loan-cows from Kush, II 556; from Zahi, II 556.
COW HIDES, IV 379, 395.
CRAFT, III 51, 52; succession of, see Coppersmiths.
CRAFTSMEN, II 371, 372, 753, 775, 801, 833; overseer of, see Index V; see also Handicraft.
CRANES, IV 242.
CRATE, IV 234, 241, 379.
CRENELATED OVAL, IV 718.
CREW, II 328; III 275; IV 212, 407, 944.
—Crews: of Egypt, IV 574; Byblos, IV 586, 591; Syrian, IV 574; Alasa, IV 591.
—Galley crew, IV 328.
—of recruits, I 343; leader of, see Index V.
CRIME, III 62, 389, 390; IV 425, 426, 427, 428, 429, 430, 431, 446, 451, 530, 880.
—Capital crime, III 64; IV 529; of death, IV 454, 456.
—Crimes: insurrection, IV 427, 428, 429, 430, 442, 443; collusion, IV 427, 428, 429, 438, 439, 440, 442, 444, 477; conspiracy, IV 430, 443, 447; not reporting conspiracy, IV 431, 432, 433, 434, 435, 436, 437, 438, 439, 440, 448, 449, 450.
CRIMINAL CASES: docket of, II 670, 683; entry of, II 683.
CRIMINALS, II 683, 767; IV 427, 428, 429, 430, 431, 432, 433, 434, 435, 436, 437, 438, 439, 440, 442, 443, 445, 448,

449, 450, 452, 453, 456; procedure of cases against, II 683; IV 423–56.

Crocodile, III 615; captured by Amenemhet I, I 483; Pharaoh as, II 659; III 117.

Crown Possessions: in the Oryx nome, I 523; of the south, building of, in Elephantine, I 650; of Thinis of the South, in Abydos, I 665 n. b; tributes distributed to, II 706.

—Overseers of, I 312; gang-overseers of, I 522; people of, IV 466; scribe of, IV 465.

Crown, Royal, II 235, 239, 314; III 267, 270, 406; of Amon, II 198; IV 246.

—Crown: "Great in Magic," I 609; cf. the same title of goddess Mut.

—the double crown, I 500; II 229; III 286, 486; IV 304.

—Etef-crown, I 168; II 292; IV 104, 186, 209, 351, 401, 411.

—Northern crown, I 609.

—Red crown, I 609, 779; II 229, 318, 815; III 414; IV 62, 104.

—Serpent crown, IV 62.

—Southern crown, I 609.

—White crown, I 609, 779; II 229, 235, 318, 636, 815; III 414; IV 62, 104, 182, 304.

—Crowns: as adornment, II 888; see also Diadems.

Crude Copper: see Copper.

Crystal, Rock, IV 373; cut, IV 233, 287, 345; beads of, IV 233, 287, 345, 377; seals of, IV 233, 303, 345, 349, 377; pendants of, IV 287; armlet of, IV 303; semdets of, IV 377; scarab of, IV 377; bracelet of, IV 303, 349, 377; finger rings of, IV 377; eye-amulets of, IV 377.

Cube, IV 378, 395.

Cubic Measures: see Measure.

Cubit, One: indicates the length of a newborn child, I 395 n. f; was the length of Tefibi's son, when he began to rule, I 395; of Kheti, III 413; see also Measures, Linear.

Cumin, IV 287.

Cup Bearer: see Index V.

Curly-haired: epithet for Negro, II 71, 657 (see corrigenda); III 155; for Kode Folk.

Curse: on violators of endowment, II 925; III 192, 194; IV 483; of treaty, III 386.

Cushion, II 675 bis.

Custom: practiced upon a king, IV 866.

Cyperus of the Shore, IV 301, 350.

D

Dagger, II 22, 254; wrought with electrum, I 682; of bronze, II 802.

Dahabiyeh, II 1034, 1039.

Dais, II 675, 981; III 13.

Damage, IV 149, 543.

Dances of the God: by the dwarf from Yam, I 353.

Dancing, II 238.

Dark Period: the second, between the Old and Middle Kingdoms, I 52, 57.

Date Grove, IV 215.

Date Palm: fiber of, IV 380, 395.

Date Trees, IV 264, 1021.

Date Wine, I 336.

Dates, IV 244, 295, 347, 944; dried, IV 299, 347.

—for divine offering, II 159; food, I 785; oblation, II 571.

Daybook of a Frontier Official, III 629.

Deben, I 785; II 377, 436 bis, 446 ter, 459 bis, 482, 486, 490, 491, 493 bis, 500, 502, 509, 514, 515, 518 bis, 522, 526, 527, 534, 536, 718, 719, 720, 721, 722, 723, 724, 726, 727, 730, 732, 733, 734, 735, 736, 737, 738, 739, 740, 744, 761, 903; III 207; IV 30, 228, 231, 232, 283, 285, 286, 287, 341, 343, 344, 345, 373, 377, 385, 386, 389, 390, 391, 566, 568, 576, 680, 681, 682, 732, 733, 734, 735, 736, 737, 949, 950, 952, 953, 954, 956, 957.

Decadence, I 22, 23.

Deceased: honors for, I 6; daily intercourse with king, I 6.

Decision, Legal, III 25.

Decoration of Soldiers and Officials with Gold, I 372; II 6, 9, 10, 11, 13, 14, 22, 23, 24, 39, 64, 81, 584, 585, 587, 588, 986, 1009, 1036; III 6, 73.

Decorations on Cattle, II 1035.

Decree, IV 630, 653, 656, 679, 992; royal, I 351; of Ramses III, IV 147–50.

Decree—
—Coptos decree, by Nubkheprure-Intef, I 773–80; dealing with a culprit, I 777.
—Coronation decree of Thutmose I, I 18; II 54–60.
—Decree for Harmhab's reforms, I 18.
—Endowment decree, I 349.
—Sealing of decrees, I 274; privy councilor of, I 336.
—Temple decrees, engraved on tablets, IV 202, 255, 265, 317, 321, 354, 360, 363, 656; concerning the sacred cattle of Apis, IV 332.
DEDICATION STELÆ, I 15; II 904–910; royal (of buildings and monuments), II 127, 301, 905.
DEDMET FLOWER, IV 215, 264, 345, 379, 393.
DEED, II 966.
DEIFICATION: of Snefru, I 722; Amenhotep, III, II 893–98, 900; Amenhotep, son of Hapi, II 911–12; Menmare, III 173; Ramses II, III 502, 504; see Apotheosis.
DEMOTIC, I 24.
DEPOSITION: of a priest of Min, I 778; of vizier, IV 361.
DEPOSITIONS: of legal documents, IV 534; taken by the vizier, II 704; IV 534.
DEPUTATION, IV 525, 526.
DESERT, IV 479; of Abydos, IV 1023.
DETENTION: unlawful, of slaves, III 55; penalty for, III 55.
DEW, DIVINE, II 197, 274, 819.
DEWAT CHAMBER, IV 866, 871.
DEWATOWE SHIPS: see Ships.
DIADEM, II 142, 145 bis, 226, 229, 231, 312 n. b, 314, 812, 831, 832–36, 838; III 16, 535, 536; IV 47, 382, 843, 988H; magic power of, II 220; king crowned in, when performing the foundation ceremony, I 506; of Re, IV 895.
—Double diadem, I 686; II 255; III 267; IV 304; double plumed, IV 401.
—Serpent diadem, II 245, 657, 925; IV 66, 127, 130.
DICTIONARY: Egyptian, I 33.
DIORITE, IV 980.
DISTRICT, II 686; III 580, 583; IV 265; of Abydos, IV 681; Aphroditopolis, IV 948; Amenopet, IV 539; Bista, IV 957; Busiris, IV 968; Gate of Ihotep, I 312; Middle of Heliopolis, IV 857; Hare nome, IV 948; Heracleopolis, IV 948, 968; Oxyrrhyncus, IV 948; town of Pesebek, IV 784; Ranofer, IV 830; Sais, IV 957; Sep, IV 948; Thebu, IV 957; see also Nome.
—Districts of the colporteurs, III 172; in Wawat, IV 479, 480, 481, 482, 483.
—Sacred districts of Mehenet (of Sais), IV 982, 1011; Resenet (of Sais), IV 1011.
—For Chief of, Officials of, Scribe of, Supervisor of, see Index V.
DIVINE BOAT: see Boat.
DIVINE COMMUNITY, IV 888.
DIVINE MEMBERS OF AMENEMHET, I 446, 492.
DIVINE OFFERINGS: see Endowment, Offering.
DIVINE OFFICE OF KINGS, III 403.
—For Divine consort, Divine father, Divine hand, Divine mother, Divine votress, see Index V.
DIVINE WATER, III 474.
"DIVINE WORDS" (Hieroglyphs), I 533.
DIVISION OF HORUS AND SET, THE TWO (when they divided the kingdom between them), II 120.
DIVISIONS OF COURT FISHERMEN, IV 466.
DOCKET, II 670; IV 535; criminal, II 683.
DOCUMENTS: written, I 1, 2, 5; mutilated state of, I 26; state, I 18; religious literature, I 2, 20; legal, I 20; IV 534; administrative, I 10; memoranda, I 20.
DODEKASCHOINOS: gift of, I 24; IV 146.
DOGS, II 413; III 475; IV 818, 1004.
—of Berber breed, I 421 n. b; from Punt, II 265.
—of King Intef I, I 421.
—Chief of Libya like a, III 580.
DOM PALM: fruit of, IV 234, 241, 294, 378, 391; from Mehay, IV 234.
DOMAIN OF PHARAOH, I 294, 309, 310, 312, 356, 382.
—for Custodian of, Scribe of, Superintendent of, see Index V.
—Royal domain, cedar from, II 157, 903; IV 15, 209, 278, 331, 970; lands of, II 186; superintendent of, III 70.

—Domain of a statue, IV 479, 480, 481, 482, 483; boundaries of, IV 479, 480, 481, 482, 483.
—Domain of Tehenut, IV 482; of pyramid, I 373; of temple, IV 141, 265.

Door Posts, III 14, 15, 236, 625; IV 311, 489; made of limestone, IV 355; 356; sandstone, III 625; stone, IV 357, 358, 362; wood, III 625; cedar, IV 406; electrum, IV 192; gold, IV 9, 197, 214, 216.

Doors: setting up of, I 328; made of cedar, IV 406, 489; door-keeper, see Index V; see also Doorpost, Doorway, Lintels, Portals.
—Palace doors: of cedar, I 148.
—Shrine doors: of cedar, II 156; of copper, IV 198, 254; of electrum, IV 5; of ketem gold, IV 251; of bronze, IV 320.
—Temple doors, III 412, 517, 528; of black granite, IV 7; of cedar, II 155, 157, 375, 611, 614, 794, 903; III 217, 245, 505, 520, 537, 625; IV 11, 355, 356, 357, 358, 362, 910, 970; of gold, IV 7, 195, 197, 214, 216; wrought with Asiatic copper, III 217; of copper, I 483; II 45, 104, 302, 390; III 525; IV 7, 14, 189, 311; of black copper, II 375; of bronze, III 528; of electrum, III 567; IV 4, 189, 191, 929; gilded with electrum, III 237; meru wood, IV 488 n. c;
—Tomb door of cedar, IV 958M.
—the great door, I 109; II 376; of temple, II 157; III 502; IV 195.
—the great double doors, of the palace were closed at death of king, I 491; of heaven, IV 216; of temple, IV 871, 929.

Doorway, I 634, 706; II 643; of tomb, I 637 bis; II 947 n. a; of fortress, I 650; of temple, II 44, 643, 662; III 227, 260, 528; IV 11; names of, II 104, 643; III 227; inscriptions of, see Inscriptions.
—Doorways: made of Benut stone, II 643; sandstone, II 794; granite, IV 197; black granite, III 528; red granite, III 528: electrum, II 903; III 227, 230, 237; bronze, III 246; gold, IV 14, 311; granite, IV 11; see also Portals.

Double Cabinet: see Cabinet; for Master of, see Index V.

Double Crown, see Crown.

Double Diadem: see Diadem.

Double Doors: see Door.

Double Façade: see Façade.

Double Gold-house, I 533, 664; II 371; see also Gold-house; for Lord of, Overseer of, see Index V.

Double Granary: see Granary; for Overseers of, see Index V.

Double Granary of Amon: see Index I; for Overseer of, see Index V.

Double House: see House; for Attached to, see Index V.

Double Plumed: see Plume.

Double Serpent-crest: see Serpent-crest.

Double Silver-house; see Silver-House; for Lord of, Overseer of, see Index V.

Double Staircase: see Staircase.

Double *w*ᶜ*b.t*-house: see House.

Double White House: see White House; for Overseer of, see Index V.

Dough, I 312.

Doves, IV 106, 242.

Dragging: of timber from Lebanon to the seacoast, IV 583.

Draughtsmen, I 447; III 271; IV 466.

Dream, III 582; IV 922, 923.

Drinking-Vessels, II 436; of silver, III 589.
—Drinking-vessel for the ka, II 32; made of gold, II 32.

Ducks, IV 992.

Dues, I 556; II 110, 149, 172, 483, 543, 596, 774, 798; III 51, 53, 273, 481; IV 878; for harem, III 54; to the gods of the deep, IV 330; to the temples, II 112, 557, 559, 597, 648; III 54; IV 283, 340, 386, 489; of local officials, II 716, 718–45; III 481; IV 958H; of Egypt, III 484; of negro lands, IV 34.
—Laws on dues, III 53, 54.

Dungeon of the Gate, III 180.

Dwarf, Dancing, I 351, 353; brought from Yam, I 351.

Dwelling of the High Priest of Amon, IV 489; see also Building, House, Palace.

Dyke, III 598; IV 724A, 795.

Dynasties:
—First: records of, I 7; length of, I 56,

58, 85 n. a; chronology of, I 57; history of on the Palermo stone, I 79, 84, 91–116.
—Second: length of, I 56, 85 n. a; chronology of, I 58; history of, on the Palermo stone, I 84, 117–44;
—Third: inscriptions of, I 168–75; records of, I 6, 24; length of, I 55, 85, 85 n. a, 86; chronology of, I 58; history of on the Palermo stone, I 79, 84, 145–48.
—Fourth: length of, I 54, 55; inscriptions of, I 176–212; chronology of I 59; accession of, I 79, 88; history of on the Palermo stone, I 79, 84, 87, 149–50.
—Fifth: records of, I 3, 7, 24; inscriptions of, I 213–81; chronology of, I 60; length of, I 54, 55; history of on the Palermo stone, I 78, 84, 87, 146 n. a, 153–67; introduction of the title, "Son of Re," II 187.
—Sixth: inscriptions of, I 282–390; records of, I 6, 8; chronology of, I 61; length of, I 54.
—Seventh: chronology of, I 53, 57, 62.
—Eighth, I 53, 62.
—Ninth: inscriptions of, I 391-414; chronology of, I 53, 62.
—Tenth: inscriptions of, I 10, 391–414; chronology of, I 53, 57, 62.
—Eleventh: inscriptions of, I 415–59; chronology of, I 63, 415–18, 423A, 424, 434; minimum length of, I 52.
—Twelfth: inscriptions of, I 460–750; their importance, I 8, 14, 17; chronology of, I 64, 460–62; rising of Sothis in, I 42, 46, 57; partially contemporary reigns of kings in, I 52; maximum length of, I 52.
—Thirteenth: inscriptions of, I 751–87; chronology of, I 65.
—Seventeenth: chronology of, I 65.
—Eighteenth: inscriptions of, II 1–1043; records of, I 13, 14, 20; succession of early kings of, II 17; dates of, I 47, 51; rising of Sothis in, I 43, 46; minimum length of, I 50; chronology of, I 65.
—Nineteenth: inscriptions of, III 1–651; importance of records of, I 13, 18, 23; minimum length of, I 50; chronology of, I 67.
—Twentieth: inscriptions of, IV 1–603; importance of records of, I 13, 22, 23; minimum length of, I 50; chronology of, I 69.
—Twenty-first, I 22, 23; inscriptions of, IV 604–92; minimum length of, I 50; chronology of, I 70; IV 604–7.
—Twenty-second, I 22; inscriptions of, IV 693–792; minimum length of, I 50; chronology of, I 71, 72; IV 693–94.
—Twenty-third, I 22; inscriptions of, IV 793–883; minimum length of, I 50; IV 793–94.
—Twenty-fourth, I 22; inscriptions under, IV 884; minimum length of, I 50; chronology of, I 73.
—Twenty-fifth, I 22; inscriptions of, IV 885–934; minimum length of, I 50; chronology of, I 74; IV 885.
—Twenty-sixth, I 22, 23, 48; inscriptions of, IV 935–1029; minimum length of, I 50; IV 1026; accession of, I 57; chronology of, I 75; IV 935–41.

E

EARRINGS, IV 876.

EARS: of grain, IV 244.
—Ears and nose cut off, as punishment, IV 451, 452, 524.

EARTH, II 139, 288, 570 *et passim*.
—Kissed, II 238, 268 *et passim*.

EBONY, II 387, 390; III 475; of best of the highlands, II 127.
—Brought from Negro lands, I 336; Punt, II 265, 272, 486; Nubia, II 375; Genebteyew, II 474; Kush, II 494, 502, 514; the south countries, II 652. Articles made of ebony: billets, III 475; chairs, II 436; chest, II 755; coffin, I 247; harp, II 32; shrines, II 127, 375, 388, 390; staff, IV 288; staves, II 802; IV 391; statue, II 436, 801; whips, II 802.

ECLIPSE, inscription of Takelot II, I 35.

EDICTS, II 705, 710; IV 354; of Harmhab, I 18; III 45–67; of mortuary endowment, II 922–27.

EDUCATION OF CHILDREN: Ptahshepses, I 256, 257; Amenemhet I, I 474–83; see also Teaching.

EGG, KING IN THE, III 267, 270, 288; IV 657, 817, 850; of Harakhte, IV 62; king, the pure egg, II 314.

ELDERS, II 916.

ELECTRUM, I 165, 167; II 155, 157, 274, 281, 302, 309, 315, 317, 319, 377, 390,

596, 608, 761; III 176, 230, 237, 285, 403; IV 7, 29, 632, 633, 721, 909, 911; in bars, II 279; in rings (commercial), II 279; weighing of, II 281.
—Articles made of: armlets of, II 376, 654; balances, IV 256; jar, II 556; vase, II 164; vessels, II 902; necklace, II 654; pendant, II 654.
—Articles decorated with, II 164, 298, 305, 309, 317, 319, 447, 775, 776, 805, 890; III 517, 525, 528, 970; barque, III 212; chariots wrought with, II 430, 447, 960, 969; ceiling, IV 958J; roof, IV 16; columns, III 512, 515; shrine door, IV 5; temple doors, III 567; IV 4, 929; doorway, II 903; III 227; great house, IV 904; great seat, IV 14, 610; image, IV 958K; portals, II 883, 895, 898; offering-tables, I 534, 610; II 164, 376; statue, I 165, 668; IV 633, 913, 958K; dagger wrought with, I 682; staff of, I 682; pyramidion, II 624, 630, 633, 834; staves, IV 912; temple walls, II 886; IV 748; shrines, II 374 bis, 776, 888; IV 1020; inlaid figures, II 375, 376; IV 910; amulets, II 376, 654; bow and stern of sacred barge, II 94; parts of doors, II 45; statue standards, II 95; flagstave tops, II 103, 883, 888, 889; the great throne, II 292; interior of holy of holies of Amon Temple, finished with, II 153, 596; portals of Amon Temple at Karnak wrought with, II 153.
—Brought from Emu, II 298, 387; the mountains, IV 28; Punt, I 161; II 272; the south countries, II 654; the highlands, II 374, 377.
—King's limbs of, III 403.
—Mine of electrum east of Redesiyeh, III 170.

Elephant: from Kush, I 510 n. b; from Retenu, II 125.

Emanation, II 991, 1000, 1029; IV 246, 817, 909, 911, 912, 913, 914, 915, 916.

Embalmers, I 370.

Embalming, of Mekhu's body, I 370.
—Embalming material: festival oil, from the double White House, I 370; secret things from the *wꜥb.t*-house, I 370; — —, from the *ꜥḳꜣ* house, I 370; clothing of the double White House, I 370; burial equipment from the court, I 370.
—House of embalming, IV 1029; name of, IV 1029.

Embankment, IV 842.

Embark, IV 571.

Emery, II 558; IV 600; from Zahi, II 460; from Retenu, II 534 (?).

Emigrants, extradition of, III 383, 385.

Emory: see Emery.

Empire: inscriptions of, I 8, 11; minimum length of, I 50.

Empty Years, IV 398.

Enactments, II 568; of Harmhab, III 45–67; form of, III 45.

Enbu Plant, IV 379, 395.
—Enbu fruit, IV 240, 393.

Encircling Wall of Temple, II 642.

Enclosure, Temple, II 164; see also Wall, and Index II.

Endowment: of Aton, II 952, 954, 958, 966; daily offerings, III 31, 515; IV 355, 1021; divine offerings, II 622, 792, 806, 900, 908; III 77, 159, 268; IV 256, 320, 335, 354, 355, 359, 654, 958M; feasts, II 569, 571, 798, 908; IV 208, 237, 290, 329, 924; the lay-priests of Amon, at Karnak, II 618; mortuary offerings, I 200, 269, 379, 562, 577, 630; II 839, 840, 908, 921, 926; III 526; IV 679, 1007; mortuary priests, I 200–9, 274, 630; II 32, 569, 571; oblations, IV 296, 329, 347; offerings for ancestors, III 23; temples, I 156, 159–61, 165–67, 213; II 163, 295, 571, 616, 617, 793; III 31, 413; IV 146–50, 755, 784, 992; tomb, I 213.

Enekh of the West (=life, euphemism for the dead), II 907.

Enemy, IV 1006.

Enfeebling by Magic Rolls, IV 454, 456.

"Enter in" to His Majesty, IV 460.

Epiphi: see Months.

Equipment, III 584.

Era of Opehtiset-Nubti, III 538, 542.

Erasure of Inscriptions, II 52, 126, 190, 192 n. d, 193, 205, 218, 290, 306, 312, 320, 612, 968.

Establishment: of the field [— —], I 302; of Osiris, IV 1021.

Estate: regulation of, I 536; private, of Sebni, I 366, 368; of Yewelot, IV

795; of Putowe, IV 948; of Kewkew, IV 948; of Nesumin, IV 948; of Harsiese, IV 948.
—Count's (*pr-ḥ ᵓ ty -ᶜ*), I 536, 551, 552, 565, 570, 574.
—Divine estate, IV 386; of Amon, IV 222–45; Ptah, IV 337–39; Re, IV 280–82; of the gods, IV 364–69; 383–85.
—Estate of Pharaoh, II 769, 871; IV 147; stewards of, II 871; reports from, II 871; harvest of, II 871; chief overseer of, II 925.
—Paternal estate (*nw-pr-yt*), I 536, 551, 552, 565, 570, 574.
—(*pr-ḏt*), I 546.

ETERNAL (=TEMPLE) AFFAIRS, I 610.
—Dwelling (=pyramid) of Sesostris I, I 509.
—Horizon (=tomb), IV 513.
—Seat (=necropolis), III 32B.

ETERNITY, CITY OF (=tomb), I 402; temple of, III 233, 240; horizon of, III 240.

ETHIOPIAN PERIOD, I 22; IV 796–934.

ÉTUI, II 1024.

EVIL SPIRIT, III 438.

EVIL-DOER, I 401, 403.

EXACTIONS, IV 266, 283, 323, 340, 341, 386, 387, 497, 958H.

EXAMINATION: of witnesses, IV 424, 486; of culprits, IV 426–56, 524, 540, 547–55; tortures used at, IV 546, 548, 549, 550, 551, 552, 553, 555.
—Court of examination, IV 425.

EXCELLENT ONES, I 623.

EXPEDITIONS, II 818; III 20; records of, II 407, 455; to Wan, II 582; to Carchemish, II 583.
—by sea: to Lebanon, I 146 n. a; to southern Palestine, time of Uni, I 315; to Punt, I 429; to Hammamat, I 442, 446; personnel of, I 447.

EXPLORATIONS, II 294; to Yam, by Harkhuf, I 333; to Sethu and Irthet, I 334; of Akhetaton, II 960

EXTORTION: laws on, III 54; penalty for, III 54.

EXTRADITION: of political fugitives, III 382, 384; of emigrants, III 383, 385.

EYE: Karnak, the eye of the All-Lord, II 316.

EYE COSMETIC: from Punt, II 265, 272; from Naharin, II 501.

EYE PAINT, IV 348, 391; from the Asiatics, I 620 n. d.

F

FAÇADE, II 374.
—the great double façade, III 412; IV 16; gate of, II 678.

FALSE DOOR: of tomb, I 212, 238, 239, 290, 405 n. e; of mastaba, I 254, 308; made of limestone, I 212, 238, 239, 254, 290, 308, 405 n. e; of granite, I 322.

FAME (*b ᵓ w*, lit. souls) OF THE KING, II 120, 413 *et passim*.

FAMILY, KING'S, IV 944.

FAMINE: of Joseph, I 483 n. b; III 10; in Lebanon districts, II 436; among Asiatics, III 11, 636, 638 n. b; in Egypt, IV 398.

FAN, II 22; as insignium of office, III 15; fan-bearers: see Index V.

FANFARE, III 40.

FASHION OF WOMEN, IV 849.

FAT, III 208, 413; IV 286, 344, 394.

FAT: goose, IV 232, 376; white, IV 233, 239, 299, 300, 350; roasts of, for mortuary oblation, II 571.

FATTENING-HOUSES, IV 217, 260, 313, 323.

FEAST-DAY ATTENDANTS: see Index V.

FEASTS, II 298, 462; IV 275, 359, 675, 926; calendar of, IV 139–45.
—Feast of New Year's day, I 40, 42, 545, 573, 583, 585, 630; II 171, 233, 239, 240; III 224; IV 144, 651, 836; fire kindled in the temple on night of, I 562, 573, 583.
—Feast: of the great year, I 630; the little year, I 630; the great feast, I 630.
—Feast of beginning of the seasons, I 668; II 45, 171, 569, 571, 615; III 526; IV 259, 289, 346, 356, 381, 396, 906; offering for, II 569; IV 208, 236; endowment of, II 571, 908; IV 208.
—Feast of "Beginning-of-the-River," II 32, 373, 596, 798, 838, 888; III 94, 568; IV 330 n. a, 358.
—of New Moon, I 46; II 430, 562, 608; the twelve monthly, I 630, 665 n. b; II 35; the twelve mid-monthly, I 630, 665 n. b.
—Fifth of the month, II 35.
—Sixth of the month, II 35, 149, 562; a feast of Amon, IV 958L.

Feasts—
—of the five intercalary days, I 630.
—of the Birth of the Gods, I 164.
—Feast-of-the-Appearance, I 261; II 544, 569; IV 200, 257, 322, 354, 356; storehouses for, IV 200, 257, 322, 354, 356.
—"Coming Forth," bread of, II 618.
—Feasts of Amon, III 32B, 439; IV 652, 777, 840; leader of, see Index V; "Gift-of-Life," IV 552; "Day-of-Bringing-in-the-God," II 551; IV 836; celebrated in the second day in the third month of the first season, IV 836; "Abiding in Thebes," IV 836; "Feast of the Valley," III 212, 215, 218, 515, 517, 522; IV 17; Tenth feast of Amon, II 608; date of II 608. See Feast of Opet.
—Birth of Anubis, I 91, 100.
—Feast of Anuket, celebrated for three days in the ninth month, II 798; extended to four days, II 798; "Feast of Nubia," a feast of Anuket, II 798; endowment of, II 798.
—Feast of Apis, I 212; of Running-of-Apis, I 114, 121, 127.
—Feast of Bast, IV 973; celebrated on the fifth day of the fourth month of the second season, IV 973.
—"Coming Forth of Harakhte," II 139.
—Worship of Horus, I 91, 94, 96, 98, 100, 118, 120, 122, 124, 126, 128, 130, 132, 133, 135, 137, 142, 144; "Worship-of-Horus-of-Heaven," I 125; feast of the great Rekeh, I 630; IV 768; the little Rekeh, I 630; a feast of Horus, IV 768.
—Feast of Khonsu, IV 753 n. c; celebrated in the first month of the third season, IV 753.
—Birth of Mefdet, I 115.
—Birth of Min, I 99, 142.
—Peret-Min (="Going-forth of Min"), II 566; offering for, II 566.
—"Altar-of-the-Feast," of Mut-Hathor of Thebes, II 622; date of, II 622.
—Feast of the Nile-god, IV 296; celebrated semi-annually at Silseleh, IV 296 n. e.
—"Great-Going-Forth" of Osiris, I 669.
—Feast of Ptah "South-of-His-Wall," III 23, 77, 159.
—Feast of Ptah, "Bringing-in-the-God," II 614, 617.
—"First-of-the-Flood," a feast of Ptah at Memphis, IV 330.
—Birth of Sed, I 113.
—Birth of Seshat, I 115.
—Feast of Seshed, I 150.
—Feast of Shed, II 240.
—Feast of Sokar, I 97, 108, [118], 123, 129.
—Urshu, feast of Sutekh, IV 726; celebrated on the 25th day, fourth month of the second season, IV 726.
—Feast of Thoth, I 222; II 35, 302.
—Birth of Upwawet, I 150; procession of, I 540; "Going Forth of Upwawet," I 669.
—Birth of Goddess Yamet, I 98.
—Feast of Zet, I 101, 107, 131.
—Feasts of Heaven, II 35; IV 236, 289, 346, 381, 396; eight in number, IV 144; minor feasts of heaven, IV 144.
—Feast of the Earth, II 35.
—Feast of the union of Two Lands, I 94, 140, 150, 164.
—Feast of circuit of wall, I 93, 140, 150, 164, 166.
—Feast of stretching the cord, I 109, 119, 143.
—Feast of bringing the wall of Dewazefa, I 138.
—Feast of "Binding-of-the-Barbarians," I 655 n. b; II 171.
—Feast of "Repulse-of-the-Troglodytes," I 655, II 171; occurs on the twenty-first day of the fourth month of the second season, II 171.
—Feast of Coronation, Shepseskaf, I 258; Sabu-Ibebi, I 286; Thutmose I, II 60; Thutmose III, II 317, 430; Ramses III, IV 237.
—Feast of Desher, I 94.
—Feast of Hakro, I 746; II 35.
—Feast of happy living, I 630; of the dead, I 630.
—"Myriad-of-years" (probably a festival of Dêr el-Bahri), II 333, 362, 375.
—"Occurrence of Jubilee," II 307, 310, 311. See Jubilee.
—Feast of Opet, II 591, 809, 887, 888; III 58, 256, 436; IV 237, 671, 836, 840, 909; celebrated on the 19th day of the 2d month, IV 144, 237. See Feasts of Amon.
—Feast of Victory, II 549, 550, 551, 552, 553.
—Feast of Wag, I 222; II 35; celebrated on the 18th day of the first month of the first season, I 550, 555, 564; night of, celebrated on the 17th day of the

first month of the first season, I 573, 577, 590.

FEATHER, IV 873; serpent and feather, signs for Aphroditopolis, I 433, n. a.

FEET (king's): companions of: see Index V.

FELDSPAR, from Retenu, II 491.

—Green feldspar, IV 287, 343, 389; statue of, IV 302; from Zahi, II 462.

FERRY BOAT, I 275; IV 863; of cedar, IV 229, 282, 387.

FERRYING, I 493.

FESTIVAL HALL, II 288, 377; offerings, II 298.

FEUDAL PRINCIPALITIES OF EGYPT, IV 746.

FICTION: state, II 187–90; see also Poetry, Hymn.

FIELD, II 966; IV 332, 893, 948, 957, 958, 1021; given away by the king to temples; II 1 n. c, 966; IV 141; for mortuary endowment, II 925, 926; III 526.

—Fields of Dodekaschoinos, IV 146; belonging to Khnum, IV 146; extent of, IV 146.

—Fields of Egypt, III 580.

—Fields of Amon, II 354; overseer of: see Index V.

—Fields: calculations of, III 275; inspectors of, II 437; III 275; renting of, IV 482; ritual roll of, III 271.

—Flax fields of Pharaoh, in Miam, IV 479, 480, 482.

—for Inspectors of, field judge of, Ruler of, Palace ruler of, Scribes of, Supervisor of, see Index V.

FIG TREES, I 496; planting of, I 173; of sand-dwellers, I 313.

FIGS, III 208; IV 240, 294, 391; impost of, IV 240.

FIGURE, III 525; of gods, III 233, 391; IV 245, 384; impost paid to, IV 225; of king, IV 514; made of gold, IV 26, 311.

—Figures outlined, IV 255.

—Inlay figures, IV 909; of costly stone, IV 7 9, 216; of electrum, II 375; IV 7, 11, 14, 214, 910; of gold, IV 205, 488 n. c, 489; ketem-gold, IV 199, 205, 311; silver, IV 489.

FINGER: skilled in, I 531; see also Measures, linear.

FINGER RINGS: of fine gold, IV 231; gold of two times, IV 231; white gold, IV 231; malachite, IV 377; rock-crystal, IV 377; red jasper, IV 377.

FIRE: day of kindling in the temple, I 545; on New Year's night, I 552; on night of Wag-feast, I 573.

FIRE CHAMBER: an apartment of the temple, III 28.

FIRE-PANS, I 795.

FIREWOOD, IV 295, 303, 380, 394; from Retenu, II 447; Naharin, II 502.

FISH, III 207, 208, 291, 404; IV 243, 394, 582, 1005; cut up, IV 243, 380; whole, IV 243, 380; in temple lakes, II 883; eating of, an abomination for the palace, IV 882.

—Champions like fishes, II 431.

—Shene fish, IV 243.

—White fish, IV 243.

FISHERMEN, III 62, 376; of Elephantine, II 650; IV 148; impost of, IV 229, 283.

—Court fishermen, IV 466; divisions of, IV 466; officers of, IV 466.

FLAGSTAFF: the northern, in the palace, II 678.

FLAGSTAVES: temple, II 103, 624, 776, 883, 888, 889, 894; III 508, 567; IV 15, 626, 632; made of cedar, III 94, 537; IV 15.

FLAT DISH, II 32, 93, 436; of costly stones and gold, I 436; gold, II 32, 447, 518, 533; of silver, II 447, 462, 518, 533.

—from Retenu, II 436, 447, 509, 518, 533 (?), 536(?); from Zahi, II 462.

FLAX, I 172; IV 229, 235, 241, 283, 295, 371, 379, 387, 392.

—Southern, IV 379, 392.

—Overseer of: see Index V.

FLAX FIELDS: of Pharaoh, in Miam, IV 479, 480, 482.

FLEET, II 304; IV 863; enormous fleet of Kheti I, I 398, 401; of Kheti II, I 405, 411; of Snefru to Syria, I 89; of Amenemhet I, I 465; Hatshepsut's, to Punt, II 251; northern, II 7; captain of, see Index V.

FLINT: sword of, II 525; from Retenu, II 525.

FLOCKS: of geese, II 559; IV 380.

—birds, II 571; IV 768.

FLOOD, IV 743; flood inscription, IV 742–44.

FLOOR: temple, II 375, 883; of adytum, II 806; adorned with silver, II 806, 883, 886, 889, 890.

FLOUR, IV 238.

FLOWERS, IV 244, 272, 274, 350, 394, 871; impost of, IV 244.
—Beautiful flowers, II 902, 903; in temple garden, II 167, 881, 887, 903; in temple lakes, II 919; IV 194.
—Flower gardens of temple, II 167, 881, 887, 903; IV 264.
—Flower offering, III 16, 626, 648; IV 194, 200, 217, 633; for oblation, II 960, 1042; IV 768; see also Blue flower, Dedmet flower, Garden fragrance, Isy flowers, Katha flowers, Lotus flower, Menhet flower, Papyrus flower; see further, Blossom, Bouquets, Clusters, Garland, Sunshade.

FLY: golden, as decoration of honor, II 23, 585, 587.

FOALS, II 435; IV 850.

FOLDS: cattle, I 281; calves, I 408.

FOLK TALES, I 24; II 188.

FOLLOWERS OF THE KING, I 492; II 423; commander of, see Index V.

FOLLOWING: of Upwawet, I 394.

FOOD: royal, I 423E.
—Food offering, II 355, 976; IV 906.

FOOTSTOOL: from Kedesh, I 436.
—Footstool of the palace, I 320; master of, see Index V.

FORAGE, II 437.

FORD: of Orontes, II 784.

FORECOURT, I 49; II 627; III 412, 458 n. b, 504, 545, 567; IV 259, 269, 274, 495, 531, 621, 970.

FOREIGNERS, IV 994; of Ayan, Eper of, IV 466; unclean, IV 905.

FORESKIN, IV 42, 52; people of Ekwesh had none, III 588; see also Hands cut off.

FORT: of Thutmose I, at Tombos, II 72, 121; on the eastern border, I 493; see also Fortress, Stronghold, Building.

FORTIFICATIONS, II 433.

FORTRESS, III 580; see also Fort, Strongholds; for Commandant of, Deputy of, see Index V.
—The Tower of Ramses, "a fortress of Abydos," (?) III 82 n. b; of city of Amor, IV 117; Beki, II 852; Bigeh, 718; Buto of Seti-Merneptah, a fortress of Seti I, III 100; Byblos, IV 573; Elephantine, I 650; II 719; Ereth, in Kheta, IV 120; Hatsho, IV 107; Khammat, II 894, 896, 897; Lebanon, II 548; Port of South, I 396; Merneptah-Hotephirma, III 638; "Satisfier of the Gods," I 1041; Semneh, I 653 n. c, 752; "Seti-Merneptah," III 86; Taroy, II 852; Tehenu, II 892; Tharu, III 88, 100, 307, 542, 631; Southern (= Thebes), 702; "Khaftet-hir-nebes," in the necropolis of Western Thebes, II 339; Thinis, I 396, 423; Tombos, of Thutmose I, called "None-Faces-Him," II 72; "Repulse of the Troglodytes," at Uronarti, I 654, n. a, 655; Wawat, II 616; of the West, III 586.
—"Fortress of Menkheprure": name of the inclosure of the mortuary temple of Thutmose IV in Thebes, II 821; peopled with captives from Kharu, II 821; from Nubia, II 823.
—Temples called fortresses, II 883, 894.
—Reports to be sent to vizier from southern fortress, II 702; from fortresses of the South and North, II 675.

FORTUNE, IV 946.

FOUNDATION, IV 355, 356, 358, 406; for ceremony of: see Ceremony.

FOUNDATION STONE, III 269.

FOUNDING: see Endowment.

FOWL, III 404; IV 62, 94, 98, 212, 230, 298, 329, 342, 345, 347, 363, 372, 388, 958M; for divine offerings, II 458, 562, 621, 629, 793; IV 200; evening offering, II 565; feast-offering, II 566; IV 208; oblation, II 553, 554, 960; IV 848, 856, 866, 869, 874, 875; mortuary offering, II 840; III 17; in temple lake, II 883.
—Hatching-fowl, IV 293, 298, 347.
—*ḥt*-ᶜ ͗-fowl, for divine offering, II 159, 793; IV 242; for oblation, II 571; IV 298, 347; mated, for mortuary offering, II 571; fattened, for mortuary offering, II 571.
—Table fowl, II 621, 622.
—*w ͗ d*-fowl, I 729.
—Water fowl, IV 229, 235, 283, 293, 298, 345, 347, 380, 387, 392.
—Wild fowl, III 276; IV 41, 44, 65,

141, 217, 265, 323, 768; from Lebanon, II 483; tomb-robbers to be slain like, I 330, 338, 378.

FOWLERS, I 281; of Elephantine, IV 148; impost of, IV 229, 283; chief of: see Index V.

FRAGRANCE, IV 843; of a god, II 196; of Punt, IV 333; see also Garden-fragrance.

FRAGRANT WOOD, IV 264; shrine of, I 667; from Punt, II 265; III 527; Retenu, II 471.

FRAUD: condemned by Amon, IV 671.

FRONT OF THE ARMY, II 427.

FRONTIER: southern, gods of, IV 34; Egyptian, in Zahi, IV 65; of Hare nome, IV 821; of Heracleopolis, IV 825.

FRONTIER OFFICIAL: see Index V; day-book of, III 629; letter of, III 636.

FRUIT, II 117, 159, 260; III 268; IV 34, 215, 217, 234, 240, 294, 300, 329, 344, 350, 363, 378, 379, 391, 394, 958H; from Zahi, II 461, 462, 472; from Retenu, II 473, 616; Naharin, II 482; of Arvad, II 461.

—Best fruit, IV 350; first-fruit, IV 906; see also Apples, Banu, Berries, Cinnamon, Cumin, Dates, Dom-palm fruit, Enbu, Figs, Grapes, Ibenu, Katha, Khenti, Khithana, Manna, Mehiwet, Minium, Myrrh, Olives, Pomegranates, Raisins, Shesa-fruit, Southern fruit, White fruit.

—Fruit for divine offering, II 562, 616, 621, 622, 798; IV 194, 200; mortuary offering, II 571; III 526; oblation, 553; IV 208.

FUEL, I 556, 557.

FUGITIVES: political, extradition of, III 382, 384; treatment of, III 389, 390.

FUNERAL: splendor of, I 382; expenses for, I 382; IV 1016, 1024.

—Funeral: of Mekhu, I 370; Zau Shemai, I 382; grandfather of Kheti II, I 413.

—Funeral functionaries: embalmers I 370; chief ritual priest, I 370; *ymy-wʿb*, I 370; —*sḏ*, I 370; mourners, I 370.

FURNITURE: temple, II 32; mortuary, II 861 n. c; IV 521, 538.

—from Kush, II 1035; III 475; from Libya, III 584.

FUTURE PUNISHMENT: red flame of fire in Heliopolis, III 180, 192.

G

GALA COSTUME, II 974.

GALLEYS, II 304; IV 9, 65, 66, 282, 407, 408.

—Galley archers, IV 407 n. a.

—Temple galley, IV 211, 226, 270, 282, 328, 337, 339, 354, 364, 383, 384; archers of, IV 211; captains of, IV 211; crews of, IV 328.

GAME OF DRAUGHTS, IV 822.

GANG-PLANKS, II 263.

GARDEN: palace, IV 215; temple garden, II 36, 295, 161, 352, 978; III 527, 567; IV 141, 189, 194, 217, 220, 226, 262, 274, 280, 282, 288, 313, 337, 339, 364, 370, 383, 384, 394, 676, 682, 687.

—Garden of Min, II 566.

—Gardens of Amon: overseer of, II 352; a Punt made in it, II 295.

—Gardens: of Arvad, II 461; Akhetaton, II 978.

—Sycamore gardens, IV 380.

—Shedeh gardens of Re, IV 262.

—Vine gardens, IV 380.

—Wine gardens of Amon, IV 213.

"GARDEN FRAGRANCE" (a flower), IV 244, 301, 350.

GARDENERS: of Amon, IV 213; of Re, IV 263; of Horus, IV 272; of Osiris, IV 682.

GARLAND: of flowers, IV 244, 295, 301, 350, 491, 871, 924, 926; of gold, IV 373; of grapes, IV 379.

GARMENTS, II 722; III 71; IV 228, 272, 283, 284, 285, 341, 344, 374, 375, 387, 390; of statues, II 571; IV 232; of youth, II 7.

—Garments made of linen, III 207, 208; of colored linen, IV 230, 284, 342, 372, 388; mek-linen, IV 284, 342, 388; royal linen, IV 284, 342, 372, 374, 375, 388, 582, 876; southern linen, IV 284, 342, 372, 375, 388; fine southern linen, IV 284, 342, 372, 374, 375, 388.

—*dw*-garments, IV 232, 239, 241, 374, 375; of thick stuff, IV 394.

—*ḥm-ḫrd*-garments: of royal linen, IV 852.

—*ḫnky*-garments: of royal linen, IV 374.

—Hamen garments, IV 232, 237.

—*kꜣ-ḏꜣ-m-rꜣ*-garment of southern linen, IV 375.

Garments—
—*rdw*-garments, IV 239.
—Sedeb garment, IV 871.
—*ydg*ꜣ-garments: of royal linen, IV 232, 374; fine southern linen, IV 232, 374; southern linen, IV 375.
—*yfd*-garments, of southern linen, IV 375; colored linen, IV 239, 375; see also Clothing, Kilts, Mantles, Raiment, Robe, Tunic, Wrapping.

GARRISONS: of residence city (Thebes), II 694; of court, II 694; stationed by the vizier, II 694.
—Egyptian garrison in the city of Ikathi, II 787.

GATES: temple, I 148, 421, 509; II 309, 376; IV 701, 756 n. a, 958L; names of, I 148; II 376; made of copper, II 376; of gritstone, III 245.
—Dungeon of the gate, III 180.
—Gate of harem, IV 441.
—Gate of life, IV 853.
—Gates for the canal at Siut, I 407.
—Gates of the netherworld, II 378.

GAZELLE, IV 160, 190, 242, 392, 553; IV 768; male, IV 242, 392; from negro lands, IV 724.
—the remarkable gazelle at Hammamat, I 436.

GEESE, IV 229, 235, 283, 293, 298, 341, 345, 347, 380, 387, 392, 944, 949, 954, 992.
—for divine offering, II 616, 621, 622, 798; IV 190.
—for mortuary offering, I 512; II 11, 356, 365; III 276, 526.
—Fat geese, IV 217, 235, 260, 298, 323, 380, 392, 768.
—*mnyt*-geese, I 729.
—*r*ꜣ-geese, IV 242.
—*Tw-r-pw*-geese, IV 235, 242, 345.

GENDARMES, II 978; officers of, II 927; captain of, see Index V; chief of, II 978; III 198; of Mazoi, IV 466; foreign, III 542.

GENII: of North and South, II 206; of the cardinal points, II 228, 231.

GEOGRAPHICAL LIST, I 26.

GEOGRAPHY: OF SOUTHERN NOMES, I 529 n. e.

GIFT LANDS, administered by the vizier, II 689.

GIFTS, III 632; IV 412; from foreign princes, II 820, 1028; III 273, 420, 436, 446; IV 207; of the king, II 986; III 66; IV 230; New Year's, I 545, 563; II 801.
—Gifts to Amon, IV 230–35; Ptah, IV 342–45; Re, IV 284–88; the gods, IV 372–80, 388–96.

GILDING, III 179.

GIRAFFE, III 475.

GIRDLE, I 294, 597; see also Index V, Girdle.

GIRLS, IV 111.

"GO IN AND GO OUT" (in the Netherworld), II 353, 378; IV 187, 382.

GOAT, I 312; IV 298, 347, 392; for mortuary offering, I 556; from Kheta, III 428; from Libya, III 584; from Meshwesh, see Index VI.
—Mountain goat, II 139, 479; III 11.
—Small goats from Zahi, II 490.
—White goats from Zahi, II 490.
—Wild goats, I 496; IV 91; from Naharin, II 501; on the highlands of Memphis, II 813.

GOLD, II 280, 281, 318, 342, 383, 389, 390, 434, 558, 596, 666, 718, 719, 720, 721, 722, 723, 724, 725, 726, 727, 730, 731, 732, 733, 734, 735, 736, 737, 738, 739, 740, 743, 744, 754, 771, 773, 838, 881, 887, 902, 906, 987, 992, 993; III 63, 71, 137, 151, 176, 192, 193, 204, 210, 229, 268, 286, 309, 401, 420, 428, 434, 453, 512, 515, 527, 601; IV 27, 31, 32, 33, 126, 141, 150, 190, 230, 256, 259, 272, 284, 285, 335, 342, 349, 354, 360, 372, 373, 383, 386, 388, 389, 494, 521, 551, 577, 580, 582, 635, 708, 732, 733, 734, 735, 736, 737, 843, 847, 852, 859, 874, 875, 876, 878, 880, 881, 883, 889, 909, 910, 911, 915, 929, 958E, G, 970; as adornments of other objects, II 32, 92, 104, 155, 165, 185, 300, 301, 373, 375, 390, 413, 436, 582, 755, 775, 790, 838, 888, 889, 890; III 412; IV 191, 199, 203, 254, 278, 287, 311, 312, 315, 343, 377, 538, 970; commercial, in rings, II 279, 436, 490, 501, 518, 1035; III 475; in scraps, IV 373, 386, 389; as decoration or reward of honor, I 372; II 6, 9, 10, 11, 13, 14, 22, 23, 24, 39, 64, 81, 584, 585, 587, 588, 986, 1009, 1036; III 6, 73; color of, IV 202, 408; numbering of, I 81; palace of Amenemhet I, decked with, I 483; for oblation, II 960 (?).
—Articles made of gold: altars, IV 735; *dw*-altars, IV 735; Thoth apes, IV 256, 735; arm rings, II 585, 587;

censers, IV 735, 736; fourfold censer, IV 735; chapel, IV 732; chariots wrought with, II 430, 431, 490; bracelets II 64, 471; IV 876; chaplets, II 32; tables, II 32; 175, 390; necklaces, II 32, 585, 587; collars, II 944, 986, 989; III 7, 8, 9, 69, 73, IV 201, 204, 493; columns, IV 315; drinking-vessel for the ka, II 32; flat dish, II 32, 447; figure, IV 26; finger rings, IV 231; flies, III 28, 585, 587; garland, IV 373; great seat, IV 7, 251; horn, II 447; lion, II 585, 587; offering-tables, II, 32; IV 610, 911, 912, 958, 1020; ornaments, IV, 231, 285, 343, 373, 386, 389, 538, 1011; pitcher, IV 735; portals, II 890; shrine, I 667; IV 209, 331; axe, II 23; armlet, II 64; sphinxes, IV 732; statue, IV 250, 268, 302, 316, 326, 349, 395; table vessels, IV 190, 269, 354, 357; temple doors, IV 7, 311; throne, III 321; vase, I 500; II 164, 754; IV 231, 269, 327, 538; vessels, II 32, 64, 162, 436, 615, 989, 1028, 1031, 1035; IV 285, 343, 497, 566, 730; whips, II 802.

—Gold from Akita, III 286; Coptos, IV 30, 228; Edfu, IV 30; Emu, IV 34; God's Land, III 116, 274; the Malachite country, IV 409; Karoy, II 889; III 285; Kush, II 502, 514, 522, 526 (?), 774; IV 30; Libya, III 584; Ombos, IV 30; of the south countries, II 652; of the highlands, II 373.

—Articles of gold from: Retenu, II 447, 471, 491, 510, 820, Zahi, II 459, 490; Naharin, II 482, 501; III 434; Kadesh, II 585; Punt, II 486; Wawat, II [515 ?], 527 (?), 539; Tikhsi, II 587.

—Gold, doubly refined, II 155 bis.

—Gold of two times, IV 231, 285, 343, 386, 389.

—Gold of three times, IV 408.

—Fine gold, IV 228, 231, 245, 327, 331, 343, 385, 389, 491, 498, 610, 389; amulet of, IV 253; barque shrine of, IV 982; in lay figures of, IV 488 n. c, 489; image of, IV 737; from Emu, IV 31; Khenthennofer, IV 770.

—Asiatic gold, IV 26.

—Green gold, from Emu; from Punt, II 265.

—Ketem gold, IV 199, 201, 204, 205, 231, 311; amulet of, IV 319; shrine doors of, IV 251.

—Gold of the mountains, IV 29, 30, 32, 228.

—Fine mountain gold, IV 285, 386; color of, IV 318.

—Native gold, IV 28, 30.

—White gold, IV 231, 285, 343, 389; beads of, IV 231.

—Gold, washed from rivers, IV 29, 30.

—Gold countries of Amon, III 647.

—Gold dust from Punt, III 37.

—Gold mines, in Akita, III 286.

—Gold mining, III 195.

—Gold ore, brought from Nubia, I 520; from Coptos, I 521; II 774; from negro lands, IV 33.

—Gold washing, III 192, 193, 285.

GOLD WORKERS, I 447.

GOLD-HOUSE, I 609; I 52, 185; III 71, 263, 484; IV 204, 214, 316, 354, 363; overseer of, see Index V; in charge of the vizier and chief treasurer II 706.

—Gold-house of the temple, IV 315.

—Double gold-house, I 533, 664; II 43, 52.

GOLDSMITHS, II 754.

GRAFFITI, III 32A–C, 642–51; IV 660, 777.

GRAIN, II 225, 319, 437, 461, 462, 465, 621, 622, 723, 727, 731, 733, 734, 738, 739, 740, 741, 743, 744, 745, 748; III 271; IV 206, 267, 362, 403, 550, 685, 859; ears of, IV 244; ground, II 462; pounding of, II 749; in the kernel, II 462, 473; transported by ship to Kheta, III 580.

—Grain for oblation, II 571, 749; for taxes, III 61; as mortuary offering, I 252; stored up for times of need, by Kheti II, of Siut, I 408; cultivated by Amenemhet, I 483.

—Grain: from Naharin, II 480; Tunip, II 530.

—for Registrar of, Overseer of, see Index V.

—Clean grain, II 434, 462, 473, 561, 806; III 275; IV 236, 257, 283, 289, 297, 313, 314, 346, 347, 371, 376, 381, 387, 396; from Zahi, II 510, 519.

—Southern grain, II 171, 737 bis, 741, 742, 743, 987.

—*dḳ*-grain, II 571.

—*sw-t*-grain, II 737, 742.

—*š* ᶜ-grain, II 737.

—*tb*-grain, II 737.

—*y* ᶜ *ḥ*-grain, II 733, 733, 748, 749.

—See also Barley, Corn, Spelt, Wheat.

GRAIN-HEAP, III 404, 526; IV 9, 325, 354.

GRANARY, II 149; III 66, 271; IV 330, 403, 851, 854, 855, 859, 868; inspection of, IV 146 n. c.
—Granary of Amon: see Index II, Karnak; Overseer of, see Index V.
—Granary of the king's estate, II 107.
—for Overseers of, Superintendent of, see Index V.
—Stronghold of granary, I 379; Commander of: see Index V.
—Temple granaries, II 43, 63, 343, 350, 806, 932; III 515, 527; IV 207, 217, 227, 250, 314, 325, 354, 355, 362, 497, 878, 906, 958G, H.
—The double granary, I 533; II 768.

GRANITE, II 601; IV 980, 1020; obelisk of, II 89, 304, 315, 318, 336, 624; III 567, IV 980, 982; shrines of, II 376, 775; IV 254, 320; portals of, II 794 n. b; III 525; chapel of, III 506; altar of, IV 900; door-lintels of, IV 311; sarcophagus of, IV 1011; stela of, II 605, 609 n. e; III 487, 538 n. f, 541, 596 n. d; IV 745 n. a, 919 n. a; statues of, I 601; II 876, 883; temple foundation of, IV 311; block of, II 846 n. a; IV 543; mountain of, IV 97; of the South, II 315.
—Black granite, II 906; temple of, IV 189, 214; temple doors of, IV 7; statue of, III 22 n. f; IV 967 n. a, 981 n. a; doorway of, III 528; stela of, II 655 n. b, 878 n. a; IV 650 n. a
—Constantinople obelisk made of, II 630.
—Granite quarry at Assuan, II 42; I 304, 876, 980; at Elephantine, I 322; IV 311, 319, 679, 982; at the First Cataract, I 324.
—Gray granite, IV 919 n. a; statue of, IV 981 n. b.
—Pink granite, II 905; jar of, II 32; doorway of, III 528; colonnade of, IV 970; lintels of, IV 970; stelæ of, I 651 n. c, 653 n. c; II 781 n. b, 810 n. a; IV 669 n. d, 795 n. a, 746 n. a, 635 n. a.

GRAPES, IV 234, 240, 378, 379, 391.

GRASSHOPPERS, III 309, 455, 592; IV 46, 91, 893.

GRAVER'S TOOL, IV 189, 202, 255, 317, 318, 321.

GREAT HOUSE (*pr-wr*), I 609; II 240 bis, 288; of silver, III 213.
—of a ⌜barge, IV 331, 354, 904; made of electrum, IV 904; of gold, IV 331.
—of a barque, IV 743.

GREEK HISTORIANS, I 23, 25.

GREGORIAN CALENDAR, I 40.

GRITSTONE, IV 246; the two Memnon colossi of, II 883 n. e; 906 n. a; temple model of, III 240 n. b; gate of, III 245; images of, IV 252; stela of, IV 724A n. b; statues of, II 883, 917; sanctuary foundation of, IV 251; temple of, III 246; IV 189, 214; mountain of, III 17; IV 79, 82, 357, 406; overseer of works in, III 17.

GROTTO: of Ellesiyeh, II 652; Silsileh, III 648 n. d.
—Grotto temples, at Abu Simbel, III 495.

GROVES, IV 67, 470, 880; of Kadesh, II 465; Arvad, II 465; Tunip, II 530.
—Date grove, IV 215.
—Temple groves, IV 220, 226, 262, 271, 272, 280, 282, 288, 339, 363, 384.

GRYPHON, IV 40, 43, 46, 90.

GUIDE, II 916.

"GUILTY": judgment of, declared by court, IV 426, 428, 429, 430, 431, 432, 433, 434, 435, 436, 437 438, 439, 440, 441, 442, 443, 444, 446, 447, 448, 449, 450.

GUM, IV 378; of god's land, IV 29; of Punt, IV 29, 31; of myrrh from Punt, II 288; III 116; from Genebteyew, II 474; ointments of gum, IV 476, 477; sweet oil of gum, IV 497, 498.

H

HAKRO: see Feasts.

HALL: Audience see Audience hall.
—Festival hall, II 288; IV 10.
—Judgment hall, I 605; II 681, 705, 706, 707, 903; for Door-keeper of, Master of: see Index V.
—Hall of the king, II 778; IV 931, 1017; of king's house, II 700; overseers of hundreds in, II 700; of royal council, IV 1000 n. a.
—Temple hall, II 165, 304; IV 489, 602, 610, 764, 889, 898, 910, 929, 971.
—Shrine hall, II 775.
—Hall of vizier, II 666, 670.
—Hall of writings of Egypt, IV 255, 321, 354, 363, 679.
—Broad hall: of the palace, III 590; IV 17; of temple, II 1018; III 515, 522; IV 7, 625; of temple militia, IV 972.

Hall—
—*ḏbꜣ·t*-hall, III 154.
—*dwꜣ·t*-hall, III 154.
—Beer-hall, IV 451 n. c, 880.
—Jubilee hall, IV 748.
—Hall of petitions, in Abydos, IV 678.

HAMMERED WORK, IV 198, 199, 201, 231, 317, 343, 732.

HAND CUT OFF: as trophy, III 587; IV 42, 52, 54; act executed on captives, who were circumcised, III 588; this was done to the following peoples, who accordingly practiced circumcision: Hyksos at Avaris II 10; Ekwesh, III 588, 601; Ibhet, II 854; Imukehek, II 42; Khenthennofer, II 14; Kush, II 59; Megiddo, II 431, 435; Meshwesh, IV 52, 54 (?), 111; Naharin, II 85, 532; Senzar, II 584; Seped, IV 52, 54 (?); Sharuhen, II 13; Shekelesh, III 588; Sherden (?), III 588; Temeh, IV 52, 54 (?); Teresh, III 588; Tikhsi, II 797.
—Hands of silver from Tinay, II 537;
—Hands and feet of witnesses, tortured, IV, 545, 548, 549, 550, 552.
—Divine hand: see Index V.

HANDICRAFT, II 352; overseer of, II 371; Ptah, creator of, III 288.

HANDLE: of wood, IV 288.

HANDWRITING: of Pharaoh, IV 110.

HANGING: head downward, II 80, 797.

HANK (of yarn), IV 375, 390.

HAPPINESS: Ptah, bestower of, III 401.

HARBOR MOUTH, IV 65, 66, 75, 77; dues for, III 54; for Deputy of, Inspectors of, Overseer of, Scribe of, Table-scribe of, Servants of, see Index V.

HARBORS, IV 944; of Dor, IV 566, 567; Byblos, IV 569; the Hare nome, IV 833; Memphis, IV 858, 863; Heliopolis, IV 873.
—Garrisons of the coast harbors of Zahi, II 468, 472, 483, 492, 510, 519, 535; for Chief of, Master of, see Index V.

HAREM, ROYAL: of Nussorre, I 256; of Sesostris I, 598; of Pepi, I 307; royal, of the queen, I 440; entered by Uni, I 310; private prosecution in Pepi I's, I 310; secret of, I 310.
—Harem conspiracy: under Ramses III, IV 416–56; court of, IV 423–24; first prosecution of, IV 425–43; second prosecution of, IV 444–45; third prosecution of, IV 446–50; fourth prosecution of, IV 451–53; prosecution of magic practicers, IV 454–56.
—Harem gate: people of, IV 441.
—Harem ladies of Naharin, II 867; chief of, II 867.
—The great harem, I 595; Scribe of: see Index V.

HARP, IV 880; of ebony, II 32; for temple of Amon at Karnak, II 165.

HARVEST: II 699; II 404, 616; IV 497; first of harvest given to the temple, I 546–47; II 274.
—Harvest: of Wawat, II 475, 487, 503, 539; Naharin, II 480; Kush, II 494, 502; Lebanon, II 518; Megiddo, II 437; Kadesh, II 465; Arvad, II 465; Retenu, II 473; Zahi, II 510, 519, 535 (?); Ibhet, II 852; Tunip, II 530; South and North, II 871; in province of Minieh, I p. 48.

HATCHET, II 254.

HAWK, IV 40.
—Divine, III 144, 285; IV 47, 54, 62, 91; of fine gold, as ornament of barge-bow, IV 331.

HAWK: sacred animal of the Cerastes, mountain nome, I 281 n. c.
—Hawk, poetical designation of the king, I 492; II 141, 145; III 598; IV 94, 106.
—Horus Hawk, III 195.

HEADDRESS, II 22; of Peleset, IV 73.

HEADS, IV 223, 224, 225, 280, 338, 365 366, 367, 368, 369; of ways, II 916; river mouths, II 916; of statue, II 436 bis; of ram, made of lapis lazuli, from Shinar, II 484; of goat from Retenu, II 509; of lion, from Retenu, II 509; of ox, from Retenu, II 518, 536 (?).

HEAP, I 785; II 265, 274, 275, 276, 288, 387, 566, 617, 618, 761.

HEARERS OF THE CALL, II 985.

"HEARING" OF JUDICIAL CASES, by Uni, I 307, 310; Amenemhet, I 445; Mentuhotep, I 531; Senmut, II 352; Rekhmire, II 670.
—Order of in the vizier's hall, II 675; of criminal cases, II 683; depositions of, II 704;

HEARSAY, II 287.

HEAVEN, II 118, 139, 141 bis, 144 bis, 195, 220, 225, 285, 288, 305, 570, 894 *et passim;* queen, mistress of, II 269;

ways of, II 257; circuit of, II 269; western corner of, I 335; doors of, II 141.

HEIFERS, IV 229, 242, 283, 293, 345, 387, 392; from Kharu, IV 229; from Zahi, II 490.

HELMET, ROYAL, III 30, 69; of bronze, I 501; from Naharin, II 501.

HEMISPEOS, III 504.

HERACLEOPOLITAN RULE, I 53, 88; length of, I 53, 63.

HERBS, IV 295, 301, 350, 394, 944.
—ʾ *ḥ*-herb, for divine offering, II 159; for oblation, II 571.

HERD, III 276, 616; IV 229, 283, 341, 387; Overseers of: see Index V; in charge of stewards, IV 294; in charge of vizier, IV 224.
—Herds of large cattle, III 428; IV 212, small cattle, IV 89, 141, 212; fowl; IV 212; goats, III 428; horses, III 359, 428; Nubian, II 645.
—Loan herds, I 522; III 57; of mountain goats, II 479; officials of, III 66.
—Temple herd, III 526; IV 141, 141 n. a, 150, 212, 217, 224, 251, 275, 283, 313, 332, 338, 340, 354, 359, 360, 362, 369, 405, 466, 929.

HERDMEN, III 616; IV 275, 481.

HERESY, ATON, I 66 n. e; II 932–1018.

HEZET PLANT, IV 235.

HIDDEN NAME, IV 753, 906, 925, 926.

HIDES: penalty for stealing of, III 56; presented to the court, I 369; given as taxes, II 718; III 56, 57.
—Hide of Panther, II 265, 272, 321; III 475; of cows, IV 379, 395; of ox, VI 582.

HIERODULES: captive women assigned as, IV 128.

HIEROGLYPHS: scribes of, 755.

HIGHLAND OF THE BLESSED (=necropolis), II 378; porters of, II 378; see also Cemetery, Necropolis, and Index VI, Highlands.

HIGHWAYS, II 285, 294, 299; of Punt, III 155.

HINDERING: by magic rolls, IV 454, 455.

HIPPOPOTAMUS: shooting of, I 110.

HOLY PLACE, III 271.
—Holy of holies, II 153, 155, 795; III 244, 246; IV 201 n. c, 865; place of stela in, I 16; "station of the king" in, II 140 n. b; of Amon at Karnak, II 153; name of, II 153; of "House of Menmare," III 215, 219.

HOMAGE, II 238.

HONEY, I 496; II 117, 727, 731, 733, 734, 736, 738, 739, 741, 743, 745, 748; III 208; IV 228, 239, 272, 283, 286, 294, 300, 329, 344, 350, 360, 376, 387, 390, 394, 491, 683, 770, 859, 992; from Retenu, II 518; Zahi, II 462 472; for mortuary offering, I 366 for oblation, II 571; IV 768.

HONEY COLLECTORS OF THE TEMPLES, VI, 149, 266, 313, 324.

HOOF, III 285; Overseer of, see Index V.

HORDE, III 473; of rebels, II 656.

HORIZON (*y*ʾ *ḫw.t*, more properly Light-sphere), II 141, 887, 991, 999, 1001; III 3, 270; IV 622, 906; Karnak is the — on earth, II 316; journeying to, by Intef I, I 423F; departing into, I 491; IV 400.
—Horizon of Aton (=Akhetaton), II 949.
—Horizon of eternity, III 240; IV 187; sem-priest of, III 623; the eternal (=pyramid), IV 513.
—Horizon of Harakhte, IV 251.
—Horizon of heaven, II 604, 755, 883, 903, 905, 984, 999; III 16, 79, 116, 230, 246, 248, 281, 412, 521; IV 8, 9, 10, 315, 356, 609, 632, 970.
—Horizon in the West, of Amon, II 375; III 261; doors of, II 375.
—Horizon of Re, III 232, IV 198, 314, 610.
—Horizon: palace of, IV 7.
—Eastern horizon, II 972, 984.
—Western horizon, II 972.
—Mysterious horizon, IV 195, 251.

HORN, III 285; IV 46; Overseer of, see Index V; lord of the two horns, a royal title, IV 921.
—of gold, II 447.

HORSE, EGYPTIAN, II 421, 424, 470, 813, 864; III 84, 88, 97, 100, 132, 134, 146, 441, 450, 584; IV 40, 46, 49, 50, 51, 65, 72, 73, 405, 724A, 822, 832, 847, 850, 852, 860, 874, 875, 876, 877, 878, 880; Master of, see Index V.
—Horses, from Bekhten, III 446; Kheta, III 343, 420, 428; Khatithana, II 729; Libya, III 589; Meshwesh, IV 86, 90, III; Retenu, II 125, 413, 447, 467, 491, 509, 518, 533 (?), 597, 790, 1028;

Kadesh, II 420, 467; Megiddo, II 431; Zahi, II 462, 490; Ullaza, II 470; Naharin, II 81, 85, 479, 482, 498, 501, 532; Nuges, II 508; Isy, II 511; Lebanon, II 783; Orontes, II 784, 785.
—See also Foals, Mares, Stallions, Steed.

HOSTAGES: foreign king's or chief's children as, II 122.

HOUND, I 483, 464; IV 514; names of, III 467; IV 514.

HOUSE, II 978; IV 357, 363, 386.
—House of the council of thirty, I 532.
—ʿḥʿ-house: things from it for embalming Mekhu's body, I 370.
—House of Enekh, I 707, 709.
—House of his father (=tomb of ancestor): of Kheti I, I 402.
—House of a god, IV 354; see also Index II.
—House of the sphinx, I 127, 180.
—the good house (=the embalmers' house), IV 1029.
—House of incense, IV 238.
—the pure house (=Serapeum), IV 977, 986, 1010.
—Southern house (=Luxor), IV 909.
—Timber house, IV 380, 394.
—House of rolls, III 264; Keeper of, see Index V.
—House of sacred writing (in Abydos), I 533; IV 445, 460, 1022; Scribe of: see Index V.
—The double house, attached to, I 284, 285, 298, 299 bis.
—See also Embalming, Fattening-houses, Great house, Gold-house, Silver-house, White House.
—Double *wʿb.t*-house: secret things of, for Mekhu's funeral, I 370.

HOUSEHOLD: of Khnumhotep, II, I 623.

HUE: of a god, III 24.

HUNDRED: part of the army, Overseer of, see Index V.

HUNT: of elephant, in Niy, II 588; of lion, II 865; of wild cattle, at Sheta, II 864; master of, IV 539.

HUNTERS OF THE HIGHLANDS (=Troglodytes), I 429.

HUS STONE, IV 191.

HUSBAND OF EGYPT: king the, III 490.

HUSBANDMEN, III 275.

HUT, IV 524.

HYMNS: of Amon, II 891–92; IV 744; of Aton, II 979, 984, 991, 992, 999–1001, 1007, 1010–11; of Re, III 15, 18, 19; in praise to Sesostris III, I 17; to Thutmose III, I 17.
—Hymns of victory, by Thutmose III, II 655–62; IV 137; Merneptah, III 602–17.
—Sun-hymn of Sute and Hor, II 299 n. e.

HYPOSTYLE, II 138, 140, 603, 805; III 222, 367 n. a, 513; IV 472, 614, 742 n. a; columns of, II 805; III 513.

I

IBENU FRUIT, IV 378, 395.

IBEX, III 475; for oblation, I 432; II 553.

IBIS, SACRED, I 281 n. c.

IDENINU PLANT, IV 235, 379, 392.

IMAGE, II 300, 812, 894, 897; III 31, 117, 179, 218, 233, 288, 486, 502, 517, 525, 622; IV 4, 9, 27, 37, 47, 62, 198, 311, 330, 363, 817, 836, 872, 909, 911, 912, 913, 914, 915, 916; of Mat, IV 458, 463; offered to gods, IV 458, 463; images made of gold, IV 204; grit-stone, IV 252; costly stone, IV 377; electrum, IV 958K.
—Portable images, IV 204, 217, 743, 958K; processional, IV 225, 315, 384, 737; impost paid for, IV 225; see also Statue.

IMPOST, III 179, 193, 210, 274, 276, 277, 481; IV 33, 141, 220, 266, 324, 686, 846, 933; imposts, II 522, 597, 601, 908, 1015.
—Impost (Egyptian), paid by officials, IV 225; standard bearers, IV 25; inspectors, IV 225; people, IV 225, 228, 283, 340, 341, 386, 387, 497; peasants, IV 229, 283, 341, 387; fishermen, IV 229, 283, 387; fowlers, IV 229, 283, 387; of leaders, mayors, etc., II 768; III 63.
—Impost remitted, I 408; III 57, 63; numbered by the herald, II 767, 768.
—Impost consisting of figs, IV 240; flowers, IV 244; malachite, I 731; wood, III 52; vegetables, III 59.
—Impost from foreign lands: Kush, II 271, 494, 502, 514, 522, 526, 538; southern counties, II 281; the south countries, II 652; III 484; Wawat, II 475, 487, 495, 503, 515, 523, 527, 539; Nubia, IV 190; Meshwesh, IV 92; Temeh, IV 92; Megiddo, II 441; Retenu, II 473, 557; Lebanon, II

483, 510; Haunebu, II 953; Kharu, IV 229, 387; Sinai mines, I 731; Syria, IV 229, 387; Retenu, IV 28; Zahi, IV 190, 328.

IMPRISONMENT: of women for theft, IV 556.

INACCESSIBLE: channels II 88; valleys, II 337; countries, III 118; IV 719, 749.

INCENSE, II 139, 288; III 268, 270, 613; IV 228, 239, 266, 272, 283, 286, 294, 299, 304, 309, 313, 324, 329, 333, 348, 360, 363, 373, 378, 387, 390, 394, 491, 611, 612, 678, 684, 736, 770, 859, 865, 870, 871.

—for divine offerings, II 562, 572, 616, 621, 798; III 40; IV 200; evening offering, II 565; feast offering, II 566, 569; mortuary offering, II 365, 571; oblation, I 453, 468; II 553, 554, 571, 960; IV 208, 468, 768.

—Inflammable incense, IV 239; incense from Punt, IV 130; Negro tribes, I 136, 369; Retenu, II 447, 473, 491, 509, 518, 525, 416; Zahi, II 462, 472, 510, 519; Naharin, II 482.

—as tribute, II 750, 771.

—Ihmut incense from Punt, II 265.

—Sonter incense from Punt, II 265.

—White incense, IV 233, 239, 299, 344, 376.

—Green incense for divine offering, II 572.

—House of incense, IV 238.

INCLOSURE, II 864; temple, II 881; III 412; made of brick, II 614; see also Wall.

INCOME, IV 948; of Amon, IV 227–29; Ptah, IV 340–41; Re, IV 283; of the gods, IV 371, 386–87; of official, II 108, 117; taxes of, II 706, 716; rank of receiver of, II 675.

INDUCTION: ceremony of, IV 988H; see also Investiture.

INFANTRY, EGYPTIAN, III 307, 311, 325, 327, 342, 365, 380, 428, 578, 583, 587; IV 71, 72, 89, 354, 402, 410, 822, 859, 1004; of the South and North, II 429; of Tunip, II 459; Egyptian, in city of Ikathi, II 787; of Libya, III 683; of Kheta, III 320, 321, 378; of Sherden, IV 72, 118; for Captains of, Commandants of, Commander of, Leader of, Lord of, Officers of, see Index V.

INHABITANTS OF EGYPT, distinguished from its people, I 445; see People.

INHERITANCE: of office, II 925, 926; of craft, coppersmiths, IV 532; of priesthood, see under Succession.

—Inheritance from the mother: of monarchy, I 398, 405, 414.

INK, III 32A n. a.

—Ink palette, I 5; III 50.

INLAY, IV 201, 269; of stone, IV 199, 311; costly stone, IV 204, 209, 231, 331, 334, 538, 904, 910, 958E, J, K, 982; gold, IV 231, 311; malachite, IV 253; lapis lazuli, IV 253, 319; see also Figures.

INSCRIPTION, TEMPLE, I 2, 13; II 472; III 517, 519; Rock, see Rock inscriptions; Building, I 4, 14, 22; Tomb, I 10; Hammamat, Ahmose II, I 75 n. h; Politarch, I 28; Greek and Latin, I 27, 28; Eclipse: of Takelot II, I 35; magical, IV 455.

—Coffin inscriptions, by Paynozem II, IV 665–67.

—Colossus inscription, at Tanis, by Ramses II, III 417.

—Column inscription, at Cairo, by Merneptah, III 593–95; in temple of Amon at Karnak, by Thutmose III, II 601; Amenhotep II, II 804–6.

—Dedication inscriptions, III 211–20, 227–42, 248–49, 409, 508, 513, 514, 516, 521, 522, 528; IV 472, 602, 603, 997–99.

—Doorway inscription: at Cairo, by Thutmose III, II 643; Coptos, by Nubkheprure-Intef, I 773–80; Sakkara, by Harmhab, III 16–17; Soleb, by Amenhotep III, II 898.

—Grotto inscription at Ellesiyeh, by Nehi, II 652.

—Mummy inscriptions, by Paynozem I, IV 637–42, 644–47; Menkheperre, IV 661; Paynozem II, IV 663; Pesibkhenno, IV 688; Yewepet, IV 700.

—Obelisk inscriptions: of Thutmose III, Constantinople obelisk, II 479 n. a; II 630–31; London obelisk, by Thutmose III, 633; New York obelisk, by Thutmose III, II 635–36; Lateran obelisk, by Thutmose III, II 627–28; Thutmose IV, II 831–38; at Elephantine, by Thutmose I, II 89; at Heliopolis, by Ramses II, III 545–48; at Karnak, by Thutmose I, II 86–88; Hatshepsut, II 306, 308–310, 314–19, 321; at Tanis, by Ramses II, III 392, 448 n. b.

—Pylon inscriptions, in temple of Amon

at Karnak, by Thutmose I, II 245; Thutmose III, II 521–23, 541–73, 594–98, 645–47; Amenhotep III, II 899–903; Roy, III 621–26; high priest of Amon, IV 671–73; Taharka, IV 889; Temple of Khonsu, Karnak by Paynozem I, IV 632–33; Medinet Habu, by Ramses III, IV 61–68; 85–92, 94–99, 101–6, 130, 132–35, 137–38; Ramesseum, by Ramses II, III 329–30, 356.

—Quay inscriptions, at Elephantine, IV 147–50; by Ramses III, IV 146–50; Karnak, IV 695–98, 794, 886–88.

—Rock inscription, at Assuan, by Hapu, I 614–16; Sesostris III, I 653; family of Neferhotep, I 753 n. b; Thutmose I, II 77; Thutmose II, II 119–22; Senmut, II 360–62; Amenhotep III, II 844 n. b; officer of Amenhotep III, II 875; Bek, II 973–76; Seti I, III 202; Ramses II, III 479; the First Cataract, by Mernere, I 317, 318; Amenhotep III, III 844; Bigeh, by Ramses II, III 553; Gebelên, by Hui, III 210; Hammamat, by Khui, I 674–75; Amenemhet, I 707; Ramses IV, IV 457–60, 461–68; Hatnub, by Nenekhseskhnum, I 304–5; Island of Konosso, by Mentuhotep I, I 423H n. d; Thutmose IV, II 825–29; Amenhotep III, II 845; Kummeh, by Amenemhet IV, I 749; Korusko, of Amenemhet I, I 472–73; Ma ͑ sara, by Neferperet, II 27–28; Redesiyeh, by Seti I, III 197–98; Sarbût el-Khadem, by Amenemhet II, I 606, Sebek-hir-hab, I 725–27; Ptahwer, I 728; Amenemhet, I 730–32; Amenemhet IV, I 750; Thutmose III, II 450 n. a; Island of Sehel, by Sesostris III, I 644, 647; importance of, I 28; family of Neferhotep, I 753 n. b; Thure, II 75, 76; Thutmose III, II 649, n. d; Ramose, II 937 n. a; Ramses II, III 553 n. b, 557; Seti (II), III 646; Semneh, by Sekhemre-Khutowe, I 751–52; Silsileh: by official of Ikhnaton, II 934–35; Seti I, III 206–8; Ramses II, III 552, 554, 555, 556, 559, 560; Roy, III 627–28; Siptah, III 648; Setemhab, IV 19, 20; Haremsaf, IV 701–8; Tell el-Amarna, by Ikhnaton, II 949–72; Tombos: by Thutmose I, II 67 n. d; Turra: by Amenemhet III, I 740; Amenhotep III, II 875; at Wadi Maghara: by Snefru, I 168–69; Khufu, I 176; Sahure, I 236; Nuserre, I 250; Menkuhor, I 263; Dedkere-Isesi, I 264–67; Pepi I, I 302–3; Pepi II, I 340–43; Khenemsu, I 713–14; Harnakht, I 717–18; Sebekdidi, I 719–20; Ameni, I 721–23; Amenemhet IV, I 750; Hatshepsut and Thutmose III, II 337.

—Shrine inscription, II 126–27, 775.

—Statue inscription: of Enebni, II 213; Harmhab, III 23–32; Sheshonk, IV 740; Hor, IV 967–73; Uzahor, IV 980; Neferibre-Nofer, IV 981–83; Nesuhor, IV 989–95; Ahmose, IV 1014; Pefnefdineit, IV 1017–25; at El Kab: by Ahmose Pen-Nekhbet, II 20–24, 41–42, 84–85, 344; Karnak: by Senmut, II 350–58; Puemre, II 380–81; Amenhotep, son of Hapi, II 912, 914–20; Luxor: by Nebwawi, II 179–83; Ibe, IV 958A–M; Thebes: by Senmut, II 364-68; Hapuseneb, II 389–90; Nebnefer, II 929–31.

—Stela of Khufu, I 177–80; Mertityôtes, I 188–89; Nenekhsekhmet, I 237–40; Enekhnes-Merire, I 344–49; Intef, I 419–20; Thethi, I 423A–G; Eti, I 457–59; Nessumontu, I 469–71; Meri, I 507–9; Mentuhotep, I 510–14; Ikudidi, I 524–28; Intefyoker, I 529; Mentuhotep, I 530–34; Simontu, I 294 n. a, 594–98; Sihathor, I 599 603; Khentkhetwer, I 604–5; Khentemsemeti, I 607–613; Khnumhotep, I 617–18; Ameni, I 649–50; Sesostris III, I 651–52; 653–60; Sisatet, I 671–72, 673; Sebek-khu, I 676–87; Harure, I 733–38; Sehetepibre, I 743–48; Neferhotep, I 753–65; I 766–72; Ameniseneb, I 781–87; Vizier of King Khenzer, I 783 n. d; Ahmose I, II 29–32, 33–37; Harmini, II 47–48; Keres, II 49–53; Thutmose I, II 54–60, 54 n. a, 90–98; Yuf, II 109–114; Nebwawi, II 184–86; Hatshepsut, II 338–39; Thutiy, II 369–78; Thutmose III, II 599–608, 609–22, 642, 655–62; Intef, II 763–71; Ni bamon, II 777–79; Amenhotep II, II 781–97, 791–98, 818; Thutmose IV, II 810–15; Semen, II 822; Pe ͗ aoke, II 839–40; Neferhet, II 839 n. d; Mermose, II 851–55; Amenhotep III, II 856–58, 877, 878–92, 904–910; Amenhotep, II 921–27; Eye, II 1042–43; Harmhab, III 2–5; Ramses I, III 74–79; Hori,

III 82 n. b; Seti I, III 82, 157–61, 203–4; Ramses II, III 282–93, 297, 392, 394–414, 415–24, 427–28, 429–47, 487–91; Seti, III 538–42; Merneptah, III 596–601, 602–617; Roy, III 627–28; Ramses IV, IV 457, 461, 469–71; Hori, IV 484–85; Menkheperre, IV 650–58; Sheshonk, IV 675–87; Sheshonk I, IV 724A; Wayeheset, IV 725–28; Osorkon II, IV 745–47; Kerome, IV 755; Pediese, IV 771–74, 778–81; Weshtehet, IV 782–84; Harpeson, IV 785–92; Yewelot, IV 795; Piankhi, IV796–883; Bocchoris, IV 884; Taharka, IV 892–96; Senbef, IV 917–18; Tanutamon, IV 919–34; Psamtik I, IV 935–58, 959–62, 963–66; Necho, IV 974–79; Apries, IV 984–88; Enekhnesneferibre, IV 988A–J; Amasis, IV 1008–1012; Stela at El Kab, I 741–42.

—Temple inscriptions, at Abu Simbel: by Ramses II, III 449–57, 496–501; Rekhpehtuf, III 642; Abd el-Kurna: by Ramses II, III 448 n. b; Abydos: by Seti I, III 227–43; Ramses II, III 251–81, 485–86; Amâda: by Merneptah, III 606 n. a; Arsinoe: by Amenemhet III, II 233; Benihasan: by Hatshepsut, II 296–303; Seti I, III 249; Bêt el-Wâli: by Ramses II, III 458–77; Bubastis: by Osorkon II, IV 748–51; Dêr el-Bahri: by Thutmose I, II 125; Hatshepsut, II 192, 194, 196–98, 200–1, 203, 205, 208, 213, 216, 219–20, 223–25, 227, 229, 230, 233, 235, 253, 255–58, 260–62, 264–66, 268–69, 271–72, 274, 276, 278, 280–82, 285–88, 290, 292–95; Derr: by Ramses II, III 503; El Kab: by Ramses II, III 505, 558; in temple of Amon at Karnak: by Thutmose III, 131–66, 415–37, 439–43, 445–49, 451–52, 455–62, 464–67, 469–75, 477–87, 489–95, 497–503, 507–515, 517–19, 529–40, 654; Hatshepsut, II 305; Amenhotep II, II 798A, 804–6; Seti I, III 82–150, 223–24; Ramses II, III 348–51, 355, 367–91, 509–13; Merneptah, III 574–92; Ramses IV, IV 472; Ramses IX, IV 492–98; Sheshonk I, IV 709–724; Osorkon, IV 753, 756–70, 777; Taharka, IV 900; Mentemhet, IV 901–16; in temple of Ptah. at Karnak: by Thutmose III, II 611; in temple of Khonsu at Karnak: by Ramses XII, IV 602–3; Hrihor, IV 609–626; Paynozem I, IV 632–33, 649; Luxor, by Amenhotep III, II 187–212, 215–42, 841; Ramses II, III 480–84, 506–8; Menkheperre, IV 659; Osorkon II, IV 743; Medinet Habu: by Thutmose III, II 638–41; Ramses III, IV 4–17, 26–34, 37–58, 70–82, 107–114, 117–29, 140–45; Paynozem I, IV 634; Ramesseum: Ramses II, III 329–32, 335–40, 365, 448, n. b, 514–15; Redesiyeh: by Seti I, III 162–95; Sebûʿa: by Ramses II, III 504; Semneh: by Thure, II 62–66; Thutmose III, II 169–72, 174–76; Nehi, II 651; Serreh: by Ramses II, III 502; Soleb: by Amenhotep III, II 894–98; Wadi Halfa: by Seti I, III 248; Neferhor, III 643; Piyay, III 644; Hori, III 645, 650, 651(?).

—Tomb inscription: Senuonekh, I 232–35; Persen, I 241; Nezemib, I 279; Kheruf, II 873; at Abd el-Kurna: Ineni, II 43–46, 99–108, 648; Puemre, II 383–87; Rekhmire, II 666–762; Menkheperreseneb, II 773–76; Khamhet, II 819, 871–72; Hatey, II 932; Ramose, II 936–48; Abusir: by Weshptah, I 243–49; Hotephiryakhet, I 252–53; Abydos: by Uni, I 293–94, 307–315, 320–24; Assasîf: by Neferhotep, III 70–72; opposite Assuan: by Harkhuf, I 328–36, 351–54; by Pepinakht, 356–60, Khui, I 361; Thethi, I 361 n. d; Sebni, I 365–74; Assiut: by Tefibi, I 394–97; Kheti I, I 399–404; Kheti II, I 407–14; Hepzefi, I 538–93; Benihasan: by Khnumhotep I, I 465; Amenemhet, I 518–23; Khnumhotep II, I 622–39; Thuthotep, I 688–706; Cairo: by Kam, I 187; unknown builder, I 290; Dêr el-Bahri, IV 668, 689, 691–92; Dêr el-Gebrâwi: by Henku, I 281; Ibi, I 377–79; El Kab: by Ahmose, son of Ebana, II 6–16, 39, 80–82; Pahri, II 3 and n. b; Ahmose-Pen-Nekhbet, II 20, 25, 344; Setau, IV 414; Gebel Marâg: by Zau, I 381–85; Gizeh: by Thenti, I 182; Ihi, I 183; Thethi, I 184; Henutsen I, 185; Zezemonekh, I 186; Nekure, I 192–99; Debhen, I 211–12; Senezemib, I 270–74; Hermonthis: by Intef, the monarch, I 419 n. c; Ibrim: by Penno, IV 476–83; Kasr-es-Saigîl: by Idu-Seneni, I 338; Kurnet-Marraï: by Huy, II 1010–41; Sakkara: by

Methen, I 171–75. Ptahshepses, I 255–62; Sabu-Ibebi, I 283–86; Sabu-Thety, I 288; Harmhab, III 3–4, 8, 11–13, 16–17, 20; Shekh Saʿîd: by Thutnakht: I 689; Tehneh, by Nekonekh, I 216–30; Tell el-Amarna: by Ani, II 977; Merire I, II 983–88, 1018; Eye, II 990–96; Mai, II 997, 999–1003; Ahmose, II 1006–8; Tutu, II 1010–13; Huy, II 1015–17; Western Thebes: by Thaneni, II 392, 820; Amenemhab, II 578–92; Woser, II 671 n. e; Amenemopet, II 671 n. e; Ramses V, IV 473; Hrihor, IV 593–94; vase inscription of Hatshepsut, at Gizeh, II 214.

INSECTS, see Fly, Grasshopper.

INSPECTION, III 94; IV 909, 913; of boundaries, I 528; II 969; cisterns, IV 726; craftsmen, II 753, 754, 775; divine fathers, I 610; flagstaves, II 776; food for divine offerings, II 752; granaries, IV 146 n. c; land, I 482; III 58; mines, III 170; obelisks, II 776; sepulchers, IV 511; shrines, II 775, 776; statues, II 752; taxes, II 717, 729; temples at Coptos, I 777; temple of Osiris at Abydos, I 787; temple of Amon at Karnak, II 383; temples of Karnak, IV 660; tombs, IV 511, 513, 514, 516, 517, 518, 519, 520, 533, 543; treasuries, IV 146 n. c; water supply, II 707; weighing, II 387; Wawat by Hapu, I 616; wells, IV 726; works of divine offerings, II 757.

INSTALLATION, IV 775, 865, 958D, 1012.

INSTRUCTION: to the court, IV 424; of children, I 413; of a king, I 413.

INSURRECTION: crime of, IV 427, 428, 429, 430, 442, 443.

INTERCALARY DAYS, I 540, 561; see also Feasts.

INTERCESSION OF THE DEAD FOR LIVING PEOPLE: by Hotephiryakhet, I 252; by Harkhuf, I 329; by Seti I, I 251; III 253; by Ramses III, IV 246.

INTERIM REIGNS: between XIX and XX Dynasties, I 50, 68, 68 n. e; of obscure period, I 52; of dark period, I 52, 57.

INTERIOR AFFAIRS: overseers of, II 677; reports to the vizier, II 687, 697, 707.

INTERMENT, IV 966, 977, 986; see also Burial, Funeral.

INUNDATION, I 83, 523; II 871; IV 47, 628, 743; to be reported to vizier, II 709; see also Index VI: Nile Levels.

INVASION OF EGYPT, III 580, 594, 595, 608; IV 1006; Libyan-Mediterranean, III 572-617; Northerners, IV 64; by Meshwesh, IV 88, 95; by unclean foreigners, IV 905, 907.

INVENTORY, IV 947; of temples, engraved on tablets, IV 202.

INVESTIGATION: of official acts, III 58; of pyramids, IV 513; of sepulchers, IV 513; of tombs, IV 513; of theft IV 566; of fraud, IV 673; of writings, I 178, 179, 756.

INVESTITURE OF VICEROY OF KUSH, II 1020.

IRON: statue of, IV 302; vessels of, from Tinay, II 537.

—King's organs of, III 403.

IRRIGATION: canal of, in Siut, I 407; chief of, IV 726.

ISI PLANTS, IV 213, 215, 244, 295, 301, 350, 394.

—Isi flowers, IV 264.

ISLANDS: given for the support of temples, IV 359.

ISRAEL STELA, III 602–617.

ITHYPHALLIC, II 104, 302 n. a, 889 n. a; Min, I 296.

IVORY, II 387, 601; III 471; IV 344, 391; brought from negro lands, I 336; Punt, II 263, 265, 272, 486; God's Land, II 265; from Tehenu, II 321; Genebteyew, II 474; Kush, II 494, 502, 514; the south countries, II 652; Retenu, II 447, 509, 525; Isy, II 493, 521.

—Articles made of ivory: chairs, II 436; tables, II 509; chest, II 755; statues, II 801; whips, II 802; see also Tooth ivory.

J

JACKAL: sacred animal of Lycopolis, I 281, n. c; southern army like, I 396.

—Southern jackal, Pharaoh like, II 661, 829.

JAR, I 430; II 159, 509, 518; IV 230, 238, 239, 243, 284, 297, 342, 388, 394; 498, 565, 589, 954.

—ʿ-jar, IV 299, 300, 301, 347, 348, 350.

—ꜣʿʿ-jar, IV 228, 233, 283, 286, 344, 376, 387, 390.

Jar—
—ʾʿʿ-*bw*-jar, IV 294, 299.
—ʿ*ḥ*ʿ-jar, II 571.
—ʿ*š*-jar, IV 924.
—*bp*ʾ-jar, IV 300, 348.
—*pw-g*ʾ-jar, IV 300, 350.
—*m-s*ʾ-*ḫy*-jar, IV 233.
—*m*ʾ*dydy*-jar, IV 376.
—*mn*-jars, II 447 bis, 462 bis, 482, 491, 501 bis, 509, 518, 571 bis, 572, 621; IV 233, 239, 292, 299, 341, 348, 376, 378, 390, 393.
—*mn.t*-jar, IV 395.
—*mrsw*-jar, IV 376.
—*mḥn*-jar, IV 301.
—*mḥtt*-jar, IV 350.
—*nms.t*-jar, IV 301, 350.
—*hbn(.t)*-jar, I 590; II 159, 164, 509, 567, 734, 736, 738, 739, 741, 743, 745; IV 950, 952, 953.
—*ḫbḫb*-jar, IV 875, 878.
—*sny*-jar, IV 378, 395.
—*st*ʾ-jar, I 569.
—*ḳby*-jar, I 550, 556.
—*k*ʾ-*bw*-jars, IV 233, 239, 292, 299, 376, 390.
—*k*ʾ-*ḥr-k*ʾ-jar, IV 294.
—*g*ʾ*y*-jar, IV 238, 241, 294, 300, 301, 350, 393.
—*ṯ*ʾ*b*-jar, II 621, 622.
—*ṯbw*-jar, IV 294.
—*ds*-jar, I 569, 585; II 113, 114, 563 bis, 620, 621; III 77, 159; IV 347.
—Jars made of alabaster, II 544; electrum, II 556; pink granite, II 32.

JASPER, RED, IV 287, 377; scarab of, IV 233, 377; statue of, IV 302; finger rings of, IV 377; semdets of, IV 377.

JOINT (of meat), II 113, 114; IV 565.

JOURNAL OF THE KINGS OF BYBLOS, IV 576.

JOURNEY, KING'S, I 309.

JUBILATION, IV 526.

JUBILEE, Sed, I 105, 296, 298, 300, 302, 305, 403, 435, 437, 443; II, 431, 873, 940, 991, 995, 1006, 1007, 1029; III 195, 240, 279, 281, 371, 399, 406, 414, 550; IV 56, 304, 331, 335, 382, 414, 468, 473, 485, 620, 653, 748, 751, 768, 848, 927; same as Royal jubilee, *q. v.*
—Explanation of, IV 750, 751, 848.
—of Re, III 28; IV 31, 704; jubilee court, IV 707; jubilee hall, IV 748; jubilee houses, IV 335, 414.
—Royal jubilee, II 608; III 28, 32; of Thutmose I, I 66 n. g; II 89; Hatshepsut, II 221, 233, 239, 241, 307, 310, 311, 328; Thutmose III, II 628, 630, 633; Amenhotep III, II 870–74; Ramses II, III 550–60; same as Sed jubilee, *q. v.*

JUDGES: impartiality of, I 357; of a god II 668.
—Corrupt judges, laws on, III 63–65.

JUDGING IN THE NAME OF THE KING, I 307; in criminal cases, II 683.

JUDGMENT-HALL, I 605; II 681, 705, 706, 707, 769, 903; III 63; appointments to, II 705; doorkeeper of, II 711; laws of, III 63; masters of, Index V; herald of, II 763, 767, 768.

JUDGMENTS: reported to the vizier, II 681; stay of, II 686; not to be passed by an official on a superior, II 681.
—Rendered by Amon, IV 650–58, 673, 676; by Sutekh, IV 727, 728.

JUDICIAL OFFICE, I 438.

JUDICIARY OFFICE: chief, vested in the vizier, II 675, 681, 685–86, 688–91, 700, 704, 705.

JULIAN CALENDAR, I 40, p. 48.

JUNIPER, II 321.

JUSTICE: courts of, IV 147; crime against, III 64.
—Six courts of justice, I 305, 307, 428, 445; II 713, 754; Chief of, see Index V.

K

KA, II 111, 235, 298; III 622 *et passim;* shaped by the god, II 202; twelve of them nursed for Hatshepsut, II 210; journeying to, I 187, 253; ka of the living king, I 324, 351, 423E, 448.

KA CHAPEL: of Amenhotep, II 923, 924, 925, 926; slaves of, II 924, 925, 926; fields of, II 925, 926.

KA HOUSE, I 550; Overseer of, see Index V; of Khnumhotep II, at Menet-Khufu, I 630; at Nehri at Mernofret, I 635.

KA TEMPLE, I 289, 290, 550; rank of the overseer of, I 550.

KARA BOATS: of Acacia, IV 229, 283, 387.

KATHA PLANT, IV 600; given as taxes, III 55 bis.
—Katha flowers, IV 294, 600.
—Katha fruit, IV 294.

KED WOOD, IV 910; mortuary chests of, IV 966.
KEEL, IV 582.
KETTLE, II 436; III 589.
KHENTI FRUIT, IV 378, 395.
KHESYT WOOD: from Punt, II 265.
KHITHANA FRUIT, IV 240, 393.
KIDET, II 436, 446 bis, 482, 484, 486, 490, 491, 502, 509, 514, 515, 518 bis, 522, 526, 527, 536 bis; IV 228, 231, 283, 285, 341, 343, 373, 377, 385, 386, 389, 682, 685, 686, 880.
—Kidet weight, IV 880.
KILTS: of Southern linen, IV 303, 350, 374; fine Southern linen, IV 232, 375.
"KINDNESS OF AMON": a greeting, IV 573.
KING: see Index V; archives of, III 643, 644.
—King's estate: Chief of, Chief overseer of, Steward of: see Index V; granary of, II 107; chief of, II 368.
—King's hall, II 778; Overseer of, see Index V.
—King's house, I 533; II 342, 389; IV 849, 958J; see also Palace; offices of, I 447; going into and out of, reported to vizier, II 676, 680; affairs of II 679; intercourse between court and local authorities, II 692; gates of, opened by command of vizier, II 680; edicts from, received by vizier, II 705, 710; messengers of, II 692.
—King's horses, master of, see Index V.
—King's property, I 745; Overseer of, see Index V.
—King's records, I 218, 221, 225, 299; III 647; Scribe of, see Index V.
—King's rolls, IV 498; Scribe of: see Index V.
—King's wardrobe, great lord of: see Index V; secret things of the king, I 608; Master of: see Index V.
—King's weapons, II 213; Master of: see Index V.
—King's works, chief of: see Index V.
—King's workmen, leader of: see Index V.
—See also Body guard, Brand, Brewery, Cattle, Domain, Chamber, Command, Concubine, Council hall, Court, Crown, Divine office, Domain, Estate, Family, Feet, Flax field, Food, Hall, Helmet, Iron.
—King's officials: see Index V, under Attached, Attendants, Beloved, Butler Companion, Confidant, Confidante, Cup-bearer, Deputy, Dignitary, Fellow, First, Following, Great Ones, Guardian, Herald, Honored, Messenger, Orderly, Prince, Scribe, Servant, Steward, Subordinate, Sunshade bearer, Treasurer, Vizier.
KIOSK, II 289, 981, 1021, 1028.
KISS THE GROUND, II 996 *et passim*.
KITCHEN OF PHARAOH, III 51, 59; of temple of Amon, III 624 n. a.
KNEADERS, III 624 n. g.
KNIFE, II 436; III 589.
KROPHI: name of a cave at Elephantine, III 171 n. a.

L

LABOR, ENFORCED, IV 147.
LADDER, SCALING, IV 118.
LAKE GARDEN, I 173, 272; Isesi's, called Nehbet, I 273; Harkhuf's, I 328.
—Pleasure lake of Queen Tiy in Zerukha, II 869.
—Temple lake, I 111, 268, 503, 509, 534; II 36, 164, 883, 919; III 567 n. c; IV 189, 194, 213, 261, 264, 363, 488 n. c, 489, 910, 912, 916, 1020; constructed of sandstone, IV 910, 912.
LAMPS: Temple, IV 992.
LANCE, II 80.
LAND CASES: first "heard" by land overseer, II 686; appealed to vizier, II 686.
LANDMARKS: of the sacred cattle of Apis, IV 332; of Menet-Khufu, I 624, 625; Oryx nome, I 626; Hare nome, I 626; Jackal nome, I 626, 632; Oxyrrhyncus, I 632; Tell El-Amarna, II 949, 1042.
—the ancient, I 625; flooded by the Nile, I 407; restored after rebellion according to old writings, I 625.
LANDS, IV 948, 957, 958; numbering of, I 81.
—Lands, citizen, IV 755, 795.
—Flax land: see Flax.
—Olive land, IV 216, 263, 288, 394.
—Gifts of, II 1, 6, 15, 16, 113, 114; for endowment of mortuary offerings, I 156, 159, 165, 202, 205, 206, 209, 546, 574, 584, 586, 591, 592; II 840; for a statue, IV 479–83; to temples, II 102, 149; III 31, 413; IV 200, 222, 226,

251, 265, 280, 282, 313, 337, 339, 354, 359, 364, 370, 380, 383, 384, 681, 687, 948, 950, 954, 957, 958, 972, 1021.
—Land overseer, II 686; hearing of real-estate cases by, II 686.
—Land, the whole: Chief of, Commander of, Supervisor of, see Index V.

LANDSCAPE RELIEF: of Punt, II 254, 259.

LAPIS LAZULI, II 280, 434, 558, 773, 775, 838, 881, 889, 902, 903; III 137, 151, 204, 453; IV 29, 31, 32, 34, 126, 230, 231, 284, 285, 342, 343, 354, 372, 373, 383, 385, 388, 389, 491, 732, 735, 847, 875.
—Articles made of lapis lazuli: amulet IV 233; beads, IV 343; inlay, IV 253; offering-tables, I 534; II 390; rosettes, II 32; scarab, IV 233, 285, 343, 389; statue, I 668; IV 302, 395; stela, II 889; ceiling, I 483; shrine, I 667; necklace, II 509; sphinxes, IV 732.
—Artificial lapis lazuli, from Shinar, II 484.
—Lapis lazuli from God's Land, III 116; Naharin, III 434; Retenu, II 447, 509, 518, 536 (?); Zahi, II 459, 462; Isy, II 493; Babylon, II 446, 484; Assur, II 446 bis; Shinar, II 484; Tefrer, III 448 n. b; IV 30.
—Sparkling lapis lazuli, IV 377.
—Vessels ornamented with, II 32, 92, 165, 185, 436, 447, 1031; IV 315.

LARGESSES OF THE KING, III 65.

LATERAN OBELISK, II 626–28, 830–38.

LAUNDERERS, TEMPLE, IV 992.

LAW, II 568; IV 38, 62; see also Legal petitions handled according to, II 667; concerning vizier's duties, II 673; the 40 skins, containing, II 675, 712; in the temples of the gods, II 757; concerning land cases, II 686.
—Administration of, III 25; by the hereditary prince, III 25.
—Laws of Harmhab, III 51–66; of Egypt, III 270; of the palace, III 101; of the judgment hall, III 63.
—Laws on robbery, III 51–52; dues, III 53–54; slave service, III 55; stealing, III 56–59; connivance, III 58; tax collectors, III 58; inspectors, III 58; judges, III 63–65; bribery, III 64.
—Lawgiver, see Index V.

LEAD, II 558; IV 32, 245, 373, 385, 389; from Zahi, II 460, 462; Retenu, II 471, 491, 509, 534 (?); Isy, II 493, 521; statue of, IV 302, 392.

LEATHER: roll of, II 392, 433; sandals of, IV 241, 394; shields of, II 802; tents of, III 589; for taxes, IV 150.

LEGACY, I 194–99, 423E.

LEGAL ENACTMENTS, I 5; III 45–67; records, I 18.

LEGAL PROCEEDINGS, I 66 n. e, 204, 310; IV 423–24; protocol of, I 310.

LEGISLATION OF HARMHAB, III 45–67.

LEGITIMISTS, II 348.

LENTILS, IV 582.

LETTERS, I 10, 18, 20, 42; III 292, 630, 632, 633, 634; IV 443, 574, 600; of Sebni, I 367; of a frontier official, III 636; copies taken of, IV 527.
—Royal letters: to Harkhuf, I 6, 351–54; Ikhernofret, I 9, 664; Sebni, I 371; Senezemib, I 271, 273; Paynehsi, IV 595–600.
—Letter scribe, IV 588, 589.

LEVY, II 916.

LIBATION, II 35, 150, 288; III 626; IV 269, 272, 612, 871; vases for, I 421; for feast offerings, II 569; mortuary offering, III 17.

LIBATION BASIN, IV 1000 n. a.

LIBRARIES: at Heliopolis, I 757; see also Archives, House of Rolls, House of Writngs.

LID OF JAR, IV 231, 243, 394; of sarcophagus, I 266, 308, 321, 436, 451.

LIE: none in Pharaoh's records, II 97 *et passim;* punishment for, II 670, 683.

LIFE, SYMBOL OF, II 195, 202, 241.

LIFETIME: of 110 years, II 926.

LIMBS, II 197, 294, 299, 544, 652, 754; Horus who has numbered his, I 502; king's, of electrum, III 403.

LIMESTONE OF AYAN, I 534, 635, 740; II 27, 44, 103, 302, 380, 390, 603, 604, 799, 800, 812, 875; III 240, 525; IV 7, 355, 356, 358, 970; temple of, II 345 n. c, bis, 390; III 240, 525; IV 216, 311, 355, 970; pylons of, II 103; hypostyle of, II 603; pyramid clothed with, I 212; sarcophagus of, I 308; gates of, I 509; temples clothed with, I 534; II 27, 44; IV 251; mortuary chapel of, I 635; doorposts of, IV 355,

356; lintels of, IV 355, 356; broad hall of, IV 7; pyramidion of, IV 982; false door, I 88 n. a; slab, I 241 n. f; stelæ of, I 419 n. a, 421 n. a, 457 n. d, 676 n. c, 766 n. b; II 29 n. d; 49 n. a, 642 n. b, 856 n. b, 921 n. b; III 2; IV 725 n. a, 782 n. a; tombs of, III n. a, IV 979; statue of, IV 958A, n. a.
—Limestone cliffs at Amarna, II 949 n. b.

LINE: extension of (=the foundation ceremony), II 152; see also Cord and Ceremony.

LINEN, I 722, 723, 725; IV 582, 639, 661, 663, 668, 688, 958M; for mortuary offering, II 365; for statues, II 571; for temple, II 301, 376, 544, 615; garments of, III 207, 208; IV 228.
—Colored linen, IV 239, 283, 286, 341, 344, 375, 387, 388; garments of, IV 284, 342, 372, 375, 388, 390; mantles of, IV 232; tunics of, IV 232, 375; *dw*-garments, IV 375; *yfd*-garments, IV 375.
—*d*ꜣ-*w*-linen, II 722, 727 bis, 736, 738, 744 bis.
—Fine linen, II 615; IV 700 bis, 823, 878, 944.
—Mek-linen, IV 230, 283, 286, 329, 344, 387, 390; clothing of gods of, IV 335; garments of, IV 284, 342, 388; robe of, IV 232; mantle of, IV 232; from the Malachite country, IV 409.
—*mt*-linen, II 719, 721, 722, 723, 726, 727 bis, 730, 731, 736, 738, 744 bis.
—*mnḫ.t*-linen, II 165.
—Mysterious linen: shroud of, IV 1011; from Mehenet, IV 1011; Resenet, IV 1011.
—Prime linen, I 382.
—Royal linen, II 171, 544, 571; III 515; IV 31, 228, 230, 232, 272, 283, 286, 329, 344, 360, 374, 375, 387, 875; from the Malachite country, IV 409; clothing of gods of, IV 335; garments of, IV 232, 284, 342, 372, 374, 388, 390, 582, 876; hamen-garments, IV 232; mantles, IV 232, 374; statue garments, IV 232; tunics, IV 232, 374; upper garments, IV 232, 374; wrappings of, IV 966; wrappings of Horus, IV 232, 374; *ḫnky*-garments, IV 374; *ydg*ꜣ-garments, IV 374; *ḥm-ḫrd*-garments, IV 582.
—Southern linen, IV 230, 239, 283, 286, 341, 344, 372, 375, 387; garments of, IV 284, 342, 375, 388, 390; kilts of; 303, 350, 375; *dw*-garments, IV 375; *ydg*ꜣ-garments, IV 375; tunics, IV *k*ꜣ-*d*ꜣ-*m*-*r*ꜣ-garments, IV 375; *yfd*-garments, IV 375.
—Colored southern linen, IV 228.
—Fine southern linen, I 382; IV 228, 230, 283, 285, 329, 341, 342, 344, 360, 371, 372, 375, 387; *dw*-garments of, IV 232, 284, 374, 388, 390; kilts of, IV 232, 374; tunics of, IV 232, 374; upper garments of, IV 232, 374; *ydg*ꜣ-garments of, IV 232, 374; hamen-garments, IV 374.
—Double fine southern linen, IV 283.
—*šḫr*ʽ*w*-linen, II 554.
—White (*pḳ*ʽ*t*) linen, I 727; II 554, 571, 615.
—*wm*ʽ*t*-linen, II 554.

LINTELS, IV 489; of granite, IV 311; of red granite, IV 970; of limestone, IV 355, 356.

LION, IV 580; captured by Amenemhet, I 483; hunted by Thutmose III, II 813; on the highlands of Memphis, II 813.
—Tame, III 450, 470; IV 49, 112, 122.
—Golden, as a decoration of honor, II 23, 585, 587.
—as adornment of temples, II 896, 897.
—Pharaoh as a, II 660, 783, 844, 853, 896 n. d, 901; III 88, 117, 144, 147, 465, 479, 489, 580; IV 40, 41, 46, 49, 51, 54, 62, 75, 104, 921, 1005.

LIPS OF COLUMNS, IV 889.

LISI, IV 209, 279, 283, 328, 336, 364, 383, 387, 770, 832; army, IV 466; tax, II 718–45, III 57.
—of Asiatic cities, II 402 n. a, 403 n. b; III 34 n. a, 114, 366; IV 712–16; booty, II 480, 500, 501, 508, 532, 790; captives, II 788; III 156, 588; countries, II 402, 798A; III 119, 156, 342; IV 138; food for the king, I 423E; Hittite lands III 321; Hittite officers, III 337; Hittite chief, III 349; monuments IV 731; Nubian regions, I 311, 336, 510, II 843, 845 n. f, 849; ornaments, IV 538; plunder, II 459, 469; III 589; princes, IV 830, 878; property, II 688; IV 140, 948; rewards, II 583, 584, 584, 585, 587; supplies, II 472; temple dues, IV 160, 227, 283, 340, 386; temple estates, IV 159, 222, 280, 337, 364; tombs, IV 513; towns, II 490; in Nubia, II 645, 646,

647; tribute, II 445, 448, 462, 466, 482, 518, 525, 533, 534.
—Karnak list, I 419, and n. d; II 605 n. i; list of Ramses II at Abydos, I 529 n. e; Abydos list, I 59, n. a, 60 n. f, 61 nn. a, c, 62 n. d; Sakkara list, I 59 n. a, 60 n. g, 62 n. d, 149 n. c.

LISTING THE NUMBER OF THE PEOPLE, II 916.

LITERARY COMPOSITIONS, I 90

LIVING STREAM (or river): water from, for the ka, II 356, 378.

LOAD, II 264; loading, IV 407.

LOAN CATTLE: see Cattle.

LOAN COWS: see Cow.

LOAN HERDS: see Herds.

LOAVES: for food, I 430; II 462; for divine offering, II 559, 560, 562, 571, 620, 621, 622, 792; for evening offering, II 565; for feast offering, II 566; for mortuary offering, I 329, 518; for obelisks, II 563; for oblation, II 749; of the fire, IV 291; makers of, III 624.
—ʿ*ḳ*-loaves, IV 238.
—Large ʿ*ḳ*-loaves, IV 238, 291, 393.
—*wdnw·nt*-loaves, IV 238, 291, 297.
—*byꜣ·t*-loaves, II 113; III 77, 159, 624 n. h; IV 238, 291, 297, 347.
—*bḥ*-loaves, IV 238, 393.
—*p*ʿ*·t*-loaves, IV 238.
—*pws*ꜣ-ʿ*ḳ*-loaves, IV 238.
—*pr·t-s*-loaves for divine offering, III 77, 159.
—*nfr·t*-loaves for food, II 462, 472.
— —*rrt*-loaves for mortuary offering, I 590.
—*syd*-loaves, IV 238, 393.
—Sweet *s*ʿ*b*-loaves, IV 238.
—*sḫt*-loaves, II 735.
—*ḳw*-loaves, II 735, 739, 743.
—*ḏdmt-ḥr-t*ꜣ-loaves, IV 238.
—Flat loaves: for mortuary offering, I 555, 556, 585, 590.
—Heth loaves: for mortuary offering, I 241.
—Kyllestis loaves, IV 238, 291.
—Oblation loaves, IV 238; large oblation loaves, IV 291, 393; white oblation loaves, II 571; IV 238, 291.
—Pesen loaves: for mortuary offering, I 241.
—Persen loaves, II 113; III 624 n. h; IV 238, 297, 347.
—Pyramidal loaves, IV 238, 347; white pyramidal loaves, IV 291; white pyramidion loaves for divine offerings, II 572 n. c.
—Round loaves, IV 291.
—Senu loaves, for divine offerings, II 378; III 624 n. h; for mortuary offering, II 353.
—Seshu loaves, IV 297.
—White loaves, I 540, 542, 544, 547, 550, 555, 556, 577, 585, 590; II 159, 565, 571, 572, 621, 622; IV 238, 297; for mortuary offering, I 540, 542, 544, 547, 550, 555, 556, 577, 585, 590; for evening offering, II 565; for divine offerings, II 159, 572, 621, 622.
—Tall white loaves, IV 291.
—White *t*ꜣ-loaves, IV 238.

LOGS, IV 232, 234, 245, 286, 288, 295, 300, 303, 348, 379, 380, 385, 390, 391, 394, 577, 578; from Retenu, II 491, 525; Arrapachitis, II 512.

LOINS, IV 634.

LOTUS FLOWER, IV 194, 213, 244, 264, 295.

LOWING OF CATTLE, I 493.

LOWLAND, II 113, 114, IV 95; *M-ḫ*ꜣ*-w*, skin of, from Assur, II 449.

M

MACE, II 225; III 117, 489; war, IV 130, 246, 718, 720.

MAGAZINE, I 172; II 356, 986; III 208; IV 330, 410, 849; Overseer of: see Index V; Scribes of: see Index V; temple, IV 313, 324, 1021.
—of the overseer of the White House, IV 512; chief scribe of, IV 512.

MAGIC: practice of, IV 454–56; prosecution for, IV 454, 455, 456; regarded as a capital crime, IV 454, 455, 456; ordered by the gods, IV 455.
—Magic power, II 235; of diadem, II 220; of a god, IV 455.
—Magical inscriptions, IV 455.
—Magical prayer, III 18.
—Mut, great in magic, I 468.

MAGIC ROLLS, IV 454; for hindering, IV 454; for bewitching, IV 455; for terrifying, IV 454; for enfeebling, IV 454, 456; for extraordinary power, IV 455.
—Magic rolls deposited with dead kings, IV 455.

MAIDENS: for the garden of Min, II 567.

Maids, IV 111.
—Maid servants: temple, IV 751, 992.
Malachite, II 280, 390, 430, 558, 773, 775, 838, 881, 902, 903; III 137, 151, 204, 453; IV 29, 32, 126, 230, 284, 285, 342, 343, 354, 372, 373, 383, 385, 388, 389, 491, 847, 874, 875, 944.
—Articles made of: finger rings, IV 377; collars, I 534; inlay, IV 253; scarab, IV 233, 285, 343, 389; statue, II 668; IV 302, 395.
—Brought from the mine-land (of Sinai) I 602, 713, 731, 736; God's Land (at Sinai), II 450 n. a, 820; III 116; the Malachite country IV 409; Naharin, III 434; Reshet, II 321; IV 31, 34; Zahi, II 459.
—Sparkling malachite, IV 377.
—Vessels ornamented with, II 32, 165, 185, 1031; IV 315.
Malachite Country, I 161; IV 409; Hathor, mistress of, I 715, 720, 722, 723, 725, 750; II 450 n. a; IV 409.
"Malachite" Terrace, I 266, 342.
Males, Captive: assigned for the storehouse, IV 128.
Manna, IV 378, 390; from Punt, IV 286, 390.
Mantles: of royal linen, IV 232, 374; mek-linen, IV 232; colored linen IV 232.
Mares, II 435, 589, 875.
Marine, I 390; IV 407.
—Marines, II 328, 332 n. d; III 197; royal, II 332, 916; for Captain of, Officers of, Scribes of, see Index V.
Marriage, II 7; III 28.
Marshes, II 966; IV 895; inclosed, III 276; temples of Thebes like, IV 743; of Delta, III 291; see Index VI: Marshes.
Marvels, II 139, 253, 265, 271, 272, 274, 277–78, 282, 285, 288, 377, 486, 513, 608, 804, 864, 867; III 274, 288, 420; IV 197, 407, 491, 618, 635.
Masonry, II 306; IV 515.
Mastaba: of old kingdom, I 181.
—at Abydos, of Uni, I 291 n. a.
—at Gizeh, of Ikhi, I 183 n. b; Thethi, I 184 n. d; Kam, I 187 n. d; Senezemib, I 268 n. i.
—at Sakhara, of Methen, I 166 n. c, 170 n. c; Nenekhsekhmet, I 237 n. c; Ptahshepses, I 254 n. a; Sabu-Ibebi, I 282, n. a; Sabu-Thety, I 287 n. a.
—Mastaba inscription: see under Inscriptions, Tomb.
Mastic Tree, IV 245.
Masts, II 492; IV 861.
Mathematics, I 20.
Matriarchate, I 398, 405, 413–14; rule of the mother of Kheti II at Siut, I 414, and she acting as lord, I 414; Nakht II inherited the Jackal nome from his mother, I 632; Khnumhotep II inherited Menet-Khufu from his mother's father, I 624, 628.
Meals, I 493, 496.
Measure, II 734, 737, 741, 742, 743; IV 582; see also Bales, Basket, Bekhen, Bolts, Bunch, Bundle, Censerfuls, Coil, Hank, Jars, and the following:
—Linear measures: cubit, I 83 n. a, 93, 95, 97, 98, 99, 100, 101, 103, 104, 105, 106, 107, 108, 109, 110, 111, 112, 113, 114, 115, 119, 120, 121, 122, 123, 124, 125, 126, 127, 128, 129, 130, 131, 133, 134, 135, 136, 137, 138, 140, 141, 142, 143, 144, 146, 147, 148, 152, 157, 159, 165, 212; II 965 bis; IV 288, 330, 343, 355, 356, 358, 406, 513, 515, 886, 887, 904, 916, 958J; finger, I 83 n. a, 97, 103, 105, 108, 113, 115, 119, 120, 121, 123, 124, 125, 127, 128, 129, 130, 133, 134, 136, 137, 140, 142, 143, 146, 147, 148, 152, 157, 159; IV 343, 886; iter, II 479, 852, 965 bis; IV 46, 216; palm, I 95, 97, 98, 100, 103, 107, 108, 109, 113, 115, 119, 121, 122, 123, 127, 128, 133, 134, 136, 137, 138, 140, 141, 142, 143, 147, 148, 152, 157; IV 288, 343, 886, 887; span, I 101, 104, 106, 112, 114; ipet-rod, II 995.
—Square measures: *ḥ ʾ·t*, I 574, 584, 586; khet (land-measure), II 965 ter; IV 479, 480, 481, 482, 483; stat (a land-measure containing 100 square cubits = 1 aroura, or about $\frac{7}{10}$ acre, more exactly $\frac{27}{40}$ acre), I 156, 158, 159, 161, 165, 166; II 15, 16, 840; IV 226, 282, 288, 339, 370, 380, 384, 394, 681, 755, 784, 795, 948, 950, 954, 957, 1021.
—Cubic measures: heket, I 545; II 171 bis, 319, 377, 437, 486, 513, 572, 733, 737, 739, 740, 742, 743, 744, 761; IV 229, 232, 234, 236, 240, 241, 283, 286, 287, 289, 294, 297, 313, 341, 344, 346, 347, 371, 378, 379, 381, 387, 390, 391, 392, 396; hin, IV 232, 239, 287,

299, 300, 345, 393, 498, 683, 949, 950, 952, 953, 954, 1021; khar, I 556; IV 955; *nḏ*ʾ, II 159 bis, 571 bis; pedet, II 572, 719, 722; *pg*-vessel, II 571; pyramid, IV 294; uhet, I 556; *yp*ʿ*t*, IV 232, 234, 238, 239, 240, 241, 244, 286, 294, 295, 297, 301, 350, 380, 390, 392, 393; ʿ-measure, IV 299, 348, 394; *ps*ʾ-measure, IV 378, 395; *msty*-measure, IV 234, 235, 240, 287, 301, 344, 350, 378, 390, 391, 392, 395, 582; *mḏ*ʾ-measure, IV 295, 347; *mḏ*ʾ*yw*-measure, IV 244; *ḥtp*-measure, IV 238, 240, 244, 291, 294, 379, 392, 393; *ḥtp-ḥr-nmtt*-measure, IV 294; *sbḫ*ʿ*t*-measure, IV 241, 379; *spr*-measure, IV 299, 348; *ḳ*ʾ-*t*ʾ-*rw-ty*-measures, IV 378; *k*ʾ-*bw*ʾ-*s*ʾ-measure, IV 240; *gs-r*ʾ-measure, IV 295, 303, 380, 394; *ṯ*ʾ*y*-measure, IV 238, 240, 294, 378, 393; *ṯmṯm*-measure, IV 238, 291; *ṯrf*-measure, IV 292; *d*ʾ-*w*ʾ-*r*ʾ-measure, IV 294; *d*ʾ*mw*-measure, IV 240; *dm*ʾ*w*-measure, IV 345; *dm*ʾ*mw*-measure, IV 379; *dydy*-measure, IV 295; *dny*-measure, IV 294, 295; *dny.t*-measures, II 621, 622; IV 240, 294, 299, 300; *ḏdm*ʿ*t*-measure, IV 244, 294, 301, 394, 768; zawet, II 995.

—Loaf-measure: of the court, IV 393; of gold, IV 393; for eating, IV 393; for the mouth of the eater, IV 393.

—Measuring, I 83 n. a; II 273–76, 377.

—Measuring-line: at foundation ceremonies, I 506, 609; II 152, 608, 795.

MEAT, II 117, 260; III 71; IV 238, 393, 467; roast of, for the altar, I 569, 571.

MECHIR: see Months.

MEDICAL PAPYRUS, I 246.

MEDICINE, I 20.

MEHIWET FRUIT, IV 240, 378, 392.

MEKHTEBET: an uncertain adornment, II 22, 24.

MEMBERS OF STATUES: of precious stones, II 376.

MEMORIAL, II 150, 286; memorial stelæ, at Abydos, I 9; memorial tablets, I 661 n. d.

MEMORIAM: monument in, II 175.

MEMORY, II 378.

MENHET FLOWER, IV 213.

MENHET PLANT, IV 295.

MENIT-UZ (metal): statue of, IV 302.

MERA WOOD, IV 288, 379, 391.

MERCENARY, III 428; IV 994; mercenary troops, III 307; IV 117.

MERCHANTS, III 274; IV 313.

MERCY: to poor, I 328, 357, 479; to orphans, I 479.

MERU WOOD, I 146; II 321; IV 378; shrine of, I 667; tent poles of, II 435; chest of, II 755; mortuary chests of, IV 966; staff of, IV 288; staves of, IV 391; temple doors of, IV 488 n. c; from Assur, II 449; from Retenu, II 435, 447.

MESDET STONE: pairs of, III 246.

MESNET STONE: offering tables of, I 727; necklace of, I 500.

MESORE: see Months.

MESSAGE, IV 819; royal, II 929; see also Index V: Messengers.

METAL, WALL OF, IV 66.

METROLOGY, EGYPTIAN, IV 151.

MICE, III 598.

MIDDLE AGES, I 3.

MIDDLE KINGDOM: inscriptions of, I 8, 9, 10; chronology of, I 42, 57; temples of, I 442

MIDWIFE: goddess acting as, II 206.

MILITARY COMMANDER: see Index V.

MILITIA OF HERACLEOPOLIS: chief of, IV 968; broad hall of, IV 972.

MILK, I 493; II 162, 566; IV 295, 301, 350, 394, 870, 929, 958M; for mortuary offering, II 571; III 17.

MINERALS: see Bronze, Copper, Electrum, Emery, Feldspar, Gold, Iron, Lapis lazuli, Lead, Malachite, Metal, Menit-uz, Natron, Silver, Stones, Stones (costly), Tin.

MINES OF COPPER: in Atika, IV 408.

—at Sinai, I 10, 12; operated in the First Dynasty, I 168; by Snefru, I 168; of Ka, I 731.

—Mine of electrum, east of Redesiyeh, III 170.

—Mines of gold, in Akita, III 286.

—Mine land (Sinai), I 353 n. c, 725, 735, 736, 737; the eternal mountain in, I 736; malachite in, I 736.

—Mine chamber excavated at Sinai by men, I 606; made for Hathor, at Sinai, I 723; name of, I 725.

—Miners, I 447; necropolis miners, I 697.

Mines of Copper—
—Mining: Snefru regarded as founder of, I 168; of gold, III 195.
—Mining work, IV 517.
MINIUM FRUIT, IV 378, 395.
MIXERS, III 624, 625.
MIXTURE OF SIX PARTS (=bronze), IV 202, 318, 320, 343, 358.
MOAT, IV 118.
MONEY, IV 683, 685, 686; of Thekel, IV 568.
MONKEYS, III 375; from Punt, II 265.
MONOLITHIC SHRINE, II 775; IV 198, 320.
MONTHS: Thoth, first month, II 933; IV 296 n. e; Paophi, second month, II 591 n. b; IV 144, 791 n. a; Tybi, fifth month, II 874; Mechir, sixth month, II 304, 318, 602; Phamenoth, seventh month, II 592 n. c, 823; IV 296 n. e; Pharmuthi, eighth month, I 655; Pakhons, ninth month, II 592 n. c; IV 144, 958L; Epiphi, eleventh month, II 410 n. a; IV 296 n. e; Mesore, twelfth month, II 304, 318.
MONUMENT, I 12, 19, 154, 158, 159, 160, 161, 165, 166, 409; II 149, 150, 152, 154, 157, 158, 164, 174, 175, 176, 192 n. d, 309, 311, 312, n. b, 317, 318, 339, 351, 383, 548, 558, 568, 571, 596, 601, 603, 605, 606, 608, 611, 624, 627, 628, 633, 638, 639, 643, 651, 654, 662, 752, 755, 759, 775, 800, 805, 832, 836, 838, 856, 883, 887, 888, 889, 890, 892, 894, 896, 897, 898, 903, 909, 912, 917, 936, 946, 960; III 17, 174, 177, 195, 200, 206, 210, 213, 215, 216, 217, 219, 223, 224, 227, 229, 232, 236, 242, 246, 248, 249, 259, 260, 269, 270, 281, 405, 414, 499, 500, 501, 502, 503, 504, 505, 510, 511, 512, 513, 515, 519, 520, 521, 522, 528, 529, 537, 544, 566; IV 4, 5, 7, 8, 10, 11, 12, 13, 14, 15, 16, 27, 28, 62, 110, 179, 191, 197, 252, 311, 357, 412, 460, 464, 465, 473, 528, 602, 603, 609, 610, 612, 620, 622, 625, 626, 632, 633, 634, 635, 649, 704, 706, 721, 731, 889, 897, 898, 899, 900, 943, 945, 980, 1011 n. c.
MOORING, IV 566, 861, 863.
—Mooring stake, I 423, 612; Intef I drove it in the sacred valley, I 423; as title of Hatshepsut, II 341.
MOPHI: name of a cave at Elephantine, III 171 n. a.
MORTAR, IV 538.
MORTUARY: ceremony of the righteous, benefit of, II 925.
—Customs, I 536.
—Endowment, I 200, 269, 379, 562, 577, 630; II 839, 907, 921; IV 679, 1007; by Hepzefi, I 535–93; by Amenhotep, II 921–27; for Osiris, II 840; for Ahmose I, II 840; edict of, II 922–27; contracts of, I 538–93.
—Furniture, II 861 n. c; IV 521, 538.
—Gods, III 278.
—Mortuary oblations, II 571, 1001.
—Mortuary offerings, I 155, 159, 161, 165, 173, 185, 201, 206, 207, 208, 209, 220, 227, 232–35, 241, 252, 349, 379, 394, II 35, 36, 52, 170, 356, 365, 389; III 271; IV 187, 485, 927, 1018.
—Mortuary priest, Mortuary prophet; see Index V.
—Mortuary prayer, I 384; II 97, 111; III 21, IV 484, 995, 1018, 1025; quaint claim of, I 278; posture in, II 37.
—Mortuary statues of: Hepzefi, I 540; Thutmose III, II 97; Seti I, III 271; placed in the temples, I 500, 540; II 52, 156, 604, 605 n. i.
—Mortuary stelæ, I 469, 507, 529, 530, 599, 671, 743; II 47, 839; IV 1026.
—Mortuary temples: see Index II; of Nemathap, I 173; at Abydos, of Seti I, III 174, 225, 226, 263, 266; a Kurna, of Seti I, II 210, 212, 213, 215–20; at Thebes, of Thutmose IV, II 821, 823; Merneptah, II 856 n. b; Amenhotep, II 921; Amenhotep III, II 904–8; of Thutmose III, II 33[illegible] n. i; of Mentuhotep III, IV 520 n. b; Ramesseum: see Index II.
MOUNTAIN, II 995; secret chambers of, II 946; of gritstone, overseer of works in, III 17; of Bethanath, III 356; of Akhetaton, II 962, 963, 964, 965, 966, 969, 971, 972, 994; of electrum, east of Redesiyeh, III 170; "Lord-of-Life," name of the mountain on the west of Thebes, III 210; the great, of Wawat, IV 480, 481.
—Obelisk, called, II 318; statue called, II 917.
MOUNTAIN GOATS: see Goats.
MOUNTAINEERS, III 178.
MOUNTINGS, II 155; IV 254, 287, 343, 355, 356, 358, 377, 406, 489, 910, 929.
MOURNING: for grandfather of Kheti II, I 414; for a king, I 491; mourners, I 370.

MUD BRICK, II 607.

MUMMY, IV 538; of Thutmose II, IV 637; Amenhotep I, IV 638, 647; Seti I, IV 639, 661; Ramses III, IV 640, 641; Ramses II, IV 642; Ahmose I, IV 645; Sitkamose IV 644; Siamon, prince, IV 646; Thutmose IV, I 15; restorations of, I 22; IV 592–94, 636–47, 661, 662–67.
—Mummy inscriptions, IV 637–42, 644–47, 661, 663, 688.

MURDER: punished with death, IV 658.

MUSICIANS: temple, II 1018.
—Musician (fem.) of Re: Teya, III 542.

MUSTERING, IV 1004; of troops, II 693; of workmen, II 935; of young men, II 329, 332.

MUTINY, IV 989.

MYRRH, I 763; II 283, 288, 387; III 475; IV 26, 232, 264, 286, 304, 333, 344, 348, 372, 390, 685, 770, 870, 875, 878; from Genebteyew, II 474; Red Land, I 429; fields of the sycamore, II 299; Punt, I 161; II 260, 263, 265, 274, 275, 276, 277, 321, 486; IV 130, 210, 407, 929; divine offering, II 572; gum of, II 288; Hathor, mistress of, II 295.
—Dried myrrh, IV 299, 329; from Punt, II 486, 513; Retenu, II 491.
—Myrrh fruit, IV 232, 286, 390.
—Myrrh resin from Punt, II 265.
—Myrrh sycamores, IV 333.
—Myrrh terraces of Punt, II 260, 284, 285, 287, 288, 294.
—Myrrh trees from Punt, II 263, 264, 265, 272, 288; IV 390.
—Myrrh-wood, IV 232, 286, 390.

MYTH: of Horus and Set, II 70 n. d.

N

NAME: beautiful, I 676; IV 943, 990, 1014; hidden, see Hidden; royal, used in oath, II 58; see Oath.

NAOPHORS: of costly stone, IV 377; explanation of meaning of, IV 377 n. c.

NATIVE VERSIONS, I 24.

NATRON, IV 235, 241, 299, 345, 350, 379, 392, 865; from Retenu, II 518.
—Natron gatherers of Elephantine, IV 148.

NAVE OF TEMPLE, III 515.

NAVY, I 405; II 591; see also Fleet, Warships; administration of, under the vizier, II 667, 710; officials of report to vizier, II 710.
—Commander of, Officers of: see Index V.

NEBDU, IV 241.

NECKLACE, II 22, 23, 24, 45, 254, 288, 376, 390, 544, 654; of *Mšn.t*-stone, I 510; *ḥm*ʾ*g.t*-stone, I 500; gold and silver, II 32; lapis lazuli, II 509; electrum, II 654; costly stone, II 545, 801, 802; IV 876; gold, II 585, 587.
—Necklaces: from Retenu, II 509; Kadesh, II 585.
—Necklace-rattles, II 93.
—Bead necklace, II 725, 731; of gold, II 722, 723, 727, 738, 740.
—Braided necklace, III 2.

NECROPOLIS, I 371; II 378; III 32B, 259; the gods, lords of, III 17; cliff, I 613; the highlands of the blessed, II 378; officer of the tomb in the, II 378; inspectors of, see Index V; soldiers of, I 710; scribes of, see Index V.
—Necropolis of Abydos, IV 1020, 1029; see Tazoser, Index VI.
—Necropolis of Benihasan, I 623; feasts of, I 630.
—Necropolis, southern, of, Dêr el-Gebrâwi, I 375 n. f.
—Necropolis of Heliopolis, II 814; sacred road to, II 814; Gizeh, probably the, II 814 n. c.
—Necropolis of Memphis, the Serapeum, IV 977, 979, 986, 1010; tomb of Apis in, IV 979; called "the western desert of Memphis," IV 977, 986.
—Necropolis of Siut, I 582; official body of: overseer, I 582, 584; chief of the highland, I 584; eight mountaineers, I 582, 584.
—Necropolis at Western Thebes, II 338; fortress of, II 338–39; goddess of, II 338–39; chief treasurer of, IV 665; inspectors of, IV 511, 512, 517, 522, 525, 533, 665; chief of police of, IV 511, 512, 525, 527; administrators of, IV 525; scribes of, IV 526, 529, 530, 640; police of, IV 525; workmen of, IV 524, 525, 526, 528, 530, 533, 543; serf-laborers of, IV 525.
—Necropolis thieves, IV 511, 513, 515, 516, 517, 521, 522, 535.

NEGE BULLS: from Khara, IV 229.

NEGLIGENCE OF NOT REPORTING CONSPIRACY: crime of, IV 431, 432, 433, 434, 435, 436, 437, 438, 439, 440, 448, 449, 450.

NEIGHBOR, IV 398, 944.

NENYBU WOOD, IV 344, 391.

NEST (of Horus hawk), II 138.

NET, IV 41, 44, 77.

NEW MOON: dates of, in reign of Thutmose III, I 46, 51.

NEW YEAR: gifts of, I 545, 563; II 801.

NEW YEAR'S DAY, I 42, 545, 563, 573, 583, 585; II 925; New Year's Night, I 573, 583; New Year's feast, 19th of July, I 40; see also Feasts.

NEYBU WOOD, IV 234; from Assur, II 449.

NIGHT WATCH, I 417.

NODDING THE HEAD OF A GOD, III 440, 444, 580; IV 615, 617, 655, 656, 658.

NOMES, IV 905, 906, 948, 957; order of southern, I 529 n. e; records of, II 703; boundaries of, II 703; Deputy of, see Index V.

—Nomes of: Abydos, IV 1020; Aphroditopolis, I 423; Apollinopolis Magna, II nome of Upper Egypt, I 500; Athribis, IV 873; Busiris, I 159; IV 830 n. a; Cerastes mountain, XII nome of Upper Egypt, I 199; Crocodile nome, I 529; Cusæ, XIV nome of Upper Egypt, I 500; II 300; Hare, I 700–6; IV 821, 848, 948; Harpoon, I 174; Heliopolis, IV 955; Hesebka, XI of Lower Egypt, IV 830; Jackal, I 626, 632; Khent, I 159, 165; Libyan, I 159; Lycopolis, XIII nome of Upper Egypt, I 280, 396; see Jackal nome; Memphis, I 159; Mendes, I 173, 174, 197, 198; IV 830; Oryx, XVI of Upper Egypt, I 518; Oxyrrhyncus, IV 818 nn. b, c, 820, 837, 948; Patoris, IV 905; Sais, I 172, 173, 174; Sekhem II of Lower Egypt, I 173, 175; Thebes, I 420, 459; Thinis, I 349; II 181, 763, 767; Upper nome, I 199; Xois, I 156, 159; IV 818; Yuna, IV 948.

—Nome of Tehenut, IV 482; see also Wawat and Libya, Index VI.

NORTH WIND: a sweet, for the ka, IV 485; as epithet of the king, II 994.

NOSE TO BE CUT OFF: as penalty for robbing, III 51; extortion, III 54; slave stealing, III 55; stealing hides, III 56.

—Nose and ears cut off, IV 451, 452, 524.

NUMBERING: occurrence of, I 84, [118], 120, 122, 124, 126, 128, 130, 132, 133, 145, 147, 148, 161, 166, 298, 303, 305, 320, 387; of large cattle, I 157, 267; of large and small cattle, I 81, 192, 266, 340; of gold and lands, I 81, 137; of all people, I 106.

O

OARS: steering, IV 331, 845.

OATH: form of royal name for legal, II, 58; in foreign lands in Pharaoh's name, II 68; by Pharaoh, II 121, 318, 422, 452, 570, 601; III 327, 365; IV 835, 850, 862, 875, 880, 881, 932.

—Oath of the king, IV 486, 524, 526, 529, 547, 548, 549, 550, 552, 553; "as the king lives for you," I 349; "as Upwawet, lord of Siut and Anubis, lord of the cave, live for you," I 394; "as my father lives for me," I 658; "as Sesostris lives," I 682; "as Re loves me, as my father Amon favors me," II 121, 318, 422, 570; "as Re loves me, as my father Atum favors me," III 327, 365.

OBELISK, II 903, 908; of Seti I, III 202.

—at Elephantine, of Thutmose I, II 89.

—in Heliopolis, erected by Seti I, III 316, 544; inscribed by Ramses II, III 545; New York obelisk, II 634; London obelisk from, II 632–33.

—of the temple of Khammat in Soleb, II 890.

—of Ramses II at Tanis, III 392, 543 n. c; Luxor, III 543 n. c, 567; Karnak III 543 n. c.

—at Karnak: of Thutmose I, II 86; two of them, II 86; only one inscribed by Thutmose I, II 86; the other inscribed by Thutmose III, I 16; II 86; obelisk, Lateran, from Karnak by Thutmose III, II 626, and Thutmose IV, II 833–34; pyramidion of, II 834; Constantinople obelisk of Thutmose III, II 479 n. a, 629–31; four obelisks of Thutmose III, II 563, 571, 776; divine offerings for, II 563, 572; obelisks at Karnak: of Hatshepsut,

II 304–21, 376; two of them, II 304, 309; one standing, II 304–319; one fallen, II 320–21; history of, II 304, 319; location of, II 304, 319; dimensions of, II 304.
—Obelisks on the sacred barge, II 888.
—Divine offerings for obelisks, II 563, 572.
—Obelisks made of black basalt, III 246; of granite, II 89, 304, 315, 318, 336, 624; III 567; IV 980, 982; of red granite, II 630.
—Obelisk inscription; see Inscriptions.

Oblation, I 432, 756; II 139, 286, 312, 355, 553, 554, 749, 814, 815, 952, 960; III 423; IV 141, 187, 208, 237, 259, 272, 290, 296, 354, 356, 383, 388, 468, 676, 768, 856, 857, 866, 870, 874, 958D.
—Festival oblation, IV 329, 330, 335, 928.
—Endowment of oblations, II 908; IV 329.
—Mortuary oblation, II 571, 1001.
—Oblation of vessels, II 654.
—Storehouse of, IV 259.

Oblation Bearer: chief of, IV 515.

Oblation Standards, II 795.

Oblation Table, II 795; of costly stones, I 764; the great, of Osiris at Abydos, I 787.

Oblation Tablets, II 795.

Obscure Period: minimum length of, I 52.

Occurrence, II 935; of numbering, I 81, 82; of royal jubilee, II 89; III 552, 553, 554, 556; of "Running-of-Apis," I 114; of Sed-jubilee, I 296, 298, 300, 302, 305, 435; IV 414.

Odor: of a god, II 196; of Punt, I 762; II 196, 274, 288; of king, III 148.

Offering, I 409; II 954; III 16, 259, 260; IV 382, 678, 767, 869, 1021; records of, IV 1022; for Aton, II 996; of the ancestors, endowments for, by Harmhab, III 23; of images, IV 458, 63; for the ka, II 333, 353, 355; see also Mortuary offerings; on king's behalf, II 57; "Offering-which-the-king-gives," II 213, 766; royal, which Amon-Re and the king give, II 365; royal, which Osiris gives, II 367; of Pharaoh's house, III 55; tax collection for, III 55; of Min to Mentuhotep IV, I 437.
—Aton-offering of Aton, II 987.
—Daily offerings, II 919; III 31, 272, 526; IV, 141, 216, 217, 236, 262, 289, 313, 335, 346, 355, 359, 360, 381, 396, 609, 763, 958M.
—Divine offerings (usual term for temple income), I 156, 159, 160, 161, 165, 166, 167, 274, 299, 437, 756; of Amon II 102, 149, 159, 160, 170, 186, 225, 286, 293, 298, 302, 352, 390, 557, 559, 560, 648, 652, 749; III 263, 275, 518, 624; IV 47, 149, 190, 207, 217, 228, 229, 236, 256, 259, 265, 266, 268, 269, 283, 289, 309, 313, 320, 321, 324, 326, 327, 334, 341, 346, 347, 356, 357, 358, 360, 362, 363, 381, 387, 396, 399, 470, 471, 573, 676, 851, 854, 855, 856, 868, 906, 910, 927, 972, 1007, 1021; dues for, collected by two deputies of the army, III 54; endowment of, II 622, 792, 806, 900, 908; III 77, 159, 268; IV 256, 320, 335, 354, 355, 359, 654, 958M; fields of, II 102, 161, 186; grain of, I 274; overseer of, I 299; "hearings" of, conducted by vizier, II 706; storehouses of, IV 258; works of, II 757; in temple of Amon, established by Intef I, I 421; for Harakhte, II 562; for Min, II 567; for Min-Amon in Bohen, III 77, 159; for Mut-Hathor of Thebes, II 622; for Ptah, II 619, 620, 621; III 413; for Wennofer, III 526; for obelisks, II 563, 571; for statues, II 564, 571, 604, 618, 619, 620; III 272, 626.
—Evening offering, II 565.
—Festival offering, IV 383, 388, 763, 924, 925; for the feast of the "Appearance," II 569; for the feast of the "Beginning of the seasons," II 569; for feast of Peret-Min, II 566;
—Food offering, III 150, 179, 204.

Offering-tables, II 93, 225, 301, 390; IV 676, 910; given to the southern gods in Elephantine by Sesostris I, I 500; for temple of Abydos, I 534; made of alabaster, I 323 bis; gold, II 175, 390; IV 610, 611, 612, 958M, 1020; Asiatic copper, II 175; copper, IV 911; costly stone, IV 958M, 1020; marvelous stone, IV 287; lapis lazuli, I 534; II 390; bronze, I 534; II 175; IV 912; electrum, I 534, 610; II 164, 376; silver, I 534; II 175, 390; IV

610, 911, 912, 958M, 1020; mesnet stone, I 727.

OFFERING-TABLET, I 308; II 35, 97; IV 199, 326; of silver, IV 735; white stone, IV 972.

OFFICE, II 926, 1040; IV 321, 357, 534, 747; inheritance of, II 53, 766, 925, 926; III 622, 626, 647, 648; assigned, II 1025; divine offices, IV 1018.

OFFICIAL BODY: of the temple of Upwawet, I 550; of the necropolis of Siut, I 584, 589; of the palace, I 631.

—Official body of Khnumhotep II, I 623; excellent ones, I 623; officers, I 623; artificers, I 623; peasant slaves, I 623.

OIL, I 496; II 117; IV 216, 228, 263, 272, 283, 286, 299, 329, 344, 360, 387, 491, 770, 859, 992; of Egypt, IV 233, 376; Kharu, IV 233; Zahi, II 462; as tribute, II 750, 771.

—Best oil, IV 300, 348, 394.

—*bḳ*-oil, IV 376; *bḳꜣ*-oil, IV 390; red *bḳ*-oil, IV 239, 376.

—Festival oil: for embalming, I 370.

—Green oil: from Retenu, II 473, 491, 509, 518; Naharin, II 482; Zahi, II 510, 519.

—Olive oil, III 208.

—*nḥḥ*-oil, IV 239, 376, 390, 394; of Egypt, IV 376; of Syria, IV 376.

—Sefet oil, I 241, 382; IV 376; from Retenu, II 509, 518.

—Sweet oil, III 208; IV 239; from Naharin, II 482; Retenu, II 491, 509, 518; of gums, IV 497, 498.

—*ṯḥnt*-oil, I 366.

OIL TREE, IV 216; Osiris, protector of, I 783.

OINTMENT, II 185, 288, 918; III 71, 207; IV 335, 497, 875, 958M; choice, II 294; prime, of the pure ox, II 293; for taxes, IV 150; for oblation, II 612; for mortuary offering, II 365; for embalming, I 366; IV 966; presents of, I 372; for the temple, II 165, 615; of gums, IV 476, 477; of divine things, II 544, 615.

OKEANOS, II 325; see also Index VI, the Great Green.

OLD AGE, I 402; II 994, 1003, 1008; IV 489, 491, 612, 657, 675, 677, 705, 740, 784.

OLD KINGDOM, I 5, 42; length of, I 56; Sothic date, I 44; calendar existed before, I 45.

OLIVE LAND, IV 216, 263, 288, 394.

OLIVE WOOD: from Assur, II 449.

OLIVES, IV 239, 241, 379, 393.

ONIONS, IV 296, 348.

OPPRESSION, III 50, 67.

ORACLE OF THE GOD, II 151, 250, 284, 285, 606, 823, 827; III 174, 534.

ORGANS, KING'S: of iron, III 403.

ORNAMENTS, II 544; IV 521, 538, 988H; of costly stones, I 534; II 545; IV 1011; gold, IV 231, 285, 343; IV 1011; of prince, IV 343; of divine consort, IV 988H; of divine votress, IV 988H.

ORYX: for oblation, IV 768.

—White oryx, IV 190, 242, 266, 392; male of, IV 242, 293.

OSTRACA, I 20; ostracon in Turin, I 69 n. j; in British Museum, 5623, 5638, I 474 n. d, 45.

OSTRICH, III 475; eggs of, III 475.

—Ostrich feathers, III 475; from Punt, III 37.

OVALS: containing names of a country, IV 130, 137, 718.

OVERLAY, IV 889, 909, 970.

OX CARTS, IV 73, 467.

OX HIDES, IV 582.

OXEN, II 719; IV 242, 293, 392, 482, 583, 859, 914, 944, 949, 954; for oblation, II 815, 960; IV 208, 329; for mortuary offering, I 518; II 111, 113, 114, 139, 149, 356, 365, 840; III 17, 526; for divine offering, II 160, 458, 616, 793, 798; IV 9, 190, 200; for feast offering, II 566; for taxes, II 719, 720, 721, 722, 723, 726, 727, 731, 734, 738, 739, 740, 741, 743; flesh of, III 207, 208; from Punt, II 468; Naharin, II 482; Retenu, II 491, 616; with carved horn, III 475; used to drag stones, II 27; Libya, III 584; Genebteyew, II 474; Wawat, II 475, 487, 495, 503, 515, 527; Kush, II 494, 502, 514, 522.

—the pure, prime ointment of, II 293.

—*sꜣ*-ox, II 723.

—*wn-dw*-ox, II 723, 742; III 413.

—White ox: offered to Re in Heliopolis, IV 870.

P

PAINT, III 625.
—Painted chariots, II 467, 491, 509; figures, II 601.
—Painters, I 784.

PAIR, IV 241, 394.
—Pairs (=flagstaves), III 244; of *msd.t*-stone, III 246.

PAKHONS: see Months.

PALACE, II 64, 72, 107, 120, 235, 236, 237, 292, 317, 337, 343, 352, 377, 389, 771, 801, 978, 990, 1013, 1026, III 16, 20, 24, 28, 30, 71, 101, 213; 219, 230, 240, 365, 421, 577, 584, 642; IV 52, 91, 99, 209, 412, 678, 749, 848, 882, 932, 944, 958E, 966, 1019; master of, II 352; daily register of, II 393; men of, I 390.
—Footstool of, I 320; Master of: see Index V.
—Palace baths, I 187; Overseer of: see Index V.
—Palace hall, I 187; Leader of: see Index V.
—Secret things of, II 936; Master of: see Index V.
—Laws of, III 101.
—Palaces: of Amenemhet, I 483; decked with gold, I 483; ceiling of lazuli, I 483; doors of copper, I 483; bolts of bronze, I 483; of Ikhnaton, II 987, 989, 990; "Sahure-shines-with-crowns," audience hall of, I 239; House of Amenopet, IV 539; Houses-of-Snefru, wall of southland and northland, I 146; "Structure-of-Beauty," palace of Neferhotep, I 755.
—for palace officials, see Index V under Butlers, Chief, Companion, Conductor, Grandees, Governors, Leader, Lords, Magnates, Master, Overseer, Princes, Ruler, Steward, Storeroom-keeper, Treasurer.
—of a god, III 240; IV 192, 215; at Dêr el-Bahri, II 375.
—Door of the dwellers of the netherworld, III 240.
—Temple palace, IV 338; Chief of: see Index V.

PALANQUIN, IV 958E; poles of, IV 958E.

PALEOGRAPHY, I 31.

PALERMO STONE, I, 76–167; description of, I 76 n. a, 78; location of, I 67 n. a; archaic character, I 77; importance of, I 3, 56, 88.

PALETTE, III 50; see also Ink.

PALM: see Measures, linear.

PALM GROVE, III 473; leaves IV 378, 395.
—Palm fiber, IV 235, 301, 350, 379, 392; see also Date palm, Dom palm.

PANELS: of cedar, IV 929.

PANNIER: of silver, IV 231.

PANTHER, II 80; III 475; IV 46; rage of, II 72, 80, 121, 792; IV 835, 841, 862; from Negro lands, I 136; IV 724; from Genebteyew, II 474.
—Southern panther, II 321; from Punt, II 265, 272; skins of, II 265, 272, 321; III 475; IV 724.

PAOPHI: see Months.

PAPYRI: Abbott, I 421; inscription of, IV 509–535.
—Amherst, I 69 n. a; IV 536–41.
—Anastasi I, IV 713 n. g.
—Anastasi II, III 425–26, 448 n. c.
—Anastasi III, III 629–35.
—Anastasi VI, III 636–38.
—Berlin, No. 3019; I 474 n. d 6.
—Berlin, No. 3029, I 498 n. a.
—British Museum, No. 10053, IV 486;
—Ebers, I 43 n. b.
—Harris 500, I 24, 31, 68 n. e; II 547; IV 35, 60, 84, 145, 151–412; discussion of, IV 151–81.
—Kahun, I 10, p. 48, 67 n. d.
—Lee, IV 416 n. a, 423–56.
—Mayer, IV 544–56.
—Millingen, I 474, n. d 1.
—Rollin, IV 416 n. a, 423–56.
—Sallier I, I 24, 67 n. b, 69 n. g, 474 n. d 2, 3; II 4 n. b.
—Sallier III, III 305 n. c, 315.
—Sinuhe, I 486 n. d.
—Turin, I 52, 53, 54, 55, 56, 59, nn. a, b, c, d, 60 nn. g, h, 61 n. c, 62 n. d, 63 n. f, 64 n. b, 69 n. i, 78 n. a, 79 n. a, 86, 88, 161 n. b, 190, 416, 427, 460, 461; IV 416–56, 595–600.
—Turin fragment, IV 542–43.
—Wenamon, IV 557–91.
—Westcar, I 24, 67 n. b; II 187, 188, 198 n. j; date of, II 188.

PAPYRUS: sandals of, IV 241, 393; rolls of, IV 582.
—Papyrus flowers, IV 244, 264, 295, 394.
—Papyrus plants, IV 215, 271.
—Papyrus rind, IV 238, 241, 294, 393.
—Papyrus stems, IV 244.

PARTIALITY: an abomination to show, II 668.
PASTURE, I 408; pasturage, III 577.
PATERNAL PROPERTY, I 423; IV 874.
PATROL, IV 147.
PAVEMENT (*sꜣ t w*), II 13; IV 958J, M.
—Temple, of silver, IV 7, 671, 672.
PAVILION, II 872.
—in Akhetaton, II 960; name of, II 960; in Medinet Habu, IV 17; name of, IV 17 n. c.
PAYMENT, IV 880, 958G.
PEASANT SERFS, II 536; II 107, 354; IV 125; given as endowment to a mortuary priest, I 630; III 413; made officials, I 281; meaning of name, I 536; duties of, I 536.
—of Amon, II 354; Chief of: see Index V.
PEASANT SLAVES, III 271, 277, 526.
PEASANTRY, III 322; Chiefs of: see Index V.
PEASANTS, IV 539, 821; impost of IV 229.
PEDET BIRDS, IV 242.
PEN, I 5; II 916.
PENALTIES, III 193; for robbing; III 51; extortion, III 54; stealing of slaves, III 55; stealing of hides by army officers, III 56; by soldiers, III 57; bribery, III 64; for stealing from the temples, IV 676; for murder, IV 658.
—Penalty on father entailed upon his posterity, I 778.
PENDANT: of electrum, II 654; rock crystal, IV 287; costly stones, IV 287, 377.
PEOPLE, IV 821, 958; given by the king to Methen, I 175; for endowment of mortuary offerings, I 202, 205, 206, 209; deeded to a god, II 966; distinguished from the inhabitants, I 445; listing the number of, II 916; of the Harem gate, IV 441; of the infantry, IV 466; Advocate of: see Index V; belonging to the temple, IV 146 n. c, 150, 223, 277, 281, 338, 354, 355, 357, 359, 365, 366, 367, 368, 369, 676, 1021.
—People (*rḫy·t*), I 445 bis; II 236, 766, 767, 768, 805, 840, 858, 993, 1002; III 59, 174, 175, 265, 268, 578, 580; IV 43, 47, 398, 921; for Chief of, Master of, see Index V.
—People of the court (*ᶜnḫw*), I 286.
—People (*ḥnmm.t*), IV 47, 188; commands laid upon, II 767; of Naharin, II 858.
—*ḥsb.w*-people, III 192.
—People (*pᶜ.t*), I 445; III 578.
—People (*rmt*), impost from, IV 225, 228.
—People of wax inscribed, for magical purposes, IV 455.
PEOPLE'S BUREAU, II 689 n. d.
PERFUME: festival, for embalmment, I 382 bis; from Retenu, II 518.
PERISTYLE COURT: at Luxor, III 506.
PERSEA TREE, II 294 n. c; IV 385; the hidden, II 298; cut, IV 288.
PESGU WOOD: from Retenu, II 447.
PETITIONER, II 667; right of, to appeal, II 668, 689, 691; summons of, II 685.
PETITIONS: to the king, by Nakht II, concerning landmarks, I 632; to the vizier, II 714, 715; to be in writing, II 691; Hall of: see Hall.
PHALLI: uncircumcised, IV 52, 54; from Libya, III 587, 588, 601 ter.
PHAMENOTH: see Months.
PHARAOH: annals of, I 3, 6, 13, 20; II 621; title applied to the Heracleopolitan kings, I 401; officials of, I 401; lineal descent of, from Re, II 187; daily report to, from vizier, II 678; from chief treasurer, II 678; crown possessions of, IV 466; see also, King's house, and Index V: King.
—Domain of, I 294, 309, 310, 312, 356, 382; Custodian of: see Index V.
PHARMUTHI: see Months.
PHOENIX, HOUSE OF, IV 818 n. e.
PHYLE: pyramid, I 356; Scribe of: see Index V; of priests, IV 468, 753.
PIETY: for departed parents, I 181–85; toward parents, II 37.
PIG (lead), II 493.
PIGEON, II 726, 727, 735, 737; IV 298.
—Pigeon (*mny·t*), IV 242.
PILLAR, III 504; four, II 1029; of heaven, II 376, 601, 656, 889; III 406, 480, 545; IV 720.
—Pillar of heaven (royal title), III 265; see also Index V: Great Pillar.
PILLAR INSCRIPTION: at Gebelên, by Nesubenebded, IV 628–30.

Pillar Inscription—
—at Wadi Halfa, by Nehi, II 412–13.
—Sebuʿa, by Ramses II, III 504.

PITCHER: of gold, IV 735; silver, IV 735.

PIVOTED, IV 343.

PLACE: the great, a part of the Theban necropolis, IV 533, 665, 667; Mut, guardian of, IV 665.
—"Place of Beauty," part of the Theban necropolis, IV 523, 525, 528, 533.
—"Place of Truth," IV 465; meaning of, IV 465 n. f.
—"Place which he knows," IV 272.

PLAN: of battle, I 312; III 307.
—of the Punt reliefs, II 252; of the reliefs of Seti I, III 81; Ramses III, IV 4.
—Plans, II 368, 371, 914, 916; III 24, 50, 180, 207, 266, 270, 510; IV 38, 41, 58, 63, 64, 65, 105, 308, 354, 485, 625.

PLANK, IV 345; see also Gang plank.

PLANTS, IV 262, 272.
—*bʾ-kʾ-yʾ*-plant, IV 234.
—See also, Beni plant, Cyperus, Enbu plant, Flax, Hezet plant, Ideninu plant, Katha plant, Menhet plant, Papyrus, Reeds, Semu plants, Sebkhet plant, Storea, Yufiti plant.

PLASTER: clay as, II 106.

PLEA, IV 351.

PLEASURE LAKE, II 869.

PLEASURE MARSHES, I 745.

PLOWMEN, IV 821.

PLUME, III 610.
—Plumes, the two, III 535; IV 988H; of Onouris, IV 365; of Tatenen, IV 62.
—Double-plumed diadem: see Diadem.

PLUNDER: by the army, II 430, 455, 459.

POEM: of Pentaur, III 305–315; Ramses III, IV 93–99.

POETRY, EGYPTIAN: teaching of Amenemhet I, I 476; tale of Sinuhe, I 486; building inscription of Sesostris I, I 499; teaching of Sehetepibre, I 747–48; hymn of victory by Thutmose III, II 655–62.
—Court poetry, II 188; see also Hymns, Literary.

POLE, IV 379, 391; chariot, II 435, 447; tent, II 435, 490; palanquin, IV 958E; carrying, I 430; IV 315.

POLE HOUSES, in Punt, II 254.

POLICE, IV, 525.
—Chief of, IV 511, 512, 525; see also Index V.

POLITARCH INSCRIPTIONS, I 28.

POMEGRANATES, IV 234, 241, 301, 379, 391.

POOL, III 84, 86, 100, 276, 291, 404; IV 141, 265, 295, 588, 681, 870, 972.
—"Ibsekeb," name of pool, III 86; "Sweet," name of a pool, III 84.
—Pools of Pithom of Merneptah, Hotephirma, III 633.
—"Pool of Horus," a place in Kush(?), tablet placed there by Amenhotep III, II 845.
—Pool of Nun, II 887.
—Pools of the marshes (=Delta), III 31.

POOR: mercy to, I 328, 357; II 767, 768.
—Poor man, laws on robbery of, III 51, 52, 58, 59, 61; on stealing from III 53; extortion from, III 54, 58, 59.

PORT, II 254.

PORTAL, II 889, 903; IV 191.
—Temple portals, II 154, 564, 601, 835, 883, 886; III 525, 528, 567; IV 10, 205, 626; see also Doorways.
—Portals of gold, II 890; electrum, II 883, 895; granite, III 525.

PORTIERS: guarding the gates of the nether world, II 378.

PORTRAIT, II 314; of the king: sphinx, II 802.

POSSESSIONS, IV 851, 874, 876, 958.
—Great in, a title, see Index V.

POST, for balances, IV 288; for scales, IV 391.

POULTRY YARDS, IV 9, 217, 260, 265, 323, 331.

POWER: Ptah, bestower of, III 403; extraordinary, given by magic rolls, IV 455.

PRACTICE OF MAGIC, IV 454–56; forbidden by the gods, IV 455; forbidden in the sacred writings, IV 456.

PRAYER, II 245, 353, 994, 995, 996, 1003, 1008, 1013; III 204, 279, 423,

648; IV 186, 246, 249, 485, 942, 969, 973, 991; inscribed on tablets, IV 202; magical, III 18.
—Mortuary, II 111; III 648, of Zau, I 384; for the Pharaoh, II 97; posture in, II 37.

PRECINCTS OF THE GODS, III 31, 223.

PREDYNASTIC AGE, I 3; kings of, I 78, 79, 90.

PRESENTS FROM RETENU, II 1030; see also Gifts.

PRISON: the great, criminals in, III 683.

PRISONERS OF WAR: brought to Egypt, from Naharin, II 81, 501, 581; III 344; Shasu, II 124; Zahi, II 392; Megiddo, II 402, 431, 435; Negeb, II 580; Tintto-emu, II 15; Negro lands, I 146; II 39, 645; Kush, II 41, 84, 122, 857; Khenthennofer, II 80; prisoners of war from Egypt, II 11; Aleppo, II 798A; Carchemish, II 583; Kadesh, II 585, 798A; Ketne, II 798A; Kharu, II 798A, 821; Kheta, III 342, 344; Niy, II 798A; Retenu the Lower, II 798A; Retenu the Upper, II 798A; Se(n)zar, II 798A; Tehenu, III 134; Thenew, II 798A; Tikhsi, II 487; Wan, II 582.
—Slain before Amon, III 113; see also Captives, Slaves.

PRIVATE AFFAIRS OF HIS LORD, I 423C; private matter (judicial cases of), I 307.

PRIVY CHAMBER, I 200; entered by Ptahshepses, I 256; Sabu-Ibebi, I 286; rank of the master of, II 675.
—Privy council, II 352.
—Privy office in charge of Thethi, I 423C.

PROCEEDINGS: legal, IV I 204, 310; IV 423–43.

PROCESSION, I 540, 669; II 357, 571, 618; III 212; IV 611, 727, 749, 761, 768, 836, 988J.
—Procession of a god, II 133, 139, 300; of Harendotes, II 181; Amon, II 608; of Hathor, II 357; of Mut, II 357; of Ptah, II 615; at feast: "Beginning-of-the-Seasons," II 615.

PRODIGIES, II 187; see also Wonder.

PROPERTY, I 551, 570; II 840; IV 767, 946; temple, IV 251, 277, 280, 927; registered in the office of vizier, II 688; confiscation of, I 779; IV 1024.

PROSECUTION: of the queen of Pepi I, I 310; in the harem conspiracy, IV 425, 444, 446, 451; of practicers of magic, IV 454–56.

PROSTRATION (in prayer), IV 1018; see also Kissing the ground.

PROVERB, III 611.

PROVISION, III 230; IV 944; see also Magazine.

PROW, II 251, 797.

PTOLEMAIC PERIOD, I 24; II 189.

PUBLIC ARCHIVES: (place of writings), I 270.

PUNISHMENT: to be inflicted when cause is given for, II 668; IV 424;
—Punishment, executed, IV 426, 427, 428, 429, 430, 431, 432, 433, 435, 436, 437, 438, 439, 440, 441, 442, 443, 452; punishment not executed, IV 444, 453; punishment of death, IV 454.
—Consisting of: placing upon the rack, IV 524; cutting off the noses and ears, IV 451, 452, 524; see also Imprisonment.

PURE HOUSE: of Debhen, I 212; see also House.

PURIFICATION, II 568; at coronation, II 216, 240; of temples, IV 905 *et passim;* of kings, IV 843 *et passim;* endowment for, I 209.

PYLON, II 889, 894, 917; III 505, 508; IV 621, 626, 632, 707; double, II 906; III 525.
—Pylon III: in Karnak, erected by Amenhotep III, II 885, 889, 903.
—Pylon IV, IV 889 n. a.
—Pylon VI, II 402 n. a, 520 n. f, 541 n. a, 646.
—Pylon VII: at Karnak, II 404, 647; fragment of, II 593–98.
—Pylon VIII, 403 n. b.
—Pylon XI, III 34 n. a.
—Pylon: in temple of Karnak, erected by Amenhotep II, II 795; made of sandstone, II 795.
—Pylons: at Karnak temple, the two of Thutmose I, II 103, 304, 317; of Hatshepsut, II 243.
—Pylon: western, built by Amenhotep III, II 885.
—Pylons: at Abydos' temple, II 246.
—Pylon towers, III 269, 356 n. a.

Pylon—
—Pylon inscriptions: see under Inscriptions.
PYRAMID, III 577; IV 539; base of, IV 517; investigation of, IV 513; upper chamber of, I 322; Attached to, Overseer of: see Index V.
—Pyramid: "Shelter-of-Shepseskaf," I 151.
—"The-Soul-of-Sahure-Shines," I 159, 249.
—of Zoser, terraced, I 170; Methen buried beside it, I 170.
—of Khufu, I 180.
—of Henutsen, daughter of Khufu, I 180.
—"Great-is-Khafre," I 184.
—"Great-is-Khafre," I 202, 205, 206, 208, 209.
—"Divine-is-Menkure," I 211 bis.
—Temple of Menkure, I 212.
—of Hir, I 212, 212 n. c.
—"Isesi-is-[Beautiful]," I 274.
—"Horizon-of-Khufu," I 275.
—Teti, at Sakkara, I 289.
—of the queen of Mernere: "Mernere-Shines-and-is-Beautiful," I 321, 322 bis, 323, 324, 345.
—"Pepi-Remains-Beautiful," I 356.
—"Neferkere-Remains-Living," I 341, 346, 356; domain of, I 374.
—"Merire-Remains-Beautiful," I 341, 345, 346.
—"Fame-of-Ity," I 387.
—Brick pyramid of Intef I, on the western plain of Thebes, I 423C n. f; containing the mortuary stela of Intef I, I 423, 424; investigated by the Ramessid inspectors, IV 514; now disappeared, I 423G n. f; of Amenemhet I, in Kenofer, I 490 n. a.
—of Sesostris I, at Lisht, I 507 n. b; pyramid chapel, of Sesostris I, at Lisht, I 507, 508 n. b; columns, lake, gates of, I 509; stairway of I 528.
—"Amenu-kherep," of Amenemhet II, I 601.
—of Tetisheri, II 36.
—of Mentuhotep II, IV 520.
—of Ahmose-Sepir, IV 519.
—of Kemose, IV 519.
—of Sekenenre-Taoo, IV 518.
—of Sekenenre-Tao, IV 518.
—of Sekhemre-Shedtowe-Sebekemsaf, IV 517.
—of Sekhemre-Upmat-Intefo, IV 516; stela of, IV 516.
—of Nubkheprure-Intef, IV 515.
—of Intefo, IV 514; stela of, IV 514; king's figure of, IV 514.
—Pyramid city, governors of: see Index V.
PYRAMIDION, I 321; II 313, 624, 630. 633; of electrum, II 624, 630, 633, 834; limestone, IV 982.
—in Mehenet of Sais, IV 982; of Sesostris I, I 503.
PYRAMIDION HOUSE: of Heliopolis, IV 871.

Q.

QUARRY: opened, IV 704, 705.
—of Gebelên, IV 629;
—of Miam, IV 474.
—of alabaster, at Hatnub, I 7, 305, 323, 695 n. b, 696; location of, I 695.
—of black basalt, at Hammamat, I 675.
—of granite, at Assuan, I 42; II 304; at Elephantine, I 322; at First Cataract, I 324; Ibhet, I 321, 322; at Silseleh, I 49.
—of gritstone, at Gebel el-Ahmar, near Cairo, II 906 n. a.
—of limestone, at Ma ᶜ sara: see Index VI; at Troja, I 210, 212, 239, 274, 289, 290, 307, 509; II 800, 875.
—of sandstone, at Silseleh, I 49; II 935; III 205 n. c; IV 18, 701 n. d.
—Quarry inscriptions: see under Inscriptions, Rock.
QUARRY CHAMBERS: opened, I 740; III 27, 799, 800, 875.
QUARRY SERVICE, I 390; II 935; men of the palace, I 390; soldiers, I 390; quarrymen of, I 390; IV 19, 537; chiefs of, II 935; IV 466, 474.
QUARRYMEN, I 390, 447, 697, 710; III 172; IV 466; works of, IV 466; master workmen of, IV 466.
QUARTERS: temple, IV 992; of foals, IV 850.
QUARTZOSE: black, stela of, III 427 n. a.
QUAY: of Elephantine, IV 146 n. c; of Karnak, I 22; IV 693 n. a.
QUEEN: titles of, I 341; herald of: see Index V.
QUIVER, II 785; III 450; IV 70; Libyan, III 584; from Meshwesh, IV 111.

R

RACK: witness placed upon, IV 524.

RAIMENT, II 719; of a god, IV 966.

RAISED WORK, IV 231, 302, 319; of costly stones, IV 315.

RAISINS, IV 301, 350.

RAM, IV 589; divine shadow in form of, II 596, 889 n. a; Ptah-Tatenen, lord of Mendes in form of a, III 400; as adornments of temples, II 894, 895; IV 635 n. d, 649.
—Rams' heads: as adornment of sacred barge, made of gold, IV 209.

RAMP, IV 189, 355, 356, 357, 358.

RAMPART, II 596, 616, IV 55, 118, 856, 861.

RANK, I 307, 312, 332; II 1040; IV 995; of the official body of the temple, I 550; III 565, 623.

RATIONS: daily, for the soldiers, I 431; III 207, 208; of meat and fowl, I 372.

REAL ESTATE: cases of, II 686, 688; see also Estate, Property.

REAP, IV 893; see also Harvest.

REAR: of the army, II 427.
—of foreign armies, IV 46; rearguard, I 680; II 421.

REBELLION: in Memphis, IV 928; Heracléopolis, I 399; Menet-Khufu, I 625; of Egyptians, II 11, 15, 16; Kush, II 844; Shasu, III 101; Oasis, IV 726; Askalon, III 355. See also Revolt, Insurrection.

REBELS, III 580; IV 62, 130, 857, 871, 990.

RECORDING, II 555; IV 679.

RECORDS: III 580; IV 178, 460; Assyro-Babylonian, I 3; Egyptian, I 3; of nomes, kept by vizier, II 703; legal, copy of, IV 535; the mysterious, III 410; in temple at Thebes, of XXI Dyn., I 22; boundary, I 531; daily, kept by Thutmose III, II 392, 433, 455, 540; for the future, II 568;
—of Pharaoh, III 647; overseer of, I 348.
—of the vizier, II 684; loan of, II 684.
—of Thoth, III 448 n. b.
—Records of Restorations: of Hatshepsut at Benihasan, I 15; of mummies, IV 592–94.
—of Nile levels, I 22, 95–169; IV 695–98; 793–94, 886–88.
—of offerings, IV 1022.

RECRUITS: crew of, I 343; II 332; III 340; IV 70; commander of, I 512; youth of, I 527, 697; scribe of, II 916; III 17.

RED CONGLOMERATE: from the Red Mountain, I 493 n. b. See Gritstone.

REEDS, IV 234, 287, 378, 391.
—Reed grass, IV 241.

REFECTORY, III 624; IV 958J.

REFORMS: of Harmhab, I 18; see also Laws, Enactments.

REGALIA, II 788; IV 29, 142, 401; of Horus and Set, IV 62; of Re, IV 142; made of costly stone, IV 9.

REGISTER: of property, II 688; of boundaries, II 689; daily, in the palace, II 393, 472.

REGULATIONS, II 568, 666; petitions handled according to, II 667; of the ancestors, III 536.
—of impost, III 210; of temple plans, III 263; of army, II 695; of prophets, II 754; of priests, IV 250; of Sed jubilees, IV 414; of commandant, II 298.
—House regulations engraved on tablets, IV 202.

RELEASE: from taxes, III 57, 63.

RELIEFS:
—Snefru, I 169.
—Khufu, I 176.
—Nekonekh, I 226.
—Sahure, I 236.
—Persen, I 241.
—Nuserre, I 250.
—Menkuhor, I 263.
—Isesi, I 264.
—Senezemib, I 276.
—Pepi, I 302.
—Mernere, I 317, 318.
—Mentuhotep II, I 425.
—Mentuhotep IV, I 435.
—Mentuhotep, I 514.
—Sesostris I, I 510.
—Sesostris I, I 510.
—Sesostris II, I 617.
—Sesostris III, I 643, 646.
—Thuthotep, I 694, 695, 699, 704–6.
—Sehetepibre, I 744.
—Yuf, II 110.
—Thutmose I, II 244.
—Thutmose II, II 125 n. e, 168, 173.
—Hatshepsut, I 13; II 192, 193, 195,

199, 202, 204, 205, 206, 208, 209, 210, 211, 212, 216, 217, 226, 228, 231, 234, 240, 241; the Punt reliefs, II 246–51, 252, 254, 259, 263, 266, 267, 270, 273, 275, 279, 283, 289, 305; obelisk, II 312, 323, 330, 336; bas-relief, II 337; stela, II 338.
—Senmut, II 359, 363.
—Puemre, II 382, 385.
—Thutmose III, II 450 n. a, 543–46, 645, 646, 653, 655.
—Rekhmire, II 712, 714, 717, 747, 752, 753, 756, 761, 762.
—Menkheperreseneb, II 773, 774.
—Amenhotep II, II 781, 791, 798A, 807.
—Thutmose IV, II 811, 819.
—Amenhotep III, II 187–212, 215–42, 841, 843, 845, 871, 872, 874, 876, 879, 904.
—Khamhet, II 870, 871, 872.
—Ikhnaton, II 933, 978, 981, 982, 986, 989, 1014, 1016, 1017, 1018.
—Ramose, II 938, 941, 944.
—Bek, II 974, 976.
—Huy, II 1014, 1016.
—Tutenkhamon, II 1021, 1028, 1035.
—Huy, II 1022–24, 1035, 1039–40.
—Harmhab, III 2, 5–9, 10–13, 15, 18, 20, 34, 37.
—Neferhotep, III 69, 73.
—Seti I, III 80–156, 163, 165, 203.
—Ramses II, III 255, 258, 284, 328–51, 354, 397, 415, 431, 450, 452, 454, 457, 460, 462, 464, 468, 470, 473, 475, 481, 485, 496, 539.
—Merneptah, III 594, 597, 628.
—Roy, III 626 n. c, 628.
—Siptah, III 647, 648.
—Ramses III, IV 25, 29–34, 49–57, 69–82, 99–114, 117–30, 132–35, 137–38, 184, 246, 305.
—Ramses IV, IV 458, 463.
—Ramses VI, IV 476, 477.
—Ramses VII, IV 484.
—Ramses IX, IV 493.
—Hrihor, IV 611, 612, 613, 614, 621, 626.
—Sheshonk I, IV 702, 709–718.
—Osorkon II, IV 749–50; 757–70.
—Pediese, IV 779.
—Weshtehet, IV 783.
—Piankhi, IV 814, 815.
—Mentemhet, IV 903, 909.

Religious Literature, I 2, 20.

Renewal of Burial, IV 499, 593.

Rent of Fields, IV 482.

Report: on battles, IV 834; on harvest, II 871; on judgments, II 681; of Wenamon, IV 557–91; from the overseers of the interior, II 677, 708.
—of chief treasurer, I 423D; II 676, 678, 679; to chief treasurer, I 428, 445; II 679.
—from vizier, II 678, 679; to vizier, II 676, 677, 679.
—from doorkeeper of judgment hall, II 711.
—from the fortresses, II 676, 702.
—from navy officers, II 710.
—from the court, II 676, 679; from the king's house, II 676, 679.

Reptiles, II 984.

Residence, III 406.
—"House-of-Ramses-Meriamon-Given-Life," name of residence of Ramses II, III 406.
—Residence city, I 628; garrison of, II 694.

Resin, of myrrh, II 265.

Resting-place: of a god, III 213, 215, 224, 246, 510, 515; of noblemen, IV 511.

Restitution: ordered in cases of robbery and theft, III 53.

Restorations: of temples, II 152, 157, 612; III 31, 537; IV 178, 179, 276, 357, 358, 359, 360, 634, 659, 897–99, 909–916, 966, 968, 1022; of tomb, II 112; III 32B; of inscription, I 15; II 192 n. d; II 573, 856, 878, 896, 968; III 200; wall of Luxor, IV 627–30; mummies, IV 592–94, 637–47.

Revenues, IV 949; for the gods, II 793.

Revolt: by Negroes, II 826; by Nubia, II 121; Kush, II 844; Ibhet, II 853; Gezer, III 606; Wawat, III 606 n. a.
—of high priest of Amon, IV 486.

Rewards, II 583, 584, 585, 587, 588, 872, 926, 944; III 6, 73, 486, 643; IV 471, 492, 494, 611, 633, 708, 879.

Rings: of silver, II 584; of *b*ꜣ-*b*ꜣ-*y*ꜣ, IV 377.
—Commercial: see Gold, Silver.
—Earrings, IV 876.
—Seal rings of Thethi, I 423D.

Rites, IV 988J.
—Ritual roll of fields, III 271.

River, the Living, II 378; water of, II 925; see Living stream.
—River-mouths, IV 44; see also Index VI.

Road, IV 1004, 1006, 1007; to Yam, I 333; of Elephantine, I 334; of

Uhet, I 335; from Yehem to Aruna, II 421; to Taanach, II 421; to Zefti, II 421.

Roast: for food, III 207; for mortuary offering, I 569, 571; II 571.

Robbery, IV 147, 150, 566; laws on, III 51, 52; by soldiers, forbidden by Uni, I 312.

Robe of Mek-Linen, IV 232.

Rock Inscriptions: see Inscriptions.

Rod, II 758; beating with, IV 548, 549, 550, 551, 552, 553, 555.
—Ipet-rod, II 995.

Roll, III 50; IV 483; of papyrus, IV 582; of names, IV 545; of testimony, IV 534; of the house of Osiris, I 758.
—House of rolls, III 264, 410.
—Leather rolls for daily records, II 392, 433.
—Ritual roll of fields, III 271.
—*šw*-rolls, II 742.

Roman Prefects of Egypt, I 28.

Roof, Temple, IV 315.

Rope of Palm Fiber, IV 235, 379, 392; coils of, IV 582.

Rosemary, IV 234, 344, 378, 392.

Rowing, II 809.

Rudder, I 493; III 291.

Rug: under the feet of the vizier, II 675.

Ruler's Table, IV 695; Commandant of: see Index V.

Rules, IV 908; obsolete, IV 908; of war IV 861.

S

Sacks, II 263, 735, 750; III 37; IV 32; of myrrh, II 263; of grain, II 319; IV 550; of gold dust, III 37; silver, IV 566.

Sacred Animals: see Animals.
—Sacred writing, II 353; forbidding practice of magic, IV 456; house of, I 533; IV 445, 460.

Sacrifice, IV 857; of the gazelle at Hammamat, I 436; of goats, I 453; of cattle, I 453. See Offering.

Sacrificial Tablet of Silver, IV 199.

Sailors, I 275, 360; IV 825, 858, 859; for Captain of, Chief of, Commander of, see Index V.

Sails, II 798; IV 578, 944.

"Salâm": said by Libyans, III 617; IV 43; by Meshwesh, IV 97.

Salt, IV 235, 241, 379, 392.
—*spr*-salt, IV 299, 348.
—Salt-gatherers of Elephantine, IV 148.

Sanctuary, II 298, 300, 540, 555, 758, 935, 987, 994; III 16, 178, 240; IV 141, 251, 471, 678.
—of the South, endowment of, I 156, 159.

Sandals, I 312, 430; II 148, 245, 268, 303, 451, 656; III 84, 156, 159, 204, 359, 371, 450, 465, 471, 584; IV 412.
—Made of leather, IV 241, 394; of papyrus, IV 241, 393.

Sandstone, II 389, 601, 775, 903; IV 914; chapel of, II 152; Holy of Holies of, II 153; pylon of, II 795; III 505; columns of, II 795; IV 910; lakes constructed of, IV 910, 912; temple of, II 157 n. c, 611, 614, 883, 886, 890, 895, 898, 905; III 216, 217, 220, 500, 507, 510, 512, 515, 521, 522; IV 4, 7, 9, 14, 189, 195, 214, 602, 603, 610, 625, 649, 897, 898, 899; adytum of, II 639; IV 14; doorways of, II 792; doorposts of, III 625; great seat of, IV 5, 14; tower of, IV 189; stelæ of, I 510 n. a, 753 n. a; II 54 n. a, 90 n. g; 109 n. b, 904 n. a; III 157 n. a.
—Sandstone from Red Mountain, II 153.
—Sandstone mountain, at Abu Simbel, III 500.
—Quarry of, at Silsileh, II 935; III 205 n. c; IV 18, 701 n. d.

Sarcophagus, I 253; presented by the king, I 269, 273, 275, 307; of Mernere: "Chest-of-the-living," I 321; of ancestor of Kheti, I 402; of Mentuhotep IV, I 436, 448; of Apis, IV 1011.

Scales, IV 391; post for, IV 391.

Scarabs: of Thutmose III, II 625 n. f; Amenhotep III, II 859, 861–62, 863–64, 865, 866–67, 868–89.
—Made of black granite, IV 191; bronze, IV 233; costly stone, IV 377, 390; lapis lazuli, IV 233, 285, 343; malachite, II 233, 285, 343; minu stone, IV 233; red jasper, IV 233, 377; rock crystal, IV 377.

Scepter (*w ˀ s*), Royal, I 646; II 436; IV 493.

Scientific Treatises, I 20; on medicine, I 20; mathematics, I 20; astronomy, I 20.

Scourge, Royal, III 69; IV 62.
—Scourging as penalty on soldiers for stealing hides, III 57.

Scout, Border, III 616; Egyptian III 321, 330, 334, 578; Hittite, III 321, 322, 330.
—Scouting, II 916.

Scraps: of bronze, IV 343; copper, IV 373, 385, 389; gold, IV 373, 386, 389; silver, IV 231, 343, 373, 386, 389.

Sculptors, IV 466; Chief of: see Index V.

Sculpture, III 517, 519; IV 311.
—Sculptured stone, I 500; IV 191.

Seal, II 182, 185, 239, 352; IV 353, 689, 871, 908.
—as pendant, of costly stone, IV 233, 377, 290.
—Hittite seal, III 391.
—Made of gold, II 32; rock crystal, IV 233, 303, 345, 349, 377; ubat stone, IV 287, 377; wrought wood, IV 234, 284, 345, 391.
—Seal of writings, I 274; royal, I 351; II 1022; of privy office, I 423C; of office, II 1024, 1025.
—Seal of *sḏm˙w*-officers, II 684.
—Seal ring, I 423 D; II 32 n. a.
—Seal-scribe: see Index V.

Sealing, II 371; of treasury, reported to vizier, II 676; of property lists by vizier, II 688; of boundaries by vizier, II 689; edicts to navy, II 710.

Seasons of the Year, I 387 *et passim*.

Seat, the Great: of a god, II 640, 901, 908, 987; III 230, 233, 237, 240, 242, 260, 269, 525; IV 5, 7, 14, 201, 251, 311, 315, 319, 331; =tomb, IV 523, 533.
—Made of alabaster, III 525, 529; electrum, IV 14, 610; gold, IV 7, 250; sandstone, IV 5.

Sebkhet Plant, IV 235, 392.

Secrets, I 755; of court, I 377; of heaven, II 936; of heaven, earth, and nether world, II 936; III 623; of the divine book, II 915; Masters of: see Index V.
—Secret chambers of the mountains, II 946.
—Secret chapel, III 412.
—Secret mine of Sinai, I 266.
—Secret things of his majesty, I 270, 285, 305, 423C, 533 bis, 534, 668; from the double *wᶜb.t*-house, for Mekhu's funeral, I 370; of the palace, II 936; of the temple, I 550, 745; IV 706, 708; of the king's wardrobe, I 608.
—Secret words, IV 321.
—Secret writings, II 355, 748.

Sedan Chair, II 981.

"Seed is Not": said of Libyans, III 604; IV 91; Seped, III 604; IV 91; Tehenu, IV 87; Meshwesh, III 604; IV 43; Amor, III 604; IV 39; Israel, III 603, 617; Temeh, IV 50, 58; northerners, IV 66.

Seher, Statue of, IV 302.

Semdets: of irer stone, IV 377; rock crystal, IV 377; hirset stone, IV 377; red jasper, IV 377; hukȧmu stone, IV 377; costly stone, IV 377.

Semu Plant, IV 240, 344, 378, 392.

Sepulchers: inspection of, IV 511, 521; investigation of, IV 513.
—Sepulcher chamber, IV 540.

Serf Laborers, III 566; IV 402; of necropolis, IV 525; of temple, IV 313, 321, 354, 358, 360, 362, 386.

Serfs, IV 932.

Serfs, Peasant, I 281, 536, 630; II 107; III 277; IV 933.

Serpent, II 300; IV 922; as adornments, II 888; as sign for Aphroditopolis, I 423 n. a.

Serpent Crest, IV 38, 130, 335, 721, 814, 882; the double, IV 895.

Servant There (=myself), I 372 *et passim*.

Servants, II 989; III 9; of the Negroes, II 854.

Sesha Birds, IV 242, 298, 347.

Setting of Tomb, I 308.

Settlements, III 141, 270; IV 147, 278, 281; of Naharin, II 479; of Kharu, II 884; of Tehenu, III 611; of women in temples, IV 321.

Shadow: king as, IV 47, 71, 72, 103, 850, 854.
—Divine shadow (term for the manifestation of a god), II 104, 302 n. a, 596, 889, 890, 907.
—Shadow of Re, name for "temple of Aton" in Akhetaton, II 956, 1016, 1017, 1018; IV 363.

SHEAF, III 404.

SHED BIRD, II 571.

SHEDEH (=wine), IV 213, 228, 233, 239, 262, 269, 272, 283, 286, 292, 299, 309, 313, 329, 335, 344, 376, 387, 390, 468, 734, 768.
—Shedeh gardens of Re, IV 262.

SHEEP, IV 41.

SHELLS: from Punt, II 272.

SHELTER, IV 992.

SHENE FISH, IV 243.

SHEPHERD, THE GOOD: royal title, II 900; III 195, 580; of the cattle of Amon, IV 212.

SHESA FRUIT, IV 378, 395.

SHIELD, III 475, 489; IV 74, 105; from Retenu, II 509; Kush, II 1035.
—Amon as, III 581; IV 72, 246.
—King as, IV 57, 62.
—Made of leather, II 802.

SHIP, IV 354, 566, 571, 576, 578, 586, 599, 678, 767, 821, 825, 831, 840, 861, 863, 864, 873, 879, 883, 1003, 1005, 1006, 1007; royal, II 7, 332; captives taken in, II 15; cabin of, IV 840; Captain of, see Index V; made of cedar, I 146, 465; II 32, 94, 492; IV 209, 574.
—Temple ship, IV 19, 147, 193, 209, 270.
—Ship (=sacred barge of Osiris), II 183.
—Ships of Ahmose I: "The Offering," II 7; "Shining in Memphis," II 8.
—"Star-of-the-Two-Lands," II 332 n. d.
—Byblos ship, IV 574; made of cedar, II 492.
—Keftyew ship in Zahi, II 492.
—Ships of Sidon, IV 574.
—Thekel ships, IV 588.
—Ships from Zahi, II 460, 492.
—Large ship, I 308; III 441.
—Dewatowe ships, I 146, 147.
—Sixteen barges, I 146.
—Sektu ship, in Sahi, II 492.
—*wsḫ*-ships, IV 19.
—*mnš*-ship, III 274.
—See also Barges, Barques, Boats, Treasure-ship, Troop-ship, Vessels, Warships.

SHIPBUILDING, I 138, 146; at Red Sea by Enenkhet, I 360 n. e; by Henu, I 432.

SHOOTING, IV 842.

SHORES, II 966.

SHRINES, I 156, 667, 787; II 126, 127, 197, 198, 201, 375, 376, 380, 390, 606, 607, 889 n. a; III 237; IV 250, 254, 312, 320, 539, 908; the seat of a god, II 374; monolithic, IV 198, 320.
—Shrine of a barge, called "great house," IV 331, 354; in the sacred barge of Amon, II 888; IV 209.
—Barque shrine, of fine gold, IV 982.
—Portable shrine, I 667; II 173; IV 315, 599.
—"The Horizon of the God," probably in Dêr el-Bahri temple, II 374; Sekhet Re, a shrine in the temple of Atum in Heliopolis, see Index II; in temple of Khonsu at Karnak, IV 609.
—Doors of, II 156, 889 n. a; IV 198; hall of, II 775; statues of, II 156, 889 n. a.
—Made of carob wood, I 667; ebony, II 127; electrum, II 374, 776, 888; IV 1020; fragrant wood I 667; gold, I 667; IV 209, 331; granite, II 376, 775; IV 198, 254, 319; lazuli, I 667; meru wood, I 667; silver, I 667; stone, II 156.
—Water carrier of, IV 539.
—Shrine chamber, III 529.
—Shrine inscription: see Inscriptions.

SHROUD OF MYSTERIOUS LINEN, IV 1011.

SIEGE, IV 861.

SIEVE OF SILVER, IV 203, 231.

SIFTING VESSEL OF SILVER, IV 203, 231.

SILVER, II 280, 342, 383, 390, 434, 558, 601, 720, 722, 723, 727, 730, 732, 733, 734, 735, 739, 740, 771, 773, 887, 902, 992, 993; III 63, 71, 137, 151, 204, 210, 309, 428, 434, 453, 512, 515, 527; IV 7, 27, 29, 30, 31, 32, 126, 141, 150, 190, 228, 230, 245, 256, 259, 272, 283, 284, 285, 313, 335, 341, 342, 349, 354, 360, 372, 373, 383, 385, 386, 387, 388, 389, 494, 521, 568, 576, 577, 580, 582, 635, 680, 681, 682, 683, 684, 685, 686, 687, 708, 732, 733, 734, 735, 736, 737, 847, 852, 859, 875, 876, 878, 881, 883, 889, 909, 958E, G.
—Commercial: in rings, II 436, 485, 490, 518, 1035; sack, IV 566; crude, IV 285; in scraps, IV 231, 343, 373, 386, 389.
—as material for vessels, II 162.
—as ardornment of other objects, II 32, 92, 165, 185, 301, 375, 435, 883,

888; IV 312, 315, 538; temple floors adorned with, II 806, 886, 889, 890.
—as reward of honor, III 6, 73.
—Articles made of silver: altars, IV 735, 736, 737; amulet IV 319, 373, 386; bowls, IV 735; candelabra, IV 735; cartouche vessel, IV 735; casket, IV 231; drinking-vessels (*ṯb.w*), III 589; IV 476, 477; flat dishes, II 447; IV 735; hin-vessel, IV 735; spouted vessel, IV 735; axe, II 24; jars, II 32; drinking-vessels for the ka, II 32; great pails, II 32; sphinxes, II 32; inlay figures, IV 489; offering-tablets, IV 735; pannier, IV 231; rings, II 584; sieve, IV 203, 231; sifting-vessel, IV 203, 231; censer, I 500: offering-tables, I 534; II 175, 390; IV 610, 911, 912, 958M, 1020; shrine, I 667; pitcher, IV 735; statues, II 436; IV 250, 268, 302, 316, 326, 349, 395; table vessels, IV 190, 269, 354, 357; tablet, III 371, 372, 373, 386, 387, 388, 391; IV 202, 231, 285, 317, 343; temple pavement, IV 7, 671, 672; vase, I 500; II 32, 164, 754; IV 203, 231, 269, 327, 538; vessels, II 615, 795, 1028, 1031, 1035; III 106; IV 343, 476, 497, 566, 730, 992; *dw*-vessels of, IV 735.
—House of silver, II 352; Overseer of: see Index V.
—Silver from the malachite country, IV 409; Naharin, II 482; III 434; Kheta, II 485; III 420; Senzar, II 584; God's Land, III 116, 274; Libya, III 584; Retenu, II 447, 491, 518, 533(?), 820; Assur, II 446; Zahi, II 459, 490.
—Silver house, the double, I 533, 664; II 43, 52, 377.

SILVERSMITHS, II 754.

SINGER, IV 589; temple, II 1018.
—Singing women: of the house of the divine votress of Amon-Re, IV 521, 543; of Amon-Re, IV 641, 755.

SIRIUS (Sothis): reappearance of, I 40; to be observed by the vizier, II 709; see also Sothic.

SISTER-WIFE, IV 774.

SISTRUM, II 995; III 414; IV 847, 943; *sḫm*, II 93; *šsy.t*, II 93.
—Sistrum-bearer: Mut, the, IV 733; of Harsaphes in Heracleopolis, IV 792.

SITTING: of the court, II 292; in the vizier's hall, II 675.

SKINS: of southern panther, II 260, 321, 474, 486; IV 724; *M-ḫ ꜣ-w-*, II 449; see also Hides.
—Water-skins of Libya, III 609, 610.

SKINS, THE 40, CONTAINING THE LAW, II 675, 712; III 45.

SLANDER, IV 533.

SLAUGHTERING BLOCK, II 149.
—Slaughter yards, IV 190.

SLAVES, III 82; king's, IV 846; for temples, II 402 n. c, 555 881, 884; III 78, 138, 160; IV 200, 217, 220, 225, 257, 322, 338, 355, 356, 359, 360, 404, 680, 682, 687, 1021; mortuary temples, II 924, 925, 926; III 271; peasant slaves, III 271.
—Slaves: from Khenthennofer, II 14; Tintto-emu, II 15; Punt, II 486; Kush, II 493, 502, 514, 522, 526; Wawat, II 487, 494, 503, 515; Asiatic, II 555, 587; IV 217; Syrian (*Ḫ ꜣ-rw*), II 555; Avaris, II 12; Sharuhen, II 13; Tikhsi, II 587; Retenu, II 436, 447, 467, 471, 491, 509, 518, 533; Zahi, II 460, 462; Naharin, II 480, 482; Arrapachitis, II 512.
—Slave service: laws on, III 55.
—Stealing of slaves, III 55; penalty for, III 55.

SLINGERS: slinging stones, IV 842.

SMITING: of the Northerners, I 81; the Troglodytes, I 81, 104, 176.

SOCIETY, CLASSES OF: count (*ḥ ꜥ ty-ꜥ*), I 536; official (*šr*), I 536; citizen (*nḏs*), I 536; peasant (*y ꜥ ḥty*), I 536; see also these subjects in Index V and under People.

SOLDIERS, I 390, 410; II 299, 335; III 40, 195, 271, 616; IV 55, 65, 71, 97, 822, 825, 838, 841, 858, 863, 878; provision of, while on march, I 430; heads cut off from, II 225; penalty for stealing hides by, III 57.
—Soldiers of Bekhten, III 442, 444, 446.

SON-IN-LAW: Ptahshepses of Shepseskaf, I 54.

SORCERESS: Mut, the great, I 141; the two great, II 314.
—Sorcery: Wereret, great in, II 288; see also Bewitching, Magic.

SOTHIC CALENDAR: early existence of, I 45.
—Sothic cycle, length of, I 44.
—Sothic date: of Amenhotep I, I 51,

64; of Thutmose III, I 66 n. h; of Kahun Papyrus, I p. 48.
—Sothic year, longer than calendar year, I 40.
—Sothis (Sirius), I 40; feast of, I 40; difference between feast and heliacal rising of, I 41; late rising of, in XII Dyn., I 42, 53; Sothic date in reign of Thutmose III, I 43, 51; II 410 n. a; Sothic date in reign of Ramses III, I 43 n. b.
SOUL: living with Osiris, II 378.
—Souls of Amon, II 154.
—Souls of Anubis: temple of Upwawet, a monument for, I 403.
SOUTHERN FRUIT, IV 240, 378, 393.
SOUTHERN PALACE, WAYS OF, I 258, 283, 286.
SPAN (of horses), III 84, 88, 97, 100, 132, 134, 312, 330, 337, 361, 486; IV 72.
—Royal, names of, III 84 bis, 88, 97, 100, 132, 134, 312, 330, 347, 361; IV 72, 73, 77, 106, 107, 120, 123.
SPAN: see Measures, linear.
SPARS, IV 861.
SPEARS, II 784; III 457; IV 70, 119; from Meshwesh, IV 111.
—of bronze: from Retenu, II 509, 525; Wan, II 582.
SPEECH OF EGYPT, I 494; correct in, I 413; II 571; throne, II 291–95; of Punt chiefs, III 37.
SPELT, I 496; II 149, 171; III 66; IV 250, 314, 325, 354, 359, 550, 859, 955, 958H, 992.
SPHINX, I 177; IV 649 n. e; of Harmakhis, I 179, 180; of Seti I, in his temple in Kurna, III 114; of Ramses II, in his temple in Memphis, III 531.
—Sphinx portraits, II 802.
—Sphinxes made of gold, IV 732; lapis lazuli, IV 732; silver, II 32.
—Stela, of Thutmose IV, II 810–15.
SPIRIT: land of, I 351; king to be a, III 511.
—Evil spirit, possessed of, III 438, 440, 444; speech of, III 444.
SPLENDORS, II 292, 308; in heaven, II 358.
SPOIL AT MEGIDDO, II 431.
SPRINGS, IV 726, 727, 728.
SPY, III 319; beating of, III 330.
STABL ANTAR: modern name of the temple of Pakht at Benihasan, II 296 n. c; names of, III 337, 347; IV 123.
STABLE, ROYAL: III 312, 330, 337, 347, 361, 635, 645; IV 106, 123, 822, 850, 852, 874, 875, 876, 877; filth of, IV 968; chief of, II 818; III 198; IV 466; charioteer of, III 635.
STAFF, III 450; king's, I 296; II 986; official's, II 385, 1039; III 13; of statue, II 436.
—Crook staff, IV 62.
—Made of carob wood, II 436; ebony, IV 288; of electrum, I 682; meru wood, IV 288; *Ṯ* ͗ *-gw*-wood, II 536.
—Staff of old age, I 692; II 916.
—See also Staves.
STAIR OF TOMB OF KHETI II, I 412; of of shrine, of alabaster, II 375.
STAIRCASE, THE DOUBLE, III 406.
STAIRWAYS OF TEMPLES, I 421, 528, 673, 684; II 150; IV 909, 915; of tomb, I 577.
STAKE: for the ground plan of the temple, I 506.
STALL, IV 874; see Stable.
STALLIONS, II 435, 875.
STANDARD (containing royal Horus name), II 143.
—Standard (for supporting the image of a god), II 303; of electrum, II 95; of Amon, IV 49.
—Standard, of drinking-vessel, for the ka, of silver, II 32.
—Standard bearers: impost from, IV 225; see also Index V.
STARS, II 886, 894; III 232; in the body of Nut, II 164; unresting, III 278; shooting, IV 62, 91.
—Pole star, IV 304; Orion, II 828; circling star, II 658; III 117; "imperishable," II 318; III 378; IV 852.
—Star of electrum: royal title, II 900.
—Star of the South, I 511.
STATE FICTION, II 187–90.
STATEMENTS, II 377, 437, 555, 788, 864, 865, 872, 995; III 600; IV 33; of oracle, II 606.
STATION OF THE KING (in the temple ritual), II 140, 791, 796, 883, 904; III 271, 537.
STATIONS OF RANK: making of, I 309.
STATUES, IV 268, 320, 326, 357, 927; of Ikhi, I 165; Debhen, I 212; Intef,

I 419; Mentuhotep, I 433; Sesostris I, I 500; Hepzefi, I 540; Amenemhet II, I 601; Khnumhotep II, I 630; Sesostris III, I 660; Thuthotep, I 694; Vizier of King Khenzer, I 783 n. d; Ahmose-Pen-Nekhbet, II 18 n. d; Queen Ahhotep, II 118, 114; Thutmose III, II 164, 165, 186; Nebwawi, II 177, 178 n. a; Enebni, II 213; Hatshepsut, II 288; Hatshepsut Meretre, II 802; Senmut, II 349, 353, 363; Puemre, II 380; Hapuseneb, II 388 n. f; Amenhotep II, II 802; Khepri (=Sphinx), II 814; Amenhotep III, II 876, 917; Amenhotep, son of Hapi, II 912, 913; Nebnefer, II 928; Harmhab, III 22 n. f; Seti I, III 202, 260, 263, 271; Ramses II, III 406; Roy, III 626; Ramses III, IV 26, 199, 201; Ramses VI, IV 477, 479; Namlot, IV 678; Osorkon II, IV 745 n. a; Amenhotep I, IV 913; Ibe, IV 958A; Hor, IV 967; Uzahor IV 980; Neferibre-Nofer, IV 981; Irhoro, IV 981; Nesuhor, IV 980, 993; Enekhnesneferibre, IV 988I n. a; Ahmose, IV 1014; Pefnefdineit, IV 1015.

—Mortuary statues of Hepzefi, I 540; Thutmose III, II 97; Amenhotep III, II 906; placed in the temples, I 500, 540; II 52, 156, 604, 605 n. i; in charge of the mortuary priest, I 542, 544, 555, 577, 590; fire kindled before it on feast-days, I 574; procession of, II 571, 618; divine offerings for, II 564, 571, 618, 619, 620; III 626; garments for, II 571; domains of, IV 479–83.

—Statues of gods, IV 250, 316; impost paid to, IV 225; of Amon, IV 190, 217, 219, 220, 245, 384, 736; of the Nile god, IV 302, 349, 395, 738; Nile goddess, IV 303, 349, 395; of Ptah, III 582; IV 315.

—Statue made of alabaster, IV 302; black granite, III 22 n. f; IV 967 n. e, 981 n. a; bronze, IV 302; copper, IV 302, 395; costly stone, II 883; IV 190, 250, 316, 349, 377, 395; ebony, II 436, 801, 802; electrum, I 165, 668; IV 633, 913; gold, IV 199, 201, 250, 268, 302, 316, 326, 349, 395; granite, I 601; II 876, 883; IV 191; gray granite, IV 981 n. b; green feldspar, IV 302; grit-stone, II 883, 906, n. a; IV 191; hirset stone, IV 302; iron, IV 302; ivory, II 801; kenmet stone, IV 302; lapis lazuli, IV 302, 395; lead, IV 302, 395; limestone, IV 958A n. b; malachite, IV 302, 395; menit-uz-metal, IV 302; mesdemet stone, IV 302; minu stone, IV 302; red jasper, IV 302; seher, IV 302; shesmet stone, IV 302; silver, II 436; IV 191, 250, 268, 302, 316, 326, 349, 395; sycamore wood, IV 303, 349, 395; tin, IV 302; tur, IV 302.

—Statues: from Kadesh, II 436; with human face, II 436.

—Statue inscriptions: see under Inscriptions.

Staves, II 493; IV 913; of ebony, II 802; electrum, IV 912; meru wood, IV 391; see also Staff.

Stealing, IV 486, 566, 676; laws on, III 54–59; penalty for, III 54, 55, 56; IV 676; of slaves, III 55; of hides, III 56, 57.

Steed, III 224, 360, 489; IV 103.

Steer, IV 9.

Steering Oars, IV 331, 845.

Stela, IV 321, 464, 531, 586, 618, 630, 656, 679, 761, 784; importance of, I 4, 9, 13, 14, 16, 22, 23, 24, 71 n. g, 72 n. b.

—Bases of, IV 205.

—Erected to Min, I 441; Harakhte, I 501; Re, IV 255, 265.

—Stela: made of alabaster, IV 988A n. b granite, II 605, 609 n. e; III 487, 538 n. f, 541, 596, n. d; 745 n. a, 919 n. a; black granite, IV 650 n. a; red granite, IV 669 n. d, 795 n. a, 796 n. a, 935 n. a; of granite of Elephantine, IV 679; gritstone, IV 724A n. d; lazuli, II 889; limestone, IV 725 n. a, 782 n. a; overlaid with gold, IV 205.

—Stela of Intefo, IV 514; Sekhemre-Upmat-Intefo, IV 516.

—See also Inscriptions, Stela.

Stems, IV 244.

Stern (=of ship), II 251, 252; IV 65, 66, 582; of fine gold, IV 331.

Stern Rope: title of Hatshepsut, II 341; of the Northland, II 885.

Sticks, IV 287.

Stipulations: for offerings, IV 678; for building, IV 707, 916.

Stock, Ancient, I 399, 400.

Stone, IV 958J *et passim*.

—Hard stone (=alabaster): statues of, I 323, 601, 696.

Stone—
—Stone of Ayan (=limestone), I 534, 635, 740; II 27, 44, 103, 302, 339.

STONE: enduring, stela of, II 606.
—Good white stone of *š*ʾʿ.*t*, in the temple of Kummeh, I 510.
—See also Alabaster, Benut stone, Quartzose, Basalt, Diorite, Flint, Granite, Gritstone, Hus stone, Limestone, Mesdet stone, Mesnet stone, Red Conglomerate, Sandstone and the following:

STONE CARRIERS, II 759.

STONE, COSTLY (rendering of ʿʾ.*t*, a word applied to all rare and costly stones and minerals, like malachite, lapis lazuli, turquoise, or amethyst, but not including pearls, rubies or diamonds, which were unknown), I 731; II 91, 92, 280, 376, 377, 383, 389, 390, 596, 773, 838, 887, 889, 902, 906, 912, 1028; III 31, 137, 151, 237, 405, 428, 453, 504, 512, 527, 537; IV 7, 26 bis, 27, 29, 32, 33, 126, 128, 190, 191, 214, 230, 245, 284, 287, 331, 335, 342, 349, 372, 383, 385, 386, 388, 394, 610, 847, 852, 876, 880, 881, 909, 911, 912, 913, 1011.
—Objects ornamented with, II 165, 185, 436, 490; III 412; IV 312, 315, 610, 843.
—Articles made of costly stones: amulets, II 376; IV 233; eye amulets, IV 29, 377, 390; inlay, IV 204, 209, 231, 331, 334, 538, 904, 910, 958E, J, K, 982; naophors, IV 377; necklace, II 545, 801, 876; offering-tables, IV 958M, 1020; ornaments, I 534; II 545; IV 1011; seal pendants, IV 287, 377; scarab, IV 377, 390; seal, IV 233, 377, 390; semdets, IV 377; statues, I 668; II 883; IV 250, 315, 349, 377, 395; vase, II 545; vessels, II 615, 1031; IV 730; from Retenu, II 491; God's Land, I 764; II 280, 820; III 116, 448 n. b; IV 34; from the Southland, IV 34; from Retenu, II 473, 518, 534 (?), 820; in secret mine at Sinai, I 266, 738; from the Two Mountains, III 448 n. b.
—*B*ʾ-*b*ʾ-*y*ʾ-stone: rings of, IV 377.
—Sparkling stone: statues of, IV 395; from Retenu, II 473, 533 (?).
—Green stones from Retenu, II 473, 491; Kheta, III 428.
—*ḥm*ʾ*g*.*t*-stone: necklace of, I 500.
—*ḥrtt*-stone: vessels of, from Assur, II 446.
—Hukamu stone: semdets of, IV 377.
—Irer stone: semdets of, IV 377.
—White stone: offering tablets of, IV 972; pylons of, III 246; from Nubia, II 176; from Hittites, II 485; from Retenu, II 518.
—*ybh*ʿ*t*-stone from Naharin, II 501.
—Kenmet stone, IV 600; statue of, IV 302.
—Mesdemet stone, IV 345; statue of, IV 302.
—Minu stone: statue of, IV 302; scarab of, IV 233; from Retenu, II 491, 518; white menu stone from Retenu, II 509, 518.
—Hirset stone, IV 287; amulet of, IV 233; statue of, IV 302; semdets of, IV 377.
—Shesmet stone: statue of, IV 302.
—Uba stone, IV 303, 350, 395.
—Ubat stone: seals of, IV 287, 377.
—Marvelous stone: offering-table of, IV 287.
—Timhy stone from Wawat, IV 373, 389.
—Uz mineral, IV 348, 377.
—Inkhu stone, IV 600.
—See also Crystal, Jasper.

STONE WORK: Overseer of: see Index V; workmen in stone, III 171.

STONECUTTERS, I 447; IV 275, 466, 539.
—Stone cutting, I 239, 343.

STORE CHAMBER, III 100; name of, III 100.

STORE CITIES: sustenance ordered out therefrom by Pepi II, I 354.

STOREA, IV 393.

STOREHOUSE, II 356, 751; III 94, 204; IV 330, 403, 576.
—Storehouse of the count, I 556; of Akhetaton, II 1015.
—of offerings of temple at Abydos, I 783.
—in the city of Wa, in Northern Syria, II 458.
—Temple, I 550, II 352, 402, 554, 645, 646, 751, 755, 884, 929; III 78, 111, 119, 138, 152, 160, 351, 453, 526; IV 47, 227, 257, 258, 259, 270, 313, 314, 324, 354, 355, 358, 489, 491, 497, 550, 910, 992; overseer of, I 550; II 352; rank of, I 550; chief measurer of, II 929; captives assigned for, IV 128.

STOREROOM, I 723, 750; Keeper of: see Index V; of dates, II 749.

STRATEGY, III 298–304; plan of, made by Uni, I 312.

STREAM: the living, II 356.

STREET, IV 968.

STRINGS: of flowers, IV 244; of beads, IV 343.

STRONGHOLDS, II 467; III 86, 270, 457, 616; IV 141, 818, 853, 854, 856, 858, 867; Sent, I 172; Hesen, I 174; cow, I 174, 187; of the Northland, I 311; of the sand-dwellers, I 313; Redesiyeh, III 174; the nomads (Asiatic), overthrown by Nessumontu, I 471; "Wall of Seshmu-towe," I 742; of Ptah-Tatenen, III 576; of Asia, IV 141; of Merneptah-Hotephirma, III 633.
—Captives settled in, IV 403, 405 n. g; for Chief of, Commander of: see Index V.
—Stronghold of granary, I 379; Commander of: see Index V.

SUBJECTS (*nḏ.t*): of Pharaoh, I 122.

SUCCESSION: of kingship from father to son, I 423A; of high priests of Amon, III 622, 626; of officers, see Office, Inheritance of; of Craft, see Craft.

SUICIDE, ENFORCED, IV 444, 446, 447, 448, 449, 450, 452, 454, 456.

SUIT, II 997; IV 958D, F; Master of, see Index V.

SUMMONS: of petitioners, II 685.

SUN, II 303, 325 *et passim;* circuit of, II 70, 98, 308; be joined with, I 491.
—Sun of the Nine Bows: royal title, II 1037; III 38.
—Right eye of, IV 678.
—Sun-disk, II 305, 941.
—Sun-hymn of Sute and Hor, II 299 n. e.
—Sunshades, II 802; IV 53, 583; of flowers, IV 244.

SURNAME ("beautiful name"), I 676.

SUSTENANCE: ordered out from the chief of New Towns, I 354.

SWADDLING CLOTHES, I 502, 635.

SWEETWOOD, II 390; IV 264, 870; from Retenu, II 509; Arrapachitis, II 509; God's Land, II 321; Punt, II 892; III 116, 527; Naharin, III 434.

SWIMMING: instruction in, I 413.

SWORD, I 409; II 225, 858, 925; III 117, 450, 455, 457, 465, 486, 489, 582, 584, 589, 597, 598, 613; IV 28, 70, 71, 80, 92, 246, 351, 362, 382, 405, 719, 720, 721, 823; of Horus, III 607; from Kheta, III 343; from Meshwesh, IV 111.
—of copper, from Meshwesh, III 589.
—of flint, from Retenu, II 525.
—*ḫpš*-swords, III 117, 163; of bronze, II 802.

SWORDSMAN, III 457; mercenary, IV 50.

SYCAMORE, I 493; II 299, 325; incense, IV 210; sycamore-gardens, IV 380; sycamores, myrrh, IV 333.
—Sycamore wood, statues of, IV 303, 349, 395.

SYMBOL OF OSIRIS, II 874.

T

TABLE: of carob wood, II 436, 509; gold, II 571; ivory, II 436, 509; silver, II 571; from Retenu, II 436, 509.
—Table of a god, II 353, 355, 367; III 16; IV 958J; for mortuary offerings, II 571.
—Table of the king, II 117; ruler's, II 695; Commandant of: see Index V.

TABLE FOWL, II 621, 622.

TABLE SCRIBE, II 977; III 58; of harem, III 58; queen's, III 58.

TABLE VESSELS, IV 334; of copper, IV 190, 354; gold, IV 190, 269, 354, 357; silver, IV 190, 269, 354, 357.

TABLET, IV 586, 672, 673; of bronze, IV 231, 318, 343; copper, IV 202; gold, IV 202; silver, IV 202, 231, 285, 317, 343.
—Silver tablet from Kheta, III 371, 372, 373, 386, 387, 388, 391.
—Tablets: erected at Abydos, by Ikhernofret, I 661 n. d; in Karnak temple, by Thutmose III, II 407, 555; in Karoy, by Amenhotep II, II 800; in Naharin, by Thutmose III, II 480; Amenhotep II, II 800; in Thebes, in mortuary temple of Thutmose IV, II 821, 824.
—Tablet: inscribed with prayers, IV 202; see also Prayers.

TALKING OF ANIMALS, I 408.

TALONS, IV 77, 86, 90.

TAMARISK, IV 241, 379, 392.

TAMBOURINE, II 1039.

TARGET SHOOTING, II 813, 900.

TASKMASTER, II 758.

TASSELS OF GOLD, IV 201, 204; of gold and rock crystal, IV 373; gold and costly stones, IV 386.

TAX, III 481; IV 141, 266, 852; upon officials, II 716, 718–45; see also Dues, Imposts and Tribute.
—Taxes levied by the vizier, II 706, 716; inspection of, II 717, 729; assessment of, II 916.
—Tax lists, I 10; II 716–45; taxes collected for funeral expenses, of Zau, I 382; remitted by Kheti II of Siut, I 408.
—Taxes, paid *in natura*, III 55; consisting of Katha plant, III 55 bis; leather, IV 150; hides, II 718; III 56, 57; vegetables, III 59; grain, III 61; IV 403; gold, II 718–45; IV 150; silver, II 720–40; IV 150; clothing, II 716–46; IV 150, 403; ointment, IV 150.
—Tax collectors: laws on, III 55, 58, 61, 62.
—Tax officials, IV 266, 324.

TEACHING: of Amenemhet I, I 474–83; of the great seer, II 985; of the Aton faith, II 987, 990, 1002, 1003, 1013.
—Teaching cometh from Egypt, IV 579.

TEMPLE, II 150, 302, 315, 389, 455, 800, 910, 978; III 178, 204, 232, 233, 234, 240, 248, 260, 269, 567, 585, 608, 613, 622; IV 62, 220, 283, 313, 354, 363, 386, 906, 908, 927; army of, III 31; captive women assigned as hierodules in, IV 118; decrees for administration of, see Decrees; wide hall of, I 550; workmen of, II 181; records of, from XXI Dyn., I 22; neglected by the Hyksos, I 15; rank of the scribe of, I 550; musicians, II 1018; singers, II 1018.
—Wardrobe of, I 550, 559, 560, 566; Keeper of: see Index V.
—Secret things of, I 550, 745; IV 706, 708; Master of: see Index V.
—Secret writings of, II 355, 748; master of: see Index V.
—Temple model of Heliopolis, III 244.
—Temple women: the pure settlement of, IV 321; administration of, IV 321.
—Temple-day: definition of, I 552, 561, 565.
—Temple walls, used for commemoration of a king's victories, I 12, 13.
—Temple inscriptions: see under Inscriptions.
—See further, Doors, Double doors, the Great Door, Field, Flagstaves, Fortress, Gate, Grove, Granary, Hall, Herd, House, Inspection, Lake, Land, Linen, Mortuary, Palace, Regulation, Record, Restoration, Sanctuary, Storehouse, Stronghold, Treasury, Wall.
—See also Cliff temples and Index II, and for Temple officials, see Index V.

TEN: Overseer of: see Index V.

TENT, I 353; II 431; III 576, 589; royal, II 425, 429, 447; III 318; poles II 435; of leather, III 589; people of Seir, living in, IV 404.

TERRACED TEMPLE OF MENTUHOTEP III, II 291 n. a; of Hatshepsut, II 291 n. a.

TERRACES: as source of cedar, II 32, 94, 103, 611, 614, 755, 794 n. b; IV 904; myrrh, II 260, 284, 285, 287, 288, 291 n. a, 294; the "Malachite," I 266, 342; of grain, at Arvad, II 461.

TERRIFYING: by magic rolls, IV 454.

TESTAMENT, I 200–9; violation of, I 204; of Nekonekh, I 213–30; of Senuonekh, I 231–35.

TESTIMONY, IV 600; of witnesses, IV 547–53.

THEFT, IV 552, 676; laws on, III 54; penalty for, III 54; IV 676; imprisonment for, IV 556.

THICK STUFF: garments of, IV 241, 394.

THIEVES, IV 511, 513, 515, 516, 517, 521, 522, 535, 537, 540, 543, 545, 548, 549, 550, 554, 556, 566.

THINGS (divine), IV 222, 227, 280, 283, 337, 340, 341, 364, 383, 386, 387.

THINITE PERIOD: Length of, I 56.

THOTH: see Months.

THROAT, II 987; IV 538.

THRONE, II 298, 341, 375; III 525; IV 62, 110, 399, 730, 896; of gold, III 321; speech from, II 291–95; the great, III 412; of electrum, II 292; III 286; Master of, see Index V; portable, IV 749, 751; Libyan, III 584; royal, II 122, 138, 149, 151, 237, 808, 871, 959; III 27, 40, 566; IV 9, 63, 188, 246, 304, 401, 411, 471, 649, 653, 677.
—Throne of a god, II 285; IV 909; of All-Lord, IV 196; Amon, II 314,

608, 805, 881; III 27; IV 40, 124, 246, 777, 836; Atum, II 832; III 272; IV 5, 67, 103, 246, 399; Harakhte, IV 66, 401; Horus, I 686, 779; II 55, 120, 151, 203, 208, 242, 302, 308, 319, 332, 443, 662, 812, 826; III 76, 158, 281, 285, 370, 486 578; IV 92, 142, 382, 411, 473, 624, 630, 895, 923, 934; Keb, II 595, 815; III 116, 267; IV 304, 400; Khonsupekhrod, IV 909; Osiris, IV 188, 401; Ptah, II 615; III 407, 615; IV 351; Re, II 303; III 16, 65; IV 57, 198, 887; Shu, III 612.
—of chiefs, III 645.
—Thrones, the two, marshal of, see Index V.

THROW STICKS: brought from Negro lands, I 336; from Punt, II 272.

THUNDER, produced by Amon, IV 578.

TIMBER, IV 563, 575, 582, 584, 586; green, II 433; felling of, by order of vizier, II 697; house, IV 380, 394.

TIN, IV 245, 385; bolts of, IV 929; statue of, IV 302.

TITHE, IV 354.

TITULARY, II 226, 303, 808; III 29, 435; royal, II 56, 120, 143–47; IV 489; of divine consort, IV 988D, I.

TOILET, ROYAL, I 609; Servant of, see Index V.

TOMB, I 5, 19; II 947; IV 585, 972; of limestone, IV 979; inspection of, IV 511; investigation of, IV 513; Foreman of, see Index V; house furniture in, IV 521; ornaments in, IV 521.
—Tombs of Senuonekh, I 231; Persen, I 241; Nezemib, I 278 n. b; Sebekemsaf, II 112; Amenhotep, II 818; Kheruf, II 873.
—at Abd el-Kurna of Ineni, II 43 n. c; Puemre, II 382 n. c; Amenken, II 801; Khamhet, II 819, 870; Hatey, II 932.
—at Abusir, of Weshptah, I 242; Hotephiryakhet, I 251.
—at Abydos, of Ikudidi, I 528; Zer, I 662; Osiris, I 669; Zaa, I 684; Keres, II 491, built by Queen Ahhotep, II 49–53.
—at Assiut, of Tefibi, I 393 n. a; Kheti I, I 398 n. d; Kheti II, I 405 n. c, 412.
at Assuan, of Harkhuf, I 325.
—at Benihasan, of Khnumhotep I, I 463 n. a; Khnumhotep II, I 179 n. e, 619 n. d, 623, 637.
—at Drah-abu-ʾn-Neggah: of Thutiy, II 369 n. c; Nibamon, II 777 n. e.
—at el-Bersheh, of Thuthotep, I 688 n. f.
—at El Kab, of Ahmose-Pen-Nekhbet, II 17 n. c, 25 n. f; Setau, IV 414, 415.
—at Gizeh, of Thenti, I 182 n. a; Henutsen, I 185 n. e; Zezemonekh, I 186 n. a; Mertityotes, I 188 n. a; Nekure, I 190 n. g; Debhen, I 210 n. a.
—at Hermonthis, of Intef, the nomarch, I 419 n. c.
—at Nekheb, of Ini, I 373.
—at Sakkara, of Harmhab, III 1.
—at Tehneh, of Nekonekh, I 213 n. a.
—at Thebes of Senmut, II 348; Thaneni, II 392, 820; Amenemhab, II 574 n. g; Amenemopet, II 671 n. e; Woser, II 671 n. e; Intef, II 763 n. e; Yuya, II 861 n. c; Thutmose IV, III 32B; Ramessids, IV 473 n. a; Amenhotep I, IV 513, 665, 667, 668, 691, 692, 700; Nebamon, IV 517; Nubkhas, IV 517; singing women of the Divine Votress, IV 521; Isis, IV 523; Ramses II, IV 545, 594; Seti I, IV 545, 593; Nesimut, IV 555; Bekurel, VI 555; Amenhotep III, IV 556. See also above Abd el-Kurna and Drah-abu-ʾn-Neggah.
—Peker, tomb of Osiris, I 669.
—Tomb inscriptions: see Inscriptions.
—Tombs of the lords of life, IV 4.

TOMB CHAMBER, IV 4, 515, 517.

TOMB CHAPEL, I 19, 20; of Tetisheri in Tazeser, II 36; lake of, II 36; garden of, II 36; offerings of, II 36; endowment of, II 36; mortuary priests of, II 36; ritual priests of, II 36.

TOMB ROBBERIES IN NECROPOLIS OF THEBES, IV 499–556.

TOMB ROBBERS, I 15; III 32; IV 499–556; punishment threatened by the great god (Osiris), I 330, 338, 378.

TOMBSTONE AT THEBES OF SENMUT, II 348.

TOOTH IVORY, II 509.

TORTURES: at examination, on hands and feet, IV 545, 552, 553; bastinado of feet, IV 548, 549, 550; beating, IV 548, 549, 550, 551, 552, 553.

TOW-BOAT, I 276, 322; of acacia, I 324; IV 229, 387; cedar, IV 229, 387.

TOWER, IV 842, 861; of Menmare, III 100.
—Temple towers, II 886, 889; IV 117, 189, 311, 355, 356, 357, 358.
TOWNS, II 966; III 62, 84, 86, 88, 90, 94, 141, 147, 613, 616; IV 54, 405, 410, 479, 948, 957, 958; of the Asiatics III 11; destroyed, III 11; Naharin, II 479; Zahi, II 490; Redesiyeh, founded by Seti I, III 172; of Tehenu (?), III 588; given for mortuary endowment, I 209; feeble towns settled with people from other nomes, I 281; given to temples, II 557; IV 222, 226, 280, 282, 339, 364, 383, 384; Commandant of, see Index V.
TOW-ROPE, II 328.
TRANSPORT: of monuments, III 206; transport (boat), IV 863; of acacia, IV 229, 283, 387; ship, III 441; IV 9, 19.
—Temple transports, IV 211, 226, 270, 282, 328, 337, 339, 384.
TRANSPORTATION ACROSS THE NILE, I 276, 308.
TRAY, IV 33.
TREASURES: of God's Land, II 271, 277; in king's house, sealing of, II 371.
—Treasure ship, IV 193.
TREASURY, II 182, 473, 750; III 274; IV 92, 566, 846, 849, 851, 852, 854, 855, 856, 859, 868, 874, 876, 879, 880; under vizier's supervision, II 676, 680, 706, 708; sealing of, II 676; captives for, III 155.
—Chief treasury: order of business, I 423E; chief of, I 713; double cabinet of, I 716, 725; affairs of, reported to the vizier, II 676, 680, 706, 708; Overseer of, Scribe of: see Index V; inspection of, IV 146 n. c.
—Gold treasury: overseer of, IV 1017.
—Temple treasuries, I 777, 778; III 515, 527; IV 9, 26, 27, 28, 31, 32, 190, 193, 195, 211, 217, 227, 250, 256, 266, 270, 340, 359, 362, 489, 497, 545, 547, 683, 684, 685, 686. See also White House.
—Treasury of the South, II 614.
TREATY, III 373, 374, 375, 391; of Kheta with Egypt, by Seplel, III 377; Metella, III 377; Khetasar, III 367–91.
TREES, II 263; IV 795; deeded to a god, II 966; fruit, II 433; planting of, I 173, 328; II 294; III 268; IV 213, 216, 410, 489, 1020; cutting down of, II 697; enduring trees of myrrh, II 288.
—Ished tree, II 310.
—Mimusop tree, II 294 n. c.
—Pleasant trees: for garden of Min, II 567; of Megiddo, II 433; of Arvad, II 461.
—See also Acacia, Cedar, Date, Myrrh, Fig trees, Juniper, Mastic tree, Oil tree, Palm tree, Persea, Rosemary, Sycamore, Tamarisk, Vine.
TRIBES, CHIEF MEN OF, IV 405.
TRIBUTE, II 225, 245, 325, 377, 385, 522, 525, 648, 657, 750, 1028, 1030, 1035; III 13, 82, 137, 138; 273, 428, 481, 484, 527; IV 28, 91, 126, 130, 141, 215, 256, 333, 360, 407, 412, 497, 734, 852, 868, 878; the heads and hands, IV 497; distribution of, II 706; inspection of, II 706, 761; reports on, to be made monthly, II 708.
—Tribute: from mayors, II 708; village sheiks, II 708; rulers numbered by the herald, II 771.
—Tribute from: Arrapachitis, II 512; Asiatics, II 120; III 453; Assur, II 445, 446, 449; Babylon, II 446; Bekhten III 435; never paid by Byblos, IV 576, 577; from Cyprus, II 493, 511, 521; Egypt, I 423D; Genebteyew, II 474; Haunebu, II 953; Isles, IV 34; Isy, II 493' 511, 521; Kadesh. II 773; Keftyew, II 761, 773; Kharu, II 1015; IV 724; Kheta, II 485, 525, 773; III 151, 421; Kush, II 891, 1015; III 42, 453, 590, 644; Mitanni, II 804; Naharin, II 482, 819; Northland, II 751; northern Oasis, II 385, 386; southern Oasis, II 385, 386; Oasis region, II 386; Nubia, III 484; Punt, II 261, 262, 268; III 39; IV 407; Retenu, II 445, 447, 448, 466, 471, 491, 509(?), 518, 525, 533(?), 534(?), 761, 820; III 106, 111; IV 219; Sea, IV 34; Shinar, II 484; south countries the, II 652 751, 761, 1038; III 116; South and North, III 13; Syria, II 1015; IV 724; Tehenu, II 321, 413; Tinay, II 537; Tunip, II 773; Zahi, II 462, 536(?); marshes of Asia, II 385; III 434; Watet-Hor, II 385, 386; ends of Asia, II 386, 891.

TRIBUTE WEIGHT: see Weight.
TRIUMPHANT: epithet received by the dead and constantly placed after their names; literally "true of voice" (*m*ᵓᶜ-*ḫrw*); later (from end of Empire on) placed also after the names of the living. *Passim.*
TROOPS, I 303, 315, 410; II 420, 916; III 577; IV 767, 768, 825, 861, 864; consultation with, II 420; headed by, I 312, 366; II 852; IV 966; proscribed from Sebni's estate, I 366, 368; officers of, II 433; two divisions of, III 56; recorder of, III 20; Commander of, Commander in chief of, see Index V.
—Elite troops of the king, II 809; mercenary troops, III 307.
—Temple troops, IV 966.
—Troop-ships, I 315.
TRUMPET, II 981.
—Trumpeter, III 40; IV 70, 118.
TUNIC: of royal linen, IV 232, 374; southern linen, IV 374; fine southern linen, IV 232, 374; colored linen, IV 232, 239, 374.
TUNNELING, IV 515, 516.
TUR: statute made of, IV 302.
TURBAN, III 460.
TUSK, III 475; IV 344, 391; presented to the court, I 369.
—from Retenu, II 525(?); Tehenu, II 321; Isy, II 493, 521; Niy, II 588.
TYBI: see Months.

U

UNCIRCUMCISED, III 587, 588, 601.
UNCLEAN: by eating fish, IV 882; foreigners, IV 905.
UPLANDS, II 966.
UPPER GARMENTS: of royal linen, IV 232; fine southern linen, IV 232.
URÆUS, II 70, 299; III 7, 12, 13, 15, 18, 21, 116; IV 209, 382, 401, 814, 815, 843, 882; the two, III 622.
URDU BIRDS, IV 345.
—with golden beaks, IV 345.
USHERS, II 925 n. a.
USURPER, SYRIAN, I 68, 68 n. e; IV 398.
UTENSILS: of silver, IV 958C; gold, IV 958G; copper, IV 958G.
UTTERANCE: of a god, II 196, 198, 199, 207, 208, 220, 286, 656, 891, 909, 910; III 105, 110, 116, 136, 150, 155, 164, 165, 223, 399, 518; IV 34, 49, 57, 78, 126, 130, 611, 612, 620, 633, 721; queen, II 197; king, III 259, 411, 486; IV 26 bis, 28, 29, 31, 32, 52, 54, 58, 63, 77, 78, 81, 109, 110, 112, 124, 128; officer, II 940; III 16, 271; IV 52, 55, 58, 71, 77, 82, 110, 123, 124, 127, 128.

V

VALLEY, SACRED: Intef I landed there, I 423.
VALUABLES, IV 580.
VASE, II 802; IV 326; given to the temple of Amon for libation, I 421; II 164.
—Made of bronze, I 500; II 164; IV 538; copper, I 500; II 164; costly stone, II 545; electrum, II 164; gold, I 500; II 32, 64, 164, 754; IV 199, 238, 269, 327, 538; fine gold, IV 334; gold of two times, IV 231; silver, I 500; II 32, 164, 754; IV 203, 231, 269, 327, 334, 538.
—ᵓ-*k*ᵓ-*n*ᵓ vase, II 518; from Retenu, II 509, 533; Kharu, II 436.
—Two-handled vase from Kharu II 436; from Retenu, II 509, 518, 533 (?).
—Denya vase, IV 238, 269.
—Enkhy vase, IV 269, 334.
—Gen vase, IV 334.
—Nemset vase, IV 269, 334.
—Heset vase, IV 269, 334.
—Vase stand, IV 199, 269, 327.
—Vase inscription: see under Inscriptions.
VEGETABLES, II 117, 159, 161; IV 244, 283, 329, 341, 371, 387, 949, 950, 952, 953, 954, 958M; for oblation, II 815; IV 335; for divine offering, II 567, 620, 621, 622; III 77, 159; IV 200, 217; IV 229, 394; for food, III 207, 208.
—Paid as impost, III 59.
—See also Beans, Cabbage, Onions, Lentils.
VESSEL (ship), IV 944; of Snefru's fleet, I 89; of Hatshepsut, II 252, 266, 288; transport vessels, of Thuthotep, I 697; temple vessels, II 162; from Genebteyew, II 474; Wawat, II 475, 487, 503; 515, 523; Punt, II 486; Kush, II 494, 502, 514.
—Eight vessel (a barge), II 917.
VESSELS, IV 231, 285, 343, 373, 385, 386, 389, 394, 876.

Vessels—
—of bronze, II 436, 459, 795; copper, II 459; from Retenu, II 491; costly stones, II 615, 1031; IV 730; gold, II 490, 615, 989, 1028, 1031; III 106; IV 285, 343, 497, 566, 730; wrought with gold, from Retenu, II 790, 1031; *ḥrtt*-stone from Assur, II 446; iron from Tinay, II 537; lapis lazuli, II 1031; III 106; malachite, II 1031; silver, II 615, 795, 1028, 1031; III 106; IV 343, 476, 477, 497, 566, 730, 992; from Zahi, II 490; Naharin, II 482; of workmanship of Zahi, II 482, 490; from Retenu, II 491, 518; III 106; of workmanship of, II 491; of the work of Keftyew, from Tinay, II 537.
—the work of Zahi, from Retenu, II 509.
—Temple vessels, IV 95M; for the temple cult, IV 268.
—Hin vessel of silver, IV 735.
—Spouted vessel of silver, IV 735.
—ᶜ-vessel, IV 238.
—Ekhu-vessels, IV 334.
—*sḥ*-vessel, IV 732, 733, 734.
—*k*ᵓ *k-mn*-vessel, IV 582.
—*ṯ*ᵓ*-pw*-vessels, III 589.
—*ṯ b*-vessel, IV 582.
—*dw*-vessels, of silver, IV 735.
VICTORY: commemoration of, in the temple, I 12; at Megiddo, II 431; see also Hymns.
VILLAGE, II 852; sheik of, II 692, 699, 701.
VIOLATORS, of mortuary endowment, II 925; III 192, 194; IV 483; of treaty, III 386.
VISION, of a god, III 445.
VINES: I 496; IV 216; planting of, I 173; of sand-dwellers, I 313; gardens, IV 380.
VINEYARD: planting of, I 173; IV 1021; vineyard estate, I 201.
—Vineyards of Amon, II 386; IV 213, 216; tribute from, II 386; of Re, IV 262.
VOTRESS: of Ptah, IV 321; divine votress of Amon-Re, IV 511, 513, 521, 522, 942, 946, 958C, M; house of, IV 511, 513, 521, 522, 958F, G, K; major domo of, IV 511, 513, 522; granary of, IV 958G, H; singing women of, IV 521; cattleyards of, IV 958G, H; tombs of, IV 522, 958M; temple of, IV 958K.
VOYAGE (festal of a god), II 94.
VULTURE, III 154.

W

WAGONS: from Assur, II 449; see also Ox-carts, Chariots.
WALL, III 84, 141, 260, 269, 567, 616; IV 65, 189, 216, 250, 271, 355, 356, 357, 358, 359, 360, 489, 654, 748, 818, 820, 853, 859, 861, 864, 879, 914, 970, 1020; of fortress inclosure, II 894; king as, IV 72, 75.
—Canal wall, IV 628.
—Siege-wall: of Megiddo, II 433.
—Temple walls: of electrum, II 886; IV 748; metal, IV 66.
—Walled towns, IV 818, 830.
—Walls of lakes, IV 910, 912; of pools, IV 972.
WAND, III 43.
WARDROBE, ROYAL, I 348, 533, 608; Great lord of, Master of, see Index V.
—Wardrobe of the temple: rank of the keeper of, I 550.
WARES, III 274.
WARS, of Pepi I, I 311; Harmhab, III 33–44; Libyan, under Merneptah, I 13, rule of, IV 861; see also Battles.
—Warrior, III 579; IV 58, 65, 75, 81, 879; of the sea, III 479; IV 44; Hittite, III 337.
—Warship: Egyptian, I 322; IV 65, 74; of Peleset, IV 74; Sherden, IV 74; made of acacia, IV 229, 387.
—War club of Snefru, I 168; of Pepi I, I 296; of Asiatics, I 365 n. a.
—War mace, IV 130, 246.
—War office: in charge of the vizier, II 693–95, 702.
—War plan, I 312; III 307; council of, II 420; III 322.
—Man of war, III 579.
WATCH, II 916; of army, II 425, 864; III 318.
WATER: of the living stream, II 356; of the living river, II 378; divine water (=semen virile), III 474, 486; of Re, IV 47.
—Libation of for mortuary offering, III 17.
—Water-supply, I 407; II 15 n. e; III 170; under charge of vizier, II 698, 707.
—Waters of Akhetaton, II 966; of Egypt, II 420; Naharin (=Euphrates), II 583.

WATER FOWL: see Fowl.

WAY OF LIFE, II 990; of heaven, II 257; of Re, II 257; to Punt, II 285, 294; the Two, II 299.

WAX, IV 240, 393.
—gods, made of, for magical purposes, IV 454; people, made of, IV 455.

WEAPONS, IV 75, 91, 410, 944; royal, II 213, 430, 784, 801; soldiers, II 429; IV 71; Asiatics, II 784; of Ikathi, II 788; of Kheta, III 310, 343.
—Weapons of war, IV 825; from Ullaza, II 470; Retenu, II 471, 534 (?); Meshwesh, III 589; Naharin, II 482; Nuges, II 508.
—See also Arrow, Axe, Baton, Bow, Dagger, Hatchet, Knife, Lance, Mace, Rod, Scourge, Shield, Spear, Sword.

WEAVER, TEMPLE, IV 552, 992.

WEIGHING, II 273–74, 281, 387; IV 256; Thoth, guardian of, IV 256.

WEIGHT, I 531.
—Cow, II 279; IV 29.
—*mḫ*ʾ-weight, IV 240.
—Kararuti-weight, IV 286.
—Nusa-weight, IV, 302, 349, 395; tribute, II 719, 720, 721, 722, 735.
—Round, II 279.
—See also Deben, Kidet.

WELL, III 84, 86, 616.
—of Ayan, IV 406; Redesiyeh, III 171, 197; of Elephantine, III 171; the oasis, IV 726, 728; "Well of Meriamon-Ramses-Mighty-in-Victory," III 293; "Menmare-is-Great-in-Victory," III 84; Merneptah-Hotephirma, III 631; located on the highland, III 631.
—Digging of, I 431; III 171, 195, 286, 287, 289, 290, 291, 292; inspection of, IV 726; seizure of, I 431; wonderful origin of, in Hammamat, I 451; temple-well masoned, I 534.
—*ww*-wells, IV 726.
—*ḥbs*-well, IV 726.

WHEAT, IV 9, 190, 193, 207, 259, 363, 958H.

WHEEL, POTTER'S, II 202.

WHIPS: of ebony, II 802; gold, II 802; ivory, II 802.

WHITE FISH, IV 243.

WHITE FRUIT, IV 30.

WHITE HOUSE, IV 958G; offerings of, I 370; departments of, I 447; chief of, I 722; overseer of, II 1014, 1020; IV 495, 511, 512; Scribe of, see Index V.
—White House of Miam (Ibrim): scribe of, IV 474.
—Double White House, I 505; festival oil from, for Mekhu's funeral, I 370; clothing from, for Mekhu's funeral, I 370; of the court, embalmment equipment from, for Zau, I 382; overseer of, I 505; see also Treasury.

WICKS FOR KINDLING FIRE IN THE TEMPLE, I 560–64, 566, 573–74, 583.

WIDE HALL OF THE TEMPLE: rank of the keeper of, I 550.

WIDOW: kindness to, I 395; Kharu a widow to Egypt, III 617.

WIFE-SISTER, IV 774; violation of, II 925.

WILD FOWL: see Fowl.

WILD GOATS: see Goats.

WILLS AND CONVEYANCES, I 5; of Prince Nekure, I 190–99; Nekonekh, I 223–25; Yewelot, IV 794; Shepnupet II, IV 946.

WIND, THE NORTH: the sweet, II 353.

WINDOW, IV 573, 871.

WINE, I 496; II 117, 159, 260, 434, 887; III 268; IV 216, 217, 228, 233, 239, 283, 299, 341, 344, 348, 363, 376, 387, 565, 589, 734, 949, 950, 952, 953, 954, 972; for divine offering, II 562, 616, 621, 622, 793, 798; IV 190, 213, 262, 269, 272, 286, 292, 309, 313, 329, 390, 958M, 1021; for evening offering, II 565; for feast offering, II 566; oblation, I 435; II 553, 554, 571, 612, 960; III 284; IV 199, 208, 335, 468, 768; for mortuary offering, II 571; III 17, 526; for food, III 208.
—as tribute, II 750, 751, 771; IV 734.
—of Arvad, II 461; Zahi, II 462, 472, 510, 519; Retenu, II 491, 509, 518, 616; southern oasis, IV 734, 992.
—Honeyed wine, from Retenu, II 447, 473.
—Hemy wine, IV 734.
—Syene wine, IV. 734.
—Wine cellar, IV 512.
—Wine gardens of Amon, IV 213.
—Wine presses, II 461.
—See also Date Wine, Shedeh.

WING, OF ARMY, II 426, 430; Pharaoh, lord of, II 661.

WISDOM, PTAH BESTOWER OF, III 402.

WISE MAN, I 697; III 434, 438, 439; of the house of sacred writings, IV 460.

WITCHCRAFT, IV 454–56.
WITNESS, IV 876; examination of, IV 424; gods as, to treaty, III 386.
WOLF, PHARAOH AS, III 144, 147.
—Wolves, I 281; III 134; see also Jackals.
WOMEN: imprisoned for theft, IV 556; bulls made into, IV 883.
—Captives, assigned as hierodules, IV 128.
—of the harem, IV 427, 428, 430, 447, 448, 449, 450, 451.
—Sacred women of Amon, IV 751; in Ptah's temple, IV 321.
—Singing women in temple of Amon, IV 521, 543.
WONDERS AT HAMMAMAT: first, I 435–37; second, I 449–51.
WOOD, handle of, IV 288; track for obelisk of, II 105.
—*ʿg.t*-wood, chariot-poles of, II 447; from Retenu, II 447; two-colored, from Retenu, II 447.
—*kꜣnk*-wood from Assur, II 449.
—*nḥb*-wood from Assur, II 449.
—*Ṯꜣ-gw*-wood, chariots of, II 491; staff of, II 536; from Hittites, II 485; Zahi, II 490; Retenu, II 491; seal of, IV 234, 288, 345, 391; block for the scales, IV 391; cases of, IV 391.
—See also Acacia, Aromatic, Black wood, Carob, Cassia, Cedar, Cinnamon, Fire wood, Fragrant wood, Ked wood, Kidet wood, Khesyt wood, Mera wood, Meru wood, Neybu wood, Neneby wood, Olive wood, Pesgu wood, Sweet wood, Sycamore wood.
WORKMANSHIP, II 754; IV 257, 489, 859, 897; of Zahi, II 482, 509; Retenu, II 490; Kharu, II 501, 509; Keftyew, II 537.
WORKMEN, II 383; III 271, 498; IV 275, 524, 525, 526, 551; in stone, III 171; master, IV 466; Chief, see Index V.
—King's: Leader of, Overseer of, see Index V.
WORKS: for the ka, III 272; of quarrymen, IV 466; for Chief of, Commander of, Overseer of, see Index V.
—King's, chief of, see Index V.
—Works of Amon: Chief of, Chief overseer of, see Index V.
WORKSHOP OF PTAH, IV 28; temple, II 775; IV 226, 280, 282, 337, 364, 370, 383.
WOUNDS, FIVE: opened on a soldier for stealing hides, III 57.
WRAPPING OF HORUS (a garment), of royal linen, IV 232, 374.
—Wrappings, burial, IV 966; of royal linen, IV 966.
WREATH, II 185; III 208.
WRIT OF CLAIM, I 205.
WRITING, II 151, 186, 606; IV 140, 564, 655, 672, 673, 964; of Amon, IV 563, 574; of Atum, I 756; of Thoth, I 531; IV 34.
—Writings, sacred, II 353; forbidding practice of magic, IV 456; house of, I 533; IV 445, 460, 1022; in charge of the prophets, II 353.
—Ancient: concerning landmarks, I 625; concerning taxes, II 717.
—of the vizier, II 684; confidential, II 684.
—King's writings, I 271, 273, 533; Master of, Chief scribe of: see Index V; of daily records, II 392, 680.
—Hall of writings, IV 255, 321, 354, 363, 768.
WROUGHT WOOD: seal of, IV 234, 288, 345, 391; block for the scales, IV 391; cases of, IV 391.
wʿb.t-HOUSE, THE DOUBLE: see House.
Wpg: a part of the temple of Osiris at Abydos, IV 1020; altars of, IV 1020; lake of, IV 1020.

Y

YARN, IV 228, 375, 387, 390.
YEAR: hieroglyphic sign for, on Palermo stone, I 81; reckoning of, in ancient Babylonia, I 81.
—Calendar year: length of, discovered in the fifth millennium, I 39; division of, I 39.
—Solar (Gregorian), I 40.
—Sothic year longer, I 40.
—the little year, feast of, I 630; the great, feast of, I 630.
—Millions of years spent by the king in the temple, I 403.
YOKE, IV 467; of bulls, I 523.
YOUTH, I 413, 697; IV 63, 111, 246, 895.
YUFITI PLANT, IV 234, 344, 378, 392.

Z

ZAWET, II 995.
ZENITH, II 815.

INDEX VIII

EGYPTIAN

ABBREVIATIONS

d. n.=divine name.
e. n.=ethnic name.
f. n.=feast name.
g. n.=geographical name.
p. n.=personal name.
r. n.=royal name.
t. n.=temple name.

ꜣ

—ꜣ, r. n., I 90.
ꜣ*-yw-rw-n*, g. n., IV 712.
ꜣ*yr-sw*, p. n. (?), IV 398 n. a.
ꜣ*-b*ꜣ*-n*, p. n., II 6.
ꜣ*-bk*, p. n., IV 682.
ꜣ*-m-w-r*ꜣ, g. n., III 310, 340, 356; ꜣ*-m-r*ꜣ, IV 64, 127; *y m-r* (read ꜣ*-m-r*), III 141.
ꜣ*-r-n-n*ꜣ, g. n., III 368, 391.
ꜣ*-r-n-ṯ*, g. n., III 308, 311.
ꜣ*-r*ꜣ*-m*, III 634.
ꜣ*-r*ꜣ*-n*ꜣ*-m*, g. n., III 310.
ꜣ*-r*ꜣ*-r-p-ḫ*, II 512 n. f.
ꜣ*-r*ꜣ*-rḫ*, g. n., H 512.
ꜣ*-r*ꜣ*-s*ꜣ, g. n., III 114; IV 64, 482, 591.
ꜣ*-r*ꜣ*-ty-wt*, g. n., II 461; ꜣ*-r*ꜣ*-ṯ-wt*, II 465; ꜣ*-r*ꜣ*-ṯw*, III 309, 312; IV 64; *Y-r*ꜣ*-ṯw* (read ꜣ*-r*ꜣ*-ṯw*), III 306.
ꜣ*-r*ꜣ*-ṯ*ꜣ, g. n., IV 120.
ꜣ*-ry-m*, p. n., IV 455.
ꜣ*-s*ꜣ*-b*ꜣ*-t*ꜣ, g. n., IV 405.
ꜣ*s-sw-r*ꜣ, see *Ys-sw-r*ꜣ
ꜣ*-s-ḳ-rw-n*ꜣ, g. n., III 355; ꜣ*-s-ḳ*ꜣ*-r-ny*, III 617.
ꜣ*-k*ꜣ*-n*ꜣ (vase), II 436, 509, 518, 533.
ꜣ*-k*ꜣ*-y-t*ꜣ, g. n., III 206; ꜣ*-k*ꜣ*-ty*, IV 477.
ꜣ*-ḳ-w-y-š*ꜣ, g. n., III 601; ꜣ*-ḳ*ꜣ*-w*ꜣ*-š*ꜣ, III 574; ꜣ*-k*ꜣ*-w*ꜣ*-š*ꜣ, III 579; ꜣ*-ḳ*ꜣ*-y-w*ꜣ*-š*ꜣ, III 588 bis.
ꜣ*-k*ꜣ*-n-š*, p. n., IV 878; ꜣ*-k*ꜣ*-n-š*ꜣ, IV 815; ꜣ*-k*ꜣ*-n-šw*, IV 868.
ꜣ*-k*ꜣ*-r*ꜣ*-ṯy*, g. n., III 306; ꜣ*-k*ꜣ*-ry-ṯ*, III 309; ꜣ*-k*ꜣ*-t-r-y*, III 312.
ꜣ*-ty*, g. n., III 576.
ꜣ*-d-m-*ꜣ, g. n., IV 714.
ꜣ*-d-r*ꜣ*-*ꜣ, g. n., IV 716.
ꜣ*-d-rw*, g. n., IV 712 n. e.
ꜣ*-d-rw-m*ꜣ*-m*, g. n., IV 712 n. f.
ꜣꜣ*t*ꜣ (enemy?), II 15 n. b.
ꜣ*y*, r. n., II 989.
ꜣꜥꜥ (a title), IV 547 n. c.,
ꜣꜥꜥ (-jar), IV 228, 233, 283, 286, 344, 376, 387, 390.
ꜣꜥꜥ*-bw* (-jar), IV 294, 299.
ꜣ*bw*, g. n., IV 679 n. c.
ꜣ*my* (or *Ḫnmy*), p. n., I 343.
ꜣ*n-yw-g-s*ꜣ, g. n., II 490, 507, 557; *Yn-yw-g-s*ꜣ, II 436.
ꜣ*n-n-r*ꜣ*-ṯ*ꜣ, g. n., III 114.
ꜣ*n-r*ꜣ*-ṯw*, g. n., II 470.
ꜣ*r* (violence), I 423 n. e.
ꜣ*rk*, g. n., II 845 n. f.
ꜣ*ḥ* (-herb), II 159.
ꜣ*ḥ·t* (field), II 1 n. b.
ꜣ*ḫ·t* (first season), I 218 n. a.
ꜣ*ty*, p. n., II 258.

Y

Y[ ], g. n., I 510.
*Y-y-r*ꜣ*-y*, p. n., IV 445.
Y-m-r, g. n., III 141; see ꜣ*-m-w-r*ꜣ.
Y-ny-ny, p. n., IV 440.
*Y-nw-*ꜣꜥ*-mw*, g. n., II 436, 557; III 90, 114, 617.
*Y-r-*ꜥ*-s-ṯ*, g. n., II 784 n. f.
Y-r-ṯw, g. n., III 306; see ꜣ*-r*ꜣ*-ty-wt*.
*Y-r*ꜥ*-ḏ*ꜥ, g. n., II 416; *Y-rw-ḏ*ꜣ*-*ꜣ, IV 714.
Y-ḥm, g. n., II 419.
Y-ḥtp, g. n., I 312.
*Y-k*ꜣ*-ṯ*ꜣ, g. n., II 787; *Y-k*ꜣ*-ṯy*, II 787.

Yꜣ-rd, g. n., IV 368.
Yꜣ-tꜣ, p. n., I 728.
Yꜣ-tw, p. n., I 723.
Yꜣ·t (cattle), IV 242.
Yꜣꜣ, g. n., I 496.
Yꜣw·t (goats), III 428 n. d.
Yꜣm, e. n., I 324; *Yꜣm*, g. n., I 333, 334, 336; *Ymꜣw*, g. n., I 510; *Ymꜣm*, I 311.
yꜣm·t, d. n., I 98.
Yꜣmw-Khk, g. n., II 42.
Yꜣnny, p. n., II 343.
Yꜣhtb, g. n., I 431.
Yꜣḫ-n-Ytn, r. n., II 959.
yꜣḫ (spirit), III 510.
Yꜣḫ-nb·t, p. n., I 230.
yꜣḫw·t (horizon), II 316 n. c.
Yꜣḫwty, d. n., II 325.
Yꜣḫw·t-n-Ytn, t. n., II 1018.
Yꜣḫw·t-ḥtp-ḥr, p. n., I 252.
yꜣsr (tamarisk), IV 241; read *ꜣsr*.
Yꜣt-Sbk, g. n., I 173.
Yꜣtw, p. n., II 912.
Yy-mrs, g. n., I 173.
Yy-ḫr-nfr·t, p. n., I 664.
Yꜥḥ, d. n., II 896.
yꜥḥ (-grain), II 733, 737, 739, 748, 749.
Yꜥḥ-wbn, p. n., IV 1029.
Yꜥḥ-mś, p. n., II 6.
Yꜥḥ-mś-nfr.t-yry, p. n., II 26.
Yꜥḥ-ms-sꜣ-pꜣ-yr, r. n., IV 519.
yꜥḥty (peasant, lit. "belonging to the field"), I 536; see *yḥwty*.
yꜣḫw-yś·t, IV 520 n. b.
Yw-wꜣ-p-ty, p. n., IV 705.
Yw-wꜣ-p·ṯ, r. n., IV 830.
Yw-wꜣ-rꜣ-ṯ, p. n., IV 794.
Yw-p-ty, r. n., IV 794.
Yw-fy-ty (-plant), IV 234, 344, 378, 392.
Yw-mytrw, g. n., I 459 n. c.
Yw-nꜣ, g. n., IV 948.
Yw-r-d-n, g. n., IV 716.
Yw-d-h-m-rw-k, g. n., IV 713.
yw-ṯꜣ (where), III 288 n. b.
Yw-ṯw, g. n., III 114.
Yw·f, p. n., II 112.
yw·ḫr, II 224 n. b.
yw-ty·sn, III 174.
yw-tw ḥr bs·k, IV 730 n. a.
Ywy, p. n., III 32B.
Ywyꜣ, p. n., II 862, 867.
ywꜥ·ty (peasantry), III 322.
Yww, g. n., II 299 n. b.
Ywfrr, p. n., IV 991.
Ywh, p. n., III 32C.
Yws-ꜥꜣs, IV 278; *Yws-ꜥꜣ-st*, d. n., IV 183.
Yb-sꜣ-kꜣ-bꜣ, g. n., III 86.
Yb-šꜣ, p. n., I 620 n. d.
Ybꜣ, p. n., IV 958B.
Ybb, p. n., I 707.
Ybby, p. n., I 283.
Ybnw, IV 378, 395.
ybh·t (-stone), II 501.
Ybh·t, g. n., II 852.
Ybhꜣ·t, g. n., I 321.
Ybdw, p. n., I 303.
yp t (measure), IV 232, 234, 238, 239, 240, 241, 244, 286, 294, 295, 297, 301, 350, 380, 385 n. a., 390, 392, 393.
Yp·t-ys·wt, g. n., III 510.
yp·w (dues), II 716 ter, 717.
Ypy, p. n., I 387.
ypy yḫt nb ypt n ḫnw m rs pn, I 320, n. b.
Ypw, d. n., I 500.
ym, I 784 n. c.
Ymꜣꜣw, g. n., I 351.
Ymy, p. n., I 450.
ymy-wꜥb, I 370.
ymy-wr·t nt Wꜣs·t, II 905 n. d.
ymy-pr (fortune), IV 946.
ymy-rꜣ ys·t m Wꜣt·t-Ḥr, II 385 n. a.
ymy-ḫnty, II 1009.
ymyw-ḫnty (courtiers), III 267.
ymyw-sṯ·t, e. n., II 658 n. d.
Ymn-ys-r-wꜣ, r. n., II 896 n. d.
Ymn-wsr-ꜥ, p. n., I 777.
Ymn-m-yn·t, p. n., IV 522.
Ymn-ḫꜥw, p. n., IV 449.
Ymnw-ḫrp (pyramid name), I 601.
Ymsw, p. n., I 529.
Yꜣḫ·t-yrny, p. n., I 387.
Yꜣḫw-mnw, t. n., IV 753 n. a.

Ymts, r. n., I 310.
yn·w (tribute), III 481; *yn·tw*, III 632.
Yn-yw-g-sʾ, g. n., II 436; see *ʾn-yw-g-sʾ*.
Yn-mw·t·f (pillar of his mother), III 155; IV 761.
Yn-ṉ-rʾ-y, p. n., IV 553.
yn-n-ḫw (-stone), IV 600.
Yntf, p. n., I 365.
Yn-tw·f-ʿʾ, r. n., IV 516.
Yn-tf-ʿʾ, r. n., I 423; IV 514.
Yny, g. n., I 459.
Yny, p. n., I 373.
ynyy (brought), II 271 n. c.
Yny·t, g. n., I 459, n. d; II 1 n. b.
Ynw-wʾww, p. n., III 635.
Ynw-Mn·t·yw, e. n., III 118 (read *Yntyw*).
Ynw-šfnw, p. n., IV 366, 367.
Ynw šmʿ, g. n., II 1018.
Ynbw-ḥḏ, g. n., IV 857.
ynm (?), I 736 n. d.
ynr-n-mʾ·t (granite), III 54.
ynr nfr n ʿnw, II 339 n.b.
yntyw, I 104.
Yr-wn, g. n., III 309 n. d; *Yr-wn·t*, III 312.
Yr-sw, d. n., II 959 n. c, 985 n. b; III 285 n. a.
Yr·t-rw, p. n., IV 792.
Yry, p. n., I 333.
Yry, p. n., I 369.
yry (to visit), I 602 n. d.
yry-ʿt-n-pr-ḥḏ (treasury official), I 718.
yry srt yrt ḳd m rs pn, I 320 n. f.
yry·w-pt (fowl), III 404 n. e.
Yry·t-s·t, p. n., II 112.
yryt·n·y pw m wn·mʾʿ (in reality), I 471 n. c.
Yrm, g. n., II 494, 845 n. f.
yrr (-stone), IV 377.
Yrrty, d. n., II 828.
Yrṯt, g. n., I 311, 317, 334 bis, 336.
Yrrṯt, g. n., I 324.
Yḥʾ, p. n., I 688 n. a.
Yḥy, p. n., I 165.
Yḥy, p. n., I 387.
Yḥw, p. n., I 298.
yḥwty (peasant), IV 229; see *yʿhty*.
yḫ·t (thing), I 652 n. a.
yḫ·t (offering), II 618.
yḫ·t-nṯr (divine offerings), IV 1020.
Yḫy, p. n., I 183.
Yḫy, p. n., I 298, 301.
Yḫrkyn, g. n., I 510.
Ys-sw-rʾ, g. n. (read *ʾs-sw-rʾ*), II 446 bis, 449.
ys-mʾ-rʾ (emory), IV 600.
ys-ḥʾ ḳ·t, II 916 n. b.
ys·t wr·t nt Wʾs·t, II 905 n. d.
ys.t-mʾʿ·t (necropolis), IV 668.
Ysy, g. n., II 493, 511, 659.
Yssy, r. n., I 351, 353.
yś (tomb), II 36.
Yś·t-yb, r. n., I 250; *Yś·t-yb-tʾwy*, r. n., I 250.
yś·t-ḏsr·t (cemetery), I 770, 771.
yświ (chamber), II 165.
Yḳn, g. n., I 652.
Yḳr-yb, p. n., I 343.
Ykw-dydy, p. n., I 526.
Ykwy, p. n., I 419.
Yty, r. n., I 387.
Yty, p. n., I 459.
ytwr (aisle), IV 971.
ytr (measure), II 479; *ytr·w*, II 852.
ytr (river), IV 831 n. f.
ytḥ (fortress), I 396 n. h.
Yṯ-tʾwy, g. n., I 608 n. c; IV 856.
yd (youth), I 257.
Ydʾht, g. n., I 431.
Ydy, p. n., I 466 n. c.
ydf (-garments), IV 239, 375.
Ydnywyw (-plant), IV 235, 379, 392.
ydgʾ (-garments), IV 232, 374, 375.

ʿ

ʿ (-jar), IV 279, 300, 301, 347, 348, 350.
ʿ (-measure), IV 299, 348, 394.
ʿ (-vessel), IV 238.
ʿ-mw (water-supply), I 407 n. c; II 15 n. c; III 170 n. a.
ʿ-n-p-rw-n, g. n., IV 716.
ʿ-pw-rʾ, IV 281.
ʿ-pr-d-gʾ-rʾ, p. n., III 632.

ʿ*-s-ṯy-r*ꜣ*-ṯ*, d. n., IV 105.
ʿ*-k-*ꜣ, g. n., III 114.
ʿ*·t* (house), III 625; IV 956, 957.
ʿ*·t nt ḫt* (arbors), IV 264 n. a, 1021 n. b.
ʿ*·t-ḥḳ·t* (beer-hall), IV 451 n. c.
ʿꜣ (chieftain), IV 111, 129 bis, 726.
ʿꜣ*-pḥty-st*, r. n., III 542.
ʿꜣ*-m-k*ꜣ*w*, p. n., I 782.
ʿꜣ*-n-k*ʿ*ḥ* (chief of a district), IV 699.
ʿꜣ*-n*ꜣ*-n*ꜣ*y*, p. n., IV 452.
ʿꜣ*-r*ꜣ*-n*ꜣ, g. n., IV 713.
ʿꜣ*-r*ꜣ*-ty* (ramp), IV 189 n. a.
ʿꜣ*-rw-n*ꜣ, g. n., II 421, 422, 425, 426, 427.
ʿꜣ*-rw-d-*ꜣ, g. n., IV 716.
ʿꜣ*-ḫpr-n-R*ʿ, II 116; IV 637.
ʿꜣ*-ḫpr-R*ʿ, r. n., IV 784.
ʿꜣ*-š*ꜣ*-ḳ* (to oppress), IV 188 n. a.
ʿꜣ*-g-m*, p. n., III 337.
ʿꜣ*-ty-k*ꜣ, g. n., IV 408.
ʿꜣ*·t* (costly stone), IV 1011 n. c.
ʿꜣ*m* (-club), I 365 n. c.
ʿꜣ*m-ḥryw-š*ʿ, e. n., I 311.
ʿꜣ*m·w*, e. n., I 360 bis, 681 bis; II 4, 296, 303, 657, 658 n. e; III 139, 457; IV 31, 72, 80, 994 n. a.
ʿꜣ*mw n šw*, e. n., I 620 n. d.
ʿꜣꜣ*bw*, p. n., I 707.
ʿꜣ*d* (stretch of land), I 430 n. h.
ʿ*w* ("doors"), I 322 n. e.
ʿ*w*ꜣ (to take), IV 1005.
ʿ*w*ꜣ (to reap), IV 893.
ʿ*yn* ("to build with limestone of Ayan"), I 212 n. c; ʿ*yn*ꜣ (limestone), IV 216, 355, 356, 358.
ʿ*wt* (tablets), IV 202 n. d, 231.
ʿ*pr* (equipment), I 366 n. a; IV 466.
ʿ*m*ꜣ*w*, g. n., II 387; IV 34; ʿ*m*ꜣ*mw*, II 298 n. c.; ʿ*mw*, II 265.
ʿ*mw*, p. n., I 512.
ʿ*n-*ʿ*nḫt*, p. n., I 360.
ʿ*n·f-sw*, p. n., IV 550.
ʿ*nw*, g. n., II 27, 103, 339; see also ʿ*yn*.
ʿ*nw* (tablets), IV 202 n. d, 231.
ʿ*nb-ṯm*ꜣ*·t*, II 726, 727.
ʿ*nbw* (-plant), IV 379, 395.
ʿ*nbw̱* (-fruit), IV 240, 393.
ʿ*nn*, p. n., II 931.
ʿ*nḫ* (citizen), III 51, 57, 59; IV 397; ʿ*nḫ·w* (people), I 286 n. e, 681 bis; III 65; IV 397 n. a.
ʿ*nḫ* (wreath), III 208 n. d.
ʿ*nḫ-nfr-yb-R*ʿ, r. n., II 896 n. d.
ʿ*nḫ-Ḥr*, p. n., IV 958B.
ʿ*nḫ·f-Ymn*, p. n., IV 689.
ʿ*nḫy* (-vase), IV 269, 334.
ʿ*nḫw*, p. n., I 783.
ʿ*nḫts*, p. n., IV 1029.
ʿ*nty*, d. n., III 467; ʿ*n-ty-t*, III 84; ʿ*nṯ*, d. n., IV 105.
ʿ*nty* (myrrh), III 116.
ʿ*n-ṯ-r*ꜣ*-ty*, d. n., III 386.
ʿ*nḏ* (safety), II 105 n. f.
ʿ*r-ḳ*ꜣ*-tw*, g. n., II 529.
ʿ*ry·t* (hall, judgment-hall), II 764, 767; IV 931; ʿ*rry·t*, II 763.
ʿ*rḳ* (measure), IV 231.
ʿ*ḥ*ꜣ*-nfr*, p. n., IV 539.
ʿ*ḥ*ꜣ*·w* (warriors), III 479.
ʿ*ḥ*ꜣ*ty-nfr*, p. n., IV 551.
ʿ*ḥ*ʿ (standing), I 317 n. c.
ʿ*ḥ*ʿ (heap), I 785 n. h.
ʿ*ḥ*ʿ (-jar), II 571.
ʿ*ḥ*ʿ (violence), I 423 n. e.
ʿ*ḥ*ʿ (palace), IV 900, 966 n. b.
ʿ*ḥ*ʿ (magazine), I 370.
ʿ*ḥ*ʿ*-stny*, II 292 n. c.
ʿ*ḫ* (altar), IV 1020.
ʿ*ḫw* (-vessel), IV 334.
ʿ*ḫm·t*, II 339 n. a.
ʿ*š* (-jar), IV 924.
ʿ*š*ꜣ*-ḥb-šd*, p. n., IV 438.
ʿ*ḳ* (-loaves), IV 238, 291, 393.
ʿ*ḳ* (-priest), IV 753.
ʿ*ḳ-ḥr* (=enter upon), IV 460 n. c.
ʿ*ḳb·t*, e. n., II 70.
ʿ*g·t*, II 447 ter.
ʿ*tḫ* (kneader), III 624 n. g.
ʿ*ḏ*ꜣ (guilty), IV 533 n. e.
ʿ*ḏd* (youth), IV 570.

W

*W*ꜣ*—*, g. n., II 457.
*W*ꜣ*-yw-h*ꜣ*-s*ꜣ*-t*ꜣ, p. n., IV 726.

Wꜣ-rꜣ-nꜣ, p. n., IV 437.
Wꜣ-rꜣ-kꜣ-ty-rꜣ, p. n., IV 574.
Wꜣ-š-š, e. n., IV 403; *Wꜣ-šꜣ-šꜣ*, IV 64.
Wꜣ-šꜣ-ty-hꜣ-tꜣ, p. n., IV 784.
wꜣ·w (officer), II 987.
Wꜣ·wt-Ḥr, g. n., II 385 n. a.
wꜣ·t, (way), IV 75 n. b.
Wꜣ·tt-Ḥr, g. n., II 385 n. a.
Wꜣy·t, g. n., II 1037.
Wꜣw, g.n., I 510.
Wꜣwꜣ·t, e. n., I 311, 317, 324, 358, 367; II 475, 487.
Wꜣrty, p. n., IV 566.
wꜣḥ (wreath), II 185.
Wꜣḥ-yb-Rꜥ, r. n., IV 958D, 960, 988F, 990, 1000.
Wꜣḥ-ys·t, g. n., II 736 bis.
Wꜣḥ-ꜥnḫ, r. n., I 396 n. h, 423, 529.
Wꜣḥ-kꜣ-Rꜥ, r. n., IV 811, 884.
wꜣḥ·t (oasis), I 335 n. h.
wꜣḥy·t (station), II 614.
wꜣs (-scepter), I 646.
Wꜣs·t, g. n., III 30; IV 913, 926.
wꜣg, f. n., II 35.
Wꜣg, g. n., I 433 n. d.
wꜣḏ (-fowl), I 729.
wꜣḏ (fresh), I 429 n. b.
Wꜣḏ-ꜥnḏ, r. n., I 90.
wꜣḏ-wr (sea), II 450 n. a; III 118; IV 921 n. e.
Wꜣḏ-ḫpr-Rꜥ, r. n., IV 519.
Wꜣḏ·t rnp·wt, r. n., II 239.
W-ꜥ-n, g. n., II 582.
wꜥsꜣwꜥ, III 622, n. b.
wꜥb (-priest), I 538, 552, 563, 564, 572, 583; II 97; III 31, 78, 160; IV 753, 958D, 988H, 1018.
[*Wꜥb-kꜣw*]-*Ḥtḥr*, p. n., I 218.
wꜥb·t (joint of beef), II 114.
wꜥb·t (pure), I 370.
wꜥb·t (kitchen), III 624 n. i; IV 958J.
Wꜥr·t (bend), g. n., I 370, 509 n. f.
wꜥrtw (commandant), I 679, 683.
ww (-well), IV 726.
wbꜣ (forecourt), II 627; IV 514.
wbꜣ (inspect), I 312 n. e; *wbꜣ* (explore), I 334 n. e; IV 720 n. e.
wbꜣ (-stone), IV 303, 350, 395; *wbꜣ·t*, IV 287, 377.
wbꜣ-ḥr (instructed), II 758 n. c.
Wbḫ·w, p. n., III 650.
wp, IV 465 n. f.
Wp-wꜣwt, d. n., I 763 n. i.
Wpg, t. n., IV 1020.
wm·t (-linen), II 554.
wn (coffin), IV 965 n. e.
Wn-pḥty, p. n., IV 552.
wn-ḥr (appearance), IV 200 n. a.
wn-ḥr (experienced), II 758 n. c.
wn [*ḥr n*] *sšꜣm yrw·t*, II 371 n. c.
wn-dw (-oxen), II 723, 742; III 413.
Wny, p. n., I 293.
Wnw, g. n., IV 833, 843 bis.
Wnšk, g. n., II 848 n. a.
Wr-Ymn, p. n., IV 512.
wr-ꜥꜣ (great chief), III 426.
wr pr ḥḏ (chief of the White House), I 722.
Wr-kꜣ, e. n., I 112.
wr·t (greatly), I 317 n. g, 493.
wr·t (princess), III 391 n. c.
wr·t-ḥkꜣw, d. n., IV 66.
Wr-m-rꜣ, p. n., IV 43.
Wrm, g. n., II 845 n. f.
Wršw, f. n., IV 727.
wrdw (-bird), IV 345 bis.
Whm-yb-Rꜥ, r. n., IV 1028.
whm ꜥnḫ nfr (repeating a happy life), I 725.
Whm-mś·wt, r. n., IV 545.
whm-śtny (royal herald), II 764; *whm-n-śtny*, II 764 n. c.
whm kfꜥ (repeating captures), II 20 n. f.
whm·sn nf (they answered him), IV 922 n. b.
whm·w (heralds), II 925 n. a.
wḥꜣ (to quarry stone), I 335 n. h.
wḥꜣ-ny ("I reaped"), I 658 n. f.
Wḥꜣ·t, g. n., I 335.
wḥꜣ·t (a measure), I 556.
wḥꜥ (to loose), II 148 n. a.
Wsr-mꜣꜥ·t-Rꜥ-P-ꜥnḫy, r. n., IV 941 n. a.
Wsr-ḥꜣ·t, II 888 n. b.
Wsr-ḫpš, p. n., IV 526.

Wsr·t-kᵓw, r. n., I 239.
wsḫ (-ship), IV 19, 720 n. d.
wsḫ-ḥb-šd (jubilee-court), IV 707 n. d.
wsḫ·t (castle), I 532 bis.
wsḫ·t (broad hall), II 1018; III 515.
Wšr-ḫᶜw, r. n., I 163.
wšmw (pail), II 32.
wtwt (to stir), II 616.
wtb (-priest), I 668.
Wṯntyw, g. n., II 660 n. e.
wṯs-nfr·t (barque-shrine), II 92; IV 982.
wṯs·t nfrwf (bearer of his beauty), II 316 n. d.
Wṯk, g. n., I 369.
Wṯs-Ḥr, g. n., I 500.
Wṯṯ, g. n., I 367.
wd (put, place), I 423E n. c; *wd·n·y* (have placed), II 198 n. h.
wdn, II 735.
wḏ (-mineral), IV 348, 377.
wdnw-nt (-loaves), IV 238, 291, 297.
wḏ (storehouse), II 751; *wḏᵓ*, II 751.
Wḏᵓ-Ḥr, r. n., IV 980.
Wḏ-Ptḥ-ᶜnḫ·f, p. n., IV 792.
wḏ·t-md·t (command, edict), I 193 n. b.
wḏᵓ (prosperity), II 105 n. f.
wḏᵓ (sacred eye), IV 201 n. b.
Wḏᵓ-rn·s, p. n., IV 951.
Wḏᵓy, p. n., I 343.
wdb (pay), I 219 n. b.
wḏḥ (offering-table), I 610; II 32.
wḏḥ (=sparkling), II 533 n. g.

B

B-ᶜ-l-tw-Rᵓ-m-g-w, p. n., III 630.
B-n-t-r-š, p. n., III 436.
Bᵓ, g. n., IV 716 n. b.
bᵓ (soul), IV 187.
Bᵓ-w-y, g. n., III 340
Bᵓ-wr-dd, p. n., I 351, 353.
bᵓ-bᵓ-yᵓ (-stone), IV 377.
bᵓ-nw (-fruit), IV 378, 395.
Bᵓ-rw-mᵓ-m, g. n., IV 713 n. f.
Bᵓ-ḥw, p. n., IV 481.
Bᵓ-kᵓ, g. n., III 285.
bᵓ-kᵓ-yᵓ (-plant), IV 234.
Bᵓ-kᵓ-nᵓ, g. n., IV 405.
Bᵓ-kᵓ-Rᶜ, r. n., IV 921.
Bᵓ-ty-ḥ-wᵓ-rw-n, g. n., IV 712.
Bᵓ-ty-šᵓ-n-r-ᵓ, g. n., IV 712; *Bᵓ-ṯ-šᵓ-rᵓ*, III 114.
Bᵓ-ty-tᵓ-rw-mᵓm, g. n., IV 713 n. h.
Bᵓ-ṯ-ᶜ-n-ṯ, g. n., III 114; *Bᵓ-y-ty-ᶜ-n-ty*, III 356.
Bᵓ-dy-rᵓ, g. n., IV 565.
Bᵓbᵓ, p. n., II 7.
Bᵓ stt nt tp-ršy, d. n., I 396 n. c.
Bᵓḳ·t, p. n., I 622.
Bᵓk, g. n., III 284.
bᵓkᵓy·t (precinct), III 31 n. b.
Byᵓ, g. n., I 353 n. c. 735.
byᵓ (iron), II 537 n. c.
Byᵓ·t (mine-land), I 602, n. d.
byᵓ·t (loaf), II 113; III 77, 159; IV 238, 291, 297, 347; *by·t*, III 624 n. h.
byᵓy·t (gritstone), IV 287 n. c.
Byn, g. n., IV 867.
Byn-m-Wᵓs·t, p. n., IV 443.
Byᵓs-tᵓ, g. n., IV 956, 957.
bᶜny (-plant), IV 380, 395.
Bw-yw-wᵓ-wᵓ, p. n., IV 792.
Bw-pn-Ymn-ḫᵓᶜ, p. n., IV 682.
Bb-rᵓ, g. n., II 446, 484.
bpᵓ (-jar), IV 300, 348.
bpᵓ-ny-ny, IV 234.
bnw·t (-stone), II 643.
bnbn (pyramidion, sanctuary), II 572 n. e, 935; *bnbn·t*, IV 982.
bnr (sweet), II 433 n. h.
brk (tribute), IV 577 n. a.
brk (to hail), IV 122; *bᵓ-rᵓ-kᵓ* (gifts), IV 207 n. e.
Bhny, g. n., III 79; *Bhn·t*, III 159; *Bwhn*, III 285.
Bhksy, p. n., I 365.
bḥ (-loaves), IV 238, 393.
Bḥ-ḥw-kᵓ, r. n., IV 514.
Bẖw, g. n., II 597.
bḫn, IV 235.
bḫn (black basalt), I 675 n. a; *bḫnw*, III 246.
bḫn·w (strongholds), IV 141.
bḫn·t (pylon), III 508.
bsn·t (tool), IV 189 n. d.
Bš, r. n., I 81.

bḳ (-oil), IV 239, 376; *bḳꜣ* (-oil), IV 390.
Bk, p. n., II 975.
bk (tower), IV 842 n. b.
bk (serve, labor, pay taxes), IV 931, 932, 933.
Bk-wr-n-rꜣ, p. n., IV 555.
Bk-n-Wr-n-rꜣ, p. n., IV 512.
Bk-n-nfy, p. n., IV 830.
Bky, g. n., II 852.
bk·w (imposts), I 731; II 716; III 481.

P

P-ꜥnḫy, r. n., IV 816.
P-wꜣ-r-mꜣ, p. n., IV 881.
P-wꜣ-r-mꜥ, p. n., IV 821.
P-n-dwꜣw, p. n., IV 430.
Pꜣ-y-yry, p. n., IV 442.
Pꜣ-y-yš, p. n., IV 444.
Pꜣ-y-sꜣ, p. n., III 337 bis.
Pꜣ-yf-rꜣwy, p. n., IV 423.
Pꜣ-ynywk, p. n., IV 429.
Pꜣ-yr-nw, p. n., IV 423.
Pꜣ-yr-swn, p. n., IV 443.
Pꜣ-ꜥ-n-bywk, p. n., IV 512.
Pꜣ-ꜥꜣ-ꜥḥ, p. n., II 839.
Pꜣ-ꜥꜣ-m-ḳꜥꜣ-yꜣ-ḏ-ꜣ, g. n., IV 715.
Pꜣ-ꜥn-ḫꜥw, p. n., IV 512.
Pꜣ-wr-ꜥꜣ, p. n., IV 511.
Pꜣ-wḏy, g. n., IV 368.
Pꜣ-bꜣ-y-ꜣ, g. n., IV 716 n. b.
Pꜣ-Bꜣ-š, p. n., IV 878; *Pꜣy-bꜣ-sꜣ*, p. n., IV 423, 452.
Pꜣ-mꜣ, p. n., IV 815, 878.
Pꜣ-mr-ḫtm, p. n., III 634.
Pꜣ-mry-Ymn, p. n., IV 546.
Pꜣ-mḥ-tꜣ-mꜣ, g. n., III 94.
Pꜣ-rꜣ-hw, r. n., II 258.
Pꜣ-rꜣ-kꜣmn·f, p. n., IV 445.
Pꜣ-Rꜥ, III 542.
Pꜣ-Rꜥ-pꜣyw-yt, p. n., IV 593.
Pꜣ-Rꜥ-m-ḥb, p. n., III 634.
Pꜣ-Rꜣ-m-ḥb, p. n., IV 423.
Pꜣ-Rꜥ-ḥtp, p. n., IV 281.
Pꜣ-rw-kꜣ, p. n., IV 439.
Pꜣ-ḥ-rꜣ, g. n., III 114.
Pꜣ-ḥw-ḳ-rw-ꜣ-ꜣ-bꜣ-rꜣ-m, g. n., IV 715.
Pꜣ-sꜣ-ꜥḳꜣ, p. n., IV 784.
Pꜣ-sr, p. n., IV 513.
Pꜣ-Šbk, p. n., IV 784.
Pꜣ-ḳnw, p. n., IV 784.
Pꜣ-ḳrr, p. n., IV 932.
Pꜣ-kꜣ-nꜥ-nꜣ, g. n., III 88; *Pꜣ-kꜣ-nꜥ-nꜥ*, III 617.
Pꜣ-kꜣwt-yw, p. n., IV 485.
Pꜣ-tꜣw-mdy-Ymn, p. n., IV 431.
Pꜣ-ṯwt, p. n., IV 792.
Pꜣ-ṯnf, p. n., IV 878; *Pꜣ-ṯnfy*, p. n., IV 815.
Pꜣ-dy-Ḥr-smꜣ-tꜣwy, p. n., IV 878.
Pꜣ-drps, p. n., IV 937 n. b.
Pꜣ-ḏdkw, g. n., II 9.
Pꜣy-bꜣ-ky-kꜣ-mn, p. n., IV 427.
Pꜣy-nfr, p. n., IV 512.
Pꜣy-rꜣ-kꜣ, g. n., III 386.
Pꜣy-kꜣmn, p. n., IV 547.
pꜣḳ (a bread), I 577.
Pꜣdy-Ymn-ns·t-tꜣwy, p. n., IV 881.
Pꜣḥꜣty, p. n., IV 726.
Py-dꜣ-sꜣ, g. n., III 306, 309 n. d, 312; *Py-d-sꜣ*, III 349.
Pyyꜣy, r. n., III 644; *Pyꜣy*, IV 224.
pypy·t (keel), IV 582 n. a.
pꜥ·t (people), I 445; III 578.
pꜥ.t, (-loaves) IV 238.
pꜥd·t (-bird), IV 242.
—*-pw*, r. n., I 90.
Pw-rꜣ-sꜣ-ty, g. n., IV 44, 82, 403; *Pw-rꜣ-sꜣ-t*, g. n., IV 64, 71, 81.
pw-gꜣ (-jar), IV 300, 350.
Pw-tꜣwy, g. n., IV 948.
Pw-tw-ḫy-pꜣ, p. n., III 391.
Pwnt, g. n., I 353.
pwsꜣ-ꜥḳ (-loaves), IV 238.
Pf-nf-dyy-Bꜣs·t, p. n., IV 852.
pn ("this"), I 353 n. c.
Pn-yṯt-tꜣwy, p. n., IV 338.
pn wntyw, II 808 n. c.
Pn-nw·t, p. n., IV 482.
Pn-Nḫb·t, p. n., II 20.
Pn-rnwt, p. n., IV 423.
Pn-ḥwy-byn, p. n., IV 442, 455.
Pn-tꜣ-wr, p. n., IV 444.
Pn-tꜣ-wr·t, p. n., III 315.
Pny-nꜣynꜣ, g. n., IV 867.

pnsw (joint of beef), II 113.
Pnty-Bḫn·t, p. n., IV 878.
pr (house), III 507, 567; IV 183, 195, 197, 215, 222, 223, 225, 227, 277, 283, 288, 340, 355, 357, 365, 366, 367, 369, 958J, 972, 988D, H.
Pr-ynbw, g. n., IV 956.
Pr-yr, g. n., III 579 n. d, 583; *Pr-yrr*, III 588.
Pr-ʿꜣ, I 148 n. c.
Pr-ʿnḫ, g. n., IV 547.
Pr-wr, g. n., I 159.
pr-wr (great house), I 609.
Pr-wr-sꜣḥ, g. n., I 174.
Pr-bꜣ-rꜣ-ys·t, g. n., III 576.
Pr-mꜣ (château), III 588 n. c.
Pr-nw, g. n., I 156.
Pr-nb-tp-yḥ, g. n., IV 818.
Pr-nsr, g. n., I 159.
Pr-Ḥ·t-ḥr-Mfk, g. n., IV 1003 n. e.
Pr-Ḥt-ḥr-rśyt, t. n., I 373.
pr-ḫꜣty-ʿ (count's estate), I 536.
Pr-Ḥʿp, g. n., IV 878.
Pr-Ḥr, g. n., II 742.
Pr-spꜣ, g. n., I 172.
pr-sn (-loaves), II 113; III 624 n. h; IV 238, 297, 347.
pr-stny (palace), III 20; IV 751, 958J.
Pr-šsṯt, g. n., I 172.
Pr-ḳd, g. n., I 172, 174.
Pr-g-wꜣ-ty, g. n., IV 405 n. c.
Pr-G-rw-rw, g. n., IV 878.
Pr-ḏꜣḏꜣ, g. n., IV 726.
Pr-Ḏḥwty-Wp-rḥwy, g. n., IV 830, 878.
pr-ḏt (estate), I 545.
pr·w (houses), III 498.
pr·t (second season), I 735.
pr·t-s (-loaves), III 77, 159.
Prww, g. n., I 510.
Pḥ-ʿn, g. n., IV 1003 n. d.
pḥ sw (foe), IV 921 n. a.
pḥrr, III 579; IV 58, 65, 75, 80.
pḫr-wr (the Great Bend), III 118.
psꜣ (-measure), IV 378, 395.
Psmṯk, r. n., IV 960.
psn (loaf), I 241.
psgw (-wood), II 447.
psḏ·t (ennead), III 533; IV 399.
pš (flax), IV 241, 379, 392; *pš·t*, IV 235.
pḳꜣ·t (-linen), I 727; *pḳ·t*, II 554, 571.
Pḳy, g. n., II 94.
pg (-vessel), II 571.
Ptn, g. n., I 493.
Ptḥ-n-kꜣw, p. n., I 387.
Ptḥ-špśś, p. n., I 256.
pd·t, II 572.
Pd·ty-šw, e. n., III 580.
Pd·tt, g. n., II 798.
pdr (crate), IV 241.

F

fꜣ (pay), IV 482 n. c; 577 n. a; *fꜣy* (to deliver), IV 266; *fꜣy·n* (we bring), IV 933.
Fꜣ·t-ʿꜣ·t-nt-Mwt, p. n., IV 641.
fꜣkꜣ·t; see *mfꜣkꜣ·t*, I 602 n. e.
Fnḫw, e. n., II 27, 529.
Fkꜣ·t ("Malachite"), g. n., I 266 n. c; see *mfkꜣ·t*.

M

mʿy (in charge of), I 423D.
m ys-ḥꜣḳ (spoil), II 431 n. f.
mʿmʿ (unclean), IV 882 n. d.
m wꜣ (from afar), IV 822 n. b.
m ws (in vain), I 637 n. a.
M-n-g-b-ty, p. n., IV 565.
m nḫt, IV 722 n. b.
m-rꜣ-y-nꜣ (lord), II 436, 585, 590.
M-rꜣ-yꜣ-yw-y, p. n., III 579; *M-rꜣ-yꜣ-y*, III 612; *Mw-rꜣ-yꜣ-y*, III 586; *M-rꜣ-yꜣ-yw*, IV 43; *M-w-rꜣ-yꜣ-y*, III 610; *M-w-rꜣ-wy-y*, III 615.
M-rꜣ-sꜣ-rꜣ, r. n., III 373, 391.
m rḫ·t, III 583 n. d.
m ḥb·f nb n ḫʿ ("at the his every feast of appearance"), IV 988J n. c.
m-ḫꜣ-w (an animal), II 449.
m ḫt (hereafter), IV 722 n. b.
M-sꜣ-bꜣ-tꜣ, g. n., IV 405 n. d.
m-sꜣḫy (-jar), IV 233.
m sp n šp (because of occasions of shame), IV 880 n. f.
m sp tpy (at the first time), IV 988J n. b.
m sn·t r (in likeness to), II 755 n. b.

M-šʾ-wʾ-šʾ, g. n., III 580, 589; IV 40, 43, 58, 405; *M-šʾ-wʾ*, IV 87 (90).

M-šʾ-šʾ-r, p. n., IV 90.

M-šʾ-k-n, p. n., IV 43.

m-šʾ-kʾ-bwy (tax-officials), IV 266, 324.

m šrt⸢—⸣, I 315, n. b.

M-k-ty, g. n., II 437; *My-k-ty*, II 402, 420 ter, 428, 430 ter, 431, 432; *My-k-ṯ*, II 437; *M-k-d-yw*, IV 712.

m-k-ty-rʾ (tower), III 100.

M-kʾ-m-rw, p. n., IV 566.

m kʾ·t yb·y, II 303 n. b.

m tyʾt (at this moment), II 36 n. c.

m ty·t (as an emanation), IV 912 n. c.

My-ṯ-n, g. n., II 659; *My-ṯn*, II 773; *My-tn*, II 804; *M-ṯ-n*, IV 722.

M-ṯʾ-dw-ty-w, p. n., III 632.

m ṯʾwt (secretly), IV 541.

mʾ (court), IV 393.

Mʾ-bʾ-rʾ, g. n., III 578.

Mʾ-nw, g. n., II 905.

Mʾ-sʾ, g. n., III 306, 312; *Mʾ-sw*, III 309.

mʾyw (copper), IV 548.

mʾʿ (offering), I 437.

mʾʿ-ḫrw (triumphant), III 280 281, 626 n. c.

Mʾʿ-ḫrw-Rʿ, r. n., I 749.

Mʾʿ·t-nfr·w-Rʿ, p. n., III 417.

Mʾʿ·t-ḫʿ, p. n., I 257.

Mʾʿ·t-kʾ-Rʿ, r. n., II 311

mʾw (new), IV 910 n. b.

Mʾwʾsn, p. n., IV 792.

Mʾwt-ḫnty, g. n., IV 368.

Mʾfd·t, d. n., I 115.

Mʾd, g. n., IV 915.

mʾdy·w (officials), III 272.

mʾdydy (-jar), IV 376.

My, p. n., IV 423.

My-yw, g. n., IV 480.

⸢*My*⸣*-pr*, g. n., I 172, 174.

My-ṯʾ-ry-m, p. n., III 337.

My·t-šry, p. n., IV 523.

Myʾ, p. n., III 32B.

Myʿm, g. n., II 1037; IV 474, 477; *Myʿmʾm*, III 285; *Myʿ·t*, IV 474, 479.

mynw (-stone), IV 233, 302.

myk, II 11 n. f.

mygʾ (archer), II 15 n. a bis.

Mʿy, p. n., II 1002.

mʿḥʿ·t (tomb or chapel), II 36.

Mʿḫr, g. n., I 334.

Mw-šʾ-n-ṯ, g. n., III 306, 309.

Mw-ṯ-n-rʾ, r. n., III 374, 375, 377.

mfʾkʾ·t (malachite), I 602 n. e.

Mn, p. n., II 975.

mn (-jars), II 447 bis, 462 bis, 482, 491 ter, 501 bis, 509, 518, 571, 621; IV 233, 239, 292, 299, 341, 348, 376, 378, 390, 393; *mn·t* (-jar), IV 395.

Mn-mʾʿ·t-Rʿ, r. n., III 169, 171.

mn-nfr·t (ornament), I 534.

Mn-ḫʿw, r. n., I 263.

Mn-ḫpr-Rʿ-P-ʿnḫy, r. n., IV 941 n. a.

Mn-ḫprw-Rʿ, r. n., II 812.

Mn-kʾw-Ḥr, r. n., I 263.

mny·t (necklace), I 500; II 93.

mny·t (-geese), I 729.

mny·t (pigeons), IV 242.

mny·t-wḏ (-metal), IV 302.

Mnʿ·t-Ḫwfw, g. n., I 624.

Mnʿ·t-Ḫfw, g. n., I 456.

mnw (-stone), II 491, 509, 518.

mnfy·t (troop, infantry), I 707; III 484, 578.

mnmn (herd), IV 212 n. d.

mnḥ (officer), IV 593.

mnḥ (-plant), IV 295.

Mnḫ-yb, r. n., IV 988C.

Mnḫ·t, p. n., I 508.

mnḫ·t (-linen), II 165.

mnḫ·t-nṯr (clothing), I 369 n. j.

mnš (-ship), III 274.

mnḳb (shrine), I 787.

Mntw, g. n., I 728; *Mn·t·yw*, e. n., III 118; *Mnty-šṯ·t*, e. n., II 14; II 721; *Mnṯw*, e. n., I 236.

Mntw-m-tʾwy, p. n., IV 423.

Mntw-ḥr-ḫpš·f, p. n., IV 512.

Mnṯw, d. n., II 844.

mr (canal), IV 853 n. a.

mr (chief, properly *ymy-rʾ*), III 322; IV 821.

mr (a wood), I 146; *mrʾ*, IV 288, 379,

391; *mry*, II 435; IV 288, 378, 391; *mrw*, II 447, 449.
Mr-yw—, g. n., II 487.
mr-ᶜprw (captain), I 606 n. d.
Mr-wr, p. n., IV 551.
Mr-Mw·t-Kꜣ-mꜣ-mꜣ, p. n., IV 696.
Mr-n-Rᶜ, r. n., I 320, 333.
Mr-sgr, p. n., II 171.
mr·t (peasant-slave), I 623; II 881.
Mr·t-wbḫ·t, p. n., IV 957.
mr·t-ntr (-priest), II 713, 936; *mry-ntr* (-priest), II 1036; IV 958B.
Mry, p. n., I 508.
Mry-Rᶜ, r. n., I 302.
Mry-ḫt, r. n., I 302.
Mry-kꜣ-Rᶜ, r. n., I 399.
mry·t (peasant-slaves), III 271.
Mryy-tꜣwy ("Beloved of the Two Lands"), r. n., I 302, 305.
mrsw (-jar), IV 376.
mrk (tribute), IV 577 n. a; see *brk*.
Mrty-wsy-Ymn, p. n., IV 446.
Mrtt-yt-ś, p. n., I 189.
mhywt (-fruit), IV 240, 378, 399.
mhn (-jar), IV 301.
mhrw (vessels), II 162.
mḥ-yb·f (favorite), IV 1007 n. b.
Mḥ·t-m-wsḫ·t, p. n., IV 958C.
Mḥy, p. n., I 276.
mḥtt (-jar), IV 350.
mḫꜣ (barge), I 423F n. c.
mḫꜣ (-weight), IV 240.
Mḫꜣ-tꜣwy, g. n., IV 864 n. a.
Mḫ, r. n., I 90.
Ms-swy, p. n., IV 445.
ms·w (children), I 456 n. c.
mśwy II 449 n. f.
mśn·t (a stone), I 500.
Mśd, g. n., IV 879.
mskt·t (morning-barque), IV 67, 73.
mstꜣ (-measure), IV 582; *msty*, IV 234, 235, 240, 287, 301, 344, 350, 378, 390, 391, 392, 395.
Msd-sw-Rᶜ, p. n., IV 428.
msd·t (-stone), III 246; *msdm·t*, IV 302, 345.
Msḏwt, g. n., I 174 n. h.
Mš, d. n., I 159.
Mš-tꜣ, g. n., IV 956.
Mšꜣ, g. n., IV 368.
mšᶜ (army), III 298 n. a.
mšd·t (channel), II 784 n. f.
mḳ-rꜣ-ḏy-nꜣ (horn), II 447.
mt (chief), IV 468 n. b.
mt (-linen), II 719, 721, 722, 723, 726, 727 bis, 730 731, 736, 738, 744 bis.
mty (customary), II 798 n. a; III 580 n. d.
Mṯr, g. n., I 368.
Mḏꜣ, e. n., I 311, 317, 324; *Mdꜣy*, e. n., IV 466.
mḏꜣ (-measure), IV 295, 347; *mḏꜣyw*, IV 244.
Mḳ[r], r. n., I 180.

N

Nꜣ-ᶜꜣ-tꜣ ys-nḫt·t, p. n., IV 918.
N-ᶜnḫ-Sḫm·t, p. n., I 250 n. c, 266 n. a.
N-ᶜnḫ-ššy, p. n., I 230.
N-ᶜnḫ-Ḫnty-ḫt, p. n., I 266.
N-wꜣ-sꜣ-ty-rw-kꜣ-nꜣ-yw, p. n., IV 784.
N-wśr-Rᶜ, r. n., I 250.
n-byꜣ y·t (marvelous stone), IV 287 n. c.
N-mꜣᶜt-Rᶜ, r. n., I 250 n. c, 673, 719.
N-mꜣᶜ·t-Rᶜ N-ḫᶜ, r. n., I 786 n. a.
N-mꜣᶜ·t-ḥꜣp, p. n., I 173.
n-n-y-bw (-wood), IV 344, 391.
N-h-r-n, g. n., II 479 n. a, 631 bis, 656, 800; III 118, 434; *N-h-r-nꜣ*, II 449, 867; *N-h-r-ny*, II 858 bis; III 114; *N-h-ry-n*, II 420, 818, 871; III 306, 309, 344; *N-h-ry-nꜣ*, II 479, 481, 485, 498, 500, 532; *N-hy-r-n*, III 321; *Nꜣ-h-ry-nꜣ*, II 85, 862; *Nꜣ-hꜣ-ry-nꜣ*, II 81.
N-⸢hb⸣, r. n., I 90.
n-ḫny-ḫny (necropolis), IV 526 n. b.
N-kꜣ-ᶜnḫ, p. n., I 343.
N-kꜣ-ᶜnḫ, p. n., I 216.
N-kꜣ-n-nbty, p. n., I 194.
N-kꜣw, r. n., IV 1028.
N-kꜣw-Ptḥ, p. n., I 250 n. c.
N-kꜣw-Rᶜ, p. n., I 250 n. c.
N-g-bꜣ, g. n., II 580.
n ṯꜣwt (secretly), IV 541 n. c.
n(y)t Nfr-kꜣ-Rᶜ mnᶜnḫ, I 341 n. b.

nw-pr-yt (paternal estate), I 536.
Nt-yḳr·t, p. n., IV 943.
nt ḫsf, I 423 D n. b.
nty m ḫt, IV 764 n. g.
nty sꜣwt, IV 726.
nꜣ-yy, IV 44 n. e.
nꜣ-ꜥḳ, IV 44 n. e.
Nꜣy-šnw-mḥ, p. n., IV 682.
Nꜣy-bw (-wood), IV 234.
Nyy, g. n., II 481, 588.
Nꜥ-nš-Bꜣs·t, p. n., IV 1025.
Nꜥr, g. n., IV 968.
nꜥryn (recruits), III 302.
nꜥḫ, (-bale), IV 371.
Nw-g-s, g. n., III 309.
nw·t (city), IV 485.
Nw·t, g. n., I 423; see *ꜣn-yw-ꜣ-sꜣ*.
nwsꜣ (-weight), IV 302.
nb (to fashion), I 610 n. c.
Nb-ꜥ, r. n., IV 945.
Nb-ꜥnḫ, IV 187 n. b.
Nb-wꜥ·wy, p. n., II 179.
Nb-wn-nf, p. n., III 255.
Nb-pḥ·ty-Rꜥ, r. n., II 7.
Nb-mꜣꜥ·t-Rꜥ, r. n., II 884, 845.
Nb-hp·t-Re, r. n., I p. 344 Add; IV 520.
Nb-ḫꜥs, p. n., IV 517.
Nb-ḫpr-Rꜥ, r. n., I 773 n. b, IV 515; *Nb-ḫprw-Rꜥ*, I 775.
Nb-ḫrw-Rꜥ, r. n., I 416; p. 344 Add.
Nb-snt, p. n., I 175.
Nb-kꜣw-Rꜥ, r. n., I 595, 600.
Nb-tꜣwy-Rꜥ, I 437, 446, 450.
Nb-ḏfꜣw, p. n., IV 445.
Nb·t, p. n., I 349.
nb·t (all), II 102 n. d.
Nb·t-ytf, p. n., I 782.
Nb·t-w, p. n., II 779.
nb·t-pr (lady), III 542.
nby (-wood), II 449.
Nbnšy, p. n., IV 792.
nbdw, IV 241.
Npt, g. n., II 797.
Nf-wr, g. n., IV 675.
Nfw-wr, g. n., III 281.
nfr, II 233 n. c.
nfr (-loaves), II 472.
nfr·t (-loaves), II 462.
Nfr-yr-kꜣ-Rꜥ, r. n., I 165, 244.
Nfr-ḥꜣ·t, p. n., II 839 n. d.
Nfr-Ḥr, p. n., IV 957.
nfr ḥtp (beautiful rest), IV 665 n. f.
Nfr-kꜣ-Rꜥ, r. n., I 340, 351.
Nfr-kꜣ-Rꜥ-Stp-n-Rꜥ, r. n., IV 493 n. b.
Nfr-tm, Ḥw-Rꜥ, r. n., IV 888.
nfr·w (base), IV 517 n. d.
Nfr·w-Rꜥ, p. n., II 344, 362.
Nfr·w-Rꜥ, p. n., III 435.
Nfr·w·s, g. n., IV 820.
nfr·wt (maidens), II 567 n. b.
Nmꜣyw, g. n., II 267.
nms·t (-jar), II 32 ter; IV 269, 301, 334, 350.
nn sn·y ym (none equal thereto), I 471 n. a.
Nrꜣw, g. n., IV 296.
nrꜣw (gazelle), IV 242.
Nḥy (Negroes?), IV 477 n. b.
nḥb (-wood), II 449.
Nḥry, p. n., I 622, 628.
nḥḥ (-oil), IV 239, 376, 390, 395.
Nḥsy, e. n., I 365 n. c.
Nḫbt, d. n., I 131 n. a.
Nḫb, g. n., II 7.
Nḫt-m-Mw·t, p. n., IV 539.
Nḫt-Ḥr-nꜣ-šnw, p. n., IV 878.
nḫt-ḫrw (strong voiced), I 171.
Ns-nꜣ-ꜥꜣy, p. n., IV 830.
Ns-nꜣ-ḳd-y, p. n., IV 830 n. c, 878.
Ns-sy-pꜣ-ḥr-n-Mw·t, p. n., IV 660.
Ns-sw-Ymn, p. n., IV 511.
Ns-sw-bꜣ-nb-dd, p. n., IV 564.
Ns-sw-pꜣ-ḳꜣ-šwty, p. n., IV 689.
Ns-sw-bꜣ-yš·t, p. n., IV 726.
Ns·wt-tꜣwy (Thebes), I 484; III 223, 503, 510; IV 900, 913, 924.
Nsṯnt, p. n., IV 844.
nš (?), I 309 n. h.
nšm·t (sacred barque), I 534, 613, 668.
nšm·t (feldspar), IV 287 n. b, 302, 243, 389.
nšn (to rage), II 828 n. g.
nšnꜥꜣ (great wrath), IV 764.

Nkry, p. n., II 1 n. c.
nkpᵓty (rosemary), IV 234.
ngᵓ (ox), IV 242, 293; *ngᵓ·w*, II 719.
Ngᵓw, g. n., I 493.
ngmgm (to plot), II 787.
ntr wᶜ nn ky ḥr sp·w·f, IV 969 n. b.
Ntr-ḫᶜw, r. n., I 340.
ntr-dwᵓ·t (divine votress), IV 942; see also *dwᵓ·t-ntr*.
Ntr·t-ḫᵓw, r. n., II 239.
ntry (divine), IV 261 n. a.
ntry·t (goddess), IV 261 n. a.
Nṯr, r. n., I 250.
nṯry (sanctuary), I 156, 159.
Nṯry-mw, r. n., I 117.
Ndy·t, I 669.
nḏ·f-rᵓ ḥr·f, II 134 n. b.
nḏ·t-rᵓ (oracle), II 606 n. c.
nḏ·ty (avenger), II 660.
nḏᵓ (a measure of capacity), II 159 bis, 571 bis.
Nḏm-yb, p. n., I 278.
nḏs (citizen), I 459, 536; III 565; IV 863.

R

R-b, g. n., IV 784; *R-bᵓ*, IV 783; *Rᵓ-bw*, III 611.
L-b-a-n, g. n., IV 716.
R-m-n-n, II 783; *Rᵓ-mn-n*, g. n., II 483 bis, 510.
r-hᵓw (over against), II 627.
r ḫt (under charge of), IV 784 n. a.
r ḏr·f (to its extent), I 468 n. d.
r-ḏᵓ·t, II 97 n. a.
rᵓ (-geese), IV 242.
Rᵓ-ᵓw, g. n., I 212, 239, 307; *Rᵓ-ᵓwy*, II 875.
Rᵓ-y, p. n., III 630.
Rᵓ-yn·t, p. n., II 975.
Rᵓ-yn·t, g. n., I 218, 221.
Rᵓ-wy-ᵓ-rᵓ, g. n., IV 131.
Rᵓ-bᵓ-yw-r, p. n., III 337.
Rᵓ-bᵓ-sw-n-nᵓ, p. n., III 337.
rᵓ-pr (temple), IV 283, 340.
Rᵓ-m, p. n., III 621.
rᵓ-ḥᵓ·wt (harbor-mouths), II 916 n. h; IV 44 n. a, 65 n. h.
rᵓ-ḥw-sw (-cakes), IV 238, 291, 393.
Rᵓ-ḥn·t, g. n., IV 853.
rᵓ-ḥr (chief), II 372; IV 398, 400; *rᵓ-ḥry*, III 25, 288 n. e.
Rᵓ-ḫᵓ-sy-nᵓ, g. n., III 386.
Rᵓ-stᵓ, g. n., I 177, 179, 180.
Rᵓ-š, t. n., I 159.
Rᵓ-šᵓ-ty, g. n., II 299 n. a; IV 31; *Rᵓ-šᵓ-ṯ*, IV 34; *Rᵓ-šᵓw*, II 299 n. a.
Rᶜ-⌈ᶜm⌉, p. n., I 281.
Rᶜ-wny(?), p. n., I 336 n. h.
Rᶜ-ms-sw-ᶜšᵓ-ḥb, p. n., III 496; IV 465.
Rᶜ-n-kᵓw, p. n., I 193.
Rᶜ-nfr, g. n., IV 830, 878.
Rᶜ-nḏr, r. n., I 786 n. b.
Rᶜy·t, d. n., II 325.
Rᶜhmn, p. n., I 375.
Rw-ᵓ-mr-s-k-n-y, p. n., IV 812; n. d.
Rw-bᵓ-ty, g. n., IV 712.
Rw-mᵓ, p. n., IV 442.
Rw-ḥᵓ-bᵓ-ᵓ, g. n., IV 712.
Rw-kᵓ, g. n., III 309; *Rw-kᵓ-t*, III 312; *Rw-kw*, III 574, 579.
rw·t (false door), I 322 n. e.
rwy·t (granite settings of doors in the wall), I 322 n. e.
rwyᵓ·t (banks), IV 405 n. b.
Rwty, I 148 n. c, 239 n. a.
rwd (shore), IV 405 n. f.
rwd·w (inspectors), II 1026.
rwd·t ("enduring or hard stone;" "alabaster," later "sandstone"), I 323 n. d, 696 n. c; II 153 n. e, 606 n. d.
rpy·t (figure), III 391 n. c.
rpᶜ·ty (hereditary prince), I 419 and n. d bis; III 132, 288 n. c; IV 124 n. b, 980.
rmṯ (people), II 257 n. e, 287, 288.
Rn-šnb, p. n., I 752.
rn·t pw (thy name, etc.), II 288 n. c.
rnp·w (young men), IV 63 n. a.
—rrt (-loaf), I 590.
rhd·t (kettle), II 436; III 589.
Rḥšᵓwy, g. n., IV 878.
rḫ, I 634 n. b; *rḫ·f* (he knows), II 233 n. c.
Rḫ-pḥtw·f, p. n., II 642.
rḫ stny, I 636 n. g.

rḫy·t (people), I 445 bis; II 236, 776, 767, 768, 805, 840, 858, 993, 1002; III 174, 175, 265, 268, 578, 580 n. e; IV 43, 47, 398, 921.
Rs-nf·t, g. n., II 731.
rš-ḏ ꜣ ḏ ꜣ (watchful head), II 28 n. c.
rśy (southern), I 396 n. h.
rśy (grain), I 459.
Rśy ynb·f, d. n., II 900 n. b; IV 866.
rkrk (to gallop), II 784.
Rkḥ, f. n., IV 768.
rkḥ (heat), I 630 n. b.
Rṯnw, g. n., I 680; II 548, 549, 616, 761; III 94, 97, 102, 103, 106, 107, 111, 112, 139, 147; IV 28; *Rtnw*, II 888, 1030, 1033; III 270, 457, 498; IV 219; *Rtnw·t*, II 413.
rdy·t m b ꜣ ḥ, IV 733 n. a.
rdyn ny yt·y, II 616 n. a.
rdw (-garments), IV 239.

H

H ꜣ -s ꜣ, g. n., IV 405.
h ꜣ·f (he descended), I 283 n. d.
h ꜣ y (laborer), III 531.
h ꜣ w-mn (-garment), IV 375.
H ꜣ n-wtn-Ymn, p. n., IV 448.
H ꜣ k-r ꜣ, f. n., I 746; II 35.
hy·t (hall), IV 889.
hbn (-jar), IV 950, 952; *hbn·t* (-jar), I 590; II 159, 164, 509, 567, 734, 736, 738, 739, 741, 743, 745.
hnn (head), II 509 n. a.
Hnkw, p. n., I 281.
hnd (to charge), III 608 n. e.
Hrw-nfr, p. n., IV 482.
hḏ·t (-plant), IV 235.

Ḥ

ḥ·t (house or temple), II 36; III 229, 232, 528, 644 n. e; IV 219, 223, 227, 274, 281, 283, 311, 338, 340, 355, 365, 366, 367, 958J; *ḥ·wt* (temples), II 358.
Ḥ·t-ybty, g. n., IV 916.
ḥ·t-ꜥ ꜣ·t, III 229, 240.
Ḥ·t-w ꜥ r·t, g. n., II 4, 8, 296; IV 820.
Ḥ·t-wr·t-Ymn-m-ḥ ꜣ·t, g. n., II 735.
Ḥ·t-Bnw, g. n., IV 839. III 16.
ḥ·t-bnbn (sanctuary), II 987.
Ḥt-nb, g. n., I 323; II 45.
ḥ·t-nṯr (temple), III 244, 507; IV 751 958K, 965 n. d.
Ḥ·t-sḫm, g. n., II 737.
Ḥ·t-stny, g. n., IV 818.
Ḥ·t-š ꜥ·t, g. n., IV 102, 107.
ḥt-k ꜣ (ka-temple), I 289.
Ḥ·t-k ꜣ -Ptḥ, g. n., III 77; IV 724.
Ḥ ꜣ, g. n., I 602 (in III 498 read *Ḥꜣ m*).
Ḥ ꜣ -y ꜣ -n-m, g. n., IV 713 n. e.
Ḥ ꜣ -pw-rw-m- ꜣ, g. n., IV 712.
Ḥ ꜣ -nbw, e. n., I 428.
Ḥ ꜣ -nfr, p. n., II 358.
Ḥ ꜣ -r ꜣ -b ꜣ -ty, g. n., III 84.
Ḥ ꜣ -ty-b ꜣ, p. n., IV 591.
Ḥ ꜣ -ty-ḥn-k-r, p. n., IV 784.
ḥ ꜣ·t (land-measure), I 574, 584 bis, 586, 591, 592.
ḥ ꜣ·w-tyw (leaders), IV 55.
Ḥ ꜣ·t-Ymn-ṯ ꜣ -nfr, p. n., IV 660.
ḥ ꜣ·tyw (officials), III 65, 103, 643.
Ḥ ꜣ·t-y ꜣ y, p. n., II 932; III 32C.
Ḥ ꜣ py, p. n., I 675.
Ḥ ꜣ pw, p. n., I 616.
Ḥꜣ m, g. n., III 498.
ḥ ꜣ ty-ꜥ (count), I 320, 348, 376, 377 385 n. c, 536, 622, 629 bis; IV 815 bis; 815 n. a, 878, 881, 902 n. a, 980.
ḥ ꜣ tyw (prime linen), I 382.
ḥ ꜥ y (rejoice), III 607 n. c.
Ḥ ꜥ ꜥ -yb-Rꜥ, r. n., IV 986, 988F, 990, 1003.
Ḥ ꜥ p, p. n., IV 818.
Ḥw-p ꜣ -n ꜣ, g. n., III 100.
Ḥw-r-n-k ꜣ -rw, g. n., II 436, 557.
Ḥw-r ꜣ -b ꜣ -s, p. n., IV 878.
ḥw-k ꜣ -m ꜣ -mw (-stone), IV 377.
ḥw-kw-kw (dom-palm fruit), IV 241.
Ḥwy, p. n., II 1029.
Ḥw ꜥ, g. n., II 848 n. a; *Ḥw ꜥ·t*, II 848 n. a.,
ḥwn (young man), I 665; III 565; IV 895.
ḥb-ꜥ ꜣ (chief fowler), I 718 n.
ḥb-sd (jubilee), II 630; IV 335; *ḥb-śd*,

II 1029; IV 750 bis, 848; *ḥb-st*, IV 335.
ḥbs (-well), IV 726.
ḥbś-bg·t (tomb), IV 972 n. d.
Ḥbnw, g. n., IV 820 n. b.
Ḥf·t, g. n., I 459.
ḥm-ḫrd, IV 582 bis.
ḥm·t-nṯr (divine consort), II 612; IV 988 H.
Ḥmy, g. n., IV 734 n. d.
Ḥmw-ḫrw, p. n., I 343.
Ḥn-Ḥtḥr, p. n., I 225.
ḥn·y (my majesty), II 617 n. g.
ḥn·t (queen), II 288 n. a; IV 958M, 988H; *ḥnw·t*, II 52.
ḥnᶜ-k, II 1007 n. a.
ḥnw (-measure), IV 393.
Ḥnw·t-nṯrw, p. n., IV 727.
Ḥnwt, p. n., I 725, 750.
Ḥnwt-sn, p. n., I 180.
Ḥnmy (or *my*), p. n., I 243.
ḥnmm·t (people), II 767, 858; IV 47, 188.
Ḥnk·t-ᶜnḫ, t. n., II 552 n. i.
ḥnty (period), IV 895, 909.
ḥntw (-dish), II 436.
ḥr (upon), II 11 n. f; *ḥr·f* (upon it), I 438 n. d.
Ḥr (name of a pyramid), I 211.
Ḥr-wr, I 637 n. a; II 203.
Ḥr-wr-Rᶜ, p. n., I 735.
Ḥr-m-y ḫw·t, d. n. (Harmakhis), I 179.
Ḥr-m-Ymn-pnᶜ, p. n., IV 593.
Ḥr-m-s·f, p. n., IV 706.
Ḥr-myny, p. n., II 47.
Ḥr-n-t-mḥw, p. n., I 718.
ḥr-nb (every man), IV 1003.
Ḥr-nb-mᶜt, r. n., I 312.
Ḥr-nḫt, p. n., I 718.
Ḥr-rn, t. n., I 119.
ḥr rśw (watchfulness), I 320 n. b.
Ḥr-ḫwf, p. n., I 332.
Ḥr-ḫb, p. n., IV 952.
Ḥr-ḫnt-ḫty, d. n., IV 369.
ḥr śḫr·t (to overthrow), I 602 n. f.
ḥr-ḏḏ, II 621 n. d; III 27.
ḥry (chief), II 389; *ḥry·w*, IV 405.
Ḥry-Ḥr, r. n., IV 615.
Ḥry-š-f, d. n., I 111.
Ḥry-šfyw, d. n., IV 368.
Ḥry-šry, p. n., IV 526.
ḥry-ḏḏ-ᶜ ("great lord"), I 381 n. b; III 267.
Ḥry·w-šᶜ, e. n., I 360; III 155.
ḥry·t-yb (hypostyle), II 603 n. d.
Ḥrrt, d. n., I 396 n. c.
ḥrst (-stone), IV 233, 302, 377; *hrs*, IV 287.
Ḥḥ, g. n., I 652, 657.
ḥs (vase), I 500 n. b; *ḥś·t*, II 32.
Ḥs-wr, g. n., I 174.
ḥsywt (-vase), IV 269, 334.
ḥsb (to reckon), I 407 n. a.
ḥsb (dues), IV 34; *ḥsb·t* (dues), III 481, 484.
ḥsb (-official), II 881.
Ḥsb-k, g. n., IV 830, 878.
ḥsb·w (-people), III 192.
ḥsp (land), IV 972.
Ḥsn, g. n., I 174.
ḥḳ·t (measure of capacity), I 408 n. f; II 274.
ḥḳ (ruler, prince), I 400 n. a, 402, 627, 628 bis, 632, 636.
Ḥḳ-yb, p. n., I 356.
ḥḳ·t (rulership), I 620 n. a, 629.
Ḥḳ·t-nfr·w-Mw·t, p. n., IV 988I; *Ḥḳ·t-nfr·w-mry·t-Mw·t*, IV 988I n. a.
Ḥk-, g. n., I 103.
Ḥkw, d. n., II 210.
Ḥkn-m-mᶜ·t, r. n., I 616.
ḥt (loaf), I 241.
Ḥtp, g. n., IV 247.
ḥtp (peace), II 105 n. f.
ḥtp (-bundle), IV 350, 949, 950, 952, 953; *ḥtp·t* (-bundle), IV 301.
Ḥtp (-measure), IV 238, 240, 244, 291, 294, 379, 392, 393.
ḥtp-ḥr-nmtt (-measure), IV 294.
ḥtr (dues), II 543.
ḥtry (span), II 784 n. e.
Ḥḏt-ḥknw, p. n., I 216.

Ḫ

Ḫ—, g. n., I 510.
Ḫ-w-k, g. n., III 386.

Ḫ-n-bꜣ-tꜣ, g. n., III 386.
Ḫ-r-pꜣ-n-ty-ry-s, g. n., III 386.
Ḫ-tꜣ, g. n., II 485; *Ḫtꜣ*, III 114, 151, 152, 306, 309; IV 64; *Ḫtꜣ·w*, III 143, 144; *Ḫy-tꜣ*, III 148; *Ḫtꜣ-tꜣ*, III 147.
Ḫ-tꜣ-š-rꜣ, r. n., III 371; *Ḫ-tꜣ-sꜣ-rꜣ*, III 372.
ḫꜣ (a measure of capacity), I 408 n. f.
ḫꜣ (hall), II 778.
Ḫꜣ-yw, r. n., I 90.
Ḫꜣ-my-h-mw, g. n., III 114.
ḫꜣ-n-rw (corselet), II 447; *ḫꜣnr*, II 785 n. h.
Ḫꜣ-rꜣ-bw, g. n., II 582; *Ḫy-rꜣ-bw*, III 312, 319; *Ḫy-rꜣ-bꜣ*, III 321, 337; *Ḫy-rꜣ-bꜣy*, III 322; *Ḫy-rꜣ-pꜣ*, III 386.
Ḫꜣ-rw, g. n., II 420, 436, 555, 821, 822, 884, 1015; III 84, 457, 617, 630, 633; IV 226, 229, 233, 398, 565, 723, 724, 883.
ḫꜣ-tpy (commander), I 410 n. c.
ḫꜣm (people), I 390.
ḫꜣs·wt (countries), III 88; *ḫꜣs·t* (desert), IV 1024.
ḫꜣš·ty (barbarian), II 849 n. c; *ḫꜣš·tyw*, I 532; II 106.
Ḫꜣsḫ·t, g. n., II 848 n. a, 849 n. c.
Ḫy-rꜣ-pꜣ-sꜣ-rꜣ, p. n., III 337.
Ḫy-sꜣ-sꜣ-pꜣ, g. n., III 386.
ḫy-ṯꜣ-nꜣ (-fruit), IV 240.
Ḫꜥ-bꜣw-Ḥthr, p. n., I 218.
Ḫꜥ-m-yp·t, p. n., IV 433.
Ḫꜥ-m-mꜣꜣ-n-rꜣ, p. n., IV 434, 466.
Ḫꜥ-m-mꜣꜥ·t, II 864, 890.
Ḫꜥ-m-ty-rꜣ, p. n., IV 466.
Ḫꜥ-šḫmwy, r. n., I 136.
Ḫꜥ-kꜣw-Rꜥ, r. n., I 647.
ḫꜥ·t-ḫꜥw my yꜣḫ·wty, II 314 n. g.
Ḫꜥꜣy, p. n., I 750.
Ḫꜥy, p. n., III 630, 632.
ḫꜥw (regalia), I 668.
Ḫꜥw-m-sḫmw, r. n., I 163.
Ḫꜥwy, p. n., I 675.
Ḫꜥww, p. n., I 305.
Ḫꜥf-Rꜥ, r. n., I 189.
Ḫꜥf-Rꜥ-[ḫ]ꜥ, g. n., I 199.
ḫꜥr (a measure), I 556.
ḫw-bꜣḳ (protector of the oil tree), d. n., I 785 n. e.
Ḫwy, p. n., I 299, 349, 361.
ḫwy mky (protected and defended), I 768 n. e.
Ḫwy·t, d. n., IV 874.
Ḫwf, p. n., I 387.
Ḫwny, p. n., I 336.
ḫbḫb (-jars), IV 875, 878.
Ḫpy, p. n., I 342.
ḫpr (carry out), I 322.
ḫpr ḥms·t, II 138 n. d.
Ḫpr-ḥḏ-Rꜥ-Stp-n-Rꜥ, r. n., IV 724.
ḫpr-sḫ, I 361.
ḫpš (-sword), II 802; III 117, 163.
ḫpr·t ḫprw my ḫpry, II 314 n. g.
Ḫf[w], r. n., I 189.
ḫft (corresponding to), II 614.
ḫft-ḥr (opposite), II 795 n. f.
ḫft ḥrs (nave), III 515.
Ḫft·t-ḥr-nbs, d. n., II 655.
Ḫmnw, g. n., IV 833, 842, 848 bis.
ḫn ("tent"), I 353 n. b, 471 n. d.
ḫn nꜥbꜥ ("without a lie"), I 658 n. h.
ḫn·t (prison, stronghold), I 471 n. d
ḫn·t (water-skin), I 471 n. d.
Ḫnw, p. n., I 299.
ḫnw (court), III 65.
ḫnwtyw, II 70 n. a.
Ḫnm-ꜥnḫ·f, p. n., I 343.
Ḫnm-n-ꜥnḫ-ss, p. n., I 305.
ḫnmt, I 431.
ḫns (to course), I 471 n. e.
ḫns·ṯ tꜣ, II 225 n. d.
Ḫnsw-ḥꜣt-ntr-nb·t, p. n., III 432.
ḫnky (-garment), IV 374.
ḫnt, II 903.
Ḫnt-yꜣwtf, d. n., I 159.
Ḫnt-ꜥbwy-ntrw, g. n., IV 369.
Ḫnt-m-smy·ty, p. n., I 608.
Ḫnt-ḥn-nfr, g. n., II 80.
ḫnt-ḥr·f (before it), I 436 n. d.
Ḫnt-ḫt-wr, p. n., I 605.
Ḫnt-ẖty, d. n., IV 874.
ḫnty, I 442 n. f.
ḫnty (a substance), IV 378, 395.
ḫnty (image), IV 988D n. b.

H̱

Ś and *S*

(NOTE.—The distinction has not been maintained after Volume I, viz., the end of the Middle Kingdom, when the Egyptian Scribe himself had entirely ceased to maintain it.)

sbḫ t (chamber), II 164 n. f.
sbḫ·t (-measure), IV 241, 379.
sbḫ·t (-plant), IV 235, 392.
sbḫ·t (towers), II 889.
Śbk-t ᵓ wy, r. n., IV 886.
Sbk-m-s ᵓ·f, r. n., IV 517.
Sbk-ḥr-ḥb, p. n., I 725.
Ś·bdš (quell), I 428.
Sp (to bind), I 323 n. g.
sp (virtue), III 626.
Sp-R ᶜ, t. n., I 156.
sp tpy (beginning), IV 958J.
sp·t (for *ś·yp·t*)(=investigation), I 178. n. e.
Sp ᵓ, d. n., I 156.
spr (-measure), IV 299, 348.
spr (-salt), IV 299, 348.
spr·n·f (he arrived), IV 1004.
śpt (harp), II 32 n. c.
spd, II 32 n. c.
sft (-oil), I 241, 382; II 509, 518; IV 376.
Sm (-priest), I 668; II 936.
Sm ᵓ-Ḥwḏ·t, g. n., II 935.
sm ᵓ·t (-bolt), II 722.
smn·n·s (she fastened), II 828 n. c.
ś·mnḫ-sw, I 420 n. f.
smd·t (-stone), IV 377.
Sn-Wsr·t, r. n., I 720.
sn-t ᵓ ("smelled the earth"=did obeisance), I 317 n. f, 468 n. e.
sn·w (loaves), II 353, 378; *sn·t*, III 624 n. h.
Śnwt, I 141 n. a, 159.
Sn-mw·t, p. n., II 361.
Sn-mw·t, g. n., II 718.
Sn-ḏ ᵓ-r ᵓ, g. n., II 584; see *Ś ᵓ-ḏ ᵓ-r ᵓ*.
Sny, p. n., IV 485.
sny (-jar), IV 378, 395.
sny·t, I 668 n. c.
snb (-berries), IV 350.
Snfr, r. n., I 189.
Snfr-R ᶜ-P-ᶜ nḫy, r. n., IV 941 n. a.
snn (orderly), II 1 n. c; III 584; IV 40, 65.
Snt, g. n., I 172.
snṯyy (chapel), I 668 n. c.
snḏs (?), I 324 n. b.
śr (official), I 281, 536, 547.
sr (decree), I 173.
s·rwd-k ᵓ (cause to grow), II 288 n. b.
shr, IV 309.
sḥ (-vessel), IV 732, 733, 734.
sḥy (boat), I 423F n. d.
sḥn (commander), IV 400.
sḥn (-vessel); see *sḥ* (-vessel).
sḥntw, II 785 n. h.
sḥtp (-bundles), IV 295.
S·ḥtp-yb-R ᶜ, r. n., I 465, 473.
S·ḥtp-ntr·w (name of fortress), II 1041.
śḥḏ (commander), I 677, 707.
—*sḥḏ*, I 370.
Sḫ·t-mfk, g. n., IV 1003 n. e.
sḫwy (list), III 343.
śḫm-yrf (ruler), I 779, n. d.
Śḫt-R ᶜ, t. n., I 159; *Sḫt-R ᶜ*, IV 918.
s·ḫpr (create), IV 141 n. c.
ś·ḫpr (to train), IV 402 n. e.
Sḫm, g. n., IV 878.
sḫm (-sistrum), II 93.
sḫm (adytum), II 806; III 244.
Śḫm-nṯrw (name of a house: "Mighty-of-the-Gods"), I 97.
Sḫm-R ᶜ-Wp-m ᵓ ᶜ·t, r. n., IV 516.
Sḫm-R ᶜ-ḫw-t ᵓ wy, r. n., I 752.
Sḫm-R ᶜ-Šd-t ᵓ wy, r. n., IV 517.
Sḫmw, g. n., I 174.
Sḫmi-n-ᶜ nḫ, p. n., I 238.
sḫr (character), I 665.
sḫt (-loaves), II 735.
śḫkr (deck), I 668.
ś·ś ᵓ ("sustenance," lit. "a causing to be satisfied"), I 354 n. e.
Ssy, p. n., I 299.
ssf (ashes), IV 67 n. a, 72 n. c.
Sssw, g. n., IV 369.
Śšd, I 150.
Sš ᵓ·t, d. n., I 109, 115.
s·šm·w (leaders), II 925 n. a.
S·šmw-t ᵓ wy, r. n., I 616.
sš-śtny-ḫry-ḏ ᵓ ḏ ᵓ (superior king's-scribe), II 916 n. d.
sš-śtny-ḫry-ḏ ᵓ ḏ ᵓ (inferior king's-scribe), II 915 n. b.

sšw (-loaves), IV 297.
sšd (window), IV 873 n. a.
Sḳnn-Rʿ, r. n., II 7; IV 518.
sk (to line up), IV 864 n. d.
Sk-tw (-ship), II 294.
Skmm, g. n., I 678.
Śkꜣ, r. n., I 90.
sksk (capture), II 822.
st ("offering-tablet"), I 322 n. e.
Sty-m-pr-Dḥwty, p. n., IV 435.
sṯ ḥḳꜣw nw (chiefs of), I 317 n. d.
stꜣ·t (a land measure), II 840.
Sty-m-pr-Ymn, p. n., IV 436.
Sty-rꜣ, p. n., I 716.
śtp-ḥꜣty-ʿ (to begin), II 303 n. c.
Śtny-mr-nṯr, p. n., I 243.
Stnḥ, r. n., I 166.
Sṯ·w, g. n., I 334, 336; *Sṯ·t*, g. n., I 728; *Sṯ·ty*, e. n., IV 72; *Sṯ·ṯyw*, e. n., I 423 H; II 784, 787; III 20, 479, 490; IV 119, 122, 246; *Sty·w*, e. n., IV 217.
sṯꜣ (-jar), I 569, 571.
sṯs (carrying pole), I 430.
sd·w ("broken"), I 657 n. e.
sḏꜣ (pleasure), II 813 n. g.
Śꜣ-ḏꜣ-rꜣ, g. n., II 798A; see *Sn-ḏꜣ-rꜣ*.
s·ḏfꜣ (plenty), III 404 n. a.
sḏm, I 598 n. a.
s·ḏd·t (proverb), III 611 n. a.
sḏm-ʿš (servant), II 854, 985.
sḏm-w (-officers), I 633; II 684; III, 55.

Š

Š—y—wt, g. n., II 465.
Š-m-šw-y-tw-my, g. n., II 783; *Šꜣ-my-ša-y-tꜣ-my*, II 783 n. b.
Š-k-rw-šꜣ, g. n., III 574; *Šꜣ-k-rw-šꜣ*, III 579, 595; IV 64; *Šꜣ-kꜣ-rw-šꜣ*, III 588 ter, 601; IV 81.
Šꜣ-y, g. n., IV 405.
šꜣ-wꜣ-b-ty, II 537.
šꜣ-wꜣ-bw (mastic tree), IV 245.
Šꜣ-b-tw-n, g. n., III 310, 319, 324; *Šꜣ-bw-dw-nꜣ*, g. n., IV 131.
Šꜣ-m-B-ʿ-rꜣ, p. n., III 632.
Šꜣ-n-m-ꜣ, g. n., IV 712.
Šꜣ-r-dy-nꜣ, e. n., III 307, 588; *Šꜣ-rꜣ-d-nꜣ*, III 601; *Šꜣ-rꜣ-d-ny*, e. n., III 491; *Šꜣ-rꜣ-dꜣ-nꜣ*, IV 129, 397, 402, 410; *Šꜣ-rꜣ-d n*, III 574, 579; *Šꜣ-rꜣ-d-n-nꜣ*, III 588.
Šꜣ-rꜣ-ḥꜣ-nꜣ, g. n., II 13; *Šꜣ-rꜣ-ḥꜣ-n*, g. n., II 416.
Šꜣ-sw, e. n., II 124, 517; III 101, 108, 457, 638; IV 404; *Šsꜣ·w*, II 170.
Šꜣ-šꜣ-n-ḳ, r. n., IV 724.
Šꜣ-kꜣ-nꜣ, g. n., III 576.
Šꜣ·t, g. n., II 661 n. g.
Šꜣ yš-ḥr·t, g. n., IV 994.
Šꜣʿ ym (beginning of), I 429 n. e.
Šꜣʿ·t, g. n., I 510 bis.
šꜣw (dues), II 110.
šꜣwt (cabbage), IV 240.
Šꜣbt, g. n., I 429 n. f.
Šꜣs-ḥtp, g. n., IV 366.
šꜣd (dig), III 173; *šd·t*, III 196.
šʿ (-cakes), IV 949, 950, 952, 953, 954.
šʿ (-grain), II 737.
Šʿd-mšḏr, p. n., IV 445.
šw, IV 929.
šw (-rolls), II 742.
šw (sun), III 198; IV 958D.
šwꜣ (citizen), II 920.
šps.w-stny, II 292 n. c.
špšš (luxuries), I 718.
Špšš-kꜣf, r. n., I 257.
šfw (doves), IV 106.
Šm-Rʿ, g. n., I 125.
šm·t (go), I 423E n. d.
Šmyk, g. n., I 510.
Šmʿ (Middle Egypt), I 396 n. h, 407.
Šmʿ·w (Middle Egypt, perhaps the "South"), I 442 n. e.
Šms, I 438 n. d.
Šn-wr, g. n., III 480; IV 45.
šnʿ (-fish), IV 243.
Šnw·t Ynbw-ḥḏ (granary of Memphis), IV 878 n. d.
Šrt-Mṯn, g. n., I 172, 173.
šḫr·w (-linen), II 554.
šs (-linen), II 554, 571.
šsꜣ, IV 378, 395.
šsꜣ-ḥr (skilful), II 758 n. c.
Šsꜣ·w, e. n., II 170; see *Šꜣ-sw*.
šsy·t (-sistrum), II 93.

šsm·t (-stone), IV 302.
šś (militia), IV 968, 972.
št (stone-cutting), I 239 n. c, 349 n. d.
Št-Mṯn, g. n., I 173 bis.
Štʾ, g. n., II 864 bis.
štʾ·t (holy place), IV 857.
štʾy, IV 726 n. b.
Šṯt, t. n., I 288.
šd (collect), I 382 n. e.
šd (gift-lands), II 689 n. e.
šd (-bird), II 571.
šd (-skin), II 675 n. d.
Šd-ybd, g. n., IV 780.
šdw (water skins), I 456.
šdh (-wine), IV 213.

Ḳ

Ḳ-bʾ-ʿʾ-nʾ, g. n., IV 712.
Ḳ-rʾ-ḳʾ-m-šʾ, g. n., IV 64. *K-rʾ-k-my-šʾ*, III 306, 309; *Kʾ-ry-kʾ-my-ʿ-šʾ*, II 583.
ḳʾ (be high), III 607 n. c.
Ḳʾ-y-ḳʾ-šʾ, g. n., IV 405.
Ḳʾ-yśwt-Ḥtḥr, p. n., I 218.
Ḳʾ-rʾ-bʾ-nʾ, g. n., IV 405.
Ḳʾ-rʾ-my-mw, g. n., III 114.
ḳʾ-rʾ-nʾ-ty (foreskin), IV 52; see also *ḳrn·t*.
Ḳʾ-rʾ-ḳy-šʾʿ, g. n., III 306; *Ḳʾ-rʾ-ḳy-kšʾ*, III 309; *Ḳy-rʾ-ḳy-šʾ*, III 349.
Ḳʾ-rw, p. n., IV 550.
Ḳʾ-ḫʿw, r. n., IV 942 n. d.
ḳʾ-tʾ-rw-ty (-measure), IV 378.
Ḳʾ-dw-rw, g. n., III 94.
Ḳʾ-ḏʾ—, g. n., II 821; *Ḳʾ-ḏʾ-rʾ*, III 606, 617.
Ḳʾ-ḏʾ-wʾ-dn, g. n., III 309; *Kʾ-ḏʾ-wʾ-dʾ-nʾ*, g. n., III 312; *Ky-ḏʾ-wʾ-dʾ-nʾ*, III 386; *Ḳy-ḏʾ-wʾ-d-n*, III 391.
ḳʾ-ḏʾ-m-rʾ (-garment), IV 375.
ḳʾ·t, II 808 n. a.
Ḳʾy, g. n., IV 948.
ḳʾy (tomb), IV 665 bis, 666 667.
Ḳy-nʾ, g. n., II 428, 430.
Ḳy-nn, p. n., I 776.
ḳʿḥ (district), IV 726.
ḳw (-loaves), II 735.
ḳwnk (-bread), IV 238, 291, 297.
ḳby (-jar), I 556.
Ḳbḥ, g. n., II 101, 844; IV 296.
Ḳbḥ-nṯrw, t. n., I 143.
Ḳbḥw-Ḥr, g. n., II 845.
Ḳbsw, g. n., III 337.
ḳmʾ-n-yb (conception of heart), II 164 n. d.
ḳnyw (portable shrine), I 667 n. b.
ḳnb·t (official staff), III 58 n. h, 63, 64, 65 bis.
ḳnb t ʿʾ·t (great court), IV 531 n. d.
ḳrn·t (foreskin), III 587 n. h; see also *ḳʾ-rʾ-nʾ-ty*.
ḳrty (bolt), IV 929.
Ḳhḳ, e. n., IV 402, 410, 747 n. c.
ḳḳ·t (transport ship), III 441.
Ḳd, g. n., III 321; *Ḳdy*, III 306, 309; IV 64; *Ḳdw*, II 420, 434.
Ḳd-nʾ, g. n., II 598.
Ḳd-š, g. n., II 430; *Ḳdš*, III 141, 306, 308, 309; *Ḳd-šw*, II 420, 465, 531, 585.
Ḳdm, g. n., I 493.

K

Kʾ, p. n., I 731.
kʾ-bw (-jar), IV 233, 239, 292, 299, 376, 390.
kʾ-bw-sʾ (-measure), IV 240.
Kʾ-pw-r, p. n., IV 90; *Kʾ-pw-rʾ*, IV 97.
Kʾ-m-Wʾs·t, p. n., IV 530.
Kʾ-my-tʾ, p. n., III 337.
Kʾ-my-dw, g. n., III 114.
Kʾ-ms, r. n., IV 519.
Kʾ-n-nbty-wr, p. n., I 197.
Kʾ-nʾ, g. n., II 529.
Kʾ-nfr, p. n., I 389.
Kʾ-nfr, g. n., I 490 n. a.
Kʾ-r-ḫ-n-—-n——, g. n., III 386.
Kʾ-r ḏʾ y-tʾ-—, g. n., III 386.
Kʾ-rʾ, p. n., IV 423.
Kʾ-rʾ (-boat), IV 387.
Kʾ-rʾ-y, g. n., II 800, 862, 889; *Kʾ-r-y*, II 818.
Kʾ-rʾ-pw-sʾ, p. n., IV 432.
Kʾ-rʾ-pw-t, g. n., III 356.
kʾ-rʾ-rw-ty (-weight), IV 286.

*k*ꜣ*-r*ꜣ*-ḥw-ty* (string, basket), IV 244, 301.
*K*ꜣ*-h-ny*, g. n., IV 873.
*k*ꜣ*-ḥr-k*ꜣ (-jar), IV 294.
*K*ꜣ*-ḳ*ꜣ*-rw-y*, g. n., IV 713 n. h.
*K*ꜣ*-km*, g. n., IV 873 bis, 874.
*k*ꜣ*-ṯ*ꜣ (-plant), III 55.
*K*ꜣ*-d-ṯ-m*, g. n., IV 712 n. a.
*k*ꜣ*·t* (design), II 303 n. b.
*K*ꜣꜣ*w*, e. n., I 311.
*K*ꜣ*y*, p. n., IV 224.
*K*ꜣ*w-k*ꜣ*w*, g. n., IV 948.
*K*ꜣ*m*, p. n., III 645.
*k*ꜣ*nk* (-wood), II 449.
*K*ꜣ*s*, g. n., I 510.
*k*ꜣ*š* (shell), II 272.
*K*ꜣ*k-mn* (-vessel), IV 582.
*K*ꜣ*k-s*ꜣ*-R*ꜥ, p. n., I 218.
ky (form), II 906 n. b.
*Ky-r-gy-p*ꜣ, p. n., II 867.
Kf-tyw, e. n., II 659.
⌜—⌝*-kf*ꜣ*-yb*, I 616 n. c; II 708.
Km-wr, g. n., I 493; IV 724A, 875.
Km·t (Egypt), g. n., I 451; II 11 n. d.
Kmy, p. n., I 755.
knm·t (-stone), IV 302.
Knm·tyw, g. n., II 808.
krty, III 171 n. b.
Kš, g. n., II 39, 845 n. f.
Kš-kš, g. n., III 309, 312.
*Kdndnn*ꜣ, p. n., IV 423.

G

G-wt-wt, g. n., IV 405.
*G-r-b*ꜣ*-tw-s*ꜣ, p. n., III 337.
*G*ꜣ*-ḳ*ꜣ*-ty*, g. n., III 632.
*G*ꜣ*-ḏ*ꜣ*-tw*, g. n., II 417; *G*ꜣ*-ḏ*ꜣ*-y*, III 630.
*g*ꜣ*y* (-jar), IV 238, 241, 294, 300, 301, 350, 393.
gmyy, I 334.
gn (-vase), IV 334.
gr (be silent), I 598, n. c; *gr mdt* (silent in a matter), I 657 n. d.
grg-ḥry (armed), IV 65 n. g.
grg·t (establishment), IV 1021.
*gs-r*ꜣ (-measure), IV 295, 303, 380, 394.

T

t-h-r (-warriors), II 459; *t-h-r*ꜣ, IV 44; *tw-hy-r*ꜣ III 337 bis, 344.
*T*ꜣ*-yry*, p. n., IV 774.
*T*ꜣ*-*ꜥ*-n-k-*ꜣ, g. n., IV 712.
*T*ꜣ*-*ꜥꜣ*-n*ꜣ*-k*ꜣ, g. n., II 421, 426.
*T*ꜣ*-*ꜥꜣ, r. n., IV 518.
*T*ꜣ*-*ꜥꜣ*-*ꜥꜣ, r. n., IV 518.
*T*ꜣ*-*ꜥ*yn*, g. n., IV 878.
*T*ꜣ*-yḥ*, g. n., III 580.
*T*ꜣ*-wr*, g. n., II 692.
*T*ꜣ*-pd·t* (Bowland; Nubia), g. n., I 500, 510, 602, 644; II 122, 176 bis, 375, 794 n. a, 828, 894; III 31, 479, 484, 499, 500, 501, 502, 643; IV 898, 900, 929, 994, 1014.
*T*ꜣ*-mry* (Egypt), g. n., I 451; II 98; III 77, 155, 159.
*T*ꜣ*-ny-s*ꜣ, g. n., III 337.
*T*ꜣ*-nṯr*, g. n., II 451 n. d.
*T*ꜣ*-r*ꜣ*-y*, g. n., II 852.
*T*ꜣ*-r*ꜣ*-ty-š-bw*, p. n., III 372.
*T*ꜣ*-s*ꜣ*-ḫ-r*ꜣ, d. n., III 386.
*T*ꜣ*-s*ꜣ*·t-nḫt*, p. n., IV 499.
*T*ꜣ*-sn·t-Ḥr*, p. n., IV 990.
*T*ꜣ*-šry*, p. n., IV 547.
*T*ꜣ*-ty*, p. n., IV 547.
*T*ꜣ*-d*ꜣ*-r*ꜣ, p. n., III 337.
*T*ꜣ*y-nḫt·t*, p. n., IV 452.
*T*ꜣ*yw-ḥnw·t*, p. n., IV 727.
*T*ꜣ*ywḏ*ꜣ*·t*, g. n., IV 818.
*T*ꜣ*f-nḫt-t*, p. n., IV 818.
*T*ꜣ*n-w*ꜣ*-ty-Ymn*, r. n., IV 921.
*T*ꜣ*dn·t-n-B*ꜣ*s·t*, p. n., IV 795.
*Ty-*ꜣ, p. n., III 542.
*Ty-y*ꜣ*-dw-r*ꜣ, p. n., III 337.
Ty-m-h-nw, g. n., III 379 n. c.
*Ty-n-r*ꜣ, p. n., II 984.
*Ty-n-r*ꜣ*-Ymn*, p. n., IV 539.
*Ty-n*ꜣ*-y*, g. n., II 537.
*Ty-r*ꜣ*-y-w*ꜣ, g. n., IV 114.
*Ty-r*ꜣ*-g*ꜣ*-n—*, p. n., III 337.
*Ty-r*ꜣ*-g*ꜣ*-n-n*ꜣ*-s*ꜣ, p. n., III 337.
*Ty-r*ꜣ*-g*ꜣ*-ty-t-ṯ*ꜣ*-s*ꜣ, p. n., III 337.
Ty-ḫ-sy, g. n., II 487.
Tyy, p. n., II 862.
Tyw, r. n., I 90.

Tynt-nw·t, p. n., IV 589.

Tynt-sꜣ-hꜣ-rw-yw, p. n., IV 784.

Tynt-tꜣ-ꜥ-mw, g. n., II 15.

tyḫty (tin?), IV 929.

Tyḫnw, g. n., II 892; III 116, 132, 134, 139, 588; *Tyḫy*, III 147; *Tyḫn*, IV 792; *Tyḫnwt*, IV 482; *Tḥnw*, IV 822; see also *Tḥnw*.

tyt, I 784 n. c.

Tw-np, g. n., II 459, 470, 530; *Tw-n-p*, III 365 bis; *Tnpw*, II 773.

tw-r-pw (-geese), IV 235, 242; *twrp* (-geese), IV 342.

Tw-rꜣ-ss, g. n., IV 114.

Tw-rw-šꜣ, g. n., III 574, 588 bis, 601; *Tw-ry-šꜣ*, III 579; *Ty-w-rꜣ-šꜣ*, IV 129.

Tw-tw, p. n., II 1009.

twr, IV 302.

twt ny (shape for me), II 200 n. e.

twt . . . . wḥꜣm rnp·t tn ("a statue . . . . quarried in this year"), I 323 n. e.

tb (-grain), II 737.

tp rśy (south), I 396 n. h, c, 529, 665 n. b; II 614, 692, 717, 726; IV 857.

Tp-ḥt, g. n., I 159.

tp·t, IV 334.

tpy-ꜥ (first), IV 822 n. b.

tpw (bullocks), IV 242.

tpḥ·t (opening), II 564, n. e; III 171 n. b.

Tf-yby, p. n., I 395.

tm ssḏr ("not causing a matter to sleep") I 657 n. c.

tmꜣ, II 735.

Tmḥ, g. n., I 335 nn. h; *Tmḥw*, I 335 n. h.

tmḥy (-stone), 373, 389.

tny·w (offering vessels?), II 93.

Tnpw, g. n., II 773.

Tnt-sꜣy, p. n., IV 695.

Tnt-spḥ, p. n., IV 792.

tnṯꜣ·t (throne), IV 401.

Trrs, g. n., I 334.

Tḥnw, g. n., IV 822; see also *Tyḫnw*.

Tty, r. n., I 294.

Tty-ꜥn, p. n., II 16.

Ṯ

Ṯ-kꜣ-n-šꜣ, g. n., IV 818.

Ṯ-kw, g. n., III 638.

Ṯꜣ-wꜣ-ṯꜣ-sꜣ, p. n., III 337.

ṯꜣ-pw-r (-vessels), III 589.

Ṯꜣ-m-rꜣ, p. n., IV 43.

Ṯꜣ-mw·t, g. n., II 641, 814 n. a; IV 634, 914.

Ṯꜣ-n-m·t, p. n., IV 792.

Ṯꜣ-rꜣ, p. n., III 633.

Ṯꜣ-rꜣ-y, p. n., IV 532.

ṯꜣ-rꜣ-ty (warship), IV 229 n. b.

Ṯꜣ-rw, g. n., II 415; III 54, 88, 100, 307, 542, 631.

ṯꜣ-sr·t (standard bearer), II 839.

Ṯꜣ-k-kꜣ-rꜣ, g. n., IV 44, 64, 77; *Ṯꜣ-kw-rꜣ*, IV 129; *Ṯꜣ-k-rꜣ*, IV 403; *Ṯꜣ-kꜣ-rꜣ*, IV 565.

ṯꜣ-kꜣ-rꜣ (tower), IV 189 n. a.

Ṯꜣ-kꜣ-rw-B-ꜥ-rꜣ, p. n., IV 566; *Ṯꜣ-kꜣ-rꜣ-B-ꜥ-r*, p. n., IV 567.

Ṯꜣ-kꜣ-rw-m, p. n., III 632.

ṯꜣ-gw (-wood), II 485, 490, 491.

ṯꜣ-tkmw, IV 217 n. k.

ṯꜣy (-measure), IV 238, 240, 294, 378, 393.

Ṯꜣꜥw, g. n., I 456.

ṯꜣb (-jar), II 621, 622.

Ṯw-rꜣ, p. n., II 55.

Ṯwyꜣ, p. n., II 862, 867.

Ṯb-nṯr, g. n., IV 878.

ṯb (-vessel), IV 582 bis; *ṯb·w* (-jars), III 589; IV 294, 476, 477.

Ṯbw, g. n., IV 957.

ṯmꜣ (district), II 686, n. b.

ṯmꜥ·t, II 743.

Ṯmḥ, e. n., I 311, 335; *Ṯ-m-ḥ*, g. n., III 580; *Ṯmḥw*, IV 944 n. a; *Ṯy-m-ḥ-w*, g. n., III 586.

ṯmṯm (-measure), IV 238, 291.

ṯnyw (flat dish), II 32.

Ṯnw, g. n., II 798 A.

Ṯnt-rmw, g. n., IV 878.

Ṯnty, p. n., I 182 n. a.

ṯrf (measure), IV 292.

Ṯrty, I 703.

Ṯḥnw, g. n., III 465; see also *Tḥnw* and *Tyḫnw*.

ṯḥnt (oil), I 366.
Ṯs-ḥn, p. n., I 186.
ṯsw (flats?), I 323 n. h, 669 n. c.
ṯś (commander), IV 821 ter.
ṯś (command), IV 747 n. a.
Ṯś-Bꜣs·t-pr·t, p. n., IV 774.
Ṯś-Rʿ-m-ynw, t. n., II 1018.
ṯś·t (troop), II 916; IV 825 n. b.
Ṯš, r. n., I 90.
Ṯṯy, I 184.
Ṯṯy, p. n., I 361.
Ṯṯy, p. n., I 423C.

D

Dꜣ-y-n-yw, e. n., IV 64; *Dꜣ-y-n-yw-nꜣ*, IV 81, 82, 403.
dꜣ-wꜣ-rꜣ (-measure), IV 294.
Dꜣ-pw-rꜣ, g. n., III 356.
dꜣmw (-measure), IV 240; *dmꜣw* (-measure), IV 345; *dmꜣmw* (-measure), IV 379.
Dꜣ-r-d-ny, g. n., III 306; *D-rꜣ-d-n-y*, III 349.
dy-rs-ḏꜣḏꜣ (taskmaster), II 758 n. f.
⌜*dy*⌝ *ḫd ḫnt*, I 459 n. g.
dy-śtny-ḥtp, II 52.
Dy-d, p. n., III 579; *Dy-dy*, p. n., IV 43.
Dyy·s-nk, p. n., I 338.
dydy (-measure), IV 295.
dw (-altar), IV 735.
dw (-garment), IV 232, 239, 241 374, 375, 394.
dw (-vessel), IV 735.
Dwꜣ-Ḥr-pt (a feast), I 125.
Dwꜣ-tꜣwy, I 146, 147.
dwꜣdwꜣ (early morning), I 468 n. b.
Dwꜣ-ḏfꜣ, I 138.
dwꜣ·t (-hall), III 154.
Dwꜣ·t (nether world), III 259, 272.
dwꜣ·t-nṯr (divine votress), IV 988G, H bis.
dwd·t, I 500.
dbḥ (to crave), IV 784 n. a.
dbḥ·t-ḥtp (offering table), II 32.
Dbḥn, p. n., I, 239, n. a.
dpḥ·t (-apples), IV 301.
dmy (town), III 84, 86, 88, 94, 141, 147; IV 52, 485.
Dnꜣ, p. n., IV 682.
dny (-measure), IV 294; *dny·t* (-measure), II 621, 622; IV 240, 294, 299, 300.
dnyꜣ (-vase), IV 238, 269.
Dnrg, p. n., II 114.
dnṯꜣ·t (palanquin), IV 958E.
dhn (forehead), IV 988H n. b.
dhn·n·f wy r nb, II 805 n. a.
Dḥwty-rḫ-nfr, p. n., IV 423.
dḫ·t (=*ḫd·t*="to sail down stream"), I 353 n. a.
ds (-jar), I 569, 585; II 113, 114, 620, 621; III 77, 159; IV 347.
ds (-stone), IV 972.
Dšr, f. n., I 94.
dḳ, II 571.
dd·t (flat dish), IV 735.
ddm·t (-flower), IV 345, 379.

Ḏ

Ḏꜣ-y-n—, g. n., III 386.
ḏꜣ-w (-linen), II 722, 727 bis, 736, 738, 744 bis.
Ḏꜣ-wꜣḏ-wr, g. n., IV 921 n. e.
Ḏꜣ-pw-yꜣ-rꜣ-n-dꜣ, g. n., III 386.
Ḏꜣ-pw-rꜣ, p. n., III 630.
Ḏꜣ-my-rꜣ, g. n., II 465; III 114.
Ḏꜣ-mw·t, g. n., IV 1002.
Ḏꜣ-n-——-nw-ty, g. n., III 386.
Ḏꜣ-rꜣ-Rw-m, g. n., III 633.
Ḏꜣ-rw, g. n., III 114.
Ḏꜣ-rw-mꜣm, g. n., IV 714.
Ḏꜣ-hy, g. n., II 20, 482, 489, 492, 497, 616, 658; III 318; *Ḏꜣ-hꜣ*, III 423; IV 219, 328; *Dꜣ-h*, IV 211.
Ḏꜣ-d-p-t-ṯ-rw, g. n., IV 713.
Ḏꜣꜣ, p. n., I 676, 683.
Ḏꜣy-yꜣ-ṯ-ḫy-r-ry, g. n., III 386.
ḏꜣmw (classes), IV 402 n. f, 1823 n. d.
ḏꜣdw (audience-hall), I 239 n. a, 423E, n. d, 500.
Ḏꜣty, p. n., I 389.
Ḏꜣtyy, p. n., I 343.
ḏꜣḏꜣ·w (courses), IV 489, 654 n. b.
ḏꜣḏꜣ·t (council), II 686 n. a.

*ḏ*ꜣ*ḏ*ꜣ·*t-wr*·*t* (great council), II 706.
*Ḏ*ꜥ*w*, p. n., I 347.
*Ḏ*ꜥ*w*, p. n., I 381.
*Ḏ*ꜥ*n*, g. n., IV 564.
*Ḏ*ꜥ*r-wḫ*ꜣ, g. n., II 869.
*ḏb*ꜣ (costume), I 366 n. a, 668.
*ḏb*ꜣ·*t* (-hall), III 154.
Ḏf-ty, g. n., II 421.
Ḏmy, p. n., I 336 n. a.
*Ḏr-n*ꜣ, g. n., II 470.
ḏrw (masonry), IV 515.
ḏś, later *dś* (-jar), I 430 n. i.
*Ḏśr-k*ꜣ*-R*ꜥ, r. n., II 39.
Ḏsr-t, g. n., IV 520.
Ḏt, f. n., I 101, 131.
ḏt (endowment), I 217 n. a.
ḏd, II 872 n. a; *ḏd-ny* (I have spoken), I 658 n. g.
Ḏd-ḫy-yw, p. n., IV 878.
*Ḏd-ḫ*ꜥ*w*, r. n., I 264, 265.
*Ḏd-k*ꜣ*-R*ꜥ, r. n., I 264, 265.
ḏdm·*t* (-measure), IV 244, 294, 301, 394, 768.
*ḏdmt-ḥr-t*ꜣ (-loaves), IV 238.
Ḏdty, p. n., IV 957.

INDEX IX

HEBREW

אָבֵל, IV 715 n. a bis.
אָבֵל כְּרָמִים, IV 715 n. a.
אֲבֵלִים, IV 715 n. a.
אַגָּן (ʾ-kʾ-nʾ), II 436 n. e.
אֲדוֹרַיִם (ʾ-d-rw-mʾ-m), IV 712 n. f.
אדל (ʾ-d-rw), IV 712 n. c.
אֲדָמָה (ʾ-d-m-ʾ (?)), IV 714 n. d.
אדר (ʾ-d-rw), IV 712 n. c.
אַדָּר (ʾ-d-rʾ-ʾ), IV 716.
אדרם, IV 712 n. f.
אֹהֶל, III 576 n. d.
איזה (yw-ṯʾ), III 288 n. b.
אַיָּלוֹן (ʾ-yw-rw-n), IV 712.
אל־רם (ʾ-r-ry-m), IV 455 n. d.
בֵּיתחֹרוֹן (Bʾ-ty-ḥ-wʾ-rw-n), IV 712.
בֵּיתְשְׁעָן (Bʾ-ty-šʾ-n-r-ʾ), IV 712.
בֵּית־תְּלָם (Bʾ-ty-tʾ-rw-mʾm), IV 713 n. h.
בלמם (Bʾ-rw-mʾ-m), IV 713 n. f.
ברך (bʾ-rʾ-kʾ), IV 127 n. a, 207 n. e.
גִּבְעוֹן (Ḳ-bʾ-ʿʾ-nʾ), IV 712.
הֲדִים (hdmw), II 436 n. k.
זכר־בעל (Ṯʾ-kʾ-rwʾ-B-ʿ-rʾ), IV 566 n. b.
זדפת־אל (Ḏʾ-d-p·t-ṯ-r w), IV 713.
חאנם (Ḥʾ-yʾ-n-m), IV 713 n. e.
חינם (Ḥʾ-yʾ-n-m), IV 713 n. e.
חנס (Heracleopolis), IV 790.
חֲפָרַיִם (Ḥʾ-pw-rw-m-ʾ), IV 712.
חקל, IV 715 n. f.
חקל אברם (Pʾ-ḥw-ḳ-rw-ʾʾ-bʾ-rʾ-m), IV 715.
חקלם, IV 715 n. f.
חָרְבָּה, III 84 n. a.
ידהמלך (Yw-d-h-m-rw-k), IV 713.
כבד, IV 410 n. d.
כִּכָּר (Kʾ-ḳʾ-rw-y), IV 713 n. h.
כֶּסֶת (kʾ-ṯʾ-ty), IV 232 n. a.
כֶּתֶם, IV 199 n. d.
מְגִדּוֹ (M-k-d-yw), IV 712.
מהר בעל (M-hʾ-rʾ-b-ʿ-rʾ), IV 423 n. a.
מַחֲנַיִם (M-ḥʾ-n-m), IV 712.
מרחשת (rʾ-ḥw-sw), IV 238 n. a.
נֶגֶב, IV 715.
סגור (ṯʾ-kʾ-rʾ), IV 189 n. a.
סִים לֵב, I 745 n. g; II 175 n. c.
עיזא (ʿʾ-yʾ-ḏ-ʾ), IV 715.
עין־פרן (ʿ-n-p-rw-n), IV 716.
עֲרָד (ʿʾ-rw-d-ʾ), IV 716.
עליה (ʿʾ-rʾ-ty), IV 189 n. a.
עצא (ʿʾ-yʾ-ḏ-ʾ), IV 715.
עַצְמוֹן, IV 715 n. d.
ערלה (ḳrn·t), III 587 n. h.
ערן (ʿʾ-rʾ-nʾ), IV 713.
עשׂק (ʿʾ-šʾ-ḳ), IV 188 n. a.
צוּרִים (Ḏʾ-r w-mʾm), IV 714.
צעק (ḏʿḳ), IV 97 n. g.
צדפתל (Ḏʾ-d-p-t-ṯ-rw), IV 713.
רַבִּית (Rw-bʾ-ty), IV 712.
רְחוֹב (Rw-ḥʾ-bʾ-ʾ), IV 712.
קל, IV 410 n. d.
שִׁבֹּלֶת, IV 715.
שׁוּנֵם (Šʾ-n-m-ʾ), IV 712.
שׂכֹה (Sʾ-yw-kʾ), IV 713.
שׁנה, IV 715 n. f.
שׁנים, IV 715 n. f.
תַּעְנָךְ (Tʾ-ʿ-n-k-ʾ), IV 712.

INDEX X

ARABIC

الفقاعى, IV 831 g. n.
دخل على (ᶜḳ ḥr), IV 460 n. c.
ضرب مثلا, III 611 n. a.

INDEX XI

LEPSIUS' DENKMÄLER AND TEXT

ABT. II

Denkmäler	*Records*
Taf. 2, a	I 169
2, b, c	I 176
3–7, 120, a–e	I 170–75
112, e	I 689
113, b	I 689
113, c	I 689
15, a	I 190–99
15, b	I 193
34, d	I 182
37, b	I 210–12
39, a	I 236
39, d	I 264
39, e	I 263
76, c–f	I 270–75
78, b	I 277
114, a	I 338
115, a	I 296
115, b	I 301
115, c	I 301
115, e	I 296
115, f	I 387
115, g	I 298
115, k	I 299
116, a	I 266, 302–3, 340–43
116, b	I 318
118, d	I 466–68
123, e	I 616
135, h	I 663–69
136, a	I 675
136, b	I 644
136, h	I 656–60
136, i	I 652
137, a	I 715
137, d	I 750
137, f	I 719–20
137, i	I 723 n. f.
137, g	I 721–23
137, h	I 721 n. b
138, a	I 707
138, c	I 710
138, b	I 707
138, d	I 711
138, e	I 708–9
138, f	I 712
140, o, p	I 750 n. e
143, i	I 740

Denkmäler	*Records*
Taf. 144, g	I 731–32
149, c	I 435–38
149, d	I 439–43, 452–53
149, e	I 433 n. e, 444–51
149, g	I 454-56
150, a	I 428–33
150, b	I 423 n. d
151, c	I 752
152, a	I 250
152, f	I 749

ABT. III

Denkmäler	*Records*
Taf. 3, a	II 27–28
5, a	II 69–73
6	II 87–88
12, a, d	II 6–16, 39, 78–82
12, c	II 6 n. a
16, a	II 120–22
17, a	II 332 n. d
18	II 245
22–24, d	II 308–319
24, a–c	II 321
25 bis a	II 348 n. b
28, 2	II 337
29, h	II 642
30, a	II 521–23
30, a, ll. 10–20	II 529–40
30, b	II 543–73
31	II 603
31, a, ll. 1–3	II 497–503
31, a, ll. 3–10	II 507–515
31, a, ll. 10–14	II 517–19
31, b, l. 167; 32, ll. 1–32	II 412–43
32, ll. 32–39	II 445–49
38, c. d	II 638–40
43, a	II 18–20
43, a, ll. 10–20	II 25
45, e	II 652
47, a	II 651
47, c	II 62–66
48, b–49, a	II 174
50, b	II 175
52, b	II 176
55, a–b	II 169–72
56, a	II 651
59, b	II 654
63, 64	II 801–2

Denkmäler	*Records*
Taf. 65, a	II 791–97
68	II 812–15
71, a–d	I 66 n. c; II 875
76, 77	II 819, 871–72
81, g	II 844
81, h	II 843 n. c
82, a	II 845
89, a	II 894
89, c	II 895
89, e	II 896
92–97, d	II 982–88
98, a	III 1007–8
100–2	II 1014–16
103–6, a, 107 a	II 989–96
107, a	II 1010–13
110, d	II 932
110, i	II 934–35
115–18	II 1019–41
119	II 844 n. b
120, a	III 44
120, b	III 43
121, a–b	III 41–2
126, a	III 87–88
126, b	III 83–84
127, a	III 85–86
127, b	III 109–112
128, a, b	III 98–103
129	III 153–56
130, a	III 142–44
130, b	III 145–48
131, a	III 114
131, b	III 213
131, c, d	III 213
132, a	III 215–16
132, d	III 218
123, e	III 217
132, g, h	III 213
138, g	III 200
138, h	III 249
138, n	III 198
139, a	III 163–64
140, a	III 165
140, b	III 169–74
140, c	III 175–94
140, d	III 195
141, h	III 204 n. b
145, c	III 355
146	III 370–91
149, a	III 507
152	III 217
152, a	III 517–18
152, d	III 218
152, f	III 521
152, g	III 521
153	III 317–27, 329–30
154	III 331–32
Taf. 155	III 339–40
156	III 356
157–61	III 335–38
159, b	III 448 n. b
159, d	III 520
164, 165	III 335–38
166	III 356, 359–62
174, d	III 558
275, b	I 75 n. h
175, f	III 552
175, g	III 479
176, a, b, d, e, f, g	III 458–77
180	III 504
182, b	III 504
183, a	III 503
187, a, b	III 499
187, c–e	III 317–27
188, a	III 452–53
189, a	III 496–99
192, b	III 501
192, c	III 500
192, d	III 500
195, a	III 392
196	III 415–24
197, b	III 297
197, c	III 297
199, a	III 574–92
200, a	III 627–28
201, c	III 641 n. a
202, a	III 648
202, b	III 646
202, c	III 647
209, b	III 129
209, c	IV 132–35
212	III 641
213, b	IV 13
213, d	IV 4
213, e	IV 14
219, c, A	III 641 n. e
219, e	IV 463–68
120, c	IV 11
223, e	IV 457–60
229, b	IV 474
229, c	IV 479–83
230	IV 476–77
231, a	IV 474
237, c	III 621–26
243, a	IV 622–25
243, b	IV 626
248, b	IV 615–18
251, a	IV 632–33
251, c	IV 649
251, d	IV 635 n. a
251, e–g	IV 634
252, 253, a	IV 709–22
255, i	IV 753

Denkmäler	*Records*
Taf. 256, a	IV 762–69
257, a	IV 760–61
258, a, b	IV 770
301–6	II 1019–41

ABT. V

Taf. 1, e	I 74 n. a
5	IV 897
7, c	IV 898
12, a	IV 899
13, b, d	IV 900

ABT. VI

Taf. 23, 8	IV 19

TEXT

Denkmäler	*Records*
Text I, 20	II 799–800
III, 43	III 574–92
Text III, 64	IV 615–18
III, 91, 92	III 64 n. a
III, 127, 128	III 356
III, 130	III 641 n. c
III, 134	III 515
III, 152	IV 889
III, 156	III 356 n. a
III, 164	IV 634
III, 170	IV 132–35
III, 172	IV 72
III, 174	IV 85–92
III, 175	IV 61–68
III, 176	IV 51
III, 177	IV 53–55
III, 178	IV 37–58
III, 209–214	III 641 n. b
III, 238	IV 513
IV, 37	III 505
IV, 49	IV 414
IV, 175	III 553

www.ingramcontent.com/pod-product-compliance
Lightning Source LLC
Chambersburg PA
CBHW040056200426
43193CB00060B/2939
* 9 7 8 1 6 3 9 2 3 6 4 6 6 *